GCSE/KEY STAGE 4

LONGMAN
REVISE
GUIDES

MATHEMATICS

Brian Speed

Longman

LONGMAN REVISE GUIDES

SERIES EDITORS:
Geoff Black and Stuart Wall

TITLES AVAILABLE:
Art and Design
Biology
Business Studies
CDT: – Design and Realisation
CDT: – Technology
Chemistry
Computer Studies
Economics
English*
English Literature*
French
Geography
German
Home Economics
Mathematics*
Mathematics: Higher Level and Extension
Music
Physics
Religious Studies
Science*
World History

* new editions for Key Stage 4

Longman Group UK Limited,
Longman House, Burnt Mill, Harlow,
Essex CM20 2JE, England
and Associated Companies throughout the world.

© Longman Group UK Limited 1988, 1993

First published 1988
Revised edition 1991
Eighth Impression 1992
3rd Edition 1993

British Library Cataloguing in Publication Data

Speed, Brian
  Mathematics – (Longman revise guides).
  1. Mathematics – Study and teaching
  (Secondary – Great Britain 2. General Certificate of
  Secondary Education – Study guides
  I. Title
  1510'.76.QA14,G7

ISBN 0 – 582 – 22830 – 1

Set by 17QQ in 10/12pt Century Old Style

Printed in Great Britain by William Clowes Ltd.,
Beccles and London

CONTENTS

EDITORS' PREFACE

Longman Revise Guides for GCSE/Key Stage 4 are written by experienced examiners and teachers, and aim to give you the best possible foundation for success in examinations and other modes of assessment. Much has been said in recent years about declining standards and disappointing examination results. While this may be somewhat exaggerated, examiners are well aware that the performance of many candidates falls well short of their potential. The books encourage thorough study and a full understanding of the concepts involved and should be seen as course companions and study guides to be used throughout the year. Examiners are in no doubt that a structured approach in preparing for examinations and in presenting coursework can, together with hard work and diligent application, substantially improve performance.

The largely self-contained nature of each chapter gives the book a useful degree of flexibility. After starting with Chapters 1 and 2, all other chapters can be read selectively, in any order appropriate to the stage you have reached in your course. As well as the examination-type questions and answers at the end of each chapter, you will also find a 'Review Sheet' to test yourself on the content of that chapter.

We believe that this book, and the series as a whole, will help you establish a solid platform of basic knowledge and examination technique on which to build.

Geoff Black and Stuart Wall

ACKNOWLEDGEMENTS

I would like to thank the following people for their valuable contribution to the production of this book. Stuart Wall and Geoff Black for their editing and most useful suggestions at each stage of production; my fifth form pupils at Pope Pius X school for their help with the questions; my mother Mrs Elsie Speed for her devoted typing and spelling corrections of the original manuscript; Gillian my wife, who very patiently looked after our children while I worked; and finally to my lads James, John and Joseph, and my daughter Joy; for their patient understanding of Dad 'not being able to play again tonight!' My thanks also go to Keith Evans whose statistical help was invaluable.

I am also indebted to the following Examination Boards for giving me permission to use some of their GCSE questions in this book:

Northern Examinations and Assessment Board (NEAB)
Midland Examining Group (MEG)
Southern Examining Group (SEG)
University of London Examinations and Assessment Council (ULEAC)
Northern Ireland Schools Examinations and Assessment Council (NISEAC)
Welsh Joint Education Committee (WJEC)

The above groups do not accept responsibility for the answers I have given to their questions, and so all suggestions and any mistakes in these answers are entirely my responsibility. I will be most grateful to any reader who informs me of any such mistakes should they occur.

Brian Speed

GCSE AND KEY STAGE 4 IN MATHEMATICS

LEVELS AND GRADES

TIERS OF ENTRY

SCHEMES OF ASSESSMENT

GETTING STARTED

In 1994 the GCSE examinations in Mathematics will assess the mathematics component of the National Curriculum. This is now called Key Stage 4 and is a move towards making sure that all students follow the same Mathematics syllabus, no matter what part of the country they live in or for which examination board they have been entered.

In this chapter we consider the new grading system in GCSE Mathematics, the different tiers that you can be entered for and the syllabuses which are available for each tier. We also look at the role of coursework in the overall assessment.

This book will cover the five *Attainment Targets* (ATs) for mathematics, namely:

- Using and applying mathematics (AT1)
- Number (AT2)
- Algebra (AT3)
- Shape and Space (AT4)
- Handling data (AT5).

The various topic-based chapters will take you through these 'targets', which set out the knowledge, skills and understanding expected of you in the various areas of mathematics. The Attainment Targets are broken down into ten *levels of attainment*. You will find frequent references in the margin of this book indicating the level at which a topic is set. You will also find at the end of each chapter a 'level checklist', stating what you must know and understand in that chapter to be awarded each

ESSENTIAL PRINCIPLES

1 > LEVELS AND GRADES

We have already mentioned that each attainment target is broken down into ten 'levels of attainment' describing what you must know and understand to be awarded a particular level. The GCSE/Key Stage 4 in Mathematics is not a system of hurdles. You will still be able to obtain a particular level in your overall assessment even if you cannot do everything described as being necessary for that level. This is because a weakness in one area at that level can be balanced by an above average performance in another area.

As a broad guide, the table below indicates the relationship between levels of attainment under the National Curriculum and the previous GCSE grading system. From 1994 onwards your GCSE in Mathematics (and other subjects) will be awarded in terms of these numbered levels instead of the previous letter grades.

The GCSE scale of awards up to and including 1993	The GCSE scale of awards from 1994 onwards.
	10
A	9
B	8
C	
D	7
E	6
F	5
G	4

Table 1.1   GCSE Scale of Awards

As you can see, Levels 9 and 10 correspond to the previous grade 'A'. The new system therefore provides a means of rewarding outstanding work at the previous grade 'A' standard. Level 8 corresponds to the previous grade B, but level 7 falls rather indeterminately between the previous grades C and D.

A 'level checklist' is provided at the end of each topic-based chapter, and frequent references are made to levels within each chapter (in the margin).

2 > TIERS OF ENTRY

It is an important feature of the GCSE that students must not be required to prepare for examinations which are unsuited to their level of attainment; nor must these examinations be of a kind that will undermine their confidence. Therefore in GCSE Mathematics you will find three *tiers* of entry: a basic tier, an intermediate tier, and a higher tier. These tiers are given different names by each Examination Board, but they mean the same thing.

Separate examination papers are written for each tier and each tier is targeted at different levels of attainment (Table 1.2)

Tier	Target levels of attainment					
Basic	4	5	6			
Intermediate		5	6	7	8	
Higher				7	8	9	10

Table 1.2   Levels covered by each Tier

If you are entered for the *intermediate tier*, then the highest level you can obtain is a level 8, and the lowest is a level 5. If you fall below the standard for a level 5, you will be unclassified. The same idea applies for the *higher tier* examination which covers levels 7 to 10 inclusive, and for the *basic tier* examination which covers levels 4 to 6 inclusive.

It is clearly important that you are entered for the appropriate tier of examination, since you cannot be entered for two tiers at the same time. Your teachers will be actively involved with you in selecting the appropriate tier for your examination.

To make sure that the confidence of the student is not undermined, the examination papers are written with a particular aim in view. Namely, to provide enough scope for the more able student at that tier to do well and to obtain the higher target levels but at the same time to allow a student at the lowest target level to obtain at least 50% of the marks. So, provided you are correctly entered, you can expect to be able to answer at least half the examination paper.

3 > COURSEWORK

Coursework has been an important element within the GCSE in Mathematics. From 1994 its maximum contribution has been set at 20% of the total marks. Chapter 15 of this book will provide you with helpful advice on approaching a coursework project. Some syllabuses provide an end-of-course examination to replace the coursework component. You need to check with your syllabus (see below) and teacher to find out how your particular course is to be assessed.

4 > SCHEMES OF ASSESSMENT

UNIVERSITY OF LONDON EXAMINATIONS AND ASSESSMENT COUNCIL (ULEAC)

Option A

Foundation tier	will sit Paper 1 and Paper 2
Intermediate tier	will sit Paper 3 and Paper 4
Higher tier	will sit Paper 5 and Paper 6.

There is no choice of question on any paper and each paper is worth 40% of the final total, with the coursework worth 20%, assessed over a two year period by your own centre.

Option B

The papers are set as for option A, but here the 20% coursework component consists of 'final tasks' to be set by ULEAC but assessed by the centre.

Option C

The papers are set as for options A and B, but here the 20% 'final tasks' are set *and* assessed by ULEAC.

SMP (see MEG SMP, below)

NORTHERN EXAMINATIONS AND ASSESSMENT BOARD (NEAB)

Syllabus A

Basic tier (P)	will sit Paper P1 and P2
Intermediate tier (Q)	will sit Paper Q1 and Q2
Higher tier (R)	will sit Paper R1 and R2

There is no choice of questions on any of the papers. Each paper is worth 40% of the total marks with coursework worth a further 20%. Coursework is given and assessed by your own centre.

Syllabus B

The papers are set as for Syllabus A and each is worth 40%. However the final 20% is obtained from a terminal examination paper, set and assessed by NEAB, rather than from coursework.

Syllabus C

This is a *modular* examination with the following features:

one terminal examination paper, worth 50%;
two modular examination papers, worth 15% each;
coursework tasks, worth 20%.

MIDLAND EXAMINING GROUP (MEG)

Syllabus Mathematics (with coursework)

Each tier, Basic, Central and Further, will take the following form:

a short and longer answer paper (40%);
a structured extended answer paper (40%);
coursework (20%).

Syllabus Mathematics (without coursework)

The papers are as above, but with each paper worth 50%.

Syllabus Mathematics (SMP 11–16)

Candidates may enter any one of 5 tiers:

Green	(level 3, 4, 5)
Blue	(level 4, 5, 6)
Red	(level 5, 6, 7)
Yellow	(level 6, 7, 8, 9)
Yellow extension	(level 7, 8, 9, 10)

For each tier there are two final examination papers (40% each) with coursework at 20%.

SOUTHERN EXAMINING GROUP (SEG)

SEG offer five versions, all of which include:

two written examination papers (40% each);
coursework at 20%.

The tiers available are   Foundation (F)
Intermediate (I)
Higher (H)

WELSH JOINT EDUCATION COMMITTEE (WJEC)

Syllabus A

This will consist of two parts, written papers and coursework, each part in the ratio of 200 : 50 (ie 80% : 20%)

a) Two written papers, each worth 100 marks. They are taken as:

Basic tier
Intermediate tier }   each tier having two papers
Higher tier

b) The coursework. This will consist of 'tasks' provided by the Examination Board, which combined together are worth 50 marks.

Syllabus B

As for syllabus A. However here there is a third paper which will assess the mathematics which would otherwise have been tested by coursework.

NORTHERN IRELAND SCHOOLS EXAMINATIONS AND ASSESSMENT COUNCIL (NISEAC)

There are *three* parts to the assessment at each level.

a) Written papers
At each level you sit *two written papers*, each of which will consist of *short answer questions* and *long questions* (most of which will be *structured*). There is no choice of question offered. Each paper is worth 35% of the final assessment.

b) Aural and computation
There will also be an aural and computation test, which is set for each level. This will test your mental arithmetic and how well you can understand a spoken instruction regarding information available on a separate document. This test is worth 10% of the assessment.

c) Coursework

You will normally have to hand in *four* assignments for assessing. Your teacher will tell you what these assignments are. They could include work on topics such as practical geometry, measurement, statistics, everyday application of mathematics and investigations. This coursework element is worth 20% of the assessment.

INTERNATIONAL GENERAL CERTIFICATE OF SECONDARY EDUCATION (IGCSE)

This syllabus has been designed to meet international mathematical needs while being based on the United Kingdom's national criteria as published by the SEAC.

There are only *two* levels available: the basic level being included in the *lower level* of the two which is called the *core curriculum* where the only grades available are C to G; the *higher level* being called the *extended curriculum*, where the only available grades are from A to E. There is also an *optional* coursework element in place of part of the written papers. The assessment will be in *three* parts:

a) a *written* paper of *short answer* questions.
b) a *written* paper of *structured* questions.
c) a *written* paper of *problems* **or** the *school based assessment*.

There is *no* choice of question on any paper. The combination of the different parts of the assessment are:

CORE: a) first paper 35%
  b) second paper 40%
  c) third part 25%

EXTENDED: a) first paper 37.5%
  b) second paper 37.5%
  c) third part 25%

The school based assessment which is *optional* consists of four coursework assignments (20%) and two aural tests (10%). The four coursework assignments will be on the four areas of:

■ statistics and/or probability;
■ geometry;
■ investigations;
■ practical applications of mathematics

The aural tests will be about fifteen minutes of single response questions aimed at each different level.

You may use a suitable calculator in each part of the assessment and, if you wish, four figure tables also. For centres that are in areas where electronic calculators are not readily and cheaply obtainable, there is an alternative version of the examination available.

ADDRESSES OF THE EXAMINATION BOARDS

ULEAC   **University of London Examinations and Assessment Council**
Stewart House, 32 Russell Square, London, WC1B 5DN
Tel: 071 331 4000
Fax: 071 631 3369

MEG   **Midland Examining Group**
1 Hills Road, Cambridge, CB1 2EU
Tel: 0223 61111
Fax: 0223 460278

NEAB   **Northern Examinations and Assessment Group**
Devas Street, Manchester, M15 6EX
Tel: 061 953 1180
Fax: 061 273 7572

NISEAC   **Northern Ireland Schools Examinations and Assessment Council**
Beechill House, 42 Beechill Road, Belfast, BT8 4RS
Tel: 0232 704666
Fax: 0232 799913

SEG   **Southern Examining Group**
Stag Hill House, Guildford, GU2 5XJ
Tel: 0483 506505
Fax: 0483 300152

WJEC   **Welsh Joint Education Committee**
245 Western Road, Cardiff, CF5 2YX
Tel: 0222 561231
Fax: 0222 571234

IGCSE   **International General Certificate of Secondary Education**
University of Cambridge Local Examinations Syndicate
1 Hills Road, Cambridge, CB1 2EU
Tel: 0223 61111
Fax: 0223 460278

When contacting the Examination Groups you will need to ask for the Publications Department and request an order form to be sent to you. On the order form indicate exactly which syllabus you are studying and be prepared to send a cheque or postal order with your order.

COVERAGE OF TOPICS

BASIC TIER
INTERMEDIATE TIER
HIGHER TIER

GETTING STARTED

This chapter considers the content of GCSE/Key Stage 4 syllabuses in Mathematics at the Basic, Intermediate and Higher tier examinations respectively. It helps you see how chapters and topics covered in this book relate to *each of these tiers*. The national curriculum now means that each examination board offers the same syllabus coverage of topics in mathematics.

ESSENTIAL PRINCIPLES

1 >   **Basic Tier**

The GCSE syllabuses at the *basic tier* are almost identical for every Examination Board.
The *basic tier* is referred to in a slightly different way by the various Examination Boards:

Northern Examinations and Assessment Board (NEAB)	– Level P
Midland Examining Group (MEG)	– Basic
Southern Examining Group (SEG)	– Foundation
University of London Examinations and Assessment Council (ULEAC)	– Level X
Welsh Joint Education Committee (WJEC)	– Basic
Northern Ireland Schools Examinations and Assessment Council (NISEAC)	– Basic
Cambridge University Examinations Syndicate (IGCSE)	– Core

Table 2.1 indicates the chapters and topics relevant to basic tier syllabuses.

4	Pattern in number	whole numbers, odd, even, prime, multiples, factors, simple sequences
	Fractions	vulgar (simple addition and subtraction), decimal (the four rules on simple cases), percentage, equivalence, conversion of vulgar to decimal, conversion between fractions and percentage
	Directed number	in practical situations
	Square root	of perfect squares
5	Approximation	of length and weight of everyday objects
	Rounding off	to nearest 10p, 100, etc., significant figures, decimal places
	General units	100 cm = 1 m, etc., and when to use them
	Time	12/24-hour clock, timetables
6	Household finance	HP, interest, taxation, discount, loans, wages and salaries, profit and loss, VAT
	Use of tables and charts	tidetables, conversion tables, insurance tables, etc.
	Reading scales	clocks, dials, scales
7	Simple ratio	sharing, recipes, scale drawing
	Rates	speed, foreign currency exchange rates
8	Formula	flowcharts and substitution
9	Cartesian co-ordinates	plotting points and joining up
	Graphs	drawing graphs from given data
	Interpretation	of given graphs
10	Angles	names and in triangles
	Plane figures	triangles, quadrilaterals, circles
	Symmetry	line, rotational
	Solid figures	names of, nets
11	Perimeter	of circles and rectilinear shapes
	Area	rectangle, triangle
	Volume	of cuboid
12	Equipment	protractor, compasses, set square and ruler
	Construction	of triangle, rectangle, and circle
	Drawings	accurate and scale drawings
	Bearings	compass points, one point from another
13	Transformation geometry	tessellations, reflections and simple enlargements; rotations of 90°, 180°
14	Charts	interpretation of bar chart, pictogram and pie charts
	Frequency distribution	construction of bar chart, pictogram and tally chart
	Average	mode, median and mean
	Probability	simple equally likely situations

Table 2.1 Chapters and topics relevant to Basic Tier examinations

2 > INTERMEDIATE TIER

The *intermediate tier* of all GCSE syllabuses are the same. Table 2.2 will indicate the chapters and topics relevant to intermediate syllabuses.

The *intermediate tier* is referred to by the different boards as:

NEAB	Level Q
MEG	Central
SEG	Intermediate
ULEAC	Intermediate
WJEC	Intermediate
NISEAC	Intermediate
IGCSE	Core

Each syllabus also includes *all of the basic tier* content.

CHAPTER AND TOPIC	NEAB			MEG				SEG	ULEAC			WJEC	NISEAC	IGCSE
	A	B	C	Maths	Mature	SMP (11–16)	SMP		A	B	SMP			
4 Integers, irrationals, prime factors, sequences	✓	✓	✓	✓	✓	✓	✓	✓	✓	✓	✓	✓	✓	✓
Standard form	✓	✓	✓	✓	✓	✓	✓	✓	✓	✓	✓	✓	✓	✓
Directed number: the 4 rules	✓	✓	✓	✓	✓	✓	✓	✓	✓	✓	✓	✓	✓	✓
5 Rounding off: significant figures, decimal places	✓	✓	✓	✓	✓	✓	✓	✓	✓	✓	✓	✓	✓	✓
6 Simple interest and compound interest	✓	✓	✓	✓	✓	✓	✓	✓	✓	✓		✓	✓	✓
7 Ratio: scale factors, best buys, proportion	✓	✓	✓	✓	✓	✓	✓	✓	✓	✓	✓	✓	✓	✓
8 Formulae: transposition of	✓	✓	✓	✓	✓	✓	✓	✓	✓	✓	✓	✓	✓	✓
Algebraic factors, simplification, quadratic expansion, brackets	✓	✓	✓	✓	✓	✓	✓	✓	✓	✓	✓	✓	✓	✓
Equations: linear, inequalities	✓	✓	✓	✓	✓	✓	✓	✓	✓	✓	✓	✓	✓	✓
Indices: integral (positive and negative), fractional	✓	✓	✓	✓	✓	✓	✓	✓	✓	✓	✓	✓	✓	✓
9 Constructing tables and graphs from equations	✓	✓	✓	✓	✓	✓	✓	✓	✓	✓	✓	✓	✓	✓
Gradient, travel graphs and conversion graphs	✓	✓	✓	✓	✓	✓	✓	✓	✓	✓	✓	✓	✓	✓
Solution of simultaneous equations by graph	✓	✓	✓	✓	✓	✓	✓	✓	✓	✓	✓	✓	✓	✓
Graphing simultaneous equations and inequalities	✓	✓	✓	✓	✓	✓	✓	✓	✓	✓	✓	✓	✓	✓
10 Angles in parallels, polygons	✓	✓	✓	✓	✓	✓	✓	✓	✓	✓	✓	✓	✓	✓
Plane figures: angles in semi-circle, tangents	✓	✓	✓	✓	✓	✓	✓	✓	✓	✓	✓	✓	✓	✓
Similarity	✓	✓	✓	✓	✓	✓	✓	✓	✓	✓	✓	✓	✓	
Axes and planes of symmetry	✓	✓	✓	✓	✓	✓	✓	✓	✓	✓	✓	✓	✓	✓
Intersecting chord (internal)	✓	✓	✓	✓	✓	✓	✓	✓	✓	✓	✓	✓	✓	✓
11 Area of circle, parallelogram	✓	✓	✓	✓	✓	✓	✓	✓	✓	✓	✓	✓	✓	✓
Area of trapezium	✓	✓	✓	✓	✓	✓	✓	✓	✓	✓	✓	✓	✓	✓
Volume of cylinder	✓	✓	✓	✓	✓	✓	✓	✓	✓	✓	✓	✓	✓	✓
Volume of prism	✓	✓	✓	✓	✓	✓	✓	✓	✓	✓	✓	✓	✓	✓
Pythagoras and trigonometry	✓	✓	✓	✓	✓	✓	✓	✓	✓	✓	✓	✓	✓	✓
Plans and elevations	✓	✓	✓	✓	✓	✓	✓	✓	✓	✓	✓	✓	✓	✓
12 Drawing quadrilaterals, bisectors, constructing angles and perpendiculars, loci	✓	✓	✓	✓	✓	✓	✓	✓	✓	✓	✓	✓	✓	✓
13 Transformations: reflections	✓	✓	✓	✓	✓	✓	✓	✓	✓	✓	✓	✓	✓	✓
rotations of 90°, 180°	✓	✓	✓	✓	✓	✓	✓	✓	✓	✓	✓	✓	✓	✓
translations	✓	✓	✓	✓	✓	✓	✓	✓	✓	✓	✓	✓	✓	✓
Vectors: graphical representation	✓	✓	✓	✓	✓	✓	✓	✓	✓	✓	✓	✓	✓	✓
Enlargement, fractional	✓	✓	✓	✓	✓	✓	✓	✓	✓	✓	✓	✓	✓	✓
14 Histogram: with equal interval	✓	✓	✓	✓	✓	✓	✓	✓	✓	✓	✓	✓	✓	✓
Frequency distribution, grouped data, cumulative frequency, quartiles	✓	✓	✓	✓	✓	✓	✓	✓	✓	✓	✓	✓	✓	✓
Scatter diagrams	✓	✓	✓	✓	✓	✓	✓	✓	✓	✓	✓	✓	✓	✓
Probability: combined events	✓	✓	✓	✓	✓	✓	✓	✓	✓	✓	✓	✓	✓	✓

Table 2.2 Chapters and topics relevant to Intermediate Tier examinations.

3 > HIGHER TIER

The *higher tier* is referred to by the different boards as:

NEAB	Level R	WJEC	Higher
MEG	Further	NISEAC	High
SEG	Higher	IGCSE	Extended
ULEAC	Higher		

Table 2.3 indicates the chapter and topics relevant to higher tier syllabuses. Each syllabus also includes all the *basic tier* content and the corresponding content at the *intermediate tier.*

CHAPTER AND TOPIC	NEAB			MEG				SEG	ULEAC			WJEC	NISEAC	IGCSE
	A	B	C	Maths	Mature	SMP (11–16)	SMP		A	B	C			
7 Ratios of similar shapes and volumes	✓	✓	✓	✓	✓	✓	✓	✓	✓	✓		✓	✓	✓
8 Quadratic factorisation, equations	✓	✓	✓	✓	✓	✓	✓	✓	✓	✓	✓	✓	✓	✓
Simultaneous equations	✓	✓	✓	✓	✓	✓	✓	✓	✓	✓		✓	✓	✓
Algebraic fractions		✓	✓	✓	✓									
Functions, combinations	✓	✓	✓			✓	✓	✓		✓	✓			
9 Area under a graph	✓	✓	✓	✓	✓	✓	✓	✓	✓	✓	✓	✓	✓	✓
Gradient at a point and interpretation	✓	✓	✓	✓	✓	✓	✓	✓	✓	✓	✓	✓	✓	✓
Cyclic quadrilaterals	✓	✓	✓	✓	✓	✓	✓	✓	✓	✓		✓	✓	✓
10 Angles in a circle from chord, double centre	✓	✓	✓	✓	✓	✓	✓	✓	✓	✓	✓	✓	✓	✓
Congruency	✓	✓	✓	✓	✓	✓	✓	✓	✓	✓	✓	✓	✓	✓
Angles in same segment, angles at centre of circle	✓	✓	✓	✓	✓	✓	✓	✓	✓	✓	✓	✓	✓	✓
11 Length of arc, area of sector	✓	✓	✓	✓	✓	✓	✓	✓	✓	✓	✓	✓	✓	✓
Area using sine rule ($\frac{1}{2}\,ab\sin C$)	✓	✓	✓	✓	✓	✓	✓	✓	✓	✓	✓	✓	✓	✓
Volume of prism	✓	✓	✓	✓	✓	✓	✓	✓	✓	✓	✓	✓	✓	✓
Volume of sphere, cone	✓	✓	✓	✓	✓	✓	✓	✓	✓	✓	✓	✓	✓	✓
Surface areas	✓	✓	✓	✓	✓	✓	✓	✓	✓	✓	✓	✓	✓	✓
3D solution using trigonometry and Pythagoras	✓	✓	✓	✓	✓	✓	✓	✓	✓	✓	✓	✓	✓	✓
Sine rule	✓	✓	✓	✓	✓	✓	✓	✓	✓	✓	✓	✓	✓	✓
Cosine rule	✓	✓	✓	✓	✓	✓	✓	✓	✓	✓	✓	✓	✓	✓
12 Constructing a perpendicular	✓	✓	✓	✓	✓	✓	✓	✓	✓	✓	✓	✓	✓	✓
13 Vectors	✓	✓	✓	✓	✓	✓	✓	✓	✓	✓	✓	✓	✓	✓
Matrices	✓	✓	✓	✓	✓	✓	✓	✓	✓	✓	✓	✓		✓
Transformations: combinations of	✓	✓	✓	✓	✓	✓	✓	✓	✓	✓	✓	✓	✓	✓
14 Unequal interval histogram	✓	✓	✓	✓	✓	✓	✓	✓	✓	✓	✓	✓	✓	✓
Probability (and/or)	✓	✓	✓	✓	✓	✓	✓	✓	✓	✓	✓	✓	✓	✓

Table 2.3 Chapters and topics relevant to Higher Tier examinations.

EXAMINATION AND ASSESSMENT TECHNIQUES

CALCULATORS

FORMULAE

REVISION

EXAMINATION STRATEGY

EXAMINATION EQUIPMENT

EXAMINATION QUESTIONS

USING AND APPLYING MATHEMATICS

PRACTICAL WORK

INVESTIGATION WORK

EXTENDED WORK

GETTING STARTED

It is helpful to remember that if you have been correctly entered (and your teachers will usually be very good at this), then you will be able to do at least half the examination questions well. This should give you a lot of confidence before you go into the examination. Being confident is helpful since, when you are anxious, you tend to make careless mistakes.

In this chapter we look at a number of practical things you can do to prepare yourself for the examination. We also look at the different types of question you may be required to answer. The chapter concludes by looking at how you can approach your coursework assignments. Chapter 15 will consider Coursework in still more detail.

ESSENTIAL PRINCIPLES

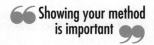
1 ⟩ CALCULATORS

All GCSE examinations allow you to have your calculator available. The questions will be set on the assumption that you have a calculator suitable for your level. So, if you know you will be asked some trigonometry questions at your level, make sure you have the appropriate calculator. If you are being entered for the *basic* tier then you will not need a scientific calculator, only a *standard* one. However, both *intermediate* and *higher* tiers will require you to have a *scientific calculator* (or to use trigonometry tables and a standard calculator). It is up to **YOU** to be responsible for your calculator and not the examination board, school or college. Do have the right one, and make certain that the batteries are not going to run out (perhaps take some spares). Do use a calculator that you are familiar with, and not a strange one borrowed at the last minute.

66 Showing your method is important 99

When using the calculator in the examination, do not forget to write out your *method of solution*, otherwise you will often lose marks. In marking exam papers this year the answer to one question should have been £1.99. Some candidates gave the answer as £1.98 *but showed no working* hence they got no marks at all even though it is quite likely that they knew what they were doing but had just made a small error, perhaps in rounding off. You will throw marks away if you do not put down your method of solution.

2 ⟩ FORMULAE

You must learn the formulae needed for each tier of the examination. It is also important that you practise using those formulae. If you have practised using the formulae *before* the examination then this will give you confidence in using them in the examination itself.

3 ⟩ Revision

There is, of course, no substitute for hard work *throughout* the course, and for regularly doing homework and classwork assignments. Revision is, however, important and should be started well before the examination, best of all *before* the Easter holiday leading to the examination. The best way to revise mathematics is to *do* it. You should try as many questions as you can beforehand; this is why there are a lot of questions at the end of each chapter. Do not be afraid of going through the same question more than once during your revision. This will be helpful practice in using the correct technique for answering that type of question, and it should help boost your confidence. Do not revise for too long at a single sitting! You are advised to revise in short periods of between 45 and 60 minutes then to have a break before doing any more. Of course, this will vary with individuals, but if you've started your revision early enough this is usually the best way rather than a last final fling!

66 Try as many questions as you can 99

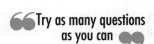

Use this book to remind you of the things you have been taught. Go through the worked examples then try the exercises for yourself, checking the answer before going any further. Finally, try the examination questions at the end of each chapter, making sure that you put down all your working, just as you will have to do in the examination.

'Review sheets' are also provided at the end of each topic-based chapter to help you check that you have understood the material presented in that chapter.

4 ⟩ EXAMINATION STRATEGY

Remember, you can do at least half the questions, and there will always be some that cause problems. You must use your time properly, so do not waste it. The majority of GCSE examinations use 'Question and Answer Books', which means there is space for you to work out your answer and to give an answer on the examination paper itself. So it doesn't matter in what order you do the questions. Go through the paper and *answer the questions you can do first*, then go back and attempt the ones you've left out. If a question causes you particular problems and you cannot see what to do then leave it, go on to another, and come back to it later. In other words, 'do what you can do well' first. This will help you 'put marks into the bank' and will help you gain confidence before you tackle the more 'difficult' questions.

Most examination papers will tell you how many marks are available to a question; the *more difficult* a question is, the *more marks* are generally given to it. So if you come across a question worth 5 marks and one worth 2 marks, you should expect the 2 mark question to be answered more easily than the 5 mark question. If you have managed to do the 5 mark question very easily, much more easily than the 2 mark question, just check that you have in fact done the question that has been set and have not misread it!

If you're answering on an answer booklet do also use *the number of lines* left for your answer as a guide. If only one line is given for working, then you should not need to do a lot of working. If however, five lines have been given for working, then you should expect to need to complete a number of stages to get to the answer.

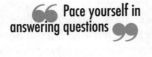

Pace yourself in answering questions

The number of marks per question will also give you some idea of how much time to spend on each question. Suppose the examination paper lasts $2\frac{1}{2}$ hours (150 minutes) and there are 100 marks, then each mark has an average time of $1\frac{1}{2}$ minutes. A 5 mark question should not take more than 8 minutes. Of course you should perhaps allow 10 minutes at the start of the examination for reading through the paper (or booklet) carefully and choosing your early questions, and perhaps 10 minutes for checking at the end. In this case you would be able to use the 'rule of thumb' that you have just over one minute per mark. Working out the *minutes per mark* should not be taken *too* far, but it does give you some idea of how to use your time well in the examination.

Check your work

Finally, do not forget to *check* those answers, especially the sense and the accuracy of your answers. If you have calculated the cost of a car to be £6, you ought to suspect that your answer is wrong and check it. Year after year examiners always mark papers where 'stupid' answers are given, such as a man being paid a salary of £45 a year! Do check your answers, it will gain you marks. Also, check that you have *rounded off* suitably. Many questions will say 'round your answers to 1 decimal place', etc., in which case you could obtain marks for rounding off. But other questions (especially at the intermediate and higher levels) might simply say 'calculate the distance … ,' and if your answer is something like 8.273419 km, you are quite likely to lose a mark for your answer since it is not given to a suitable degree of accuracy. Use the guidelines indicated in Chapter 5 to round off, or be prepared to lose marks.

You ought to be doing many of these checks while answering the question the first time, but do go through the routine as a check at the end. It may at the end be boring, but if it gains you a number of marks you would otherwise lose, and this makes the difference between grades, it will have been well worth doing.

5 > EXAMINATION EQUIPMENT

You will be required to *calculate, draw* and *construct*. You must therefore have the right equipment for the job. Do not rely on the school providing it, since if you provide the equipment you are familiar with, you can be more confident that you can use it and rely on it. Make certain you have the following:

- calculator
- batteries for calculator
- ruler
- sharp pencils
- pen (and a spare pen)

- pencil sharpener
- rubber
- protractor
- pair of compasses
- set square

6 > EXAMINATION QUESTIONS

There are different *types* of question that you could meet, e.g. short answer, structured or combination.

SHORT-ANSWER QUESTIONS

This type of question is usually given one or two marks and you may only have a line or two on which to answer the question. You will be able to assess what you have to do, then be sure to write down the *method* you are using as well as the *answer*, suitably *rounded off* if necessary.

Example

A rock group from America came to Britain on tour and went home with £14 000 profit made on all the concerts. The exchange rate was £1 to $1.12 at the time they set off from Britain. How many dollars would this make their profit?

Here you need to sort out that it is necessary to multiply the £14 000 by 1.12 which is best done on the calculator to give $15 680. Your answer should include the statement 14 000 × 1.12 as the method you have used. You take the risk of losing marks here if you give only the answer without the statement.

STRUCTURED QUESTIONS

These are the longer questions that will use one answer as part of the *next question*. This may occur perhaps two or three times in the one question. It is also vital that you show *all* your *method of working* here as one wrong answer early on will make all subsequent answers wrong and to gain your marks you must now show exactly what you have done.

Example
John and his wife Mary wanted a new carpet measuring 4 m by 5 m for their lounge. They chose an Axminster carpet priced at £12.75 per square metre, with an extra charge for fitting of £1.75 per square metre. John and Mary agreed hire purchase terms with the shop of 10% deposit and the remainder to be paid in 12 equal monthly amounts.

a) What is the area of the lounge floor to be carpeted?
b) What would be the total cost of a fitted carpet for the lounge?
c) Find out what deposit is paid on the carpet.
d) Calculate the monthly payment on the carpet.
e) After a while, Mary wanted to clean the carpet with 'Kleenit'. A packet of 'Kleenit' is sufficient to clean 6 m² of carpet. How many packets should Mary buy in order to clean the whole carpet?

You can see how one answer leads on to the next and that any mistakes made in the first answers will make a wrong answer appear later … so it is vital that you show all your method of solution in *each section* of the question. If you did this problem correctly then you would find that your answer to part d) was £21.75.

COMBINATION QUESTIONS

A longer question is often a combination of short answer and structured questions.

Example
A Girl Guide leader had to share a full cylindrical tin of cocoa into small cuboid boxes for her Girl Guides to use. The large cylindrical tin was 15 cm tall and had a diameter of 10 cm. Each cuboid box measured 4 cm by 4 cm by 3 cm.

a) Calculate the volume of the cylindrical cocoa tin.
b) Calculate the volume of one small cuboid box.
c) How many boxes can she fill from the full cocoa tin?

You should set out the first two parts as short questions with your method clearly stated. Then the final part is done by dividing the answer to a) by the answer to part b). This must be very clearly written down since it is possible for you to have made a mistake in one of the two parts, and the examiner marking your paper needs to be able to see what you've done and not to have to do *your* sum himself just to check what you've done.

SUMMARY

To summarise this section we can simply say that at all stages you should show the method of solution, unless you are certain that there is only one mark for the question and that no method is being looked for.

C O U R S E W O R K

7 > USING AND APPLYING MATHEMATICS

As we have already seen, Attainment Target 1 (AT1) involves 'using and applying mathematics'. This Attainment Target can be assessed either by coursework activities or by an examination at the end of the course. Table 3.1 provides a more detailed breakdown of the skills and understanding you need to display to reach Levels 4 to 10 in this attainment target.

	i) Applications	ii) Communication	iii) Reasoning, logic and proof
Level 4	Identify and obtain information necessary to solve problems	Interpret situations mathematically, using appropriate symbols or diagrams.	Give some justification for their solutions to problems. Make generalisations.
Level 5	Carry through a task by breaking it down into smaller, more manageable tasks.	Interpret information presented in a variety of mathematical forms.	Make a generalisation and test it.
Level 6	Pose their own questions or design a task in a given context.	Examine critically the mathematical presentation of information.	Make a generalisation giving some degree of justification.
Level 7	Follow new lines of enquiry when investigating within mathematics itself or when using mathematics to solve a real-life problem.	Use appropriate mathematical language and notation when solving real-life problems or commenting on generalisations or solutions.	Examine and comment constructively on generalisations or solutions.
Level 8	Make reasoned choices when exploring a mathematical task.	Use mathematical language and symbolism effectively when presenting logical accounts of work stating reasons for choices made.	Understand the role of counter-examples in disproving generalisations or hypotheses.
Level 9	Co-ordinate a number of features or variables in solving problems.	Use mathematical language and symbolism effectively when presenting logical accounts of work and produce concise justifications of their solutions to complex problems.	Justify their solutions to problems involving a number of features or variables.
Level 10	Explore independently and constructively a new area of mathematics.	Apply mathematical language and symbolism confidently when handling abstract concepts. Present logical and concise accounts of work resulting from an independent exploration of a new area of mathematics, commenting on alternative solutions.	Handle abstract concepts of proof and definition when exploring independently a familiar or new area of mathematics.

Table 3.1 Levels of Attainment in 'Using and Applying' Mathematics.

Coursework is often an important part of the assessment (see Chapter 2), accounting for 20% of the total marks, so it is important that your assignments are well planned throughout the course rather than an unwelcome burden at the end of the course.

Your school or college will be responsible for deciding upon the actual nature of the coursework and the way in which it is organised. There are many different tasks you could be asked to do. Whatever the nature of the coursework, the assessment will be made in three main areas: *Practical, Investigation* and *Extended pieces of work*.

8 > PRACTICAL WORK

You will be assessed on:

a) How you planned the task, how you carried it out and how accurate you were. Evidence of these three stages is necessary.
b) Whether you have demnstrated that you understand the use that can be made of equipment. For example in weighing, that you have used an appropriate set of scales.
c) Your actual skill in using the equipment.
d) Your ability to communicate what you are doing. You could well be asked to explain *why* you did a certain thing, or *why* you used a piece of equipment in a particular way.

The tasks set will be at the level for which you are being considered. If you move up a level during the course then you should be given an opportunity of doing the practical work appropriate to this higher level.

9 > INVESTIGATION WORK

You will be assessed on:

a) How you *planned* and *prepared* the set task.
b) How much *relevant information* you were able to obtain and use.
c) Your ability to *communicate* what you have done. You could be asked to talk about the investigation as well as to write a clear solution.
d) The extent to which you were able to *draw a valid conclusion*.
e) How *far* you went with the investigation. Was it exhaustive?

Very often the same investigation will be set for all levels. It is up to you to demonstrate how well you have been able to pursue the investigation and to decide the point at which you stop.

EXAMPLE INVESTIGATION

Four straight lines all intersect each other. How many intersections will there be for other numbers of lines?

a) This work can be planned in such a way that it can become an *investigation*. First you can draw two lines, then three, then four, and so on.
b) You now need to look for a *pattern*. If you can identify a pattern you can start predicting how many intersections there will be for the next sets of lines without having to draw them.
c) The work must be written up clearly. Start with an *introduction*, telling the assessor what you were trying to do. Follow this by outlining the *method* you have chosen to pursue your investigation. Present a *table of results* giving an indication of any patterns you noticed.
d) Can you draw a *conclusion*? For example, can you find the number of intersections for any given number of straight lines, say 50?
e) How far have you been able to see a pattern? Can you write a *formula* for n lines, and the number of intersections this will give?

In an investigation it is up to you to go as far into the investigation as you can. But do be clear and logical in how you set about conducting the investigation. Make sure that you write up your results neatly and on the lines suggested:

introduction → method → results → conclusion.

10 > EXTENDED WORK

Usually, the task set will be defined by the school or college from some particular starting point. It is then up to you where you take it and how far you develop it. The main points that will be looked for in an extended piece of work are given below.

a) *The comprehension of the task.*
Did you understand the problem and were you able to define what you were going to do?

b) *Planning*
Were you able to plan out the task into different set stages to enable you to complete the task?

c) *Performance of the task.*
How well did you undertake the set task? Did you choose appropriate methods? Did you use appropriate equipment? How have you interpreted the results from that equipment?

d) *Communication.*
This will be both written and oral. Again a well set-out introduction → method → results → conclusion will be important. Have you used helpful diagrams/tables etc? In oral work were you able to respond to unexpected queries?

EXAMPLE PIECE OF WORK

Plan a return journey from your home to the nearest zoo, or country park, for yourself and some children, in one day.

That is a straightforward task, and the main points looked for in the assessment would be:

a) Were you able to obtain bus/train timetables, opening hours of the zoo and prices?
b) How well did you link the times together for setting off, for lunch and for returning?
c) How appropriate is the actual solution? Does it give adequate time to get there, to enjoy the day, and return? How accurate are the prices, and how practical is the suggested journey? In fact, has the journey actually been made?
d) How well is the task written up, and can you talk about it? In fact, if you actually undertook the task you could comment on the accuracy of the planning.

Your coursework tasks should be assessed at frequent, but appropriate, times during the course. Assessed coursework will help you to be aware of how well you are doing. If you do have shortcomings you can then work on improving them before the next time such material is assessed. Yet in every case, the coursework component comes down to *you*, since it really does assess the way in which you:

- plan the work
- do the work
- communicate the work.

It is all up to you!

You can find more specific help on your approach to Coursework topics in Chapter 15 of this book. Chapter 15 also looks at oral and aural aspects of the assessment in mathematics.

GETTING STARTED

You will be required to recognise the *patterns* that arise in numbers as a result of many different situations. You will also have to actually work out some calculations. In the vast majority of examinations you are allowed to use a *calculator*. Even so, you must be very careful to check your answers to see that they make sense. You should round your answers off to a suitable degree of accuracy, as you will see in the next chapter.

Many of the ideas in this chapter will, of course, be used in later chapters and will not necessarily be examined on their own.

USEFUL DEFINITIONS

Integer	A whole number.
Fraction	A part of a whole.
Equivalent	Having the same value but looking different.
Factor	An integer that exactly divides another integer.
Multiple	The result of multiplying an integer by an integer.
Prime	A number that has two factors only.
Sequence	A list of numbers that follow a pattern or rule.
Square	To multiply a number by itself.
Finite	Of known number.
Infinite	When the number is too large to be countable.

ESSENTIAL PRINCIPLES

MULTIPLES

There are, as you know, *odd* numbers (1,3,5,7 etc.) and *even* numbers (2,4,6,8, etc.). *Even* numbers are *multiples* of 2. In other words, 2 divides *exactly* into each *even* number. Other examples of multiples could be of 4 (e.g. 4,8,12, …,96, 100, …), of 5 (5,10,15 …,185 …), or of any whole number.

FACTORS

The factors of a whole number *N* are the *whole numbers* that will *divide* into *N* exactly. So the factors of 12 are 1,2,3,4,6 and 12. The factors of 16 are 1,2,4,8 and 16.

WORKED EXAMPLE 1

A sweet manufacturer wanted to put his chocolate bars into packs of more than 1 bar, and pack them into a box that could contain 100 bars of chocolate. What possible numbers can he put into a pack?

He can put any number into a pack as long as that number is a *factor* of 100. The factors of 100 are 1,2,4,5,10,20,25,50 and 100. Since there must be more than 1, he has the choice of any of the others.

EXERCISE 1

Find the factors of 72

PRIME NUMBERS

A prime number is a whole number that has *two*, and only two, *factors*. For example, 7 has only two factors: 1 and 7; 13 also has only two factors: 1 and 13. The number 1 is not a prime number as it has only one factor, 1, and not two. Try to write down the first ten prime numbers, 2 is the first, and 29 is the tenth.

WORKED EXAMPLE 2

In one school year there were four classes. Class M4A had 29 pupils, Class M4B had 27 pupils, Class M4C had 23 pupils, and Class M4D had 22 pupils. Two of the teachers said they always had problems when trying to put the children into equal groups. Which classes did these teachers take and how could the Headmaster have avoided the problem?

The classes with 29 and 23 pupils cannot be divided into equal groups because they are prime numbers. So the teachers from M4A and M4C would have complained. To avoid the problem, the Head could change the numbers in each class so that none contains a prime number.

SEQUENCES

Sequences are lists of numbers that follow a pattern. For example, in the sequence 3, 7, 11, 15, 19 … you add 4 each time. In the sequence 3, 6, 12, 24 … you double the figure each time, and in the sequence 1, 1, 2, 3, 5, 8, 13, 21 … you add the last two terms to get the next in the sequence.

WORKED EXAMPLE 3

Find the next three numbers in the sequence 1, 2, 4, 7, 11, 16 …

Look at how the pattern builds up. You add on 1, then 2, then 3, then 4, etc., so the next three numbers will be 22, 29 and 37.

SQUARE NUMBERS

A square number is a number that can be formed by multiplying a whole number by itself. For example, 25 is a square number because 5 multiplied by itself is 25. Try to write down the first ten square numbers, 1 is the first and 100 is the tenth.

1 ▷ PATTERN IN NUMBER

Level 4

SQUARE ROOTS

Square roots are numbers which, when multiplied by themselves, give you a particular number. For example, the square root of 36 is 6, since 6×6 is 36. We use a special mathematical sign for square root, it is $\sqrt{}$. Find it on your calculator. So $\sqrt{9}$ means 'the squareroot of 9'. Now, on your calculator press 9, followed by $\sqrt{}$ and you get 3, so $\sqrt{9} = 3$.

EXERCISE 2

Find both the square and the square root of: i) 16, and   ii) 0.9.

NEGATIVE NUMBERS

We use negative numbers most often in winter when we talk about the temperature, since temperatures below freezing point are negative numbers.

Look at this thermometer, Fig. 4.1. It shows a reading of 7° below freezing point. We call this minus 7 °C and write it as –7 °C.

To work out the difference between two temperatures we can consider a temperature scale such as the one in Fig. 4.1a).

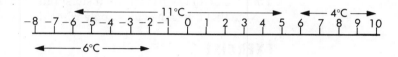

Fig. 4.1a)

Fig. 4.1

You can see that the differences between:

a)   10 °C and 6 °C is 10 – 6 which is 4 °C
b)   5 °C and – 6 °C is 5 + 6 which is 11 °C
c)   –2 °C and –8 °C is 8 – 2 which is 6 °C

It is necessary to be able to calculate new temperatures when we are given a rise or fall from a previous temperature. For example, if the temperature is 8 °C and falls by 10 °C, then by counting down 10 °C from 8 °C we come to –2 °C which is the new temperature. Also, if the temperature is –10 °C and rises by 4 °C, then by counting up 4 °C from –10 °C we come to the new temperature of –6 °C.

You need to be able to add, subtract, multiply and divide with negative numbers.

2 ▷ NEGATIVE NUMBER ARITHMETIC

ADDING AND SUBTRACTING

There are some *rules* that you ought to know:

> 66 This is where a lot of errors are made so read this part carefully. 99

+ – is the same as –
– – is the same as +

So, for example,

   5 + –2 is the same as 5 – 2, which is 3, and
   5 – –2 is the same as 5 + 2, which is 7.

You can see from the thermometer that by going up and down the temperature scale you get:

   3 + 8 = 11,   3 – 8 = –5,   –3 + 8 = 5,   –3 – 8 = –11.

In the same way,

   3 + –8 = 3 – 8 = –5 and 3 – –8 = 3 + 8 = 11.

Fig. 4.2 illustrates how we calculate –3 + 5 to be 2, or –3 – –5 to be 2.

a)   The first thing to do is to start with the first number on the number scale; here it is – 3.
b)   Since the second number is '+' or '– –' (+5 or – –5 in this case), count 5 numbers up the scale and you see that you come to 2.
   Note that when the second number is '–' or '+ –' you go down the scale.

Fig. 4.2

MULTIPLYING AND DIVIDING

Here are some more *rules* you ought to know:

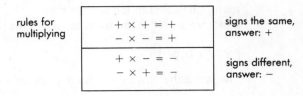

| rules for multiplying | $+ \times + = +$
$- \times - = +$ | signs the same, answer: + |
| | $+ \times - = -$
$- \times + = -$ | signs different, answer: − |

Fig.4.3

That is: when the signs are the *same*, the answer is +

when the signs are *different*, the answer is −

For example,

$$5 \times 3 = 15 \qquad 2 \times -3 = -6 \qquad 8 \div 4 = 2 \qquad 6 \div -2 = -3$$
$$-5 \times -3 = 15 \qquad -2 \times 3 = -6 \qquad -8 \div -4 = 2 \qquad -6 \div 2 = -3$$

This will be of use to you when substituting into given formulae in later chapters.

Note that the same rules apply when dividing.

EXERCISE 3

Calculate: i) $-3 + 5$; ii) $-3 - 5$; iii) -3×-5; iv) -3×5; v) $15 \div -3$.

3 > FRACTIONS

You should be familiar with two types of fractions, *vulgar fractions* and *decimal fractions*.

VULGAR FRACTIONS

A vulgar fraction is always expressed using two numbers, one above the other, for example $\frac{3}{5}$

The shaded region of the rectangle in Fig. 4.4, represents $\frac{3}{10}$, or three tenths. The 10 comes from the fact that the rectangle is divided into 10 equal pieces and the 3 because 3 pieces are shaded. We use this idea when finding a fraction of a given amount.

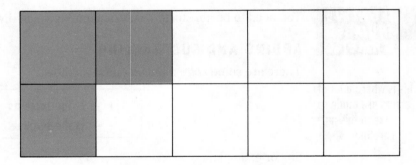

Fig.4.4

WORKED EXAMPLE 4

Find $\frac{2}{5}$ of £8.

First divide £8 by 5 to find $\frac{1}{5}$, which will be £1.60. Now multiply this by 2 to find $\frac{2}{5}$ giving a total of £3.20.

EQUIVALENT FRACTIONS

Many vulgar fractions are the same as each other, or, as we would say, are *equivalent*. The diagrams in Fig. 4.5 illustrate some fractions all equivalent to $\frac{3}{4}$.

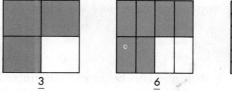
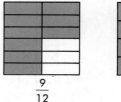
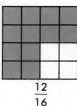

$$\frac{3}{4} \qquad \frac{6}{8} \qquad \frac{9}{12} \qquad \frac{12}{16}$$

Fig.4.5

You can find a lot more equivalent fractions just by multiplying the top part of the fraction and the bottom part by the same number.

We use this idea in what we call *cancelling down* to the simplest equivalent fraction. You may use other phrases for this, like 'simplifying' or 'putting into lowest terms'. We do this by dividing the top and the bottom, by the same number. For example $\frac{12}{20}$ will simplify down to $\frac{3}{5}$, since we can divide both the top and the bottom by 4.

| **WORKED EXAMPLE 5** | Mat has just lost 24 sheep from his flock of 80 through foot and mouth disease. What fraction of his flock, written as simply as possible, has he lost? |

Level 6

The fraction lost is 24 out of 80, or $\frac{24}{80}$. Both top and bottom can be divided by 8, so we can cancel using 8 to give us $\frac{3}{10}$.

ADDITION AND SUBTRACTION

You need to be able to add and subtract simple *vulgar* fractions. Remember that it is only easy to do this when the bottom numbers are the same. For example, $\frac{3}{10}$ added to $\frac{4}{10}$ is $\frac{7}{10}$, or $\frac{3}{5} - \frac{1}{5} = \frac{2}{5}$. So if the bottom numbers are *not* the same then you need to change them by using equivalent fractions. For example, if we want to add $\frac{1}{2}$ and $\frac{3}{8}$, we need to make both bottom numbers the same; we can make both of them 8 by multiplying, hence $\frac{1}{2}$ becomes $\frac{4}{8}$ while $\frac{3}{8}$ stays as it is. This gives us $\frac{4}{8} + \frac{3}{8}$ which is $\frac{7}{8}$.

| **WORKED EXAMPLE 6** | Kevin sold $\frac{1}{4}$ of his stamp collection to Brian, and gave $\frac{3}{8}$ of it away to Malcolm. How much of his collection had he left? |

We need to add together $\frac{1}{4}$ and $\frac{3}{8}$. We can change $\frac{1}{4}$ to $\frac{2}{8}$ by thinking about the equivalent fractions, then add $\frac{2}{8}$ and $\frac{3}{8}$ to give $\frac{5}{8}$. Now we think about $1 - \frac{5}{8}$ to find out what fraction is left. The 1 can be written as $\frac{8}{8}$, hence the sum becomes $\frac{8}{8} - \frac{5}{8}$ which is $\frac{3}{8}$.

MIXED NUMBERS

When adding two vulgar fractions, say $\frac{7}{8}$ and $\frac{5}{8}$, we get $\frac{12}{8}$ which is *top heavy*. In other words, more than a simple fraction, with one or more 'whole numbers' involved. Top heavy fractions can be simplified to what we call mixed numbers.

| **WORKED EXAMPLE 7** | Ross bought 7 bottles of ginger beer, each containing $\frac{3}{4}$ pint. How much had he altogether? |

We need 7 lots of $\frac{3}{4}$ or $7 \times \frac{3}{4}$ which is $\frac{21}{4}$. As four quarters make a whole item we divide 21 by 4 to get 5 remainder 1, which would be 5 whole items and 1 quarter. So Ross had $5\frac{1}{4}$ pints altogether.

FURTHER ADDITION AND SUBTRACTION

You must also be able to add two fractions like $\frac{2}{5}$ and $\frac{1}{3}$ where we need to change both fractions to get the same bottom number. Look for the LCM of 5 and 3, which is 15, and make both fractions into fifteenths. We can illustrate this by:

$$\frac{2}{5} + \frac{1}{3} \rightarrow \frac{6}{15} + \frac{5}{15} = \frac{11}{15}$$

In a similar way we can illustrate $\frac{5}{6} + \frac{1}{8}$ where 24 is the LCM of the bottom numbers:

$$\frac{5}{6} + \frac{1}{8} \rightarrow \frac{20}{24} + \frac{3}{24} = \frac{23}{24}$$

If one or both of the numbers being added is a mixed number, then we add the whole ones separately then add the fractions, as illustrated in the next example:

$$2\frac{3}{4} + 1\frac{1}{2} \rightarrow 3 + \frac{3}{4} + \frac{1}{2} \rightarrow 3 + \frac{5}{4} \rightarrow 3 + 1\frac{1}{4} = 4\frac{1}{4}$$

EXERCISE 4

Calculate: i) $\frac{3}{5} + \frac{1}{4}$; ii) $3\frac{1}{2} + 2\frac{4}{5}$; iii) $\frac{7}{8} - \frac{5}{6}$.

MULTIPLICATION OF FRACTIONS

You may well need at some time to *multiply* two fractions, for example $\frac{4}{5} \times \frac{1}{6}$. We do this by simplifying the question first by 'cancelling', to see if anything will divide into any of the top numbers and also any of the bottom numbers. Here we can *cancel* both the 4 and 6 by 2 to give the product $\frac{2}{5} \times \frac{1}{3}$ which we now multiply by first multiplying the top numbers then multiplying the bottom numbers to give $\frac{2}{15}$. We can summarise this by:

$$\frac{4}{5} \times \frac{1}{6} \rightarrow \frac{\overset{2}{\cancel{4}}}{5} \times \frac{1}{\underset{3}{\cancel{6}}} \rightarrow \frac{2}{5} \times \frac{1}{3} \rightarrow \frac{2}{15}$$

In a similar way we can illustrate $\frac{4}{9} \times \frac{3}{10}$, where more 'cancelling' can be done:

$$\frac{4}{9} \times \frac{3}{10} \rightarrow \frac{\overset{2}{\cancel{4}}}{9} \times \frac{3}{\underset{5}{\cancel{10}}} \rightarrow \frac{2}{\underset{3}{\cancel{9}}} \times \frac{\overset{1}{\cancel{3}}}{5} \rightarrow \frac{2}{3} \times \frac{1}{5} \rightarrow \frac{2}{15}$$

You certainly would not be expected to write all this down as a solution. It has been written out in full here simply to illustrate what is done.

If one, or more, of the numbers is a mixed number then it needs changing to a *top heavy* fraction before we can multiply.

For example, $2\frac{1}{2} \times \frac{4}{5}$ can be shown as

$$2\frac{1}{2} \times \frac{4}{5} \rightarrow \frac{5}{2} \times \frac{4}{5} \rightarrow \frac{\overset{1}{\cancel{5}}}{\underset{1}{\cancel{2}}} \times \frac{\overset{2}{\cancel{4}}}{\underset{1}{\cancel{5}}} \rightarrow \frac{2}{1} \rightarrow 2$$

DIVISION OF FRACTIONS

To cut a long story short, you divide two fractions by turning the second one upside down and then multiplying.

WORKED EXAMPLE 8

Calculate: $\frac{4}{5} \div \frac{2}{3}$.

Change the $\frac{2}{3}$ to $\frac{3}{2}$ and multiply, so

$$\frac{4}{5} \div \frac{2}{3} = \frac{4}{5} \times \frac{3}{2} = \frac{12}{10} = \frac{6}{5} = 1\frac{1}{5}$$

DECIMAL FRACTIONS

The other type of fraction is a decimal fraction. This is shown by the numbers on the right-hand side of a decimal point.

For example, 5.62 shows 5 whole ones and .62 is the decimal fraction. You need to be familiar with these equivalent fractions which help to show what decimal fractions are:

$$\frac{1}{10} = 0.1, \ \frac{3}{10} = 0.3, \ 4\frac{7}{10} = 4.7, \ \frac{1}{100} = 0.01, \ \frac{27}{100} = 0.27, \ 26\frac{15}{100} = 26.15$$

ADDING AND SUBTRACTING

You may say: 'But I have my calculator.' This may be true, but will you always have it wherever you are? I doubt it, so it is important that you know how to do decimal arithmetic.

When adding or subtracting decimal numbers you must first line up your numbers so that the decimal points are underneath each other, then add or subtract, depending on the sum given.

<table>
<tr><td>**WORKED EXAMPLE 9**</td><td>A metal bar of usual length 23.4 cm expands by 1.76 cm when it is heated to 100 °C. What is its length at this temperature?</td></tr>
</table>

Add together 23.4 and 1.76 as
$$\begin{array}{r} 23.4 \\ 1.76 \\ \hline 25.16 \text{ cm} \\ \hline \end{array}$$

Try to do this first without a calculator.

<table>
<tr><td>**WORKED EXAMPLE 10**</td><td>Gillian went into a shop with £15 and came out with £7.60. How much had she spent?</td></tr>
</table>

Subtract 7.60 from 15 as
$$\begin{array}{r} 15.00 \\ -7.60 \\ \hline 7.40 \\ \hline \end{array}$$

So Gillian had spent £7.40. Note that it helps to change the 15 to 15.00.

MULTIPLICATION

To multiply two decimal numbers, or more, you can follow the simple process outlined in Fig. 4.6.

<table>
<tr><td>**WORKED EXAMPLE 11**</td><td>Find the cost of 0.4 kg of meat at £1.65 per kg.
You want to calculate 0.4 × 1.65; it has three decimal places. Ignore the decimal points and calculate 4 × 165 to give 660; give the answer to three decimal places which will be 0.660. The cost is £0.66.</td></tr>
</table>

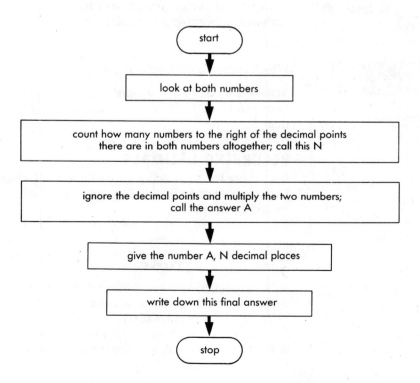

Fig. 4.6

WORKED EXAMPLE 12

Find the total length of three lengths of garden fencing each 1.6 metres long.

You want to calculate 3×1.6; it has just one decimal place. Ignore the decimal points and calculate 3×16 to give 48; give the answer to one decimal place, which will be 4.8 m.

DIVISION

You are only expected to be able to divide a decimal number by a whole number without a calculator. This is done in the same way as a *normal* division, except that the decimal point of the answer will appear directly above the decimal point of the question.

WORKED EXAMPLE 13

How much will each child get if £21.50 is divided between five children?

Calculate $21.50 \div 5$ as
$$5 \overline{\smash{)}\,21.50}^{\,4.30}$$

The answer is £4.30.

MENTAL CALCULATIONS

Naturally, wherever possible you would try to do these calculations on the calculator, but there are some very easy ones that can be done *in the head* or *mentally*.

For example, when multiplying by 10 simply move the decimal point one place to the right, as in the sums $5.67 \times 10 = 56.7$, and $3 \times 10 = 30$. When multiplying by 100 simply move the decimal point two places to the right, as in the sums $4.67 \times 100 = 467$, $0.597 \times 100 = 59.7$, $2.7 \times 100 = 270$ and $1.09 \times 100 = 109$.

It is similar when dividing by 10; we simply move the decimal point one place to the left. For example, the sums $57 \div 10 = 5.7$ and $81.97 \div 10 = 8.197$. For dividing by 100, we move the decimal point two places to the left, as in the sums $271 \div 100 = 2.71$, $25.9 \div 100 = 0.259$, $5 \div 100 = 0.05$ and $2.79 \div 100 = 0.0279$.

You can practise these decimal type calculations by setting yourself some similar problems, calculating them and then checking the answers on your calculator.

CONVERSION BETWEEN VULGAR AND DECIMAL FRACTIONS

It is necessary for you to be able to *convert* vulgar fractions to decimal fractions. This helps you to compare fractions with each other and also to add or subtract awkward vulgar fractions.

Level 6

To convert a vulgar fraction to a decimal fraction you just divide the top number by the bottom number, using a calculator if you have one available.

WORKED EXAMPLE 14

Which is the bigger fraction, $\frac{7}{8}$ or $\frac{17}{20}$?

Make each one into a decimal fraction: $\frac{7}{8}$ will become $7 \div 8$ which is 0.875, whilst $\frac{17}{20}$ becomes $17 \div 20$ which is 0.85, and since 0.875 is bigger than 0.85, then $\frac{7}{8}$ is bigger than $\frac{17}{20}$.

RECURRING DECIMALS

Both these last two fractions are what we call *terminating decimals*, because they have a fixed number of decimal places, but some fractions are not like that; they just seem to go on and on for ever.

For example, try working out $\frac{1}{3}$. Do it on the calculator and you get 0.3333333, but do it the long way
$$3 \overline{\smash{)}\,1.000000\ldots}^{\,0.333333\ldots}$$
and you will see it goes on and on for ever. We write this as $0.33\dot{3}$, the dots mean this goes on and on for ever and we call these types of decimal numbers *recurring decimals*.

Try $\frac{1}{11}$, do you get $0.09090909\ldots$? We would write this as $0.0\dot{9}0\dot{9}$. Note where the dots are this time, they show which figures repeat for ever. Try some more for yourself and make a list of the vulgar fractions that give terminating decimals and those that give recurring decimals.

4 > PERCENTAGE
 Level 5

One per cent is written as 1%, which means 1 out of 100 or $\frac{1}{100}$ or 0.01. So 2% is the same as $\frac{2}{100}$ or 0.02, and 15% is the same as $\frac{15}{100}$ or 0.15.

Using percentage with money can be simplified if we recognise that 1% of £1 is 1p and so 8% of £1 is 8p, etc. It follows then that, for example, 15% of £5 is $15 \times 1\%$ of £5, i.e. $15 \times 5p$ which is 75p.

WORKED EXAMPLE 15

Joseph the paper boy, who earned £6 a week, was given a 12% pay increase. What is his new pay per week?

An increase means *gets bigger*, and 12% of £6 is $12 \times 1\%$ of £6, i.e. $12 \times 6p$ which is 72p. So Joseph's new pay is £6 + 72p, which is £6.72.

WORKED EXAMPLE 16

A shop reduced its prices by 10% in a sale. What was the new price of a radio that was previously marked £25?

A reduction means *gets smaller* and 10% of £25 is $10 \times 1\%$ of £25, i.e. $10 \times 25p$ which is £2.50, so the new price of the radio is £25 – £2.50, which is £22.50.

EXERCISE 5

Find 15% of £5.60.

FRACTIONS INTO PERCENTAGES

To *change* a fraction to a percentage, simply multiply by 100. For instance, if Arun scored 18 out of 20 in a test, the percentage he would have got would be found by multiplying $\frac{18}{20}$ by 100. The easiest way to do this is on your calculator, as $(18 \times 100)/20$, which will come to 90%.

Level 6

PERCENTAGE INCREASE

If we want to increase by, say, 5% we really need to calculate 105% (100 + 5) which will simply mean multiplying by 1.05.

A quicker way

For example, to increase £7 by 8% we can calculate $£7 \times 1.08$, which is £7.56. This is a far quicker way than finding 8% and adding on, but you can check that you get the same answer.

PERCENTAGE DECREASE

If we want to decrease by, say, 7%, we really need to calculate 93% (100 – 7) or multiply by 0.93.

For example, £9.20 decreased by 20% is found by calculating $£9.20 \times 0.80$, which is £7.36. Again, check you get the same answer by the long method of finding 20% and subtracting.

EXERCISE 6

i) Increase £50 by 6%; ii) decrease £800 by 17%.

5 > SPECIAL NUMBER NAMES

You need to be familiar with various types of numbers.

INTEGER

Integers are *whole numbers*, either positive or negative, and zero.

For example. … –4, –3, –2, –1, 0, 1, 2, 3, 4 …

Remember, prime numbers can only be divided exactly by themselves and 1

PRIME FACTORS

The prime factors of an integer (whole number) are factors that are prime numbers. For example, the prime factors of 35 are 5 and 7, which, for convenience, we usually write as 5×7, and the prime factors of 12 are $2 \times 2 \times 3$ (note how we put the 2 down twice so that the product of these factors gives the integer we start with). You can check for yourself

Level 7

that the prime factors of 72 are $2 \times 2 \times 2 \times 3 \times 3$, which we would shorten to $2^3 \times 3^2$, and that the prime factors of 90 are $2 \times 3^2 \times 5$.

EXERCISE 7

Find the prime factors of   i) 100 and   ii) 130.

COMMON FACTORS AND HCF

Common factors are the factors that two integers have in common. For example, the common factors of 16 and 24 are 2, 4 and 8, since all three numbers divide exactly into 16 and 24. Here 8 is the HCF, since it is the *highest common factor*.

One way to find the HCF is to consider the prime factors. For example, to find the HCF of 72 and 90, we break each number into its prime factors, $2 \times 2 \times 2 \times 3 \times 3$ and $2 \times 3 \times 3 \times 5$, then look for the figures each has in common. Here both have in common $(2 \times 3 \times 3)$, hence the HCF is 18.

EXERCISE 8

Find the HCF of 36, 90 and 108.

COMMON MULTIPLES AND LCM

Common multiples are the multiples that two integers have in common. For example, the common multiples of 6 and 8 are 24, 48, 72, … Here 24 is the LCM since it is the *lowest common multiple*.

Again, we can use prime factors to help us find the lowest common multiple. For example to find the LCM of 75 and 90 we break each number into its prime factors, $3 \times 5 \times 5$ and $2 \times 3 \times 3 \times 5$ then look for the smallest combination of both, which here is $2 \times 3 \times 3 \times 5 \times 5$. Notice you can find both previous prime factors here. The LCM of 75 and 90 is 450.

EXERCISE 9

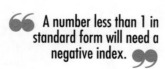

Find the LCM of 18 and 30.

 **Level 8**

STANDARD FORM

Standard form is a convenient way of writing very large or very small numbers. It is always expressed in the terms of:

$a \times 10^n$,

where a is a number between 1 and 10 and n is an integer.

For example: 200   would be written as 2.0×10^2

617000   would be written as 6.17×10^5

8431.3   would be written as 8.4313×10^3

Notice how the number on the 10, called the *index*, tells you how many places to move the decimal point. If the number is less than 1 to start with then we use negative indices on the 10.

 **A number less than 1 in standard form will need a negative index.**

For example: 0.015   will be 1.5×10^{-2}

0.000000783   will be 7.83×10^{-7}

EXERCISE 10

Rewrite in standard form: i) 568900;   ii) 0.000527

RATIONAL NUMBERS

Level 9

Rational numbers are all the numbers that *can* be expressed as a vulgar fraction of two integers.

For example, 5 is a rational number, since 5 can be written as $\frac{5}{1}$

9.16 is a rational number since it can be written as $\frac{916}{100}$.

$\sqrt{9}$ is a rational number since it is 3 or –3.

It is worth remembering that all the *recurring decimals* you came across earlier came from fractions.

For example, $\frac{2}{11}$ is $0.18\dot{1}\dot{8}\cdot$, $\frac{5}{7}$ is $0.\dot{7}1428\dot{5}\cdot$, and in fact all recurring decimals can be shown to be *rational* numbers.

IRRATIONAL NUMBERS

Irrational numbers are all numbers that *cannot* be expressed as a vulgar fraction of two integers.

For example, $\sqrt{2}$ cannot be expressed as a vulgar fraction, π cannot be expressed exactly as a fraction ($\frac{22}{7}$ is only an approximation to it).

---

6 > USING THE CALCULATOR EFFICIENTLY

66 Level 7 99

Many of us can use a calculator, but at level 7 you need to be able to demonstrate 'efficiency' in its use. This means that you must show that you can accurately use a variety of time-saving keys on the calculator.

THE MEMORY BUTTONS

At this level you should be using a scientific calculator with two main memory buttons. These are most likely to be:

$\boxed{\text{Min}}$ for putting numbers or answers into the memory.

$\boxed{\text{MR}}$ for 'recalling' or 'bringing out' what's in the memory.

WORKED EXAMPLE 16

Use your calculator efficiently, to solve the problem:

$$\frac{3.4 \times 5.7}{7.5 - 2.4}$$

You have to show your good use of memory. So here you can calculate the denominator (bottom number) first, putting the answer into the memory. Then you can calculate the numerator (top number), and divide by the memory. You then have your final answer.

66 Make your method clear 99

$\boxed{7.5}$ $\boxed{-}$ $\boxed{2.4}$ $\boxed{=}$ $\boxed{\text{Min}}$ $\boxed{3.4}$ $\boxed{\times}$ $\boxed{5.7}$ $\boxed{\div}$ $\boxed{\text{MR}}$ $\boxed{=}$ 3.8

It is most helpful in answering a question of this type to present your working out as above. By identifying the buttons you have used you show how you got to your answer.

WORKED EXAMPLE 17

Use your calculator to find the answer to:

$$\frac{75^2 - 21^2}{20^2 + 15^2}$$

Round your answer off to two decimal places.

Here you can use the $\boxed{x^2}$ button on your calculator. This is sometimes accessed by $\boxed{\text{INV}}$ $\boxed{\sqrt{}}$ (check this on your calculator).

Start by calculating the denominator (bottom), putting this into memory. Then calculate the numerator (top), and divide by the memory. You then have your final answer.

$\boxed{20}$ $\boxed{x^2}$ $\boxed{+}$ $\boxed{15}$ $\boxed{x^2}$ $\boxed{=}$ $\boxed{\text{Min}}$ $\boxed{75}$ $\boxed{x^2}$ $\boxed{-}$ $\boxed{21}$ $\boxed{x^2}$ $\boxed{=}$ $\boxed{\div}$ $\boxed{\text{MR}}$ $\boxed{=}$

This should bring you to the answer 8.2944, which rounds off to 8.29.

BRACKETS

You can also use the brackets of your calculator, where appropriate. Sometimes the brackets can be used instead of the memory button.

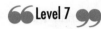

**WORKED
EXAMPLE 18**

Calculate $(2.5 \times 15.6) - (6.7 - 3.893)$

Calculate from left to right, using the brackets as necessary.

| 2.5 | × | 15.6 | − | [| 6.7 | − | 3.893 |] | = |

This should give you the answer 36.193.

EXERCISE 11

Use your calculator to efficiently calculate

i) $\dfrac{7^2 - 5^2}{2.5 \times 1.5}$ ii) $5.87 + (9.13 - 4.75) + 1.3$

INEQUALITIES

Level 7

You should be familiar with the four signs:
>   which means *greater than*; e.g. $8 > 3$
<   which means *less than*; e.g. $1 < 5.6$
⩾   which means *greater than or equal to*.
⩽   which means *less than or equal to*.

SOLUTIONS TO EXERCISES

S1

Written in pairs the factors will be 1, 72; 2, 36; 3, 24; 4, 18; 6, 12; 8, 9. A systematic search is this way from 1, through to $\sqrt{72}$ which is 8 to the nearest whole number, will give all the factors that could now be written in order as:

1, 2, 3, 4, 6, 8, 9, 12, 18, 24, 36 and 72.

S2

i) square = $16 \times 16 = 256$;
$\sqrt{16} = 4$ and -4.

ii) square = 0.81;
$\sqrt{0.9} = 0.9486833$
or a suitably rounded off answer.

S3

i) 2; ii) −8; iii) 15; iv) −15; v) −5.

S4

i) $\dfrac{3}{5} + \dfrac{1}{4} \rightarrow \dfrac{12}{10} + \dfrac{5}{12} = \dfrac{17}{20}$

ii) $3\dfrac{1}{2} + 2\dfrac{4}{5} \rightarrow 5 + \dfrac{5}{10} + \dfrac{8}{10} = 5 + \dfrac{13}{10} = 6\dfrac{3}{10}$

iii) $\dfrac{7}{8} - \dfrac{5}{6} = \dfrac{21}{24} - \dfrac{20}{24} = \dfrac{1}{24}$

S5

$\dfrac{15}{100} \times 5.6 = 0.84$

So the answer is given as £0.84.

S6

i) £50 × 1.06 = £53;   ii) £800 × 0.83 = £664.

S7

 i) $100 = 2 \times 2 \times 5 \times 5 = 2^2 \times 5^2$;
ii) $130 = 2 \times 5 \times 13$.

S8

$36 = 2 \times 2 \times 3 \times 3$;
$90 = 2 \times 3 \times 3 \times 5$;
$108 = 2 \times 2 \times 3 \times 3 \times 3$;
So HCF $= 2 \times 3 \times 3 = 18$.

S9

$18 = 2 \times 3 \times 3$;
$30 = 2 \times 3 \times 5$;
So LCM $= 2 \times 3 \times 3 \times 5 = 90$.

S10

i) 5.689×10^5 ii) 5.27×10^{-4}

S11

 i) 6.4
ii) 11.55

E X A M   T Y P E   Q U E S T I O N S

Q1

Tom is talking to his teacher about a number.

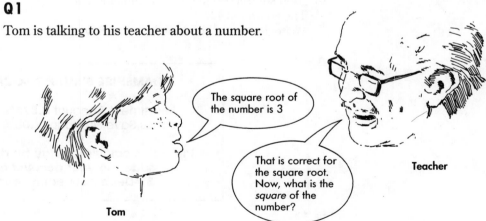

The square root of the number is 3

That is correct for the square root. Now, what is the *square* of the number?

Tom

Teacher

Fig. 4.7

Write down the square of the number.   (WJEC)

Q2

A tank was $\frac{3}{4}$ full of oil. 100 litres of oil were used. It was then $\frac{2}{3}$ full.
How much does the tank hold when full?   (NISEAC)

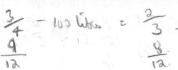

81

$3\frac{3}{4} - 100\text{ litres} = \frac{2}{3}$

$\frac{9}{12}$ $\frac{8}{12}$ 1200 litres

Q3

Look at the following pattern and complete the next three rows.

$$1 \qquad = 1 = 1^2$$
$$1 + 3 \qquad = 4 = 2^2$$
$$1 + 3 + 5 = 9 = 3^2$$

[handwritten: $1 + 3 + 5 + 7 = 4^2$]
[handwritten: $1 + 3 + 5 + 7 + 9 = 5^2$]
[handwritten: $1 + 3 + 5 + 7 + 9 + 11 = 6^2$]

(NEAB)

Q4

1   3   8   9   10

From these numbers, write down:

a) the prime number (note: 1 is NOT a prime number); *[handwritten: 3]*
b) a multiple of 5; *[handwritten: 10]*
c) two square numbers; *[handwritten: 1 & 9]*
d) two factors of 32; *[handwritten: 8 & 1]*
e) find two numbers m and n from the list such that $m = \sqrt{n}$ and $n = \sqrt{81}$

Q5

[handwritten: $n = 9$, $m = 3$]

A decorator used $2\frac{1}{4}$ tins of gloss paint and $1\frac{5}{8}$ tins of undercoat paint.
How much paint was used altogether?

Q6

[handwritten: $3 + \frac{1}{4} + \frac{5}{8} = \frac{2}{8} + \frac{5}{8} = \frac{7}{8}$ tins of paint. $3\frac{7}{8}$ tins]

Look at this list of numbers:
   2, 5, 8, 11, 14, 17, 20.

a) Which of these numbers are prime? *[handwritten: 2, 5, 11, 17]*
b) Which of these numbers is the cube of another number in the list? *[handwritten: 8]*
c) The numbers form a pattern.
    Write down the next two numbers in the pattern. *[handwritten: 23, 26]*

(MEG)

Q7

Three friends are using their calculators.

a) Mari multiplies two numbers. *[handwritten: 0.6×0.6 1.2×3]*
    The answer is 3.6
    Write down **two** numbers she could have multiplied together.
b) John subtracts one number from another.
    The answer is 4.2
    Write down **two** numbers he could have used. *[handwritten: $5 - 0.8$]*

(WJEC)

Q8

LOAMSHIRE BUILDING SOCIETY

Investment Account **8.875% p.a.**
Bonus Saver Account **8.00% p.a.**

**Interest is calculated day by day and
added to your account on
31 December each year.**

Fig. 4.8

Loamshire Building Society advertises two savings accounts, see Fig. 4.8.

Miss Blake has £500 to invest for a period of 3 years and she is going to put it into one of the Loamshire Building Society accounts on 1 January. If she uses the Investment Account she will withdraw the interest at the end of each year. If she uses the Bonus Saver Account she will leave the interest to be added to the capital at the end of each year.

[handwritten in margin: 133.125]

i)   Calculate the total interest she will receive if she uses the Investment Account.
ii) Calculate the total interest she will receive if she uses the Bonus Saver Account.
iii) State which scheme gives more interest to Miss Blake, and by how much.

(NEAB)

Q9

The mass of an electron is 0.000 000 000 000 000 000 000 000 000 91 grams. *9.1×10⁻²⁸·*

a) Express this number in standard form.
b) What would be the mass of i) 10 electrons; ii) 3 electrons? *9.1×10⁻²⁷   9.1×10*

9.1×10⁻²⁷   2.73×10⁻²⁷   2.73⁻²⁷

Q10

The prime factors of a certain number are
$2^3 \times 3 \times 11$

a) What is the number? *264*
b) Write down all the prime factors of 70. *2×5×7*   (ULEAC)

Q11

Fig. 4.9

a) From the map, Fig. 4.9 how much warmer is Wales than Scotland? *9 °C*
b) The temperatures drop by 5 °C from those shown on the map. What is the new temperature in i) Scotland; ii) England? *−10°C   −4°C.*   (MEG)

Q12

We guarantee 5 windows (opening out) and a front or back door in uPVC or Aluminium, supplied and fitted for only –

£1,750 +V.A.T. (at 15%)

Fig. 4.10

Gwen buys five windows and a front door. What is the total amount Gwen has to pay?
(WJEC)

500×8.875×3
———————
100   = £133.125

500×8×1 = 40.
540×8×1 = 583.2.
583.2×8×1 = 46.656.
583.2

£629.856.
129.856

1.750×0.15 = 262.5
+1750 = 2012·5
262.5 +1750 = 2012.5

Q13

A ball is dropped from a height of 200 cm. On each bounce the ball rises to $\frac{3}{5}$ of its previous height. To what height will it rise on the fourth bounce?　　　(SEG)

120, 72, 43·2, 25.92

Q14

Five of the numbers below are rational and five are irrational.

　i) $\pi\sqrt{5}$　　　　　　ii) $\sqrt{2}+1$

iii) $(\sqrt{2})^3$　　　　　iv) $16^{-\frac{1}{2}}$

　v) $\frac{\sqrt{3}}{\sqrt{2}}$　　　　　　vi) $2^0 + 2^{-1} + 2^{-2}$

vii) $(\sqrt{3})^4$ ✓　　　　viii) $\sqrt{3} - 1.732050808$

ix) $\sqrt{3}.\sqrt{12}$ ✓　　　x) 0.3 ✓

a) Write down the five **rational** numbers.
b) Give an example of two different **irrational** numbers, a and b, where $\frac{a}{b}$ is a **rational** number.　　　(ULEAC)

OUTLINE ANSWERS TO EXAM QUESTIONS

A1

$9 \times 9 = 81$

A2

The difference between $\frac{3}{4}$ and $\frac{2}{3}$ is $\frac{3}{4} - \frac{2}{3} = \frac{9-8}{12} = \frac{1}{12}$.

So 100 litres is $\frac{1}{12}$ th of the tank, so the tank holds $100 \times 12 = 1200$ litres.

A3

The first sums are odd numbers, the totals are square numbers, so the next three rows will be:

$$1 + 3 + 5 + 7 \qquad\quad = 16 = 4^2$$
$$1 + 3 + 5 + 7 + 9 \qquad = 25 = 5^2$$
$$1 + 3 + 5 + 7 + 9 + 11 = 36 = 6^2$$

A4

a) 3
b) 10
c) 1 and 9
d) 1 and 8
e) $m = 3, n = 9$.

A5

$2\frac{1}{4} + 1\frac{5}{8} = 3 + \frac{2}{8} + \frac{5}{8} = 3\frac{7}{8}$
Add whole numbers first.

A6

a) 2, 5, 11, 17
b) 8 (since $2^3 = 8$)
c) 23, 26

A7

There are millions of possible answers to both these questions, so, as long as:

a) they do multiply to give 3.6,
   e.g. 1.2×3 or 3.6×1;
b) they do have a difference of 4.2,
   e.g. $5 - 0.8$ or $4.3 - 0.1$
   then you will be correct.

A8

i) Since she withdraws her interest each year she will receive the same amount of interest each year which will be: $500 \times \frac{8.875}{100} = £44.37$ (the 0.005 will have been kept by the society).
   So in three years she will have received $3 \times £44.37 = £133.11$.

ii) At the end of the first year she will have in her account $500 \times 1.08 = £540$.
   At the end of the second year, she will have $£540 \times 1.08 = £583.20$.
   At the end of the third year, she will have $£583.20 \times 1.08 = £629.85$ (the 0.006 being kept by the society).
   So the interest gained will be $£629.85 - £500 = £129.85$.

iii) The Investment Account is the greater by £3.26.

A9

a) There are 27 zeros, so the decimal point needs to move 28 places to the 9.1 position, making the standard form number 9.1×10^{-28} and negative since it is less than 1.
b) i) Multiply by 10 just by moving the decimal point one place to the right; here it would be one less zero, so standard form number will be 9.1×10^{-27}.
   ii) $9.1 \times 10^{-28} \times 3$ will be 27.3×10^{-28}, which is $2.73 \times 10 \times 10^{-28}$ which will be 2.73×10^{-27}.

A10

a) $2^3 \times 3 \times 11 = 8 \times 3 \times 11 = 264$
b) $2 \times 5 \times 7$

A11

a) The difference is between $4\,°C$ and $-5\,°C$. Start at either point on the temperature scale and count to the other, you should get $9\,°C$. So, on the map, Wales would be $9\,°C$ warmer than Scotland.
b) To find the new temperature in Scotland, count down $5\,°C$ from $-5\,°C$ and you come to $-10\,°C$. To find the new temperature in England, count down $5\,°C$ from $1\,°C$ and you come to $-4\,°C$.

A12

$1750 \times \frac{15}{100} = 262.5$, so the total paid is £2012.50. The quickest way to the final answer is 1750×1.15.

A13

$$200 \times \frac{3}{5} \times \frac{3}{5} \times \frac{3}{5} \times \frac{3}{5} = 25.92 \text{ cm}$$

A14

a) $16^{-\frac{1}{2}}$, $2^0 + 2^{-1} + 2^{-2}$, $(\sqrt{3})^4$, $\sqrt{3} . \sqrt{12}$, 0.3
   (or iv, vi, vii, ix, x)

b) $\dfrac{\sqrt{12}}{\sqrt{3}}$ or, $\dfrac{\sqrt{3}}{\sqrt{12}}$

LEVEL CHECKLIST

For the level   You should be able to do the following.

4   Solve problems without the aid of a calculator.
Use fractions, decimals or percentages to describe situations.
Solve number problems with a calculator.

5   Use non calculator methods to multiply or divide.
Find fractions or percentages of quantities.
Recognise prime numbers, squares and square roots.
Use negative numbers.

6   Calculate with fractions, decimals, percentages as appropriate.
Convert between fractions, decimals and percentage.

7   Use your calculator efficiently.
Find prime factors.

8   Calculate with standard form.
Calculate with fractions.

9   Distinguish between rational and irrational numbers.

A STUDENT'S ANSWER WITH EXAMINER'S COMMENTS

Question
The local cricket team has arranged to play some friendly games in Australia, combining this with a package holiday. There is a weight limit for passengers on package holidays of 20 kg of luggage per person. The night before they leave the team members are asked to report to the club pavilion with their luggage for weighing. The club secretary makes the following list.

G. Boycott	20 kg	B. Statham	18 kg
G. Gooch	25 kg	F. Trueman	19 kg
D. Gower	19 kg	N. Cowans	20 kg
D. Randall	18 kg	J. Laker	17 kg
D. Bairstow	22 kg	H. Larwood	14 kg
I. Botham	25 kg		

i) Who should be sent home to repack?

G. Gooch, D. Bairstow, I. Botham

ii) How many kilograms overweight are each of them?

G. Gooch was 5 kg overweight
D. Bairstow was 2 kg overweight
I. Botham was also 5 kg overweight

iii) The club secretary, having second thoughts, suggests that the overweight luggage could be shared among those whose luggage is not overweight. This they do and, in consequence, no player has to be sent home. Explain why.

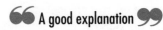

Some players had lightweight below 20 kg mark so they could take some overweight from their colleagues and make it even. The whole team was 15 kg less but there were 3 players with extra 12 kg. This 12 kg was taken by 15 kg they can spare and still the team had 3 kg to spare.

R E V I E W   S H E E T

✏ If a number _divide_ exactly into another number, then the second number is a _factor_ of the first number.

✏ The whole numbers which will divide exactly into another number are said to be _factors_ of that number.

✏ A prime number has __2__ factors, itself and __1__.

✏ The first twelve prime numbers are:

_2, 3, 5, 7, 11, 13, 17, 19, 23, 29, 31, 37._

✏ Find the next two numbers in each sequence
   a) 3, 8, 18, 38, 78, _158_ , _318_   b) 625, 125, 25, _5_ , _1_
   c) 1, 10, 100, 1000, _10000_ , _100000_   c) 0, 1, 4, 9, 16, _25_ , _36_
   _3 5 7 9 11_

✏ Which of the following statements are true?
   a) All odd numbers are prime numbers. _✗_
   b) All even numbers are prime numbers. _✗_
   c) All prime numbers are odd numbers. _✗_
   d) All prime numbers between 10 and 100 are odd numbers. _TRUE_
   e) The number 2 is the only even prime number. _TRUE_
   f) There are five prime numbers less than 10. _✗_

✏ Which of the following statements are true?

   a) $4\frac{1}{2} \div 2 = 7\frac{2}{4} \times \frac{1}{3}$ _✗_   b) $\frac{1}{2} \times \left(\frac{1}{8} + \frac{1}{16}\right) = \frac{3}{32}$ _TRUE_

   c) $\frac{1}{4} + \frac{1}{8} - \frac{1}{12} = \frac{3}{4} \div \frac{2}{6}$ _✗_   d) $2 \times \left(\frac{1}{3} + \frac{1}{9}\right) = \frac{6}{15}$ _✗_

✏ Which is the larger of the following pairs of fractions?

   a) $\frac{3}{8}$, 0.4 _0.4_   b) $\frac{7}{10}$, 0.69 _$\frac{7}{10}$_   c) $\frac{7}{11}$, 0.815 _0.815_

   d) 0.91, $\frac{17}{19}$ _0.91_   e) 0.2, $\frac{2}{13}$ _0.2_   f) 0.605, $\frac{5}{8}$ _$\frac{5}{8}$_

✏ Put the following fractions into order, with the smallest first.
   $\frac{1}{2}$, $\frac{3}{8}$, $\frac{7}{10}$, 0.73, $\frac{5}{12}$, $\frac{4}{9}$, 0.4, $\frac{5}{8}$, 0.1, $\frac{7}{16}$, 0.0999
   _0.5 0.375 0.7   0.416 0.44   0.625   0.4375_

✏ Of the numbers 0.75, $\frac{1}{3}$, π, $\sqrt{4}$, $\sqrt{2}$, $\frac{4}{11}$
   write down
   a) all the irrational numbers _π $\sqrt{2}$_
   b) all the numbers that give recurring decimals _$\frac{4}{11}$ $\frac{1}{3}$_
   c) all the numbers that give terminating decimals. _$\sqrt{4}$ 1.75_

✏ a) Increase 5 kg by 17% _5.85 kg_   _✗_   _5 × 0.17 = 0.85 + 5 = 5.85 kg_
   b) Decrease 5 km by 21% _5 × 0.21 = 1.05 → 5 = 3.95._

✏ Find the prime factors of each of the following:

   a) 216 _____   b) 405 _____

   c) 528 _____   d) 784 _____

✎ Find the Highest Common Factor (HCF) of each of the following:

a) 46, 75 ___1___   b) 135, 162 _____

c) 28, 70, 98 _____   d) 36, 144, 198 _____

✎ Find the Lowest Common Multiple (LCM) of each of the following:

a) 27, 54 _____   b) 64, 72 _____

c) 6, 9, 15 __90__   d) 4, 12, 24 __48__

✎ Convert the following numbers into standard form.

a) 9684 __9.684×10^3__   b) 500 000 __5×10^5__   c) 38 200 __3.82×10^4__

d) 0.009 5 __9.5×10^{-3}__   e) 8 million __8×10^6__   f) 0.867 __8.67×10^{-1}__

✎ Write down 5 rational numbers __$\sqrt{9}, 5, 2, 6$ 9.16.__

✎ Write down 5 irrational numbers __π $\sqrt{2}$__

✎ Use your calculator to solve the following (to 2 decimal places).

a) $\dfrac{23.1 \times 8.3}{4.2 - 1.6}$ 73.74   4.2−1.6 MIN 23.1×8.3 ÷ MR = 73.74

b) $\dfrac{55^2 - 18^2}{37^2 - 21^2}$ 2.91   37² 37²−21² MIN 55²−18² ÷ MR

c) $8.23 + (11.31 - 4.25) + 16.12 =$ 8.23+ 11.31−4.25 MIN 8.23+ MR+16.12=   31.41
  31.41

APPROXIMATION

GETTING STARTED

We use some kind of estimations or approximations every day. 'I'll need about £5 tonight, Dad', or 'There were about 200 at the disco tonight.' In many situations it is much more helpful to use approximations than to try to be exact. Only a Mr. Spock would say, 'You've got 36 hours, 53 minutes and 8 seconds before it rains!' So in this chapter we look at the rules we use to approximate. We then apply these rules to real situations as well as to examination questions. If you fail to round off to a suitable degree of accuracy you will lose marks in the examination.

USEFUL DEFINITIONS

Digits	A symbol that forms part of a number; for example, in the number 1625 there are four digits. The ordinary (decimal) number system has ten digits (0–9).
Imperial	Belonging to the official British series of weights and measures.
Metric	Based on the metre as a standard of measurement.
Significant figures	The non-zero digits in a number. The zero digit is only significant when it is in-between non-zero digits.
Upper and lower bounds	The minimum and maximum values for an item.
$\simeq$	A symbol used to mean 'is approximately equal to'.

E S S E N T I A L   P R I N C I P L E S

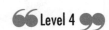

WEIGHT

At some time we all estimate weight, as when we are in a supermarket buying the vegetables. A good standard to use is a bag of sugar because it weighs 1 kg or approximately 2 pounds.

WORKED EXAMPLE 1

Estimate the weight of a brick.

If you've never held a brick find one, and make a guess as to how much it weighs. Try holding a bag of sugar in one hand and the brick in the other. If your guess was about 3 kilograms then you were about right.

LENGTH

Lengths of objects or distances are other common estimations. Do you know approximately how far it is to your school? Try estimating how far it is to the nearest pub or to the next town or village. Some kind person might check your estimate on a car's mileometer.

> **Units are important**

The units you use to estimate are important, since you would be rather foolish to try to estimate your height in kilometres or the distance travelled to school in centimetres. You have to use sensible units, like kilometres, or miles, for long distances, metres for large object lengths, e.g. cars and buses, and centimetres for small objects like pencils, books or feet.

WORKED EXAMPLE 2

Estimate the length of a bus.

A sensible unit will be metres. Try to imagine that you are walking from the back of the bus to the front. How many paces will you take (about 12?) – how long is each step (about half a metre?). That makes the bus about 6 metres long.

LIQUID

How many times have you had to estimate half a pint or a litre for some instant food that needs cooking? To estimate pints is quite easy, since most of us can find or recognise a point milk bottle. But what about a litre? A litre is about $1\frac{3}{4}$ pints; an estimate of 1 litre to 2 pints is reasonable.

A millilitre is one thousandth of a litre and almost exactly the same as one centimetre cubed, 1 cm³. A good estimate for millilitres is that 1 cup holds about 200 millilitres.

You need to be familiar with everyday units both metric and imperial, as well as the approximate links between them.

> **Level 5**

METRIC

You do need to know that the word *kilo* means *thousand* so that:

1 kilogram	= 1000 grams	or	1 kg	= 1000 g
1 kilometre	= 1000 metres	or	1 km	= 1000 m
1 kilowatt	= 1000 watts	or	1 kW	= 1000 W

Other essential units you need to know are:

1000 kilograms	= 1 tonne	or	1000 kg	= 1 t
10 millimetres	= 1 centimetre	or	10 mm	= 1 cm
100 centimetres	= 1 metre	or	100 cm	= 1 m
1000 millilitres	= 1 litre	or	1000 ml	= 1 l

Some mathematics syllabuses will tell you these, others will expect you to know them. It is very useful for you to know them all yourself.

IMPERIAL

Other common units that you should still be familiar with are:

12 inches = 1 foot
3 feet = 1 yard
16 ounces = 1 pound
8 pints = 1 gallon

 You need to remember these facts

You are probably used to these words and perhaps you even use these units more than the metric ones. So it is very useful to be aware of the approximate conversions. We say:

2 pounds weight	is approximately	1 kilogram
3 feet	is approximately	1 metre
5 miles	is approximately	8 kilometres
1 gallon	is approximately	$4\frac{1}{2}$ litres

3 ▷   TIME

SHEFFIELD–BRISTOL
Sunday
SHEFFIELD 0948
Chesterfield.............................. 1013
DERBY 1056
Burton-on-Trent....................... 1113
BIRMINGHAM, New Street..... 1203
BRISTOL, Temple Meads........ 1457

 This type of question will often appear on the basic and intermediate level papers.

With digital watches, videos and timetables we are often faced with the problem of reading from a 24 hour clock and converting the time to our regular 12 hour clock.

A digital 24 hour clock will usually display time as 09:14 where 09 refers to the hour of the day and the 14 refers to the minutes after the hour. When the hour is greater than 12, take 12 off to find the afternoon hour, e.g. 15:25 refers to twenty five past three in the afternoon.

Fig. 5.1

If we wish to find how long it takes to go from Sheffield to Chesterfield from the timetable, Fig. 5.1, then count on from the Sheffield time of 0948 to the Chesterfield time of 1013. There will be 12 minutes up to 1000, plus 13 minutes to 1013, which gives 25 minutes journey time.

The time from Sheffield to Derby can be found by noticing that the Derby time of 1056 has 8 more minutes than the 48 at Sheffield with just 1 more hour, giving a 1 hour 8 minute journey time.

The time from Sheffield to Birmingham will be a combination of the previous two methods. Count 12 minutes up to 1000, then 2 hours to 1200, then 3 minutes to 1203, giving 2 hours 15 minutes.

WORKED EXAMPLE 3

A man who was going to catch the 0948 to Bristol as in the timetable above got up late, had a puncture and finally arrived at the railway station at 12.45 pm just in time to get the next train to Bristol. Estimate about what time he would get into Bristol.

From the given timetable we can work out that the train takes 5 hours 9 minutes to get to Bristol. 5 hour 9 minutes after 12.45 pm gives us 1754, so we could round this up to 1800, which is 6.00 pm, early evening.

WORKED EXAMPLE 4

A train arrives in Sheffield at 2.10 pm, after a journey lasting 6 hours 25 minutes from Tenby. At what time did it set off?

We need to work back from 2.10 pm, or 1410. First the hours; take 6 hours off which gives us 0810, then go back 25 minutes to 0745.

EXERCISE 1

A film starts at 2150 and finishes next morning at 0115. How long does the film last?

4 ▷ ROUNDING OFF

 Level 5

We often do this when estimating; we try to be as accurate as we can to start off with, and then round off the number. To round off to the nearest 10 we need to look at the unit digit; if it's below 5 we round *down*; if it's 5 or above we round *up*. For example:

Rounding to nearest 10

21	rounds down to	20	the 1 being less than 5
138	rounds up to	140	the 8 being more than 5
285.9	rounds up to	290	the 5 being equal to 5
397	rounds up to	400	the 7 being more than 5

To round off to the nearest 100 we look at the tens digit; once again, if it's below 5 we round down; if it's 5 or higher we round up.

For example:

Rounding to nearest 100

| 283 | rounds up to | 300, | the 8 being more than 5 |
| 5749 | rounds down to | 5700, | the 4 being less than 5 |

WORKED EXAMPLE 5

What is the approximate weight of a milk crate containing 20 pint bottles of milk?

Each pint of milk is approximately the same weight as a 1 kg bag of sugar, so making 20 kg of milk. The plastic crate itself would also be around 1 kg in weight, but an estimate of 21 seems too specific, and so an estimated weight of 20 kg is the expected answer.

WORKED EXAMPLE 6

Maureen sorts magazines into envelopes to be posted. In a morning from 9.00 till 12.00 she manages to sort 253 magazines.

a) Approximately, to the nearest 10, how many magazines does she sort in 1 hour?
b) How many magazines will she sort out in a week when she works for 16 hours? Give your answer to the nearest 100.

a) Use a calculator or try a division of 253 ÷ 3, and you will get an answer like 84.333. It doesn't matter what numbers we have after the unit figure of 4, since the 4 shows us that we round down to 80, to the nearest 10. So, the answer is 80 magazines an hour.
b) We can use our answer of 80 and multiply by 16 to get 1280, which will round up to 1300, to the nearest 100, *or* you could have used the accurate answer of 84.333 multiplied by 16, which would still round off to 1300.

5 > SIGNIFICANT FIGURES

Level 5

When we estimate or approximate we generally use *significant figures*. A number having a specific significant figure will have that many *actual digits*, with the rest being zeros to keep place value.

'The crowd at the football match today was about 30 000.' This estimation is to one significant figure, since the 3 is significant and all the other digits are 0.

'His age is about 45'. This is to two significant figures, since two non-zero digits are used.

'The distance between Sheffield and Tenby is about 250 miles.' This also is two significant figures as the 0 is only used to keep place value.

A simple table, Table 5.1, may help you to see this more easily:

One significant figure	8	30	500	9000	0.003
Two significant figures	13	370	2100	45000	0.071
Three significant figures	217	36.5	1.05	4710	20 800

Table 5.1

Notice that the numbers 1.05 and 20 800 are to *three* significant figures. When the zero is *in-between digits* we *do* count it as a significant figure. When the zero is used at the end of a number (as a 'trailing zero'), we do *not* count it as a significant figure. Again, when the zero is used before a digit in a number less than 1 (e.g. 0.071) we do *not* count it as a significant figure.

Look carefully at the zeros

By now you should be using a calculator competently. This means that you should be pressing the right buttons for the right calculation. But mistakes are made! So you must always be prepared to estimate your answer to see if the figure given by the calculator is about right. One way of estimating an answer to a calculation you have to do is to round every number off to one significant figure, then to do the calculation to one or two significant figures.

Rounding to significant figures

It may be helpful here to practice *rounding off* a number to various *significant figures*. The rule for rounding off to a certain number of significant figures is very similar to that for rounding off to a certain number of units.

a) Look at the digit that 'has to go'.
b) If this is less than 5, then leave the digits on the left (if there are any) alone. If this is a 5 or more, then add 1 on to the digit on the left.
c) Put zeros in to keep the place value.

For example, look at the table below to see how this has worked out for the numbers chosen.

Number	correct to 1 s.f.	correct to 2 s.f.	correct to 3 s.f.
34.87	30	35	34.9
159.2	200	160	159
10 942	10 000	11 000	10 900
0.07158	0.07	0.072	0.0716

This topic is seldom examined on its own; it will come into a question as 'give your answer to two significant figures'. If you don't follow such instructions then you will lose marks.

WORKED EXAMPLE 7

Estimate the cost of 83 packets of crisps at 17p each.

Round off 83 to 80, and 17 to 20 to give an answer to $80 \times 20p = £16.00$. So, we would estimate the cost to be around £16.

WORKED EXAMPLE 8

A family went from Scotland to Cornwall covering 571 miles in $9\frac{1}{2}$ hours. What was their approximate average speed?

Round 571 up to 600 and $9\frac{1}{2}$ to 10, to give an answer of $600 \div 10 = 60$ mph.

EXERCISE 2

About how many cars can park on one side of a road that is 100 metres long?

6 ▷ DECIMAL PLACES

When we do want an accurate answer, using a calculator can often give us an answer that is *too* accurate and we need to round off the display to a suitable number of decimal places. *Decimal places* are the places to the right of the decimal point.

A simple table, Table 5.2, may help you to see what this means:

One decimal place	3.6	574.9	0.7	300.5	29.0
Two decimal places	135.05	2.75	31.32	219.47	8.00
Three decimal places	0.763	3.009	41.699	0.056	10.008

Table 5.2

Errors in rounding off are one of the most common made in the exams, so be warned!

The earlier principles for rounding off still apply with decimal places. Consider p, which when put into your calculator display is 3.1415927:

π, to one significant figure is 3
π, to one decimal place is 3.1
π, to two decimal places is 3.14
π, to three decimal places is 3.142

WORKED EXAMPLE 9

Find the circumference of a circle with diameter of 8 cm. Use the formula C = πD

Use your calculator to work out π × 8, and you will be shown the display 25.132741 (at least). A suitable degree of accuracy here would be to one decimal place, i.e. 25.1 cm.

WORKED EXAMPLE 10

Karen, who earns £37.60 a week, has been given a 7.8% pay increase. Calculate her new pay.

Karen's pay rise would be $\frac{7.8}{100} \times 37.60 = 2.9328$. As we are dealing with money this needs rounding to two decimal places, thus giving an increase of £2.93. So, her new pay will be £37.60 + £2.93, which is £40.53.

7 › ESTIMATION TO CHECK CALCULATIONS

 Level 6

Either before or after a calculation a good practice is for you to *estimate* the result to check whether your answer is roughly the right size.

You are warned that this only checks that you *might* have the right answer. It is certainly no guarantee that you are correct!

The usual way of estimating a calculation is to round each number off to one or two *significant figures*, as necessary, and to estimate from there.

WORKED EXAMPLE II

i) Find an approximate answer to $\dfrac{3.62 \times 15.8}{4.7}$

ii) Calculate the exact value to two decimal places.

i) Round each number suitably to $\dfrac{4 \times 16}{5} = \dfrac{64}{5} \simeq 13$.

The approximate value is 13

ii) Putting the calculation into the calculator gives the result 12.169362, which rounds off to 12.17.

Notice how the *approximate value* helps us to be confident that the answer to part (ii) is indeed correct.

EXERCISE 3

i) Approximate the value of $\dfrac{29.6 \times 0.48}{6.08 \times 1.92}$

ii) Calculate the exact value to 1 decimal place

SUITABLE ACCURACY

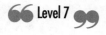 Level 7

When you calculate the answers to many problems, especially on the calculator, you often get an accuracy of far too many decimal places or significant figures than the problem merits. You are then expected to round off any answer to a suitable degree of accuracy. As a *general rule* you should round off answers to no more than one significant figure *extra* to the figures given in the calculation.

WORKED EXAMPLE 12

A length of wood 140 cm is cut into three equal pieces. How long is each piece of wood?

140 ÷ 3 = 46.66.

But, since the largest number of significant figures in the question is two (the 140) we round off to three significant figures, giving us 46.7 cm.

GEOMETRICAL ACCURACY

Questions involving the use of trigonometry and Pythagoras, which you will meet in Chapter 11, are where this problem is most likely to be faced.

In Fig. 5.2, $x = 5 \sin 76 = 4.8514786$.

Since the largest number of significant figures given is two (the 76) we round off to three significant figures, giving us 4.85 cm.

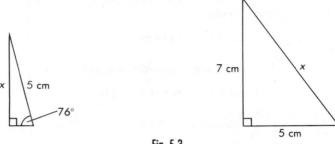

Fig. 5.2   Fig. 5.3

In Fig. 5.3, by Pythagoras' rule, $x = 8.6023253$.

Since the largest number of significant figures given in the diagrams is one, we round off to two significant figures, giving us 8.6 cm.

 **8 > LIMITS OF ACCURACY**

66 Level 9 99

If an object is measured and we are told that to the nearest centimetre it is 5 cm, then the object itself could be as small as 4.5 cm, and no smaller, or as large as 5.499, but not 5.5 cm. Or, in other words, 4.5 cm $\leqslant$ object $<$ 5.5 cm. Note the use of the inequality sign at each side. Here we might call 4.5 cm the *lower bound* and 5.5 cm the *upper bound*.

WORKED EXAMPLE 13

If a marble is said to weigh 7.8 grams, what is a) the maximum and b) the minimum weight of 100 similar marbles?

If one marble weighs 7.8 grams, then since this is written to one decimal place we may assume that the marble can weigh between the limits 7.75 g $\leqslant$ marble weight $<$ 7.85 g. So, 100 of them will be within limits.
775 g $\leqslant$ marble weight $<$ 785 g. Therefore,

a) the maximum weight will be just under 785 g,
b) the minimum weight will be 775 g.

EXERCISE 4

£5 worth of tenpenny pieces should weigh 540 grams to the nearest 10 grams. What is the minimum weight of one tenpenny piece?

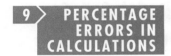 **9 > PERCENTAGE ERRORS IN CALCULATIONS**

66 Level 10 99

When you are given a length or a weight it is quite usual for you to be given a value that has already been rounded off. There is therefore already some error in the figures due to the process of rounding off.

Take, for example, the piece of card shown in Fig. 5.4.

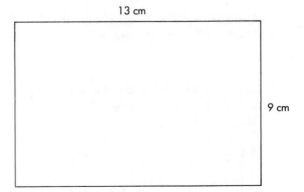

13 cm

9 cm

Fig. 5.4   (drawn to 1/2 scale)

Here the dimensions are given as 13 cm by 9 cm. In actual fact the original dimensions *before* rounding off could be as small as 12.5 cm by 8.5 cm. On the other hand, the original dimensions before rounding off could be as large as 13.49999 cm by 9.49999 cm. These different possibilities give possible areas for the piece of card ranging from 106.25 cm² to 128.24999 cm². The dimensions actually given as the rounded figures give an area of 13 cm × 9 cm = 117 cm². The calculation we have therefore made from the rounded figures could be either:

   10.75 cm² too large

or

   11.25 cm² (approx) too small

These *percentage errors* would be:

i) $\dfrac{10.75}{106.25} \times 100 = 10.12\%$ ii) $\dfrac{11.25}{128.25} \times 100 = 8.77\%$

Notice that in this case it is the smaller of the two *absolute* errors (namely 10.75 cm²) which gives the largest *percentage* error. This is because the smaller error takes place from (is divided by) a much smaller value.

WORKED EXAMPLE 14

The radius of a ball is given as 11 cm. What is the greatest possible percentage error of the calculated volume?

The largest *percentage error* in the *calculated volume* will occur when we set our answer against the *smallest possible volume* for the ball before the figures were rounded.
The *calculated volume* is $\frac{4}{3}\pi r^3 = \frac{4}{3}\pi \times 11^3$
The *smallest possible volume* is $\frac{4}{3}\pi r^3 = \frac{4}{3}\pi \times (10.5)^3$

The *largest percentage error* $= \dfrac{\frac{4}{3}\pi(11^3 - 10.5^3)}{\frac{4}{3}\pi 11^3} \times 100$

$= \dfrac{(11^3 - 10.5)^3}{11^3} \times 100$

$= 14.98\% \ (15\%).$

EXERCISE 5

A cone has base radius 5 cm and a height of 9 cm. What is the largest possible percentage error of the calculated volume?

SOLUTIONS TO EXERCISES

S1

Up to midnight is 2 hours 10 minutes, then 1 hour 15 minutes after midnight, giving a total length of 3 hours 25 minutes.

S2

Imagine one car; it is about 3 metres long. Allow 1 metre for space between cars and we are using 4 metres per car. Since 100 ÷ 4 = 25, we would say that about 25 cars would be able to park.

S3

i) $\dfrac{30 \times 0.5}{6 \times 2} = \dfrac{15}{12} \simeq 1.25$ ii) 1.2

S4

The least weight of the £5 will be 535 grams. Hence 535 ÷ 50 gives the minimum weight of 10.7 grams.

S5

30.7 %

EXAM TYPE QUESTIONS

The majority of this topic is tested within other topics so that it is put into its proper context.

Q1

Fig. 5.5 shows a woman of average height standing next to a lamp post.
  i) Estimate the height of the lamp post. *5×3 =15 feet .*
 ii) Explain how you got your answer.

(NEAB)

Q2

On a foreign holiday a motorist was warned that the speed limit was 130 kilometres/hour. What is this speed to the nearest 10 miles per hour? *80mph   8km approx 5miles*

 50 $\frac{130}{8}$ *×5 = 81.25 = 80 mph*

Fig. 5.5

Q3

Lena divides £14.30 by 3.
The answer appears as shown in Fig. 5.6

Write down the answer correct to the nearest penny. *£4.77*

(WJEC)

Fig. 5.6

Q4

Given that $y = \dfrac{9}{x}$ complete the table of values, Table 5.3, stating the values, where appropriate, to two decimal places.

x	1	2	3	4	5	6	7	8	9
y	9	*4.50*	3	*2.25*	*1.8*	*1.5*	1.29	1.13	*1*

Table 5.3

(NEAB)

Q5

Rick set off at 11.25 am on his motorbike up the M1. He averaged about 50 miles per hour. At approximately what time would you expect him to arrive at his destination 120 miles away?

11.25   2h 24min   Approximately 2·00pm.
1.49

Q6

A shop was having a closing down sale over a period of one month. It advertised 20% off most prices **each** week.
The manager is given very clear instructions on how to find the new sale price of each item on a Monday morning.
'Using the price of the item on Sunday, take off 20%; then round off to the nearest £10; you now have the new sale price.'

★★★★ per litre

43.4p
Esso

Fig. 5.7

At the beginning of the sale on Sunday, 6 May, a 'music centre' was priced at £115.

a) What would be the sale price on Monday 7 May? *92*
b) What would be the sale price after three reductions, as on Monday 21 May?

(NEAB)

73.6
40 *58.38*
56 *appro60*

Q7

A motorist buys 26 litres of petrol at the garage which displays the sign shown in Fig. 5.7
How much will he be asked to pay for the petrol?

(NEAB)

26 × 0.434 = 11.284 = £11.28.

Q8

A rectangular carpet remnant is 4.5 metres long and 1.3 metres wide. Both measurements
are given correct to one decimal place.

a) State the **minimum** possible width of the carpet. *1.25*
b) Calculate the **maximum** possible area of the carpet.

(ULEAC)

4.55 × 1.35 = 6.08m³
6.1423

Q9

Some years ago, the height of the letters and figures on car number plates was increased
from $3\frac{1}{8}$ inches to $3\frac{1}{2}$ inches.

The distance from which drivers must be able to read number plates was also increased
in the same ratio.

After the increase it was 75 feet.

What was it before?
Show clearly how you found your answer.

(ULEAC)

Q10

Albert works out $612 \div 29$ on his calculator. He gets the answer 211.103448. *Without using
a calculator* do a rough check to see if Albert's answer is correct. You must show all your
working.

(SEG)

600 ÷ 30 = 20   *Wrong in*

Q11

A set of electronic scales record weights in kilograms correct to one decimal place.
An article is placed on the scales and the scales record 2.8 kg.
When ten identical articles are weighed together, the scales record 27.9 kg.

a) Explain why the scales record 2.8 kg for one article and 27.9 kg for ten identical such
   articles weighed together.
b) If the recorded weight of one article is 2.8 kg, find the lower bound and the upper
   bound for the recorded weight of ten identical such articles weighed together.

(ULEAC)

OUTLINE ANSWERS TO EXAM QUESTIONS

A1

i) 15 feet or 4.5 metres.
ii) The height of the woman was estimated at 5 feet or 150 cm, then the lamp post was
    estimated to be 3 times higher.

A2

Since 8 kilometres is approximately 5 miles, 130 kilometres will be $\left(\dfrac{130}{8} \times 5\right)$ miles, which is 81.25. Therefore, to the nearest 10 this will be 80 mph.

A3

£4.77

A4

x	2	... 4	5	6	... 9
y	4.5	... 2.25	1.8	1.5	... 1

A5

120 miles at 50 mph will give us $120 \div 50 = 2.4$ hours, which is about $2\frac{1}{2}$ hours.
Rick's expected time of arrival then is 11.25 am + $2\frac{1}{2}$ hours, which is about 2.00 pm. We might say 'we expect him just before two'.

A6

a) $115 \times \frac{20}{100} = £23$, so, £115 − 23 = £92, this rounds off to £90.
b) Start with £90, reduce by 20% to give $90 \times 0.8 = £72$, this rounds off to £70.
Repeat the process just once more to give the third reduction; this gives £70 × 0.8 = £56 which rounds up to £60.

A7

26 × 43.4p = 1128.4p = £11.28

A8

a) 1.25 m
b) $1.35 \times 4.55 = 6.1425 \text{ m}^2$.

A9

$$\frac{3\frac{1}{8}}{3\frac{1}{2}} \times 75\text{ft} = 67\text{ft}.$$

A10

$600 \div 30 = 20$.
Albert is wrong; he has got the decimal number in the wrong place.

A11

a) If each article weighed 2.79 kg, this would round off to 2.8 kg, but ten would weigh 27.9 kg.

b) $2.75 \leqslant$ weight < 2.85
hence $27.5 \leqslant$ ten weights < 28.5
lower bound = 27.5 kg
upper bound = 28.5 kg.

LEVEL CHECKLIST

For the level	You should be able to do the following
4	Make sensible estimates.
5	Use significant figures and decimal places. Use imperial units in use today and know their equivalence. Convert one metric unit to another.
6	Use estimations to check calculations.
7	Recognise that measurement is approximate.
8	Estimate and approximate to check that the results of calculations are of the right order.
9	Understand upper and lower bounds of numbers expressed to a given degree of accuracy.
10	Determine the possible effects of errors on calculations.

A STUDENT'S ANSWER WITH EXAMINER'S COMMENTS

Question

Kleenup washing powder is sold in 800 g packets which cost 87p each. The instructions on the packet state:

1 cup of powder weighs approx. 100 g ($3\frac{1}{2}$ oz)

Quantity to use:

	HARD WATER	SOFT WATER
Top loading automatics		
8 gallon size	3 cups	2 cups
10 gallon size	4 cups	3 cups
15 gallon size	5 cups	4 cups
Soak and handwash		
Average sink (5 gallons)	2 cups	1g cups
Average bowl or bucket (2 gallons)	$\frac{3}{4}$ cup	$\frac{1}{2}$ cup

i) What is the approximate cost of the washing powder for an 8 gallon size wash in a soft water area?

_800 ÷ 8 = 100 g   88 ÷ 8 = 11 × 2 = 22p_

> **Correct method shown, but no final answer.**

Joseph lives in a hard water area and always uses the soak and handwash method, using the sink every other week for a large wash and a bowl twice every week for a small wash. On average how many weeks will one packet of Kleenup washing powder last Joseph?

W1 2 cups 1·5 cup.   Just under 3 weeks

W2   1·5 cups.

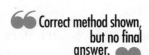

W3 2 cups 1·5

> **A correct answer, but the method does not clearly show *why* the answer is 3 weeks. You will therefore lose marks even though you have the right answer.**

REVIEW SHEET

✎ Correct each of the following to the number of decimal places (d.p.) indicated.

a) 2.643   (2 d.p.) _2.64_   b) 1.338   (2 d.p.) _1.34_

c) 17.64   (1 d.p.) _17.6_   d) 42.79   (1 d.p.) _42.8_

e) 1.7342   (3 d.p.) _1.734_   f) 1.5628   (3 d.p.) _1.563_

g) 13.652   (1 d.p.) _13.7_   h) 25.375   (2 d.p.) _25.38_

i) 8.0547   (2 d.p.) _8.05_   j) 24.073   (1 d.p.) _24.1_

k) 5.1043   (2 d.p.) _5.10_   l) 4.5071   (2 d.p.) _4.51_

m) 27.899   (2 d.p.) _27.90_   n) 5.099   (1 d.p.) _5.1_

o) 1.999   (2 d.p.) _2.00_   p) 3.987   (1 d.p.) _4.0_

✎ Change the following to decimals and round them all off to 3 decimal places.

a) $\frac{1}{3}$ _0.333_   b) $\frac{2}{3}$ _0.667_   c) $\frac{2}{7}$ _0.286_   d) $\frac{5}{9}$ _0.556_

e) $\frac{7}{13}$ _0.538_   f) $\frac{7}{9}$ _0.778_   g) $\frac{5}{13}$ _0.385_   h) $\frac{4}{17}$ _0.235_

✎ State the number of significant figures in each of the following:

a) 1.325 _4_   b) 320 _2_   c) 5.24 _3_   d) 0.509 _3_

✎ Correct each of the following to one significant figure:

a) 357 _400_   b) 3 760 _4,000_   c) 60.8 _60_   d) 0.9137 _0.9_

e) 0.0853 _0.09_   f) 227 _200_   g) 68.9 _70_   h) 3 650 _4000_

i) 0.7396 _0.7_   j) 9.52 _10_   k) 583.2 _600_   l) 0.084 _0.08_

✎ Correct each of the following to two significant figures:

a) 5 329 _5300_   b) 49.7 _50_   c) 752.2 _750_   d) 752.2 _750_

e) 0.08256 _0.083_   f) 735.6 _740_   g) 353 _350_   h) 6 492 _6500_

i) 4 880 _4900_   j) 94.4 _94_   k) 86.9 _87_   l) 5.57 _5.6_

✎ Correct each of the following to the number of significant figures (s.f.) indicated.

a) 3.223   (2 s.f.) _3.2_   b) 7.5474   (2 s.f.) _7.5_

c) 13.56   (2 s.f.) _14_   d) 17.21   (3 s.f.) _17.2_

e) 31.49   (2 s.f.) _31_   f) 36.99   (2 s.f.) _37_

g) 0.06371   (2 s.f.) _0.064_   h) 0.00714   (1 s.f.) _0.007_

i) 0.0088   (1 s.f.) _0.009_   j) 1.0097   (2 s.f.) _1.0_

k) 19.07   (2 s.f.) _____   l) 3.195   (3 s.f.) _3.20_

✎ Find approximate answers to the following questions:

a) $5\,345 \times 1.37$ _5,000 × 1.5 = 7,500_   b) $6\,307 \times 1.29$ _6000 × 1 = 6500.500_

c) $8\,520 \times 2.133$ _8500 × 2_   d) $27.1 \times 2.352 \times 3.25$ _____

e) $36.42 \times 1.534 \times 2.4$ ___ × 1.5 × 2.0_   f) $350 \times 2.75 \times 4$ _____

g) $37.8 \div 1.002$ _____   h) $6\,536 \div 70$ _6500 ÷ 70 = 100_

i) $35\,300 \div 8\,410$ _____   j) $51\,000 \div 837$ _50,000 ÷ 800 =_

k) $\dfrac{35.27 \times 9.56}{8.25}$ _____   l) $\dfrac{86.2 \times 20.55}{51}$ _80 × 20 = 1800 ÷ 90 / 70 / 50_

✎ Complete the following:
1 kilogram = _1000_ grams
1 kilometre = _1000_ metres
1 kilowat = _1000_ watts

Other essential units to know are:

1 000 kilograms = 1 _Tonne_

10 millimetres = 1 _cm ._

100 centimetres = 1 _Metre_

1 000 millilitres = 1 _Litre_

✎ Use the y^x button on your calculator to find the following squares, giving your answers to 1 decimal place.

a) 1.7^2 _2.9_   b) 3.46^2 _12.0_   c) 19.3^2 _372.5_   d) 1.08^2 _1.2_

e) 0.952^2 _0.9_   f) 3.072^2 _9.4_   g) 14.22^2 _202.2_   h) 1.98^2 _1.9_

i) 0.909^2 _0.8_   j) 1.234^2 _1.5_   k) 20.34^2 _413.7_   l) 31.7^2 _1004.9_

✎ Use the y^x button on your calculator to find the following cubes, giving your answer to 3 significant figures.

a) 1.3^3 _2.20_   b) 7.2^3 _373_   c) 5.2^3 _141_   d) 11^3 _1330_

e) 1.09^3 _1.30_   f) 14^3 _2740_   g) 27^3 _19700_   h) 1.65^3 _4.49_

i) 0.8^3 _0.512_   j) 0.51^3 _0.133_   k) 0.33^3 _0.0359_   l) 0.072^3 _3.73×10^{-4}_

✎ Use the y^x button on your calculator to find the following, giving your answers to 2 significant figures.

a) 1.5^4 _5.1_   b) 0.9^5 _0.59_   c) 2.3^6 _150_   d) 4.6^4 _450._

e) 5.3^5 _4200_   f) 6.1^4 _1400_   g) 7.5^3 _420_   h) 1.8^5 _19._

i) 3.2^4 _100_   j) 9.4^5 _73,000_   k) 2.1^7 _180_   l) 8.2^4 _4500._

APPLICATION

GETTING STARTED

It is an important part of the GCSE examining system that as many questions as possible have some *real-life* application. Throughout this book, many of the settings used are those of real-life situations. However in this chapter we focus on the *applications* which are specially highlighted in the National Curriculum for GCSE/Key Stage 4.

To answer many of the examination questions you must be able to obtain information from a *table* or *chart*, so we illustrate ways of doing this. We also include the different types of *scales* with which you should be familiar. A lot of this chapter uses ideas of number and approximation that have already been met in previous chapters.

USEFUL DEFINITIONS

Allowances (personal) The amount of income an individual is allowed to earn before paying tax.

Chargeable Income The amount of a person's income that he must pay tax on (Income – Allowances).

Commission A sum of money received by a salesman or agent on the value of goods he sells.

Compound Interest Where interest is calculated on the principle amount *and* on the earlier interest earned on that amount.

Deposit Money paid as an initial payment on a hire purchase agreement.

Discount A sum of money taken off the price of goods (List price – Selling price).

Hire Purchase A way of spreading payment for goods over a period of time.

Interest The amount of money received as a result of leaving some money with a borrower; or the amount of money given as a result of taking some money from a lender.

Loss Cost price – Selling price.

Principal Amount The original amount of money left with a lender or a borrower.

Profit Selling price – Cost price.

Salary The amount earned in a period of time (usually month or year). The salary is often paid in 12 equal monthly instalments.

Simple Interest Where interest is calculated only on the original principal amount.

ESSENTIAL PRINCIPLES

1 ⟩ HIRE PURCHASE

❝ **Level 6** ❞

Many people buy on what is called the *never never*, or *buy now pay later* schemes. These are alternative phrases for hire purchase, HP, which is a convenient way to spread out a large payment over a period of time. It usually requires a *deposit* to be paid before the goods are taken out of the shop, and a promise, or contract, to pay so much a week or a month for a number of weeks or months.

WORKED EXAMPLE 1

TV cash price £450
HP 10% deposit and 18 monthly payments of £24
Calculate how much higher the HP price is than the cash price.

The deposit is 10% of £450, which is $\frac{10}{100} \times 450 = £45$

The total of the 18 payments is	$18 \times £24 = £432$
So the total HP price is	$£45 + £432 = £477$
Therefore the HP price is higher by	$£477 - £450 = £27$

EXERCISE 1

Calculate the total HP price on a microwave bought for a £35 deposit followed by 9 monthly payments of £24.

2 ⟩ DISCOUNT

Discount is an amount of money that the shopkeeper will give you for buying goods in a particular way. The discount is not paid in actual cash but is a way of reducing the price of the goods to you. Often people are given a discount if they pay cash for their purchase, or if they open an account, or even if they work for a particular firm or are members of a particular union.

WORKED EXAMPLE 2

James is a *Young Owl*, and as such is entitled to a 5% discount on any purchase at the *Owls souvenir shop*. How much would he pay for a badge priced at £2.60?

The 5% discount on £2.60 will be $\frac{5}{100} \times 2.60 = £0.13$

So James will pay $£2.60 - £0.13 = £2.47$

EXERCISE 2

What is the price paid for a £310 washer with a discount of 10%?

3 ⟩ INTEREST

Interest is what we call the amount of money someone will give you for letting them borrow your money, or what you pay for borrowing money. So you can be given interest and you can also be asked to pay interest. Banks and building societies give you interest if you let them borrow some of your money.

For example, a well-known bank will pay you 6% interest per annum, that is per year, so if you leave £20 in their bank for one year they will pay you $\frac{6}{100} \times £20 = £1.20$.

WORKED EXAMPLE 3

I, Payup Limited offer loans of £1000, with repayments of £68.75 each month for 16 months. What is the interest paid on the loan?

16 payments of £68.75 = £1100, which is £100 more than the amount borrowed. Therefore, £100 is the interest paid on the loan.

TYPES OF INTEREST

You have just met the idea of interest, but there are two types of interest. One is *simple* interest and the other is *compound* interest. It will be interesting to see the difference between the two!

SIMPLE INTEREST

Formula for Simple Interest

Simple interest is calculated on the basis of having a principal amount, say, P, in the bank, for a number of years, T, with a rate of interest, R. There is then a simple formula to work out the amount of interest your money will earn. It is $\text{SI} = \dfrac{PRT}{100}$ which means that simple interest is found by multiplying the principal by the rate, then by the time, and then dividing by 100.

WORKED EXAMPLE 4

John had £16.40 in an account that paid simple interest at a rate of 9%. Calculate how much simple interest would be paid to John if he kept the money in the account for 5 years.

The principal is £16.40, the rate is 9% and the time is 5 years.
So, using the formula:

$$\text{SI} = \frac{16.40 \times 9 \times 5}{100} = £7.38.$$

EXERCISE 3

What is the simple interest on £250 over 3 years at 8.75% interest rate?

COMPOUND INTEREST

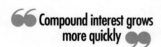
Compound interest grows more quickly

Compound interest is the interest most likely to be paid to you by banks and building societies. It is based on the idea of giving you the simple interest after 1 year and adding this on to your principal amount, sometimes every 6 months. The money then *grows* more quickly than it would with just simple interest.

WORKED EXAMPLE 5

Elsie won £60 in a beauty contest and put it into a building society account that paid 8% compound interest annually. How much would she have in this account if the money was left there for 3 years?

After 1 year the simple interest will be:

$$\frac{60 \times 8 \times 1}{100} = £4.80$$

This is added to the account. So the second year starts with a principal amount of £64.80. At the end of the second year the simple interest will be:

$$\frac{64.80 \times 8 \times 1}{100} = £5.184$$

This would be rounded off to £5.18 and added to the £64.80 to give a new principal amount of £69.98. At the end of the third year the simple interest will be:

$$\frac{69.98 \times 8 \times 1}{100} = £5.5984$$

This would be rounded off to £5.60 which, when added to £69.98, will give a final figure of £75.58.

EXERCISE 4

£60 is invested for 3 years at a rate of 9% compound interest. How much interest is this altogether?

5 > PROFIT AND LOSS

A shopkeeper usually sells his goods for more than he paid for them and this is called his *profit*. If he sells for less than he paid then he makes a *loss*.

WORKED EXAMPLE 6

Jim Karna sold second-hand cars and always tried to make about 25% profit on the cars he bought for resale. He bought a nice yellow Hillman Hunter for £650. What price would you expect him to sell it for?

66 The examiner will expect you to include the 25% profit margin you have already been told about 99

25% of £650 is £162.50, which added to £650 gives £812.50. We would expect this price to be rounded down to £800 as the selling price.

WORKED EXAMPLE 7

The Hot House Fuel Company made a total loss of 8% on their transactions of £500 000 in 1993. How much loss did they make?

The loss is just 8% of £500 000, which is £40 000.

6 > TAX

Tax is the amount of money that a government tells its people to pay in order to raise sufficient funds for that government to run the country. The tax system is generally complicated, but you are only expected to be familiar with two major types of tax which we will look at here.

VAT

VAT, or *value added tax*, is the tax put on to the price of goods sold in shops, restaurants, etc., that is then paid to the government. The tax is usually a *percentage* and can vary from year to year. The tax also depends on the *type* of goods sold, with some goods, such as books, having a zero rate of VAT, and others the usual $17\frac{1}{2}$% rate.

WORKED EXAMPLE 8

In 1993 an electrical shop bought cassette players from a warehouse in boxes of 10 for £90. To work out their selling price the shopkeeper added on 37% for his profit, then added on the VAT. The VAT on these goods in 1993 was $17\frac{1}{2}$%. Calculate the selling price and the amount of VAT on each cassette player.

The shopkeeper bought each player for £90 ÷ 10 = £9.
His profit of 37% gives him a profit of £3.33 on each one.
The VAT on this new total of £12.33 at $17\frac{1}{2}$% is £2.15775 which, when rounded off, becomes £2.16.
    The selling price is now £14.49, including VAT of £2.16.

INCOME TAX

Income tax is the type of tax that everyone who receives money for working or from investments has to pay to the government. Here again the amount can change every time the government decides to alter it. To calculate how much tax you should pay you first need to know the rate of tax, a percentage, and your personal allowances.

    Personal allowances are the amounts of money you may earn before you start to pay any tax; they are different for single men and married men, and for women in different situations, and can be increased for quite a number of different reasons.

    You only pay tax on your *taxable pay*, which is found by subtracting your personal allowances from your total actual annual pay. If your personal allowances are greater than your actual pay then you would pay no income tax.

    The *rate of tax* is expressed either as a percentage, for example 20%, which means that you would pay a tax of 20% on your taxable income, or it may be expressed at a certain rate in the £. For instance, if it was 25p in the £ you would pay 25p for every £1 of taxable pay (this is equivalent to 25%).

WORKED EXAMPLE 9

When the rate of tax is 25% find the income tax paid by Mr Dunn who earns £18 600 per annum and has personal allowances of £5800.

Mr Dunn's taxable pay is: £18 600 – £5800 = £12 800.

The rate of tax is 25%, so he would pay: $\dfrac{25}{100} \times$ £12 800 $=$ £3200.

EXERCISE 5

Mr. Palfreyman is paid a salary of £14 492 per annum which he receives in 12 monthly payments. He has personal allowances amounting to £3860. If tax is payable at the rate of 25p in the £, calculate his monthly pay.

7 > WAGES AND SALARIES

WAGES

Wages are the amounts people earn, in a week, for working. Wages usually vary with the number of hours worked. People normally have a basic week, that is, a set number of hours to be worked in a week, and receive a basic pay calculated on an hourly basis.

For example, Jane is paid £3.20 per hour for a basic week of 38 hours, so her normal wage for the week is £3.20 × 38 = £121.60.

Any extra time worked is called overtime, and is paid by various overtime rates:

time and a quarter is basic hourly rate $\times 1\frac{1}{4}$;
time and a half is basic hourly rate $\times 1\frac{1}{2}$;
double time is basic hourly rate $\times 2$.

WORKED EXAMPLE 10

Ethel, whose basic week consists of 32 hours at £2.10 per hour, works for 40 hours one week. The overtime rate is time and a half. Calculate Ethel's wage for that week.

The basic week is 32 × £2.10, which is £67.20.
The overtime of 8 hours (40 − 32) will be 8 × 1.5 × £2.10, which is £25.20.
Therefore £67.20 + £25.20 is Ethel's wage for the week, which is £92.40.

SALARIES

Salaries are the amounts people earn in a year. They are usually paid in either 12 monthly payments throughout the year, or 13 payments made every 4 weeks. So when people say they are paid monthly you need to know if they are paid for 12 calendar months, e.g. paid on 5 January, 5 February and so on every month, or if they are paid every 4 weeks, a lunar month, which will give them 13 regular payments throughout the year.

WORKED EXAMPLE 11

Joe has a salary of £16 380. What would be the difference in the amounts received if Joe was paid a) each calendar month, or b) every 4 weeks?

a) The pay for each calendar month would be £16 380 ÷ 12 = £1365.
b) The pay every 4 weeks would be £16 380 ÷ 13 = £1260. The difference therefore would be £105 per payment.

PIECEWORK

Piecework is what we call payment for each piece of work done. This means that some people are paid purely for the amount of work they actually do!

For example, Ned is paid 68p for every complete box he packs. If, in a week, he packs 160 boxes he will be paid 160 × £0.68 which is £108.80.

8 > USE OF TABLES AND CHARTS

We are confronted all the time with many types of tables and charts, from bus timetables to post office charges, and they are easy to read if you look at them in a clear logical way. You used a bus *timetable* in the previous chapter; the extract shown here is a *tidetable*.

The *tidetable* in Fig. 6.1 shows the approximate times of the high tides for the Sundays in 1993. You will read that the high tides on 5 September will be at 0354 which is 6 minutes to 4 in the morning, and at 1605 which is 5 minutes past 4 in the afternoon.

1993

Jan	3	06.28	19.19	Jul	4	**01.29**	**13.50**
	10	01.47	14.08		11	**05.49**	**17.55**
	17	06.56	19.33		18	–	**12.23**
	24	01.14	13.38		25	**05.55**	**18.12**
	31	05.25	18.01	Aug	1	–	**12.29**
Feb	7	00.43	13.10		8	**04.55**	**17.03**
	14	05.37	18.04		15	**10.42**	**23.10**
	21	00.01	12.35		22	**04.52**	**17.06**
	28	04.31	17.01		29	**10.18**	**23.10**
Mar	7	11.58	–	Sep	5	**03.54**	**16.05**
	14	04.31	16.54		12	**08.54**	**21.29**
	21	11.02	23.20		19	**03.51**	**16.05**
	28	**04.34**	**17.00**		26	**08.17**	**21.04**
Apr	4	**11.26**	–	Oct	3	**02.49**	**15.01**
	11	**04.32**	16.50		10	**07.28**	**20.02**
	18	**09.46**	22.00		17	**02.49**	**15.05**
	25	**03.30**	15.58		24	05.44	18.19
May	2	**09.44**	22.14		31	00.38	12.50
	9	**03.36**	15.54	Nov	7	05.27	17.56
	16	**07.55**	20.00		14	00.42	13.00
	23	**02.23**	14.54		21	04.40	17.11
	30	**08.19**	20.40		28	11.22	–
Jun	6	**02.35**	14.55	Dec	5	04.30	16.57
	13	**06.44**	18.49		12	11.44	–
	20	**01.05**	13.45		19	03.48	16.16
	27	**07.04**	**19.21**		26	09.25	22.19

Fig. 6.1

Fig. 6.2 is a different kind of chart. It is used in garages to help you *convert* litres to gallons, and the other way round. You can read off from the chart that 30 litres is approximately 6.6 gallons, or that 8 gallons is approximately 36 litres.

Fig. 6.2

To post a letter weighing 275 g, you need to look at the line *not over 300* in Fig. 6.3, since the previous line is lower than the 275. This letter will cost you 53p for first class post or 40p for second class.

Letter Post

Rates for letters within the UK and from the UK to the Isle of Man, the Channel Islands and the Irish Republic

Weight not over	First Class	Second Class	Weight not over	First Class	Second Class
60 g	17 p	12 p	400 g	69 p	52 p
100 g	24 p	18 p	450 g	78 p	59 p
150 g	31 p	22 p	450 g	78 p	59 p
200 g	38 p	28 p	750 g	£1.28	96 p
250 g	45 p	34 p	1000 g	£1.70	Not admissible
300 g	53 p	40 p	Each extra 250 g or part thereof	42 p	over 750 g
350 g	61 p	46 p			

Monthly insurance premiums

Age (next)	£1000	£2000	£5000	£10 000
20	1.60	3.15	7.78	15.50
25	1.85	3.40	8.05	15.75
30	2.35	3.95	8.75	16.60
35	3.40	5.10	9.95	17.90
40	6.50	9.80	18.54	33.70
45	15.70	20.56		

For female, subtract 5 years from current age.

Fig. 6.3   **Fig 6.4**

You can see from the *insurance table* in Fig. 6.4 that the costs vary for different ages and the amounts of insurance required.

For instance, you will see that it costs £9.95 per month to insure a man aged 33 for £5000. We call this monthly amount the *premium*.

EXERCISE 6

What is the montly premium for a woman aged 40 to be insured for £2000?

9 > **READING DIALS AND SCALES**

DIALS

We sincerely hope that you can read a clock; well, it's time you could! But many meters use *anticlockwise dials*. Look at the electricity meter in Fig. 6.5.

Fig. 6.5

| 10 000's | 1000's | 100's | 10's | units |

Although the faces are different the hand on each clock goes from 0 to 1 to 2 and so on up to 9, then to 0 again. Hence the correct reading of this meter will be 21 397. Take a close look at the 1000 and the 10 dials and confirm the reading.

EXERCISE 7

See if you have an electric meter like the one in Fig. 6.5, and if so then read it.

SCALES

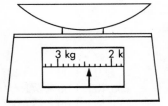

Fig. 6.6

Fig. 6.6 is a set of weighing scales; notice how the scale reads from right to left. Between each kilogram the space is divided into ten parts, and as one tenth of 1 kg is 100 grams, each small line represents 100 g. You can see that the pointer is on the fourth line between the 2 kg and 3 kg marks so the object we are weighting is 2 kg 400 g, or 2.4 kg.

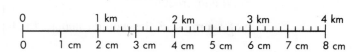

Fig. 6.7

Fig. 6.7 is the sort of *scale* you might find on a *map*. It indicates that 2 cm on the map represents 1 km in reality. The space between each kilometre is divided into ten equal parts, so each small line will represent one tenth of a kilometer which is 100 metres. Therefore a distance on the map of 3 cm will represent 1.5 km, and a distance of 3.6 cm on the map will represent 1.8 km.

Notice how on the weighing scales in Fig. 6.8 the space between each kilogram is divided into five parts, each line representing one fifth of a kilogram which is 200 grams. Hence the pointer is pointing to 3 kg 600 g or 3.6 kg.

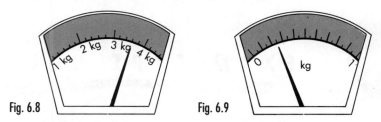

Fig. 6.8   Fig. 6.9

Now look at the weighing scales in Fig. 6.9. The space between the kilogram is divided into ten large parts (longer lines) each one now representing 100 g, or 0.10 kg, and each of these spaces is divided into two parts, each one 50 g, or 0.05 kg. The pointer on the diagram is pointing to 0.25 kg.

EXERCISE 8

Have a look at the scales in your kitchen, and look in the shops to see how many different types there are in use today.

This part of the syllabus could also be assessed in a practical examination. You will need to find out whether your syllabus contains such a practical assessment or not.

S O L U T I O N S   T O   E X E R C I S E S

S1

£35 + (9 × £24) = £251.

S2

The discount is £310 × $\frac{10}{100}$ = £31.

So, the price paid will be £310 − £31 = £279

A quicker, more acceptable way, would have been to evaluate £310 × 0.9, which also gives £279.

S3

$$SI = \frac{250 \times 8.75 \times 3}{100} = £65.62$$

Rounding off in this case will always be down.

S4

After 1 year the total in the account is	£60 × 1.09 = £65.40
After the 2nd year the total in the account is	£65.40 × 1.09 = £71.28
After the 3rd year the total will be	£71.28 × 1.09 = £77.69
So, the interest is	£77.69 − £60 = £17.69

Note: some societies would calculate the final figure to be 60 × (1.09)³ = £77.70.

S5

Mr Palfreyman's taxable pay will be £14 492 − £3860, which is £10 632.

Tax paid over the year will be 25p × £10 632 = £2 658. The net salary left over the year will be £11 834.

This divided by the 12 calendar months will make his monthly pay £986.17.

S6

£5.10

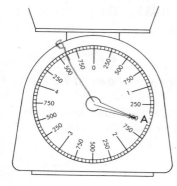

E X A M   T Y P E   Q U E S T I O N S

Q1

The kitchen scales shown in Fig. 6.10 can be used for weighing items up to 5 kilograms. A large graduation mark appears every 250 grams.

a) Write down the weight of items when the pointer is at *A*.

Answer a) ... kg ... g   1.5 kg.   *(1)*

b) On the diagram draw a pointer *B* indicating a weight of 4 kg 600 g   *(2)*

(*Total 3 marks*)

(MEG)

Fig. 6.10

Q 2

The dials on the electricity meter at the home of Mrs Sing on 31 December are shown in Fig. 6.11. What reading is shown by the dials?

Fig. 6.11

| 1000's | 100's | 10's | 1 |

7901

Q 3

a) A girl earns £1.56 an hour as a part-time waitress. If she works for 5 hours, how much does she earn?   *£1.36 × 5 £4.90*

b) A boy works in a shop on one day from 9.30 am to 12.30 pm and from 1.15 pm to 4.45 pm. He is paid £9.62.
   i) How long does he work?   *6½ hours.*
   ii) How much is he paid per hour?   *£9.62 ÷ 6.5 = £1.48 per hour* (MEG)

Q 4

During the rush hour, it takes a telephonist 40 minutes to travel the 5 miles from home to work. Find the telephonist's average speed in miles per hour.   (ULEAC)

40 ÷ 5 = 8   60 ÷ 8 = 7.5

Q 5

Imran has a copy of the timetable of trains between Doncaster and Scunthorpe. Unfortunately it is torn and stained with coffee. The legible parts are shown in Fig. 6.12. All trains stop at each station and take the same time between corresponding stations.

Doncaster	0650	*930*		1151
Stainforth	*0659*			1200
Thorne South	0705	*0040* *837*	0945	
Crowle	0713 *143*	0856	*953*	
Althorpe	*0726*	0903	*10 00*	
Scunthorpe	0727			*1221*

Fig. 6.12

a) Imran catches the 0945 train at Thorne South. At what time is he due to arrive in Althorpe?   *10.00*

b) His friend James lives in Doncaster. James catches the earlier train which arrives in Althorpe at 0903. At what time does this train leave Doncaster? *08.30*

c) After visiting a friend in Althorpe, they travel on to Scunthorpe, catching the train due to leave Doncaster at 1151. At what time is this train due to leave Althorpe?

12.21   (NEAB)

Q 6

> **Read the question and the table carefully. Then answer the question set and *not* your own.**

Travel Protector Insurance issued the table of premiums for holiday insurance shown in Fig. 6.13, in 1992.

£16.90
4.32
£20.52
2,915

Winter Sports
Cover is available at 3 times these premium rates.

(Source: *Travel Protector Insurance,* published by National Westminster Bank PLC.)

Fig. 6Q.4 Premiums
per injured person

Period of Travel	Area 'A' UK *	Area 'B' Europe	Area 'C' Worldwide
1–4 days	£3.60	£5.40	£16.90
5–8 days	£4.50	£7.80	£16.90
9–17 days	£5.40	£9.95	£21.45
18–23 days	£6.30	£12.30	£27.95
24–31 days	£7.20	£15.25	£32.50
32–62 days	–	£24.10	£44.20
63–90 days	–	£34.50	£53.95

* Excluding Channel Islands

Discount for Children
Under 14 years at date of Application – **20% reduction**
Under 3 years at date of Application – **Free of charge**

Fig. 6.13

Find the premium paid by Mr. Jones, holidaying in Blackpool with his wife and three children, aged 2, 9 and 15, from 2 August to 16 August. (NEAB)

Q7

The following information is from the 1984–85 Rates of Tax leaflet:

Basic rate	30% for taxable incomes between	£1	and £15 400
Higher rates	40% for taxable incomes between	£15 401 and £18 200
	60% for taxable incomes between	£18 201 and £23 100

In other words, in that year you would have paid tax at a rate of 30% on your first £15 400 of taxable income and at a rate of 40% for the next £2800, and 60% for the next £4900. Sir Keith Jarvis was overheard one evening to say 'I paid £6820 tax during the year 1984–85'. What was his taxable income?

Q8

The diagram below (Fig. 6.14) shows how the 55p cost of a bottle of mineral water is made up.

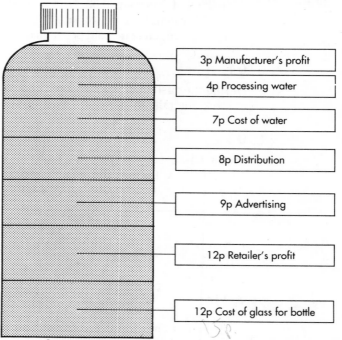

3p Manufacturer's profit

4p Processing water

7p Cost of water

8p Distribution

9p Advertising

12p Retailer's profit

12p Cost of glass for bottle

Fig. 6.14

a) Express the cost of water as a percentage of the total cost of a bottle of mineral water. Give your answer correct to one decimal place.

The cost of glass for the bottle increases by 25%. The cost of all other items is unchanged.

b) Calculate the new cost of a bottle of mineral water. (ULEAC)

Q9

Two shops sell the same model of television for the prices shown (Fig. 6.15). VAT is charged at 17.5%.

Telesales

Bettervision

Fig. 6.15   **£250 plus VAT**   **£290 including VAT**

Which shop offers the better buy? You must show all your calculations. (SEG)

Q10

DIESEL FUEL

Fig. 6.16

Capacity
600 litres

1 gallon = 4.54 litres.
Find the capacity, in gallons, of the diesel tank.   (ULEAC)

132 GALLON.

Q11

Here is an extract from a London to Bicester train timetable.

London Marylebone	1548	1613	1633	1655	1717	1742
Wembley Stadium	1558	–	–	1705	1727	–
Sudbury & Harrow Road	1601	–	–	1708	–	–
Gerrards Cross	1628	1641	1658	1735	1751	1813
Beaconsfield	1637	1648	1707	1745	1759	1823
High Wycombe	1645	1658	1715	1752	1808	1837
Princes Risborough	1659	–	1726	1806	–	1851
Little Kimble	1706	–	–	1814	–	1858
Aylesbury	1718	–	–	1825	–	1909
Haddenham	–	–	1734	–	–	–
Bicester	–	–	1749	–	–	–

a) How long does it take the train which leaves London at 1548 to get to Aylesbury? 1½ hrs.
b) The train journey to Aylesbury is 45 miles. What is the average speed of the train
    which leaves London at 1548? 30 mph
    Give your answer in miles per hour.   (SEG)

OUTLINE ANSWERS TO
EXAM QUESTIONS

A1

a) 1.5 kg, or 1.500 kg
b) See Fig. 6.17

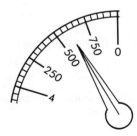

Fig. 6.17

A2

7902

A3

a) £1.56 × 5 = £7.80
b) i) 3 hours + 3½ hours = 6½ hours
    ii) £9.62 ÷ 6.5 = £1.48

A4

If it takes 40 mins to travel 5 miles; then in 20 mins she will travel $2\frac{1}{2}$ miles, or half of 5; so in 60 mins she will travel $7\frac{1}{2}$ miles ($2\frac{1}{2} \times 3$). So, her average speed is $7\frac{1}{2}$ mph

A5

a) It takes 8 minutes (0713 – 0705) to Crowle, and a further 7 minutes (0903 – 0856) to Althorpe, so it will take 15 minutes altogether. He will arrive at Althorpe at 1000.
b) It takes 23 minutes (0713 – 0650) from Doncaster to Crowle. So, from Doncaster to Althorpe it takes 23 + 7 = 30 minutes. So the train must have left Doncaster at 0833.
c) 1151 + 30 minutes = 1221

A6

The holiday is in UK, Area A, premium is £5.40.
Premiums are: Mr (£5.40); Mrs (£5.40); child aged 15 (£5.40).

Child of 9 = £5.40 $\times \dfrac{80}{100}$ (20% reduction) = £4.32.

Child of 2 free

Hence total premium = ($3 \times$ £5.40) + £4.32 = £20.52.

A7

The maximum tax at the basic rate was 30% of £15 400 which is £4620, so the taxable income was higher. The maximum tax at the rate of 40% was 40% of £2800 which is £1120, still not enough to top Sir Keith's £6820, so the remainder of the tax was paid at the rate of 60%. This remainder will be £6820 – £(4620 + 1120) which is £1080, representing 60% of the income higher than £18 200. As 60% represents £1080, then 1% represents £1080 ÷ 60 = £18. Hence 100% will be £1800. The total taxable income, therefore, would be £18 200 + £1800 which is £20 000.

A8

a) $\dfrac{7}{55} \times 100 = (12.7272) = 12.7\%$

b) $55 + \dfrac{25}{100} \times 12 = 55 + 3 = 58$p

A9

Telesales = £250 + 250 $\times \dfrac{17.5}{100} = $ £293.75

Hence, Bettervision is the better buy.

A10

600 ÷ 4.54 = 132 (after rounding)

A11

a) 1718 – 1548 = 1 hour 30 minutes
b) 45 ÷ 1.5 = 30 mph.

LEVEL CHECKLIST

For the level   You should be able to do the following:

5	Use fractions and percentages. Use units in context
6	Calculate percentage increases and decreases.
7	Solve problems using multiplication and division with numbers of any size.

A STUDENT'S ANSWER WITH EXAMINER'S COMMENTS

Question
For a motorway lamp, the length of the
motorway lit by the lamp is equal to two
thirds of the height of the lamp

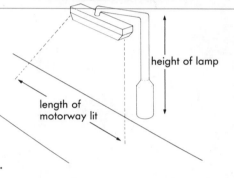

height of lamp

length of
motorway lit

a)   Copy and complete the following table.

66 Good, all correct. 99

Lamp	Height (metres)	Length Lit (metres)
X	6	4
Y	9	6

b)   Two X lamps are positioned 6 metres apart. What length of motorway is unlit
between the lamps?

66 Poor answer as it is wrong
and there is no
indication of *how*
the answer has
been found. 99

X lamps = 4 metres length lit   6-4=2m.

c)   Two Y lamps are positioned 5 metres apart. Draw a diagram showing clearly the
section of the motorway lit by *both* lamps. How long is this section?

66 Again, the answer is
incomplete. There are no
measurements. 99

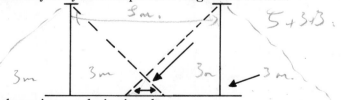

5+3+3 = 11m.

d)   The cost of a lamp, in pounds, is given by:
     Cost = 700 + (175 × height) where the height is measured in metres.
     Find the cost of lamps X and Y.

66 Good, both parts
are correct. 99

X = 700 + (175 × 6) = £1750 .

Y = 700 + (175 × 9) = £2275.

e) A planning officer is trying to decide what lamps to buy for a new motorway junction of total length 100 metres. She has to make sure that the whole length of the junction will be lit and that the total cost is as low as possible.
Should she buy lamps X or lamps Y? Explain your answer fully.

> Good answer, except that the 16.67 should have been rounded up in the calculation.

X lamp cost = 100 ÷ 4 = 25 × $1750 = $43,750

Y lamp cost = 100 ÷ 6 = 16.66 17 × $2275 = $38,675.

Lamp Y would be cheaper by $5075 -

R E V I E W   S H E E T

✎ _Hire purchase_ is a convenient way of spreading out a large payment over a period of time and usually requires a _deposit_ to be paid before the goods are taken away.

✎ If you buy goods with cash or buy many items you may be given a _discount_

✎ Write down the formula for Simple Interest (SI).

SI = $\dfrac{P \times R \times T}{100}$ where   P = principal amount
                     R = rate of interest (%)
                     T = number of years

✎ What is the *simple interest* earned on £1750 invested for 4 years at 6% interest?

$\dfrac{1750 \times 6 \times 4}{100}$

✎ Banks and building societies are likely to pay you _COMPOUND_ interest and not _SIMPLE_ interest. This means that your money will grow _quicker_ than it would otherwise grow.

✎ What is the *compound interest* earned on £1750 invested for 4 years at 6% interest?

$\dfrac{1750 \times 6 \times 4}{100} = 420$ $\dfrac{2170 \times 6 \times 4}{100} = 520.8$ $\dfrac{2690.8 \times 6 \times 4}{100} = 645.79$ $\dfrac{3336.59 \times 6 \times 4}{100} = 800$

£2690.731   4132.37 − 1750 = 2382   3336.59 + 800.78

✎ A shopkeeper will make a _profit_ if the goods are sold for more than he paid for them, and a _loss_ if they are sold for less than he paid for them.

✎ An item costing £25 to produce is sold at £30 and another costing £50 is sold at £58. Find the percentage profit on each article.

20% increase. $\dfrac{30}{25} \times 100 = 120$ $\dfrac{58}{50} \times 100 = 1.16$ 16% profit

✎ To make a profit of 8% I must sell a picture for £86.40. What is its cost price?

£86.40 × 0.92 = £79.49

✎ To make a loss of only 12% I must sell my deluxe camera, for £132. What is its cost price?

£132 × 1.12 = £147.84

✎ Most goods pay VAT at _17.5_% but books have a _0_ rate of VAT.

✎ Your *taxable pay* is given by your actual pay _and_ your personal allowances in any year.

✎ If you are paid by the *lunar* month you will receive _13_ payments in a year.

✎ _Piecework_ is a method of payment for work you actually complete.

✎ Look back at Fig. 6.1. What is the *difference* in time between the two high tides on these days?
a) 9th May _12_ hrs _30_ mins   b) 7th Nov. _12_ hrs _24_ mins.

✎ Look back at Fig. 6.2.
a) What is 40 litres approximately equivalent to in gallons? _10_ gallons.
b) What is 4 gallons approximately equivalent to in litres? _20_ litres.

✎ Look back at Fig. 6.3.
What is the cost of posting a letter weighing:
a) 325 grams second class __46p__   b) 1,200 g first class __£2.12__

✎ Look back at Fig. 6.4.
What is the monthly premium for a woman aged 35 to be insured for £5000? __£8.75.__

✎ Look back at Fig. 6.5. Draw exactly the same dials as shown in the figure.

Now put in the hands of the clock to represent:
a) 43206
b) 86789

✎ Look back at Fig. 6.7. Using the same scale, how far would be represented by a distance of 2.8 cm

on the map? __1,400 metres or 1.4 km__

RATIO
SCALE FACTOR
BEST BUYS
RATE
VARIATION
(PROPORTION)
SIMILAR SHAPES

GETTING STARTED

A lot of everyday arithmetic is to do with *ratio*, though we tend to deal with it in a common sense sort of way. Ratio is a comparison between two amounts, often written with *to*, or a colon (:). One part milk *to* two parts water is a ratio. Many mathematical problems are sorted out by the formal use of ratio, which has strong links with fractions, and ultimately with algebra.

USEFUL DEFINITIONS

Enlargement	Where all the respective dimensions of two shapes are in the same ratio, then each shape is an enlargement of the other.
Similar	Two shapes are similar if one is a mathematical enlargement of the other.
Scale factor	The ratio which links two similar figures.
Proportion	The relation of one number with another to form a ratio.
Rate	A fixed ratio between two things.
Cube root	A number which when multiplied by itself twice is a given number, the symbol of which is $\sqrt[3]{}$.
	Example: the cube root of 8 is 2 since $2 \times 2 \times 2 = 8$.

ESSENTIAL PRINCIPLES

 RATIO

 **Level 5**

You mix things in certain *ratios* every day. Tea is often made with one part of milk mixed with about eight parts of tea from the pot. Of course this mix varies with taste, but certain mixtures need to be quite accurate. Take, for example, dried baby food. The directions on a packet I used read, 1 teaspoon of dried food to 2 teaspoons of boiled water. This mix made 3 teaspoonfuls of nice food for the baby! As the baby grew he wanted more, and I would use a bigger spoon while my wife would double up the ratio given. The initial ratio of 1 to 2 was now increased to 2 to 4 which, although being more in total quantity, was in the same ratio as 3 to 6 would be to make an even greater quantity.

WORKED EXAMPLE 1

A well-known recipe for pancake mix is: 1 egg, 6 dessertspoons of flour, $\frac{1}{2}$ pint of milk and a pinch of salt. This will make enough mix for 4 pancakes.

a) What will be the recipe for 8 pancakes?
b) What will be the recipe for 6 pancakes?

a) As the recipe given is for 4 pancakes, then just double the quantities for 8. So the recipe will be: 2 eggs, 12 dessertspoons of flour, 1 pint of milk and 2 pinches of salt.
b) This time you need to add half as much again to the original recipe. This presents problems with the egg, and although $1\frac{1}{2}$ eggs is what you ought to use, I would use 2 eggs, so the recipe will now be: 2 eggs, 9 dessertspoons of flour, $\frac{3}{4}$ pint of milk and $1\frac{1}{2}$ pinches of salt.

EXERCISE 1

Here is the recipe for a cake: 3 eggs, 200 grams of flour, 100 grams of margarine, 150 grams of sugar and a pinch of salt. This will make enough for 12 people. Mavis wants to make this cake but only has two eggs, so she makes the largest cake she can to the recipe given.

a) For how many people will this smaller cake be enough?
b) Write down the recipe for this smaller cake.

WORKED EXAMPLE 2

At a camp a guide leader bought a 1 litre bottle of concentrated orange juice. On the bottle it gave directions to make up with water in the ratio of 1 part concentrated orange to 6 parts water. How much orange juice will be made up altogether using all the concentrate?

7 litres of orange will be made altogether, 1 litre of the concentrate plus 6 litres of water.

OTHER USES

This idea of ratio is also met with on a building site, where concrete mix is made using sand and cement in the ratio of 4 to 1. You will still have to mix in the water to give you the ready-to-use concrete.

WORKED EXAMPLE 3

You are told to get 100 kg of concrete mix ready with sand and cement in the ratio of 4 to 1. How much of each part, sand and cement, will you need?

By adding the 1 to the 4 you find you need 5 parts for the ratio. 100 kg ÷ 5 parts = 20 kg, so 1 part is 20 kg. Hence 4 parts of sand to 1 part of cement will be 80 kg sand to 20 kg cement.

EXERCISE 2

In 1993 Anna and Beth invested in a new company to make special baby seats for cars. Anna invested £900 and Beth £500. They decided that the end-of-year profits would be divided between them in the ratio of their investment. At the end of 1993 they had made a profit of £12 000. How much of the profit would each woman receive?

MAP SCALES

Maps very often have the scale written down as a ratio, for example 1 : 50 000, which means that 1 cm on the map would represent 50 000 cm in reality, which is 500 metres or 0.5 kilometre.

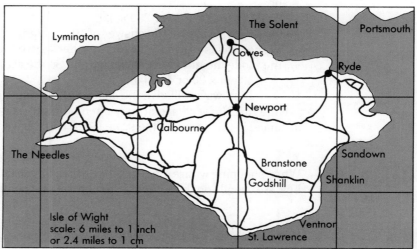

Fig. 7.1

WORKED EXAMPLE 4

The scale in Fig. 7.1 is approximately in the ratio of 1 : 400 000. Estimate the actual distance between Cowes and Newport to the nearest kilometre.

Using a ruler to measure round the slight curve, the distance on the map is 2 cm, hence the actual distance is 2 × 400 000 = 800 000 cm. Divide by 100 to change to 8000 metres, then divide by 1000 to change to kilometres, this gives 8 km.

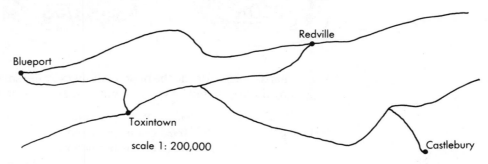

Fig. 7.2

EXERCISE 3

Use the map in Fig. 7.2 with the given scale to estimate the distance of the shortest journey from Blueport to Castlebury.

2 > SCALE FACTOR

If you enlarge a photograph then you will find that both the length and the breadth have been increased by the same scale factor. That is, a number by which the original lengths are multiplied to find the enlarged lengths.

The scale factor of the enlargement shown in Fig. 7.3 is 2, since the original lengths have been multiplied by 2 to find the enlarged lengths.

Model villages and model trains also have scale factors. Many model railways use the scale factor $\frac{1}{100}$ or 0.01, so reducing the size from the original but still *multiplying* the original length by the scale factor.

Fig. 7.3

WORKED EXAMPLE 5

Mr Shuttleworth built a model of his church using a scale factor of $\frac{1}{20}$ or 0.05.

a) How big is the model front door if the actual front door is 2 m high?
b) How high is the actual roof if the model roof is 40 cm high?

Level 6

a) The model door will be the original height multiplied by $\frac{1}{20}$ or 0.05. Change the 2 m to 200 cm, because the answer will obviously be in centimetres. So the model door will be:

$200 \times \frac{1}{20}$ or $200 \div 20$ or 200×0.05

All these ways will give the answer of 10 cm high.

b) We need to use the scale factor the other way round this time, since we are going from the model height to the actual height. So the actual height of the roof will be:

$40 \text{ cm} \times 20$ or $40 \div 0.05$

Both ways will give the answer of 800 cm, which is 8 metres.

Note that the scale factor may often be given as it is on maps, that is, as a ratio. For instance, in this example the scale factor could have been given as 1 : 20.

3 > BEST BUYS

When shopping we are often faced with deciding which jar of the same product is the best buy. We usually do this either by finding the cost per unit weight or the weight per penny.

WORKED EXAMPLE 6

Which of the tins of beans in Fig. 7.4 would represent the best buy?

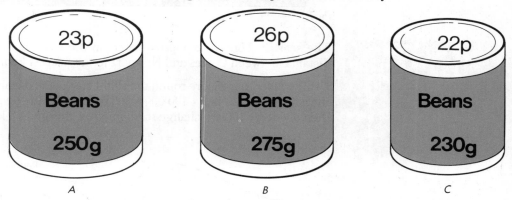

Fig. 7.4   It is perhaps easier to divide the bigger numbers by the smaller ones, so we will divide the weight by the cost to tell us what weight we get per penny.

Tin A: $250 \div 23 = 10.869565$ grams per penny.
Tin B: $275 \div 26 = 10.576923$ grams per penny.
Tin C: $230 \div 22 = 10.454545$ grams per penny.

So we see that tin A gives most weight per penny and so represents the best buy.

WORKED EXAMPLE 7

Which of the packets in Fig. 7.5 represents the best buy of butter?

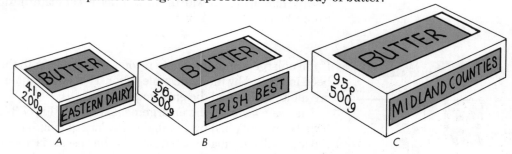

Fig. 7.5

It is convenient here to calculate the cost per 100 grams.

You could very well be asked to give a reason like this to justify your answer.

Packet A will be $41p \div 2 = 20.5p$ per 100 grams.
Packet B will be $56p \div 3 = 18.666p$ per 100 grams
Packet C will be $95p \div 5 = 19p$ per 100 grams.

So we see that packet B costs less per 100 grams, so representing the best buy.

EXERCISE 4

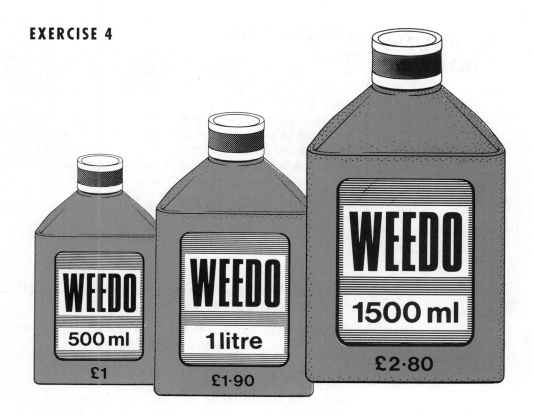

Fig. 7.6

Tom used the 1500 ml bottle of *Weedo* on his lawn which had an area of approximately 12 square metres. He suggested to Ken, who had a lawn of approximately 20 square metres, that he also should use *Weedo*. How much should Ken buy and what will be the best way for him to buy it?

4 ⟩ RATE

66 Level 7 **99**

We use the idea of rate quite a lot, from speed, which is the rate of distance travelled per unit of time, to costs of, say, hiring a tennis court, which may be at the rate of 50p per half hour. We shall look at various examples which use the idea of a rate as a description of how something is changing.

SPEED

Speed is the rate of change of distance.

For example, if you are walking at 5 miles per hour we mean just that. Every hour you walk you will have covered 5 miles, so in 2 hours you will have walked 10 miles, in 3 hours you will have walked 15 miles and so on.

If we know the distance travelled and the time taken to do it, then we can find the speed by dividing distance by time, being careful with the units.

It is useful to remember that

66 A useful definition of speed **99**

speed = distance travelled ÷ time taken.

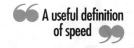

WORKED EXAMPLE 8

The 0815 train left Sheffield and arrived in Penzance, 370 miles away, at 1315. What was the average speed of the train?

The distance is 370 miles, and the time is from 0815 to 1315, which is 5 hours. Hence the average speed is 370 ÷ 5 = 74 miles per hour.

EXERCISE 5

The train in the previous example stopped at Birmingham, 87 miles from Sheffield. At approximately what time would it stop there?

THE POUND ABROAD

AUSTRIA	Sch21.90
BELGIUM	Fr65.10
CANADA	C$2.030
DENMARK	DKr11.750
FRANCE	Fr10.100
GERMANY	DM3.1300
GREECE	Drc203.00
HOLLAND	Gld3.5300
HONG KONG	HK$11.400
IRELAND	I£1.0435
ITALY	L2138.00
JAPAN	Y229.00
NORWAY	NKr10.950
PORTUGAL	Esc213.00
SPAIN	Pes200.00
SWEDEN	SKr10.350
SWITZERLAND	Fr2.520
USA	$1.4700

Fig. 7.7

EXCHANGE RATES

The exchange rates shown in Fig. 7.7 were for the British pound in the late 1980's. The table indicates the amount of each foreign currency you would have received for £1. As these rates change slightly day by day, the table is obviously out of date, but, nevertheless, it will illustrate the point.

If you were going to France on holiday and wanted to take £50 with you, the money would not be much use in France unless you exchanged it for their currency, francs. The exchange rate given is 10.1 francs to the £1. So £50 will be exchanged for 50 × 10.1 francs, which is 505 francs. To exchange back again we need to divide by the exchange rate.

WORKED EXAMPLE 9

Freda came back from Switzerland with 68.6 francs. Using the table in Fig. 7.7, how much could she exchange this for in Britain?

The exchange rate is 2.52 francs to the £1. So 68.6 francs will be exchanged for 68.6 ÷ 2.52 = £27.22 (when rounded off).

EXERCISE 6

Gary went on holiday to Sweden, exchanging £105 into Swedish krona. Using the exchange rate table in Fig. 7.7 how much would he get?

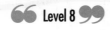

5 > VARIATION

There are three types of *variation*, or *proportion*, that we need to consider – direct, inverse and joint.

66 Level 8 99

DIRECT PROPORTION

Direct proportion is when there is a simple *multiplying* connection between two things, so as one increases so does the other. For example, the amount of paint needed to paint a wall is *directly proportional* to the area of wall. The bigger the wall, the more paint will be needed.

The variation can be, and often is, related to the *square* or the *cube* of something. For example, the volume of a sphere varies directly with the cube of the radius. The alternative ways of saying 'varies directly with' include the following:

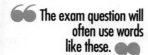
The exam question will often use words like these.

- the amount of paint *varies directly with* the area of the wall
- the amount of paint is *directly proportional to* the area of the wall
- the amount of paint ∝ the area of the wall
- the amount of paint = K × (the area of the wall).

The last two are mathematically the most convenient and we will use this shorthand a lot. The K is a constant value called the *constant of proportionality.*

WORKED EXAMPLE 10

Stanley was appointed to paint the bridges in his home town. He found that on average he managed to paint 18 feet of bridge in a 6 hour day. How long would it take him to paint the longest bridge in his town, which was 68 feet?

We can find a multiplying connection between feet and hours by saying he will paint 3 feet in an hour, or that 1 foot will take 20 minutes. If 1 foot takes 20 minutes then 68 feet will take 68 × 20 minutes = 1360 minutes. Divide by 60 to change to hours and this rounds off to 23 hours. Since he works 6 hours a day it will take him 3 days and 5 hours. He'll probably say it takes him 4 days!

WORKED EXAMPLE 11

The mass of a sphere varies directly with the cube of the radius. A sphere with radius 5 cm has a mass of 523.6 g.

Here we replace ∝ by = K×, i.e. we use the × constant of proportionality method

Find the mass of a similar sphere with radius 8 cm.

Since $V \propto r^3$ then $V = Kr^3$,
and then $V = 523.6$ g when $r = 5$ cm
hence $523.6 = 125K$, or $K = 4.1888$.
So when $r = 8$, $V = 4.1888 \times 8^3 = 2144.7$ g

EXERCISE 7

i) If the cost of washing a wall 2 m long is 75p, what would you expect to be the cost of washing a similar wall 3 m long?

ii) The square of the orbital period, P days, of a planet varies directly with the cube of its mean distance, d km, from the sun. The earth has an orbital period of 365.25 days, and has a mean distance of 149.7 million kilometres from the sun.

Calculate the orbital period of Mercury, the closest planet to the sun, with a mean distance of 58 million kilometres from the sun.

INVERSE PROPORTION

Inverse proportion is when there is a *dividing* connection between two things, so that as one increases the other decreases. For example, as I drive home and decide to increase the *speed*, then the *time taken* for the journey decreases. So speed and time taken are inversely proportional.

WORKED EXAMPLE 12

If I drive from home to work at an average speed of just 30 miles per hour it takes me 40 minutes. How long would it take me if I drove at 50 miles per hour?

Clearly, as the speed gets bigger, the time will get smaller. This time we would say that if at 30 mph I take 40 minutes, then at 1 mph I would take $30 \times 40 = 1200$ minutes. So if I drive at 50 mph I will take $1200 \div 50 = 24$ minutes.

WORKED EXAMPLE 13

The time taken to dig a field of potatoes varies inversely with the square root of the number of people digging. If it takes 8 men 6 hours to dig out a field of potatoes, then how long will it take 10 men?

Remember we can replace ∝ by K×

Since time $(t) \propto \dfrac{1}{\sqrt{(\text{number of men } (n))}}$

then $t = \dfrac{K}{\sqrt{n}}$

When $t = 6$, $n = 8$ then $6 = \dfrac{K}{\sqrt{8}} \rightarrow K = 6.\sqrt{8}$

(Keep in this surd form until we need to calculate it.)

So when $n = 10$, $t = \dfrac{6\sqrt{8}}{\sqrt{10}} = 5.367$ hours, which will be 5 hours 22 minutes. However, this time seems a bit too accurate, hence I would give the answer as $5\frac{1}{2}$ hours.

EXERCISE 8

i) Five men can assemble a car in 6 hours. How long will it take seven men?

ii) The cost each for a party of youths to go to America for a Bruce Springstein concert varies inversely with the number of people in the party. When the original 25 booked the trip to America the cost each was £375. What will be the cost for each if three less go on the trip?

DIRECT OR INVERSE?

So, when you meet a problem that involves proportion as we've described here, you need to think carefully whether it is direct or inverse so that you approach the problem the right way up!

EXERCISE 9

In an average 4 hour evening at her fish 'n' chip shop, Auntie Beattie will serve 72 portions of fish and chips. She decides to try opening her shop for 5 hours. How many portions of fish and chips would she expect to sell during the 5 hours?

JOINT VARIATION

Joint variation is where three things (or more) vary with each other in combinations of direct and/or inverse proportion.

WORKED EXAMPLE 14

Heat, C, in calories in an electrically heated wire varies directly as the square of the voltage, v, directly as the time, t, and inversely as the resistance, r ohms. Suppose 57 calories are produced by 4 volts in 15 seconds for a wire with resistance of 20 ohms. How many calories will be produced in a wire with a resistance of 30 ohms, in 20 seconds by 10 volts?

Since $\quad C \propto \dfrac{v^2 t}{r} \quad$ then $\quad C = \dfrac{Kv^2 t}{r}$

$C = 57$ when $v = 4$, $t = 15$ and $r = 20$

hence $57 = \dfrac{K \times 16 \times 15}{20}$ and so $K = 4.75$.

So when $v = 10$, $t = 20$ and $r = 30$, $C = \dfrac{4.75 \times 100 \times 20}{30}$, which is 317 calories.

WORKED EXAMPLE 15

The volume of a cone varies jointly with the square of the base radius and the height. How will the volume change if the base radius is increased by 70% and the height decreased by 10%?

Since $V \propto r^2 h$, then $V = Kr^2 h$
So when $V = V_1$ $r = r_1$ and $h = h_1$, we start with $V_1 = Kr_1^2 h_1$
So, if the radius is increased by 70%, $r_2 = 1.70 r_1$
and if the height is decreased by 10%, $h_2 = 0.90 h_1$
Hence $V_2 = K \times (1.7 r_1)^2 \times (0.9 h_1)$
$\qquad V_2 = 2.601 \, Kr_1^2 h_1 = 2.601 \, V_1$
Hence the % increase is given by:

$$\dfrac{(2.601 \, V_1 - V_1)}{V_1} \times 100 = \dfrac{(2.601 - 1)V_1}{V_1} \times 100 = 160.1\%$$

Hence the percentage increase is 160%
(Yes, you should really have noted this straight from the $V_2 = 2.601 V_1$, but I wanted it to be made clear to those with any doubts.)

EXERCISE 10

It was noted in a botanical garden that during the summer the number of insects in flight per m^3 in the greenhouse is directly proportional to the temperature and inversely proportional to the square root of the average centimetres of rainfall so far that summer.

   It was noted early in the summer while the average rainfall was 0.3 cm per day, and when the temperature was 16 °C, there was an average of 4 insects in flight per m^3 in the greenhouse. If at the end of the summer it was noted that when the temperature was 12 °C there were 2 insects in flight per m^3, what was the average rainfall for the summer?

6 > **SIMILAR SHAPES**

Two shapes are said to be similar if all their corresponding angles are equal and the ratios of the corresponding lengths are also equal, see Fig. 7.8.

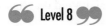 Level 8

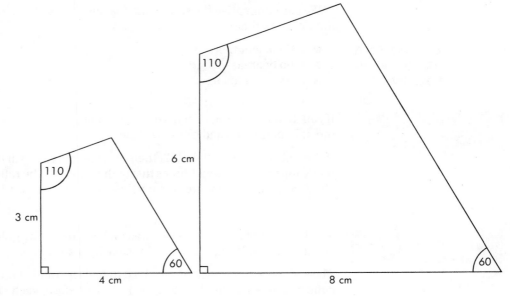

Fig. 7.8

All the corresponding angles you can see are equal and the ratio of each pair of corresponding sides is 1 : 2.

WORKED EXAMPLE 16

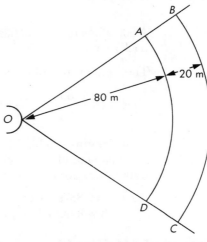

Fig. 7.9

Fig. 7.9 shows a *javelin field OABCD*. The arc length *AD* is 50 metres. How long is the arc length *BC*?

We have two similar sectors here, *OAD* and *OBC*. Draw them separately if it will help you.
  The ratio of the lengths of *OAD* to *OBC* is 80 m : 100 m, which will simplify to 4 : 5.
  Hence the ratio of *AD* to *BC* is also 4 : 5, which gives 50 : *BC* = 4 : 5.
  If we rewrite these ratios as fractions the problem is simplified to:

$$\frac{BC}{50} = \frac{5}{4} \text{ which then gives us } BC = \frac{5 \times 50}{4} = 62.5 \text{ metres.}$$

RATIOS OF SIMILAR SHAPES

Consider the two shapes shown in Fig. 7.10.

 Level 9

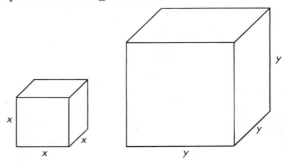

Fig. 7.10

Both these shapes are *cubes*; hence each *corresponding angle* is the same, and each *corresponding side* is in the ratio $x : y$. We can now also see that by considering any *face*, the ratio of the *areas* is $x^2 : y^2$. The ratio of the *volumes* is $x^3 : y^3$.

We can summarise the situation by saying that for any similar solid that has lengths in the ratio $x : y$ then:

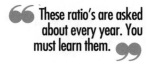
These ratio's are asked about every year. You must learn them.

- ratio of lengths $x : y$
- ratio of areas $x^2 : y^2$
- ratio of volumes $x^3 : y^3$

WORKED EXAMPLE 17

If you doubled the dimensions of a 1 pint milk bottle, what would happen to a) the area of the milk bottle top, and b) the volume?

If the ratio of the length is 1 :2, then the ratio of areas will be $1^2; 2^2$, i.e. 1 : 4, so the milk bottle top will be an area 4 times that of the original. The ratio of the volume will be $1^3 : 2^3$, i.e. 1 : 8, so the volume would be 8 times bigger, that is, a 1 gallon bottle.

WORKED EXAMPLE 18

A gold statue of height 3 metres was melted down. The gold was then cast into 64 small similar statues. What is the height of each small statue?

The ratio of volumes will be 64 : 1, so to find the ratio of the lengths we need to find the cube root of each number, to give 4 : 1. Therefore, each small statue will be of height 3 m ÷ 4 which is 0.75 m or 75 cm.

WORKED EXAMPLE 19

A 500 g box of Brekko has the dimensions 8 cm by 20 cm by 30 cm. The firm wanted to pack a similar box with 350 g of Brekko. What would be the dimensions of this new box?

The ratio of the volumes of the box will be in the ratio of 500 : 350. This ratio can be simplified to $\dfrac{500}{500} : \dfrac{350}{500}$ which is 1 : 0.7. Hence if the ratio of the volumes is 1 : 0.7 the ratio

of the lengths will be $\sqrt[3]{1} : \sqrt[3]{0.7} = 0.8879$.

So each side of the larger box will be reduced by a factor of 0.8879, hence the new dimensions are found by:

8 cm × 0.8879, 20 cm × 0.8879, 30 cm × 0.8879
which will be: 7.1 cm, 17.8 cm, 26.6 cm.

EXERCISE 11

i) Two similar tins of soup have similar labels on them of areas 15 cm² and 20 cm² respectively. If the smaller tin contains 400 g of soup, how much will the larger tin hold?

ii) For a stage production of Jack and the Beanstalk, all the giant's furniture was larger than ordinary furniture but of a similar shape. For example, his coffee table, which was 270 cm long, was copied from a real coffee table 90 cm long. How much heavier should his portable TV have been than an ordinary one, and do you think the dressed up giant would be able to carry it?

SOLUTIONS TO EXERCISES

S1

a) Since 3 eggs will make a cake sufficient for 12 people, 1 egg will be enough for 4 people, and 2 eggs will be enough for 8 people.

b) Each ingredient will require $\frac{2}{3}$ of the given recipe, but we need to round off to sensible proportions. Therefore the actual $\frac{2}{3}$ recipe of 2 eggs, 133.3 g of flour, 66.67 g of margarine, 100 g of sugar and $\frac{2}{3}$ of a pinch of salt will, in practice, be 2 eggs, 130 g flour, 70 g margarine, 100 g sugar and 1 pinch of salt.

S2

The ratio of the investment is 900 : 500, which is the same ratio as 9 : 5. Hence the profit of £12 000 needs to be divided into 14 parts, 9 parts for Anna and 5 parts for Beth. Each part is £12 000 ÷ 14 = £857.14, rounded off. So Anna will receive £857.14 (...) × 9 = £7714.29.

It is important to use the exact value of £12 000 ÷ 14 here for accuracy, but then round off. Similarly Beth will receive £857.14 (...) × 5 = £4285.71.

S3

The shortest route is from Blueport, through Toxintown then on to Castlebury. Using a ruler and measuring roughly round the roads gives 4 cm from Blueport to Toxintown and then 10 cm from Toxintown to Castlebury, a total of 14 cm. With a scale of 1 : 200 000, the actual road distance will be 14 × 200 000 cm = 2 800 000 cm. Divide by 100 to change to 28 000 metres, then divide by 1000 to change to 28 kilometres.

S4

If Tom's 12 m² needs 1500 ml of *Weedo* then 1 m² will need 1500 ÷ 12 = 125 ml. Hence Ken's 20 m² will need 125 ml × 20 = 2500 ml. The cheapest way for Ken to buy his *Weedo* would be one 1500 ml bottle and one 1 litre bottle.

S5

The train is travelling 74 miles per hour so will cover 74 miles every hour. So divide 87 by 74 to see how many hours it takes to travel this distance – this is 1.1756757 hours. You may remember we've met this problem before (see S8). We have 1 whole hour, so take 1 away on the calculator to leave 0.1756757, multiply by 60 to get 10.540541 which rounds off to 11 minutes. Therefore the train takes 1 hour 11 minutes. Add this time on to 0815 and you get 0926, the approximate time of arrival at Birmingham.

S6

Multiply 105 by the exchange rate of SKr 10.35 to give SKr 1086.75 which is the amount Gary would take on holiday.

S7

i) Cost $= \dfrac{3}{2} \times$ 75p $=$ £1.13 (we've assumed that the wall is the same height)

ii) We note from the question that $p^2 \propto d^3$, hence $p^2 = Kd^3$ and for Earth, when $p = 365.25$, $d = 1.497 \times 10^8$, hence $(365.25)^2 = K(1.497 \times 10^8)^3$, so $K = 3.9766 \times 10^{-20}$ (kept in calculator memory).

So for Mercury, where $d = 5.8 \times 10^7$, we have $p^2 = K.d^3$
which gives $p^2 = K \times (5.8 \times 10^7)^3$
$$= 7758.9$$
$$p = \sqrt{7758.9} = 88$$

Therefore the orbital period of Mercury is 88 days.

S8

i) We can see that more men will take less time, and so if we consider 5 men assembling a car in 6 hours, then 1 man will take $5 \times 6 = 30$ hours. So 7 men will take $30 \div 7 = 4.28$ hours, which is about 4 hours 20 minutes.

   Note that to calculate $30 \div 7$ exactly, your calculator will give you 4.2857143. We know the 4 is 4 hours, but what about the 0.2857143? This is a decimal fraction of the hour, and to change it to minutes you need to first subtract the 4 in your calculator to give the decimal fraction part only of 0.2857143. Now multiply this by 60 to give you 17.142857 which rounds off to 17 minutes.

ii) Let number of youths in party = Y, the cost each be C, then

$$C \propto \frac{1}{Y} \quad \text{hence} \quad C = \frac{K}{Y}$$

When Y = 25, C = 375, so $375 = \dfrac{K}{25} \rightarrow K = 9375$

so when Y = 22, $C = \dfrac{9375}{22} = 426.14.$

The cost therefore is £426.14.

S9

During 1 hour Auntie Beattie serves $72 \div 4 = 18$ portions of fish and chips, so during 5 hours she would expect to serve $18 \times 5 = 90$ portions.

S10

> You must state what your variables are as I have done here or risk losing marks.

From the question we note where I = insects in flight per m³
t = temperature °C
r = average cm of rainfall

Then $I \propto \dfrac{t}{\sqrt{r}}$; hence $I = \dfrac{Kt}{\sqrt{r}}$

When $r = 0.3$, $t = 16$, I = 4

so $4 = \dfrac{K \times 16}{\sqrt{0.3}} \rightarrow K = \dfrac{4 \times \sqrt{0.3}}{16} = 0.137.$

So when $t = 12$ and I = 2, then $2 = \dfrac{0.137 \times 12}{\sqrt{r}}$

$\rightarrow \sqrt{r} = \dfrac{0.137 \times 12}{2} = 0.82$

$r = 0.675$ cm per day.

S11

i) The ratio of the areas is 15 : 20, which simplifies to 3 : 4, hence the ratio of lengths is $\sqrt{3} : \sqrt{4}$ which is $\sqrt{3} : 2$. Hence the ratio of volumes is $(\sqrt{3})^3 : 2^3$ which is $(\sqrt{3})^3 : 8$.

   So if the smaller tin contains 400 g, the larger tin will contain $400 \times \dfrac{8}{(\sqrt{3})^3} = 616$ g.

   (*Note:* one of the simplest ways to evaluate $(\sqrt{3})^3$ on your calculator is to recognise $(\sqrt{3})^3 = 3^{1.5}$, then press the sequence of buttons $3 \rightarrow x^y \rightarrow 1.5 \rightarrow =$ to give 5.196 ...)

ii) Ratio of lengths is 270 : 90, which cancels to 3 : 1. Hence the ratio of the weights, which is the same as the ratio of volumes, will be $3^3 : 1^3$ which is 27 : 1. So the portable TV would have to be 27 times heavier, far too heavy to be carried about.

EXAM TYPE QUESTIONS

Q1

1 pint = 0.568 litre
£1 = 9.30 francs

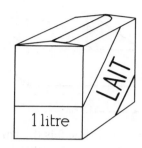 

Fig. 7.11

Which is cheaper, 1 pint of milk for 25p or 1 litre of milk for 4.20 francs? Write down each step you take.   (MEG)

45p litre

Q2

A multi-storey car park takes two hours to fill at the rate of 9 cars per minute. How long would it take to fill at the rate of 6 cars per minute?   (SEG)

120 ⨯ 9 = 1000 = 6 ⨯ 3 hour

Q3

a) Fig. 7.12 is a plan of a park. Sarah takes $3\frac{1}{2}$ hours to mow the larger grass play area. How long will it take her to mow the smaller grass area? (scale: 1 cm : 1 m)

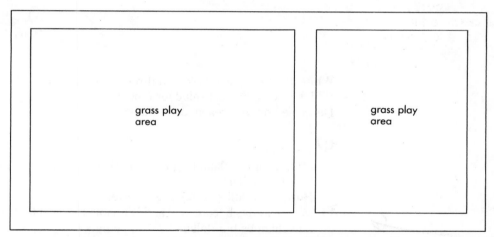

Fig. 7.12

b) There are railings all round this park which Andrew, Charles and Diane paint between them in 7 hours. How long would it have taken had Sarah been helping them also?

Q4

This recipe is enough for 8 scones.
 i) How much flour is needed for 12 scones?
 ii) How much milk is needed for 12 scones?

SCONES

8 oz plain flour   *12 oz*
1 teaspoonful salt
1 teaspoonful bicarbonate of soda
2 teaspoons cream of tartar
$1\frac{1}{2}$ oz margarine
About $\frac{1}{4}$ pint milk

(NEAB)

Q 5

Jack has two square cake tins of the same depth. The sides are 15 cm and 20 cm long, see Fig. 7.13.

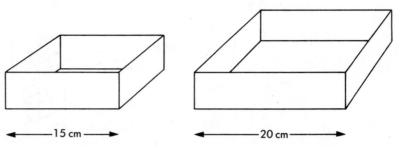

Fig. 7.13

His favourite recipe just fills the smaller tin.
This recipe uses 200 g of self-raising flour.
How much self-raising flour will be needed if the recipe is to be made to fill the largertin?

(MEG)

15:20   3:4.

3² : 4²   200 × 16/? =

9   16

Q 6

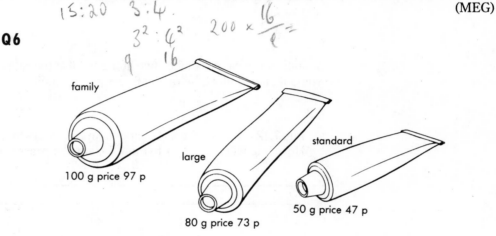

family

100 g price 97 p

large

80 g price 73 p

standard

50 g price 47 p

Fig. 7.14

Whiteside toothpaste is sold in three sizes, see Fig. 7.14.
Which size is the best value for money?
Describe how you reached your answer.

(SEG)

97 ÷ 100 = 0.97   73 ÷ 80 = 0.9125   0.94

Q 7

a) Mrs. Thomas plans to go to America. She changes £1000 into dollars at a rate of £1 = 1.56 dollars.   *1000 × 1.56. = 1560 dollars.*
   How many dollars does she receive?

b) Mrs. Thomas becomes ill and is unable to travel to America.
   She changes her dollars back to pounds.
   The exchange rate now is £1 = $1.72 dollars.
   Calculate the profit or loss that she makes.

1560/£1.72 = 906.98

Loss £93.02.

(WJEC)

> **Try to recognise this type of situation, it very often crops up on your examination papers.**

Q 8

In Fig. 7.15 the top part A of a cone is removed to leave the lower part B. The vertical heights of A and B are equal. If the volume of A is 3.14 cm³, what is the volume of the whole cone?

(SEG)

⅓ π r² h

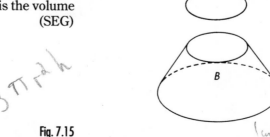

Fig. 7.15

Q9

The scales in Fig. 7.16 show that 9 marbles balance with 6 balls. Two balls are removed. How many marbles must be removed so that the scales will balance? (NEAB)

6 : 9

2 : 3

3

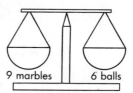

Fig. 7.16

Q10

Fig. 7.17 shows a bus drawn to scale.

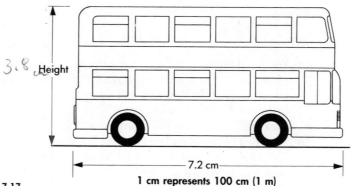

3.8 Height

7.2 cm

1 cm represents 100 cm (1 m)

Fig. 7.17

Use the diagram to find:
a) the true length of the bus, giving your answer:
   i) in centimetres;   7.2 × 100 = 720 cm
   ii) in metres.   7.2 × 1 m = 7.2 m.
b) the true height of the bus, giving your answer in metres. (WJEC)

3.8 m   9 m

Q11

Gunpowder is made up of potassium nitrate, sulphur and charcoal mixed in the ratio 33 : 5 : 7   × 2 : 66 : 10 : 14

a) 10 kg of sulphur and 14 kg of charcoal are mixed. How much potassium nitrate must be added to make gunpowder? 66 kg.
b) How much charcoal is needed to make 900 kg of gunpowder? 140 kg
c) What percentage of gunpowder is made up of sulphur? (ULEAC)

11.1%.

Q12

The 'size' of a television screen is the length of a diagonal of the screen.
   The width of a 19 inch television screen is 16.2 inches.
   Calculate the width of a similar 23 inch screen. (ULEAC)

16.2 ÷ 19 × 23 = 19.6 inches

16.2
19

OUTLINE ANSWERS TO EXAM QUESTIONS

A1

The one pint will be 0.568 litres costing 25p.
So, 1 litre (bottle rate) would cost $25 \div 0.568 = 44$ pence.
Convert this to francs, $0.44 \times 9.30 = 4.09$ francs.
Therefore the pint bottle is cheaper than the litre carton.

A2

(2×9) hours at a rate of 1 car per minute, so $(2 \times 9) \div 6$ at a rate of 6 cars per minute = 3 hours.

A3

a) You need to use a ruler and measure the sides of each grass area. The area on the plan of the large grass area is 5 cm $\times$ 7 cm = 35 cm². So Sarah mows 35 m² in $3\frac{1}{2}$ hours, which is 210 minutes. She will therefore mow 1 m² in $210 \div 35 = 6$ minutes. The size of the small grass area is 4 cm $\times$ 5 cm = 20 cm². Hence the time taken to mow the 20 m² area will be $20 \times 6 = 120$ minutes, which is 2 hours.

b) If three people paint the fence in 7 hours, then one person will paint it in 21 hours. Hence if Sarah helps out, the four of them will paint the fence in $21 \div 4 = 5.25$ hours, which is $5\frac{1}{4}$ hours.

A4

Ratio of menus is 8 : 12 or 2 : 3; hence
 i) 12 oz
 ii) $\frac{1}{4} \times \frac{3}{2} = \frac{3}{8}$ pint.

A5

Ratio of lengths = 15 : 20 $\qquad\qquad$ = 3 : 4
So the ratio of areas (since same depth of tins) = $3^2 : 4^2$
$\qquad\qquad\qquad\qquad\qquad\qquad\qquad$ = 9 : 16
Therefore a larger tin needs $200 \times \dfrac{16}{9}$ $\qquad$ = 356 g of self-raising flour.

A6

Calculations in pence per gram:
Family: $\dfrac{97}{100} = 0.97$ pence per gram.

Large: $\dfrac{73}{80} = 0.9125$ pence per gram.

Standard: $\dfrac{47}{50} = 0.94$ pence per gram.

Best value: Large. The answer would only be accepted if the calculations were shown.

A7

a) $1000 \times 1.56 = 1560$ dollars
b) $1560 \div 1.72 = £906.98$, she makes a loss of £93.02

A8

Ratio of heights for top cone : whole cone = 1 : 2
So, Ratio of volumes = 1 : 8;
Volume of whole cone = $8 \times 3.14 = 25.12$ cm³.

A9

They balance in the ratio of 9 : 6, which is 3 : 2. So, if 2 balls are taken, this balances with 3 marbles taken.

A10

a) i) $7.2 \times 100 = 720$ cm   ii) 7.2 m

b) Height measured on scale drawing is 4 cm, giving a true height of 4 m.

A11

a) $33 \times 2 = 66$ kg

b) $\dfrac{7}{45} \times 900 = 140$ kg

c) $\dfrac{4}{45} \times 100 = 11.1\%$

A12

$$\dfrac{23}{19} \times 16.2 = 19.610$$

rounded off to 19.6 inches.

LEVEL CHECKLIST

For the level   You should be able to do the following

5	Understand scale in maps and drawings.
6	Calculate with ratios in a variety of situations. Enlarge a shape by a whole number scale factor.
7	Enlarge a shape by a fractional scale factor.
8	Understand direct and inverse proportion. Use mathematical similarity to solve problems. Know that in similar shapes the corresponding sides are in the same ratio.

A STUDENT'S ANSWER WITH EXAMINER'S COMMENTS

Question

A sealed hollow cone with vertex downwards is partially filled with water. The volume of water is 250 cm³ and the depth of the water is 60 mm. Find the volume of the water which must be added to increase the depth to 80 mm.

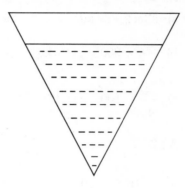

Answer

Using similar shapes

Ratio of length is $60:80$

Ratio of volume is $250:x$

$$= 60^3 : 80^3$$

So $\dfrac{x}{250} = \dfrac{80^3}{60^3}$

$$x = \dfrac{80^3 \times 250}{60^3} = \underline{592}$$

> **A good explanation of what is happening.**

> **Shame, the final question has not been answered. To answer the question you must subtract 250 from this. Still, the method will get you high marks for this answer.**

R E V I E W   S H E E T

✎   **x** *to* **y** or **x** : **y** are examples of _____

✎   Find the missing number in the following ratios:

a) _2_ : 8 = 3 : 12   b) 2 : 11 = _6_ : 33

b) _12_ : 18 = 16 : 24   d) 12 : 28 = 18 : _42_

✎   A length of 36 m is increased so that the ratio of the new length to the old length is 13 : 8. Find the increase in length.

36 ÷ 8 = 58.5

✎   A recipe for a cake big enough for 12 people is:
3 eggs, 200 grams of flour, 100 grams of butter, 150 grams of sugar and a pinch of salt.
Write down the recipe with the ingredients in the same ratio, but for a cake big enough for:

a) 4 people _1 egg 66.67 (rounded to 67 grams) 33.33 gms, 50 grams sugar ⅓ pin_

b) 8 people _2 eggs 133.333 (.. 133) 66.67 , 100 grams sugar ⅔ pinch_

c) 20 people _5 eggs 2c_

✎   Express the following ratios in their simplest form.

a) $1\frac{2}{3} : \frac{1}{4}$ _1.67_ ... b) $2\frac{1}{5} : 1\frac{1}{3}$ _1.65 : 1_

c) 65.1 : 2.1 _31 : 1_   d) 18.2 : 27.3 _0.66 : 1_

✎   The scale of a map is shown as 4 cm : 1 km   4

a) Rewrite the ratio as simply as possible _100000_

b) What is the actual length of a road 3.2 cm long on the map? _____

c) How long on the map should a road be that is 3.7 km long? _____

✎   Two quantities are directly proportional if, as one quantity _____ the other quantity increases, and vice versa. There is then a simple _____ connection between two things.

✎   A van uses 70 litres of diesel on a 315 km trip.

a) How much diesel would be used on a journey of 180 km?

40

b) How far would the van get on 100 litres of diesel?

450 km

✎   We can replace α by '= K×' where K is called the _____

✎   The mass of a sphere varies directly with the cube of the radius. A sphere with radius 4 cm has a mass of 200 g. Find the mass of a similar sphere with radius 5 cm.

_____

_____

✎   Two quantities are inversely proportional if, as one quantity _____ the other quantity increases, and vice versa. There is then a simple _____ connection between two things.

✎   If a builder needs 40 men to build a block of houses in 33 days.

a) How long would it take 60 men to build the block of houses?

22 days

ISLE COLLEGE
RESOURCES CENTRE

b) How many men would the builder need to complete the block of houses in 10 days?

_____

The time taken to dig a field of potatoes varies inversely with the square root of the number of people digging. If it takes 9 men 8 hours to dig out a field of potatoes, then how long will it take 16 men?

_____

_____

_____

_____

Two shapes are said to be *similar* if:

_____

_____

If the ratio of lengths for a similar shape is $x : y$ then:

a) the ratio of areas = _____   b) the ratio of volumes = _____

If you trebled the dimensions of a 1 pint milk bottle, what would happen to:

a) the area of the milk bottle top?

_____

b) the volume of the bottle?

_____

ALGEBRA

GETTING STARTED

All the GCSE courses have a common aim for *Algebra*. This is that the emphasis within algebra should be on the use of letters or words to *communicate mathematical information* and not simply to solve equations. If you intend to go any further in mathematics after this course, it is essential that you appreciate the use of algebra. You need to be confident in your ability to represent general situations in algebraic terms and then to manipulate those terms.

USEFUL DEFINITIONS

Constant	Not changing, as in $y = x + 5$, the 5 is always 5.
Domain	The sets of numbers that a function can work on.
Expand	To multiply out the brackets.
Factorise	Split into expressions that multiply together to make the whole.
Function	An algebraic *happening*; a rule for changing numbers.
Generalise	Express in general terms, usually using an algebraic formula.
Image	The *result* of a function being applied to numbers.
Index	The raised figure that gives the power, e.g. the 3 in y^3.
Linear	An expression involving single variables of power 1, e.g. $x + y = 3$.
Quadratic	An expression involving a squared term as the highest power or index, e.g. $3x^2 - 5x = 7$.
Range	The set of numbers to which a function takes the domain (initial set of numbers).
Simplify	To make easier; in this chapter it will mean to multiply out brackets and to collect like terms.
Simultaneous	At the same time.
Solve	To find the numerical value of the letter.
Transposition	To change the subject of a formula or equation.
Variable	A letter which may stand for various numbers.

ESSENTIAL PRINCIPLES

1 > FORMULAE

66 **Level 5** 99

If you can follow through a *flowchart* like the one shown in Fig. 8.1, then you can easily substitute numbers into simple formulae which are written out.

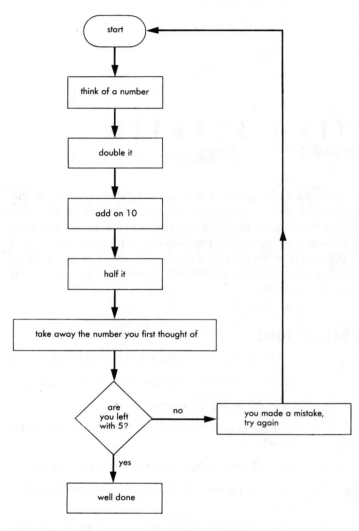

Fig. 8.1

For example, Gladys, the office secretary, paid wages to the workers using this formula:

wage = £40 + £10 multiplied by the number of years worked.

So to find Kevin's wage when he has worked for 15 years we need to substitute 15 into the formula. This will then give Kevin the wage of £40 + £10 × 15 = £40 + £150 = £190. This example could have been done with a flowchart such as the one in Fig. 8.2.

Sometimes the formula is not in words and not in a flowchart, but in what are called *algebraic terms*.

For example, the area of a rectangle is given by the formula

$A = bl$

where A = area, b = breadth, l = length.

For this type of formula we need to remember the basic rules of algebra. For example:

$3t$ means 3 multiplied by t

xy means x multiplied by y

$\dfrac{p}{3}$ means p divided by 3

Fig. 8.2

WORKED EXAMPLE 1

The cost of a pot of coffee in a cafe is calculated by using the formula: $C = 25 + 15n$, where C is the cost of the pot of coffee in pence and n is the number of people sharing the pot of coffee. Calculate the cost of a pot of coffee for 6 people.

We substitute $n = 6$ into the formula $C = 25 + 15n$. The $15n$ means multiply 15×6 in this case, which is 90. Hence the cost is given by $C = 25 + 90$, which is 115p or £1.15.

EXERCISE 1

A bank pays car expenses to its inspectors when they travel to various branches around the country. The expenses work out as follows:

For journeys of 50 miles or less: Amount = £ $\dfrac{24N}{100}$ and

For journeys of more than 50 miles: Amount = £12 + $\dfrac{£20(N - 50)}{100}$

Where N is the number of miles travelled.
How much will be paid for a journey of i) 30 miles; ii) 80 miles?

BRACKETS

We often need to make sure that in a formula certain numbers are calculated first. We do this by the use of brackets.

66 Solve brackets first 99

For example, in the formula $A = (d + e) \div 2$, it is important to add together d and e before dividing the answer by 2, or else you will get quite a different number. So if a bracket appears in a formula, work out the bracket first.

For example, $9 - (5 - 2)$ is equal to $9 - 3$, which is 6, whereas without the bracket this would be read from left to right and be $9 - 5 - 2$ which is $4 - 2$, giving us 2.

BODMAS

This brings us to what do we do when there are no brackets to indicate what to do first. Do we always work from left to right, or is there some other rule? The answer is that if we follow the rule of BODMAS this gives us the order. BODMAS stands for the phrase.

Brackets, Of, Division, Multiplication, Addition, Subtraction and we should do the things in that order.

For example, the horrible sum of
$10 \div 2 + 8 \times 3 - \frac{1}{2}$ of $6 + (4 - 2)$ is done like this:

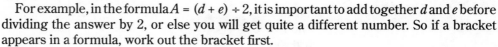

Brackets	$10 \div 2 +$	$8 \times 3 -$	$\frac{1}{2}$ of 6	$+2$	
Of	$10 \div 2 +$	$8 \times 3 -$	3	$+2$	
Division	5 $+$	$8 \times 3 -$	3	$+2$	
Multiplication	5	$+ 24$	$-$	3	$+2$
Addition		31	$-$	3	
Subtraction			28		

If any two or more of the same signs are next to each other we work from left to right.
For example, $10 - 6 - 2$ will be $4 - 2$ which is 2.

EXERCISE 2

Evaluate $\frac{1}{2}$ of $12 \div 6 + 2 \times (3 - 1) - 4$.

APPLICATION

You might use some of these ideas if you do any computer programming, since the letters we have used in this section can be put into computer programs as *variables*. They are called variables because they will vary, that is, be different at different times.

66 Level 6 99

To put a formula into a computer program we need to establish which language we are using, as this could make a difference, but we shall assume that we are using BASIC.

For example, to put the formula $t = \dfrac{d}{v}$ into a computer program we recognise that d is being divided by v, and so we would write a line:

LET $t = d/v$ (you see, it is BASICALLY the same).

Of course the computer needs to know what the letters 'd' and 'v' stand for, so we need to write a line: INPUT d, v, then print out the answer with PRINT t. A nice little program that will do all this is:

```
10 PRINT    "Tell me what d and v are"
20 INPUT    d,v
30 LET      t = d/v
40 PRINT    "t is"; t
RUN
```

If you can, try this program out, then write your own using your own formulae and your own variables.

GENERALISATION

We also use algebra to help us show a pattern.

For example, in the sequence 2, 4, 6, 8, …, we can see that the first number is 1×2, the second is 2×2, the third is 3×2 and so on, so the nth number will be $n \times 2$ or $2n$. Hence this pattern can be described as $2n$ where $n = 1, 2, 3, 4, …$

WORKED EXAMPLE 2

Pascal's Triangle

Look at this number pattern:

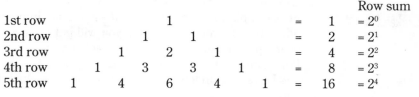

											Row sum
1st row				1				=	1		$= 2^0$
2nd row			1		1			=	2		$= 2^1$
3rd row		1		2		1		=	4		$= 2^2$
4th row	1		3		3		1	=	8		$= 2^3$
5th row	1	4		6		4	1	=	16		$= 2^4$

Now write down: a) the 6th row sum; b) the 11th row sum.
a) This is Pascal's triangle, and you should be able to see how the pattern builds itself down to give the 6th row as $1 + 5 + 10 + 10 + 5 + 1$, with a row sum of $32 = 2^5$.
b) Look at the number of the row and the row sum, and you should see that the row sum of the nth row is 2^{n-1}. Hence the row sum of the 11th row will be 2^{11-1} which is 2^{10}. Now, 2^{10} is $2^5 \times 2^5$ which will be 32×32 which is 1024, i.e. the row sum will be $1024 = 2^{10}$.

FURTHER APPLICATIONS

You also need algebra when trying to describe an observed relationship. For example, a shop selling marbles had a notice (Table 8.1) saying how much you would have to pay to have your marbles polished!

Number of marbles	5	10	15	20	Other prices
Cost (pence)	15	25	35	45	on request

Table 8.1

If you look carefully at the numbers you can find the simple formula that the shop is using to calculate its prices. As the number of marbles increases so too does the cost, but the shop is not simply adding each time nor just multiplying, so it looks like a combination of the two. By trial and error, you can work out that they double the number of marbles and add 5:

cost = 2 × number of marbles + 5.

As you will see in Chapter 9, you could find this by drawing a graph.

2 > EQUATIONS

Level 7

Equations are mathematical statements with one or more letters in place of numbers, but most importantly they contain an equals sign. *Formulae* are equations which can contain any number of letters in place of numbers, as you have already seen.

There are many different types of equations that you will come across, and when you are asked to solve an equation you are expected to find the value of the letter, or letters, that make the mathematical statement true.

For example, $50 = 16y + 2$ is an equation, and if we were to solve it we would find that $y = 3$, since that is the only value of y that will make both sides of the equation equal.

LINEAR EQUATIONS

Linear equations are equations that involve *single* variables of power 1. They contain no expressions such as

$$x^2, \; y^3, \; \frac{1}{x}, \; xy, \; \text{etc.}$$

 Linear equations have 1 as the highest power

Some examples of linear equations of the type you will meet are:

$$x + y = 10, \quad C = D, \quad W = 50 + 10N.$$

We move numbers around in an equation in exactly the same way as we moved letters around in a formula.

WORKED EXAMPLE 3

Solve the equation $18 = 5x + 7$.

As before, we can change $18 = 5x + 7$ into $18 - 7 = 5x$, which then becomes $\frac{11}{5} = x$. Hence $x = 2.2$.

So remember the rules applying to formulae also apply to equations and can be summarised as:

 A useful rule

If it's doing it to all the rest, you may move it and make it do the opposite to the other side.

EXERCISE 3

The circumference of a wheel is approximately 3.1 multiplied by its diameter. What will be the diameter of a bicycle wheel with circumference 56 inches?

$$C = 3.1 \times D \qquad 56 = 3.1d \qquad \frac{56}{3.1} = d$$

3 › SIMULTANEOUS EQUATIONS

Simultaneous equations are where we have a pair of equations that both need solving at the same time (hence simultaneous). There are two methods: the *elimination* method and the *substitution* method.

ELIMINATION METHOD

The technique is initially to eliminate one variable to find a solution to the other one, and then to substitute the found variable to complete the solution.

WORKED EXAMPLE 4

Solve the simultaneous equations $\quad 4x + y = 14 \quad \dots (1)$
$\qquad\qquad\qquad\qquad\qquad\qquad\quad 2x + y = 8 \quad \dots (2)$

To eliminate one of the variables, subtract the equations, bottom from top, which will give:
$\quad 2x = 6$, so $x = 3$.
Now, we substitute this answer in the simplest equation, (2) above, to give $6 + y = 8$, so $y = 2$. Therefore the solution of the simultaneous equation is $x = 3$ and $y = 2$.

Note that you should always check this solution and see that it works with the other equation.

WORKED EXAMPLE 5

Solve the simultaneous equations $\quad 4x - y = 3 \quad \dots (1)$
$\qquad\qquad\qquad\qquad\qquad\qquad\quad 3x + 2y = 16 \quad \dots (2)$

To eliminate y we need to double the whole of equation (1) to give

$$8x - 2y = 6$$
$$3x + 2y = 16$$

Now we can add the equations to eliminate y, to give $11x = 22$, making $x = 2$, which is substituted into equation (1), being the simplest, to give $8 - y = 3$, or $y = 5$. So the final solution is $x = 2$, $y = 5$.

EXERCISE 4

Meg, with 36p, and Dudley, with 34p, go into a sweetshop and spend all their money on sweets. Meg buys 5 chews and 3 fudge bars, while Dudley buys 2 chews and 4 fudge bars. Find the price of chews and fudge bars.

SUBSTITUTION METHOD

This is an alternative method for solving simultaneous equations. For example, solve the two equations:

$$4x - 2y = 11 \ldots (1)$$
$$3x + y = 12 \ldots (2)$$

Then from (2), $y = 12 - 3x$. Now substitute this into equation (1) to give

$$4x - 2(12 - 3x) = 11$$
$$\rightarrow \quad 4x - 24 + 6x = 11$$
$$\rightarrow \quad 10x = 35$$
$$\rightarrow \quad x = 3.5$$

and we are where we arrived at before; we now need to substitute $x = 3.5$ into one of the equations to complete the solution.

This method really becomes more useful when only one equation is linear.

WORKED EXAMPLE 6

66 A simultaneous equation involving a quadratic expression, i.e. power 2 99

Solve the simultaneous equations $\quad x^2 + y = 8 \ldots (1)$
$$x - 3y = 1 \ldots (2)$$
From equation (1), $y = 8 - x^2$, so substitute into equation (2) to give

$$x - 3(8 - x^2) = 1$$
$$x - 24 + 3x^2 = 1$$
$$3x^2 + x - 25 = 0$$

66 Read through the work on quadratic equations first 99

This is a *quadratic* equation and can be solved by one of the methods considered below to give $x = 2.72$ and $x = -3.06$ (2 decimal places). Substitute each into equation (1) which gives the final solution that

$$x = 2.72; \quad y = 0.60$$
$$\text{and } x = -3.06; \quad y = -1.36$$

EXERCISE 5

Solve the simultaneous equations $\quad x - y = 5 \ldots (1)$
$$x^2 + 2y = 24 \ldots (2)$$

 **4 ⟩ EXPANSION**

66 Level 8 99

We first met brackets when we were told to work out the brackets first. In algebra we extend the use of brackets to keep terms together or to factorise.

But first let us look at *expansion of brackets*. This usually means *multiply out*.

For example, $6(x + 3)$ would be expanded to $6x + 18$, so you see why it is sometimes called 'multiply out'.

WORKED EXAMPLE 7

Solve the equation $6x = 4(x + 5)$.

Expand the bracket first to give $6x = 4x + 20$. Then we can solve in the same way as before to give $2x = 20$, so $x = 10$

WORKED EXAMPLE 8

Expand $x(x + y)$.

This will *multiply out* to give $x^2 + xy$.

MULTIPLYING BRACKETS

The most difficult type of bracket expansion you will meet *at all but the highest level* is that of the type $(x + a)(x + b)$, where everything in the first bracket has to multiply everything in the second bracket. We can illustrate this best with a diagram:

$$(x + 6)(x + 4) = x^2 + 4x + 6x + 24$$
$$= x^2 + 10x + 24$$

EXERCISE 6

Expand: i) $(x + 2)(x + 3)$; ii) $(t - 1)(t + 2)$

5 > FACTORISATION

You are also expected to be able to factorise a simple algebraic expression.

For example, by looking at the formula $A = \pi r^2 + \pi d$ we notice that on the right hand side both terms contain π, and so this can be rewritten as $A = \pi(r^2 + d)$. Some more examples to illustrate this are:

$P = 2l + 2b$ can be factorised to $P = 2(l + b)$
$D = \pi r - r^3$ can be factorised to $D = r(\pi - r^2)$

The way to check your answer is to expand the bracket out again to see if you get the same as you started with.

EXERCISE 7

Factorise: i) $A = \pi R^2 - \pi r^2$; ii) $T = 5pq + 10p^2$

6 > SIMPLIFICATION

This means what it says! It is what we do to make an expression more simple.

For example, to simplify $t = 3(x + y) + 4(2x + y)$ we would expand both brackets to give $t = 3x + 3y + 8x + 4y$, which will then simplify to $t = 11x + 7y$ by combining similar terms.

EXERCISE 8

Simplify: i) $y = 4(x + t) + 2(4x - t)$; ii) $p = 3(x - y) - 2(3x - y)$.

FURTHER EXPANSION

You should remember from the previous sections how to expand $(x + a)(x + b)$. Well, in exactly the same way at the higher levels you are expected to be able to expand $(ax + b)(bx + c)$, for example:

$$(3x + 2)(4x + 7) = 12x^2 + 21x + 8x + 14$$
$$= 12x^2 + 29x + 14.$$

QUADRATIC EQUATION OR EXPRESSION

A quadratic equation or expression is where the highest power involved is a 2 and no negative powers are used, for example:

$3x^2 + 6x - 7$ or $5x^2 - 2y^2$

QUADRATIC FACTORISATION

Factorisation means putting a quadratic back into its brackets if at all possible, although in an examination situation you are not likely to be asked to factorise a quadratic that will not do so.

It is helpful when factorising to first consider what the signs may be.

Rule 1

> Relax; if you've been asked to factorise then it will work out if you follow these simple rules.

When the last sign in the quadratic $ax^2 + bx + c$ is positive, both signs in the brackets are the same as the first sign in the quadratic, for example:

$$6x^2 + 7x + 2 = (\ +\ )(\ +\ )$$
and
$$6x^2 - 7x + 2 = (\ -\ )(\ -\ )$$

Rule 2

When the last sign in the quadratic $ax^2 + bx - c$ is negative, the signs in the brackets are different, for example:

$$6x^2 + x - 2 = (\quad + \quad)(\quad - \quad)$$

and

$$6x^2 + x - 2 = (\quad - \quad)(\quad + \quad)$$

Once you've sorted out the signs then you need to look at the numbers. Follow through these examples for the general way to do this.

WORKED EXAMPLE 9

Factorise $6x^2 + 7x + 2$

By looking at the signs we see that the brackets both contain a '+', so $6x^2 + 7x + 2 = (+)(+)$. We see that the end numbers in each bracket must multiply to give 2, and the only way to do this is to have 2×1. Hence $6x^2 + 7x + 2 = (\quad + 2)(\quad + 1)$.

Now we see that the first numbers in each bracket must multiply to give 6, and we could have 6×1 or 3×2, but the combination we need is to multiply with the 2 and the 1, so that their sum is 7. We ask ourselves which of

$$\begin{Bmatrix} 3 \times 2 \\ 2 \times 1 \end{Bmatrix} \begin{Bmatrix} 2 \times 2 \\ 3 \times 1 \end{Bmatrix} \begin{Bmatrix} 6 \times 2 \\ 1 \times 1 \end{Bmatrix} \text{ or } \begin{Bmatrix} 1 \times 2 \\ 6 \times 1 \end{Bmatrix}$$

give a combined total of 7, and we see that the only one which does is

$$\begin{Bmatrix} 2 \times 2 \\ 3 \times 1 \end{Bmatrix}$$

so the factorisation is $(3x + 2)(2x + 1)$.

WORKED EXAMPLE 10

Factorise $2x^2 + 5x - 3$

We factorise by looking at the signs and noticing that both signs will be different, hence $(\quad + \quad)(\quad - \quad)$. The -3 indicates we need a 3 and a 1 at the end of each bracket to give $(\quad + 3)(\quad - 1)$ or $(\quad + 1)(\quad - 3)$. Now, a product of 2, i.e. 2 and 1, combining with 3 and 1 in such a way to give a difference of 5, will give us $(x + 3)(2x - 1)$.

EXERCISE 9

Factorise: i) $x^2 + 8x + 12$; ii) $2x^2 + 5x - 3$.

DIFFERENCE OF TWO SQUARES

If you expand $(x + y)(x - y)$ in the usual way you get $x^2 - xy + xy - y^2$, which is $x^2 - y^2$. This is called the difference of two squares. It is very valuable to be able to recognise this situation either way, so that when you are faced with any example of the type, say, $9x^2 - 25$, you recognise both terms are squares and you can write down

$$9x^2 - 25 = (3x + 5)(3x - 5).$$

EXERCISE 10

Factorise: i) $x^2 - 16$: ii) $4y^2 - 9$; iii) $\pi(R^2 - r^2)$.

7 QUADRATIC EQUATIONS

 Level 7

A quadratic equation is an equation involving a quadratic expression e.g. $2x^2 - 3x + 6 = 0$. To *solve* a quadratic equation, for example $x^2 + x - 6 = 0$, we initially need to factorise to give $(x + 3)(x - 2) = 0$. Then since the product of the two numbers is zero, one bracket or both must be equal to zero. In this case either $x + 3 = 0$ or $x - 2 = 0$, and we have two simple linear equations which solve to $x = -3$ or $x = 2$.

WORKED EXAMPLE 11

Solve the equation $2x^2 + 5x + 4 = 7$

You must remove the 7 to make the quadratic equal zero. This will give us $2x^2 + 5x - 3 = 0$, which factorises to $(2x - 1)(x + 3) = 0$. This give $2x - 1 = 0$ or $x + 3 = 0$. Therefore the solution is $x = \frac{1}{2}$ or $x = -3$.

66 You may have learnt the formula method, if so the formula will be given to you on a formula sheet and you simply substitute into it. 99

EXERCISE 11

Solve: i) $y^2 + y - 6 = 0$; ii) $16x^2 - 9 = 0$; iii) $x^2 + x = 20$.
We look at solving quadratic equations in more detail later in the chapter.

TRANSPOSITION

66 Level 8 99

It is often necessary to be able to change a formula round to help you find a particular piece of information.

For example, if I used the formula $C = \pi D$, where C is the circumference of a circle and D is the diameter, then to find the diameter when the circumference is 100 cm, it would be more convenient to change the formula round to give:

$$D = \frac{C}{\pi}.$$

I then have only a simple substitution to do.

This changing round of formulae is called *transposition* of formulae and what we are doing is changing the subject of a formula. The subject of a formula is the single letter, or word, usually on the left-hand side all by itself.

For example:

t is the subject of the formula $t = \dfrac{d}{v}$

Here are some rules for changing the subjects of formulae:

Rule 1

66 This is the very basis of most of your algebra. Understand this and you're almost home! 99

You can move any letter, or word, from one side of the equation to the other as long as it is operating on *all* the rest of that side.

For example, in the formula $v = u + 6t$, the u can be moved since it is adding to the rest of that side, but the t cannot be moved yet as it is only multiplying the 6.

This simple list of formulae should help you see when we can move terms:

$v = u + 6t$	we could move either the u or the $6t$
$A = lb$	we could move either the l or the b
wage = hours × hourly rate	we could move either hours or hourly rate

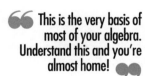

$t = \dfrac{d}{v}$	we could move either the d or the v
$x = \dfrac{y + 1}{7}$	we could move either the 7 or the $(y + 1)$
$w = n(y - 10)$	we could move either the n or the $(y - 10)$

Rule 2

When a letter, or word, has been moved from one side to the other, it does the *opposite thing* to the other side.

For example, if something was added, then when it moved it would be subtracted, or if something was multiplied then when it moved it would divide.

These examples will help to illustrate these points:

$v = u + 6t$ can be changed to $v - u = 6t$
or $v - 6t = u$

$A = lb$ can be changed to $\dfrac{A}{l} = b$

or $\dfrac{A}{b} = l$

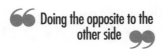
Doing the opposite to the other side

wage = hours × hourly rate

can be changed to $\dfrac{\text{wage}}{\text{hours}}$ = hourly rate

or $\dfrac{\text{wage}}{\text{hourly rate}}$ = hours

$t = \dfrac{d}{v}$ can be changed to $tv = d$

or $\dfrac{t}{d} = \dfrac{1}{v}$

$y = 6x - 10$ can be changed to $y + 10 = 6x$

or $y - 6x = -10$

WORKED EXAMPLE 12

A firm calculates wages using the formula:

Wage $= £15 +$ hours × hourly rate

Change the formula to make hours the subject, and so find the number of hours that Philip will have to work to earn £180 when his hourly rate is £5.50.

From: Wage = 15 + hours × hourly rate, we change to;
Wage − 15 = hours × hourly rate, which we then change to;
(Wage − 15)/hourly rate = hours.
    Now, substitute Wage = 180 and hourly rate = 5.50, to give hours equal to 30.

EXERCISE 12

You are given the simple interest formula:

$$I = \dfrac{PRT}{100}$$

Where I = interest, P = the principal amount, R = rate of interest, T = time.
    Change the formula to make R the subject, and hence find the rate that gives an interest of £6 when the principal amount is £20 and the time is 4 years.

9 > INEQUATIONS

Level 8

Equations with inequality signs in them are called *inequations*, but are often referred to as *inequalities* also, and are solved in exactly the same way, except that when you have to multiply or divide *both* sides by a negative number the inequality sign turns round.

    For example, if we have −2 < 5, then 2 > −5.

WORKED EXAMPLE 13

Find the range of value for which $5x + 3 > 4(x - 2)$

Using normal equation techniques we can calculate $5x + 3 > 4(x - 2)$
to give $5x + 3 > 4x - 8$, so $x > -11$.

EXERCISE 13

Find the smallest integer which satisfies the inequality $6x - 8 > 3x + 9$.

10 > ALGEBRAIC SHORTHAND

You should be familiar with the shorthand we use in algebra.
    For example, ab meaning a multiplied by b, $\frac{3}{x}$ meaning 3 divided by x, and combining similar terms as meaning, for example, $5x + 3x$ to give $8x$.
    There are other very common things that we have a special shorthand for, and those are *indices*.
    For example, we use the shorthand a^4 to mean $a \times a \times a \times a$.
    We also have a very easy way to multiply and divide two similar index terms which should be remembered:

❝ Level 8 ❞

$a^x \times a^y = a^{x+y}$;   for example $2^7 \times 2^5 = 2^{12}$
$a^x \div a^y = a^{x-y}$;   for example $y^6 \div y^3 = y^3$

You also need to know that for any number x, then $x^1 = x$ and $x^0 = 1$.

We also use negative indices to show numbers of a fractional form, for example:

$$x^{-2} = \frac{1}{x^2} \text{ and } 5^{-1} = \frac{1}{5}$$

EXERCISE 14

Write down the value of: i) $6^2 \times 6^4$;   ii) $x^5 \div x^6$.

11⟩ FRACTIONAL INDICES

❝ Level 9 ❞

❝ Do work all these out on the calculator with the correct buttons … it's so much easier ❞

The use of the *fractional index* is used to denote a root,

e.g. $9^{\frac{1}{2}} = \sqrt[3]{9} = 3$ and -3
   $8^{\frac{1}{3}} = \sqrt[3]{8} = 2$

NB. $8^{\frac{2}{3}} = (\sqrt[3]{8})^2 = 2^2 = 4$ **or** $\sqrt[3]{8^2} = \sqrt[3]{64} = 4$

Use the $x^{\frac{1}{y}}$ button on your calculator to calculate the answers. For example, to calculate $9^{\frac{1}{5}}$, just press 9 followed by $x^{\frac{1}{y}}$, followed by 5 = ⎕, this should give you 1.55.

Similarly, if you need to calculate a cube root, maybe from a similar shape situation, then use the $x^{\frac{1}{y}}$ button on your calculator followed by a 3.

WORKED EXAMPLE 14

Which is the larger? $18^{\frac{2}{3}}$ or $8^{\frac{2}{3}}$
$18^{\frac{2}{3}} = (\sqrt[3]{18})^2 = 6.868$
$8^{\frac{3}{2}} = (\sqrt{8})^3 = 22.63$
hence $8^{\frac{3}{2}} > 18^{\frac{2}{3}}$

EXERCISE 15

Calculate   i) $5^{\frac{2}{5}}$;   ii) $\sqrt[3]{11}$;   iii) $8^{-0.7}$

12⟩ FUNCTIONS

The only *functions* we are going to consider are *algebraic functions* which give a rule for changing one number to another.

For example $f : x \rightarrow 3x$ is the function f where any number is multiplied by 3 to obtain its image. Another way of denoting the same function is to say $f(x) = 3x$.

Again, where $f(x) = 2x^2 + 5$, then $f(3) = 23$, since substituting $x = 3$ into $2x^2 + 5$ gives us 23. In other words, it is another way of writing $y = 2x^2 + 5$ where we talk about $f(x)$ instead of y.

WORKED EXAMPLE 15

For the function $f : x \rightarrow \sin(2x)$ find $f(40)$.

   $f(40) = \sin(2 \times 40) = \sin 80 = 0.9848$.

EXERCISE 16

Where $f : x \rightarrow (x - 1)^2$, what is   i) $f(1)$;   ii) $f(0)$;   iii) $f(-1)$?

DOMAIN AND RANGE

The set of numbers that the given function is applied to is called the *domain*. The set of numbers that the function takes numbers to is called the *range*.

For example, in the function $f(x) = x^2 + 3$, the domain can be the whole set of numbers, positive and negative, while the range is only the positive numbers equal to or larger than 3, since the lowest value of x^2 is zero.

WORKED EXAMPLE 16

If the domain of the function $f : x \to \dfrac{1}{x+1}$ is $\{x : 2 \leqslant x \leqslant 10\}$ find the range of the function.

We need to find all the possible images from x between 2 and 10 inclusive. Looking at the function tells us that as x gets bigger then $f(x)$ gets gradually smaller.

Hence $f(2)$ will give the upper limit of the range $f(2) = \dfrac{1}{3}$

and $f(10)$ will give the lower limit of the range $f(10) = \dfrac{1}{11}$

so the range will be $\left\{ x : \dfrac{1}{11} \leqslant x \leqslant \dfrac{1}{3} \right\}$

---

13 FURTHER TRANSPOSITION

66 This is your basic rule to follow, learn it and use it. 99

 Level 10 99

All your manipulation of algebra lies in being able to understand the principle of:

If it's doing what it's doing to everything else on that side of the equation, then it can be moved to the other side and perform the opposite job.

Work through the following changes of subject of formula and then try them yourself to make absolutely certain that you can confidently cope with this basic requirement of algebra.

WORKED EXAMPLE 17

Change $x = 5y - 7$ to make y the subject.
$$x + 7 = 5y$$
$$\to \frac{x+7}{5} = y; \text{ hence } y = \frac{x+7}{5}$$

WORKED EXAMPLE 18

Change $p = \dfrac{t}{4} + 7$ to make t the subject.

$$p - 7 = \frac{t}{4}$$
$$\to 4(p-7) = t \text{ ; hence } t = 4(p-7)$$

WORKED EXAMPLE 19

Change $v = p(4t + 1)$ to make t the subject.

$$\frac{v}{p} = 4t + 1$$

$$\to \frac{v}{p} - 1 = 4t$$

$$\to \frac{v-p}{p} = 4t \quad \text{(easier to cope with if we simplify the LHS)}$$

$$\to \frac{v-p}{4p} = t$$

WORKED EXAMPLE 20

Change $t = \dfrac{3w+4}{5-w}$ to make w the subject.

$$t(5-w) = 3w+4$$
$$5t-wt = 3w+4 \quad \rightarrow 5t-4 = 3w+wt$$
$$\rightarrow 5t-4 = w(3+t)$$
$$\rightarrow \frac{5t-4}{3+t} = w$$

hence $w = \dfrac{5t-4}{3+t}$

WORKED EXAMPLE 21

Change $x = y^2 - 7$ to make y the subject.

$$x+7 = y^2 \rightarrow \sqrt{(x+7)} = y$$

hence $\quad y = \sqrt{(x+7)}$

---

14 ⟩ SOLUTIONS TO QUADRATIC EQUATIONS

❝ In the exam it will not matter which way you have solved it, as long as the method is clearly shown, and it helps if the answer is right! ❞

Quadratic equations are those that involve no higher power than a 2, nor any less than a 1. For example, $3x^2 + 6x - 1 = 0$.

They can be solved in a number of different ways depending on the particular combination of numbers they contain. Here we take our earlier work on quadratic equations a little further.

SOLVE BY SIMPLE FACTORISATION

There are times (and generally these are the only ones you are likely to be asked in the GCSE examination), when the quadratic equation will go nicely into two brackets to solve. We have already looked at the process of factorisation (p. 95).

WORKED EXAMPLE 22

Solve the equation $6x^2 + 5x - 6 = 0$.

Factorise by trying to put into two brackets ( )( ). The −6 indicates that the signs are different, hence (+)(−) or (−)(+). Now the first number in each bracket (the coefficients of x) must multiply to give 6, whilst the end two constants in each bracket must also multiply together to give 6. This gives us quite a few possibilities, e.g. $(2x + 2)(3x - 3)$, but the *combination* of the outer two and the inner two must give us $+5x$.

So the factorisation is $(3x - 2)(2x + 3)$, the positive sign is with the largest combination, since the $5x$ is positive.
So $(3x - 2)(2x + 3) = 0$
which gives us $3x - 2 = 0$ and $2x + 3 = 0$
$$3x = 2 \qquad 2x = -3$$
$$x = \frac{2}{3} \text{ and } \qquad x = \frac{-3}{2}$$

Solution is $x = \dfrac{2}{3}$ and $\dfrac{-3}{2}$

This method works very well when your solution gives two brackets with integers in them, and when you happen to 'spot' the right combination. Try the following exercise.

EXERCISE 17

Solve the equations   i) $30x^2 + 19x - 4 = 0$;   ii) $12x^2 + x - 6 = 0$.

SOLVE BY COMPLETING THE SQUARE

You may have done that last exercise quite quickly, or you may have taken quite a time to solve it. It can be a quick method, but only if you *spot* the connection and even then only if the thing does give two nice brackets.

Another way of always finding a solution (if there is one) is the method of *completing the square*. This follows through the simple procedure:

$$ax^2 + bx + c = 0$$

Divide throughout by 'a' to give $x^2 + \dfrac{b}{a}x + \dfrac{c}{a} = 0.$

Move the constant term to the other side, to give $x^2 + \dfrac{b}{a}x = -\dfrac{c}{a}$

On the Left Hand Side (LHS) drop the square term add half the co-efficient of x, place within brackets, and square.

$$\text{LHS} = \left(x + \dfrac{b}{2a}\right)^2$$

On the Right Hand Side (RHS), add $\left(\dfrac{b}{2a}\right)^2$

$$\text{RHS} = -\dfrac{c}{a} + \left(\dfrac{b}{2a}\right)^2$$

This gives $\left(x + \dfrac{b}{2a}\right)^2 = -\dfrac{c}{a} + \left(\dfrac{b}{2a}\right)^2$, which will have given you an equation like

> **Don't give up yet, this really is a good method**

$$(x + d)^2 = e$$
$$\rightarrow x + d = +\sqrt{e} \text{ and } -\sqrt{e}$$
$$\rightarrow x = +\sqrt{e} - d \text{ and } -\sqrt{e} - d.$$

It looks worse than it actually is. Follow through worked example 23, then try this method in Exercise 18; then try it again in Exercise 17 above.

WORKED EXAMPLE 23

Solve the equation $2x^2 + 5x - 3 = 0$.

Divide throughout by 2 to give $x^2 + \dfrac{5x}{2} - \dfrac{3}{2} = 0$.

Move the constant term to the other side, to give $x^2 + \dfrac{5}{2}x = \dfrac{3}{2}$

$$\left(x + \dfrac{5}{4}\right)^2 = \dfrac{3}{2} + \dfrac{25}{16} \text{ (look where things have come from)}$$

> **Halve the co-efficient of x and follow the procedure above.**

hence $\left(x + \dfrac{5}{4}\right)^2 = 3.0625$

$$\rightarrow x + \dfrac{5}{4} = 1.75 \text{ and } -1.75$$
$$x = (1.75 - 1.25) \text{ and } (-1.75 - 1.25)$$
$$= 0.5 \text{ and } -3$$
$$x = 0.5 \text{ and } -3.$$

EXERCISE 18

Solve the equations   i) $6x^2 + 7x + 2 = 9$;   ii) $2x^2 - x - 6 = 0$.

Of course this method is only useful when solving and not when just factorising, where you do need two complete brackets; but it is worth familiarising yourself with the method.

SOLVE BY THE FORMULA

There is a well known, loved and trusted *formula* which will also always work to solve equations of the type $ax^2 + bx + c = 0$.

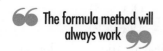
The formula method will always work

This is $x = \dfrac{-b \pm \sqrt{b^2 - 4ac}}{2a}$

(it is the formal next stage to completing the square).

WORKED EXAMPLE 24

Solve the equation $2x^2 + 5x - 3 = 0$.

Using $x = \dfrac{-b \pm \sqrt{(b^2 - 4ac)}}{2a}$, where $a = 2$, $b = 5$ and $c = -3$

then $x = \dfrac{-5 \pm \sqrt{(25 + 24)}}{4} = \dfrac{-5 \pm \sqrt{(49)}}{4} = \dfrac{-5 \pm 7}{4}$

$x = \dfrac{-12}{4}$ and $\dfrac{2}{4}$

$x = -3$ and 0.5.

Try this method on Exercises 17 and 18 if you wish to compare. All three methods are good and useful. You need to use the method that you are most confident with, or which best suits the situation at the time.

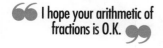
15 ALGEBRAIC FRACTIONS

You really must be confident with normal fraction arithmetic to stand a chance of being successful with *algebraic fractions*. This is because you have to apply the normal fraction rules without being able to resort to 'common fractions'.

I hope your arithmetic of fractions is O.K.

ADDING AND SUBTRACTING

As in normal fractions you need a *common denominator*, after which you can either add or subtract.

WORKED EXAMPLE 25

Level 10

Simplify $\dfrac{x}{2} + \dfrac{1}{x + 1} = 5$.

To get a common denominator on the left hand side multiply each fraction top and bottom by the numerator of the other fraction

hence $\dfrac{x(x + 1)}{2(x + 1)} + \dfrac{2 \times 1}{2(x + 1)} = 5$

$\rightarrow \dfrac{x(x + 1) + 2}{2(x + 1)} = 5$

$\rightarrow x(x + 1) + 2 \quad = 10(x + 1)$
$\rightarrow x^2 + x + 2 \quad = 10x + 10$
$\rightarrow x^2 - 9x - 8 \quad = 0$

EXERCISE 19

Solve the equation $1 + \dfrac{1}{x} = x$

MULTIPLYING

It is the cancelling here that seems to mystify most people. You must remember that when *multiplying fractions* you can cancel any factor on the top with any factor on the bottom,

$\dfrac{\cancel{2}^{1}}{3} \times \dfrac{5}{\cancel{6}_{3}} = \dfrac{5}{9}$.

WORKED EXAMPLE 26

Factorise and hence simplify: $\dfrac{(x^2 - 5x + 4)}{(x^2 + x - 6)} \times \dfrac{(x^2 + 4x + 3)}{(x^2 - 2x - 8)}$

Factorise each quadratic to obtain $\dfrac{(x - 4)(x - 1)}{(x - 2)(x + 3)} \times \dfrac{(x + 1)(x + 3)}{(x - 4)(x + 2)}$

The $(x - 4)$ will cancel top and bottom, as will the $(x + 3)$, leaving the expression as

$\dfrac{(x - 1)(x + 1)}{(x - 2)(x + 2)}$ which is $\dfrac{x^2 - 1}{x^2 - 4}$

DIVIDING

Remember the rule to turn the second fraction upside down and multiply.

WORKED EXAMPLE 27

Solve $\dfrac{(x + 1)}{3} \div \dfrac{4}{(x + 1)} = 1$

Turn the second fraction upside down and multiply, which gives us

$\dfrac{(x + 1)}{3} \times \dfrac{(x + 1)}{4} = 1$

$\rightarrow (x + 1)^2 = 12$
$\rightarrow x + 1 \quad = \sqrt{12} = 3.46 \text{ and } -3.46$
$\quad\quad x \quad = 3.46 - 1 \text{ and } -3.46 - 1$
$\quad\quad x \quad = 2.46 \text{ and } -4.46$

EXERCISE 20

Find i) the product: ii) the quotient of $\dfrac{x + 1}{x - 1}$ and $\dfrac{x^2 - 1}{x^2 + 1}$

16 **TRIAL AND IMPROVEMENT METHOD FOR SOLVING EQUATIONS**

Level 6

This method does not imply random trial and error, but rather 'intelligent detective work' to find a good solution to a problem.

For example, find the solution to $x^3 + x = 100$

■ The first thing to do is to try some whole numbers,

try $x = 3 \ldots 3^3 + 3 = 27 + 3 = 30$ … too small
try $x = 5 \ldots 5^3 + 5 = 125 + 5 = 130$ … too large

■ I now know the solution is somewhere between 3 and 5, so try halfway between, which is 4

try $x = 4 \ldots 4^3 + 4 = 68$ … too small.

■ I now know the solution is somewhere between 4 and 5, so try halfway between 4 and 5 which is 4.5

try $x = 4.5 \ldots 4.5^3 + 4.5 = 95.625$ … too small.

■ The solution is between 4.5 and 5, but an intelligent look will suggest that it is nearer to 4.5 than 5. Since half-way between 4.5 and 5 goes to two decimal places, we choose a digit nearer to 4.5, say 4.7.

try $x = 4.7 \ldots 4.7^3 + 4.7 = 108.523$ … too large.

■ We continue trying out values in this way, getting closer and closer to our solution all the time.
try $x = 4.6 \ldots 4.6^3 + 4.6 = 101.936$ … too large.

The solution is clearly between 4.5 and 4.6, so now we must move the search into two decimal places.

try $x = 4.55 \ldots 98.746 \ldots$ too small

try $x = 4.58 \ldots 100.652 \ldots$ too large

try $x = 4.57 \ldots 100.014 \ldots$ too large.

We can sensibly stop here, because the answer is *very* close to 100.

Solution: $x = 4.57$

Note. We could have continued as long as we wanted, getting more and more accurate with each try.

WORKED EXAMPLE 28

Susan has to find, correct to one decimal place, the solution of the equation

$x^2 + x = 1$

By trying values of x and showing your working clearly, find a solution to Susan's equations.

Try $x = 1$	$1^2 + 1 = 2$	too big
try $x = 0.5$	$0.5^2 + 0.5 = 0.75$	too small
try $x = 0.7$	$0.7^2 + 0.7 = 1.19$	too big
try $x = 0.6$	$0.6^2 + 0.6 = 0.96$	too small
try $x = 0.65$	1.0725	too big

hence $x = 0.6$ is the solution to 1 decimal place.

EXERCISE 21

Find the solution to $x^3 - x = 50$ correct to two decimal places.

SOLUTIONS TO EXERCISES

S1

i) Use the first formula to give amount = $(24 \times 30) \div 100$, which is £7.20.

ii) Use the second formula to give amount = $12 + 20(80 - 50) \div 100$, which is £18.

S2

1

S3

If $C = 3.1 \times D$, then $D = \dfrac{C}{3.1}$;

so where $C = 56$, $D = \dfrac{56}{3.1} = 18.1$ (rounded off).

S4

Let the price of a chew be c, and the price of a fudge bar be f, and then we can write down a pair of simultaneous equations:

$5c + 3f = 36$ (from Meg's information)

$2c + 4f = 34$ (from Dudley's information).

   Work these out and we get $c = 3$ and $f = 7$, so the price of a chew is 3p and the price of a fudge bar is 7p.

S5

From equation (1) $x = 5 + y$, substitute this into equation (2) to give $(5 + y)^2 + 2y = 24$

$$\rightarrow 25 + 10y + y^2 + 2y = 24$$
$$\rightarrow y^2 + 12y + 1 \qquad = 0$$

This will solve to give $y = -0.08$ and -11.9.
So from equation (1) we can now give the full solution of

$$x = 4.92, y = -0.08$$
$$\text{and } x = -6.9, y = -11.9.$$

S6

i) $x^2 + 5x + 6$;   ii) $t^2 + t - 2$.

S7

i) $A = \pi(R^2 - r^2)$:   ii) $T = 5p(q + 2p)$.
(See difference of two squares.)

S8

i) $y = 4x + 4t + 8x - 2t = 12x + 2t = 2(6x + t)$;
ii) $p = 3x - 3y - 6x + 2y = -3x - y$.

S9

i) $(x + 2)(x + 6)$;   ii) $(2x - 1)(x + 3)$.

S10

i) $(x + 4)(x - 4)$;   ii) $(2y + 3)(2y - 3)$;   iii) $\pi(R + r)(R - r)$.

S11

i) We can see that the signs will be different, so we need factors of 6 with a difference of 1 to give the answer of $(y + 3)(y - 2)$.
ii) This is recognised as the difference of two squares: the square root of $16x^2$ is $4x$., the square root of 9 is 3. So the solution is $(4x + 3)(4x - 3)$.
iii) $x^2 + x - 20 = 0$
$(x + 5)(x - 4) = 0$
$x = -5$ and $+4$

S12

From $I = \dfrac{PRT}{100}$ we can change to $100I = PRT$, which we can then change to $\dfrac{100I}{PT} = R$.

So the new formula is $R = \dfrac{100I}{PT}$. Substitute into this $I = 6, P = 20$ and $T = 4$, which will give you $R = 7.5$.

S13

Solve the equation $6x - 8 > 3x + 9$ to give $3x > 17$, and hence $x > 5.66$, so the smallest integer, whole number, will be 6.

S14

i) 6^6;   ii) $x^{-1} = \dfrac{1}{x}$.

S15

i) Use calculator as $5 \rightarrow x^y \rightarrow 0.4$ (i.e. $\frac{2}{5}$) $= 1.9$
ii) Use calculator as $11 \rightarrow x^{\frac{1}{y}} \rightarrow 3 = 2.22$
iii) Use calculator as $8 \rightarrow x^y \rightarrow 0.7 \rightarrow {}^+/- = 0.23$
Do try to become familiar with the use of x^y and $x^{\frac{1}{y}}$ buttons on your calculator.

S16

i) $f(1) = 0$; ii) $f(0) = 1$; iii) $f(-1) = 4$.

S17

i) $(6x - 1)(5x + 4)$
→ $6x - 1 = 0$ and $5x + 4 = 0$

ii) $(4x + 3)(3x - 2)$
→ $4x + 3 = 0$ and $3x - 2 = 0$

$x = \dfrac{1}{6}$ and $x = \dfrac{-4}{5}$

$x = \dfrac{-3}{4}$ and $x = \dfrac{2}{3}$

S18

i) $x = -0.67$ and -0.5; ii) $x = -1.5$ and 2

S19

Find a common denominator x to give $\dfrac{x}{x} + \dfrac{1}{x} = x$

→ $\dfrac{x + 1}{x} = x$ → $x + 1 = x^2$ → $x^2 - x - 1 = 0$

This will solve to give 1.62 and -0.62.

S20

i) product $= \dfrac{(x + 1)}{(x - 1)} \times \dfrac{(x^2 - 1)}{(x^2 + 1)} = \dfrac{(x + 1)}{(x - 1)} \times \dfrac{(x + 1)(x - 1)}{(x^2 + 1)} = \dfrac{(x + 1)^2}{(x^2 + 1)}$

ii) quotient $= \dfrac{(x + 1)}{(x - 1)} \div \dfrac{(x^2 - 1)}{(x^2 + 1)} = \dfrac{(x + 1)}{(x - 1)} \times \dfrac{(x^2 + 1)}{(x + 1)(x - 1)} = \dfrac{x^2 + 1}{(x - 1)^2}$

S21

3.59

EXAM TYPE QUESTIONS

Q1

Work through the flow chart in Fig. 8.3 using your calculator.

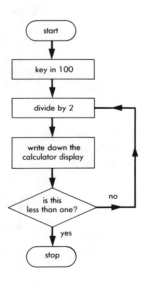

Fig. 8.3

(MEG)

Q2

Use the flow diagram in Fig. 8.4 in each of the following questions:

Fig. 8.4

a) When the input is 4, calculate the output *10*
b) When the input is 5.73, calculate the output ~ (MEG) *15.19*

Q3

A pattern of blocks is laid out as shown in Fig. 8.5.

Fig. 8.5

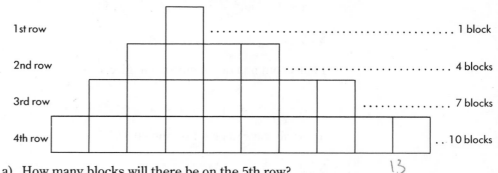

1st row	.... 1 block
2nd row	.... 4 blocks
3rd row	.... 7 blocks
4th row	.. 10 blocks

a) How many blocks will there be on the 5th row? *13*
b) How many blocks will there be on the *n*th row? *multiply the previous row number*
by 2 then add the row number
c) Which row has 28 blocks on it?   (NEAB) *after this you get n...*

Q4

Write down a possible value of *x* so that $2x < 4$ and $x > 1$.   (SEG)

Q5

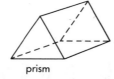
prism

cuboid

pyramid

Fig. 8.6

a) Complete Table 8.2 for the solids shown in Fig. 8.6.

Name	Number of vertices	Number of faces	Number of edges
Prism	6	5	9
Cuboid	8	6	12
Pyramid	4	5	8

Table 8.2

b) How many edges would you expect on a shape having 10 vertices and 7 faces?
(NEAB)

Q6

Let f be the function $x \rightarrow \dfrac{4 - 3x}{2}$.

a) Calculate f(–2).   b) Find the value of *x* for which f(*x*) = –7.

(MEG)

Q7

At a particular disaster relief depot, the daily weight of grain supplied can be estimated during the first month by using the following formula:

$s = 13n + nt.$

where s = number of tonnes of grain supplied,
n = number of days since the disaster,
t = number of times TV coverage has been made. *6*

a) Factorise the right-hand side of the formula.
b) Transform the formula to make n the subject.
c) What was the date of the disaster if on 28 May, after 5 TV coverages, the depot was supplied with 198 tonnes of grain?

(NEAB)

Q8

a) At the moment, Paul is six times as old as his daughter Jane.
    i) If Jane's present age is x years, write down, in terms of x, the age Paul will be in 12 years' time. *$x6 + 12$*
    ii) In 12 years' time, Paul will be three times as old as Jane. Write down an equation for x and hence find Jane's present age.
b) Solve the equation $(x - 1)^2 = 3$, giving your answers correct to two decimal places.

(MEG)

$6x + 12 = 3(x + 12).$
$6x + 12 = 3x + 36.$

Q9

Which is the larger, 5^4 or 4^5?

$3x = 24.$
$x = 8.$

Q10

a) Find the value of k such that: *bxings.* *$x = 2$*
    $(x - 3)(2x + 5) = 2x^2 + kx - 15.$
a) Solve the quadratic equation: *$k9 = 16 + (kx2) - 15$*
    $x^2 - 2x - 24 = 0.$

$4 = 7$

(ULEAC)

Q11

The amount of sleep a child needs (S hours) depends upon its age (A years) and is given approximately by the formula:

$S = 17 - \frac{1}{2} A$

a) How many hours' sleep should a child of 6 years have each night? *$17 - \frac{1}{2} \times 6$* *14*
b) When a child is born, how many hours per day should it sleep? *1~*

(NISEAC)

Q12

The stopping distance, d feet, at various speeds, v miles per hour, is given in the highway code as shown in Table 8.3.

Speed (mph)	30	50	70
Stopping distance (feet)	75	175	

Table 8.3

The stopping distance for 70 mph has been torn out. You are told that d and v are connected by the relation $d = av + bv^2$ where a and b are numerical constants.

a) Use the table to find the values of a and b.
b) Find the value of the stopping distance for 70 mph which has been torn out of the highway code table.

Q13

A babycare book gives the following formula to work out the size of a baby's meal.

$$M = \frac{150W}{N}$$

where M is the size of the meal in grams
W is the weight of the baby in kilograms
N is the number of meals per day.

Work out the size of a meal for a baby of 4 kg having 5 meals a day.

(ULEAC)

Q14

a) Look at this computer program:

```
10    FOR NUMBER = 1 TO 6
20    PRINT NUMBER * 2 + 3
30    NEXT NUMBER
40    END
RUN
```

Write down the numbers the computer will print.

b) Write down a similar program so that the computer will print the numbers 1, 4, 9, 16, 25.

(MEG)

Q15

Andrew goes shopping for his mother. He is told to buy 3 biros and 2 pencils which would have cost 68p altogether. By mistake he buys 2 biros and 3 pencils for 62p.

Take x pence to be the cost of one biro and y pence to be the cost of one pencil.

a) Write down two equations in x and y.
b) Solve your equations to find the cost of one biro.

(MEG)

Q16

A $(1, 0, 0)$ B$(6, 0, 0)$ C$(6, 3, 0)$ and D$(1, 0, 2)$ are four vertices of a cuboid.

a) Label these four vertices on the diagram.

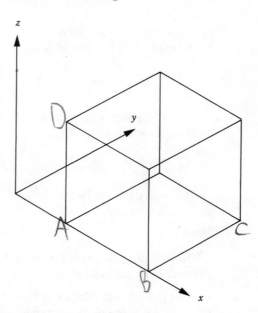

Fig. 8.7

b) Write down the co-ordinates of the other vertices of the cuboid.
c) Write down the co-ordinates of the centre of the cuboid.

(ULEAC)

OUTLINE ANSWERS TO EXAM QUESTIONS

A1

50; 25; 12.5; 6.25; 3.125; 1.5625; 0.78125.
You should have written all the above numbers in a list.

A2

a) $(4 \times 3) - 2 = 10$;   b) $(5.73 \times 3) - 2 = 15.19$.

A3

a) Add on another 3 to give 13 blocks.
b) The pattern builds up like this: $1 + 3(n - 1) = 3n - 2$.
c) Set up the equation $3n - 2 = 28$, and solve it to give $n = 10$.
   You could go the long way round and keep drawing and adding until you come to the correct number.

A4

If $2x < 4$ then $x < 2$, hence $1 < x < 2$. So any value of x between 1 and 2 (but NOT equal to them) will do.

A5

a) The completed table will be

	Vertices	Faces	Edges
Prism	6	5	9
Cuboid	8	6	12
Pyramid	5	5	8

Table 8.4

b) By looking at the numbers you will find that in each case the number of vertices, V, added to the number of faces, F, is more than the number of edges, E. In other words, $V + F = E + 2$. So, with $V = 10$ and $F = 7$ we have the equation $10 + 7 = E + 2$ which will give us $E = 15$.

A6

a) $(4 + 6)/2 = 5$.   b) Solve $\dfrac{4 - 3x}{2} = -7$, hence $4 - 3x = -14$.
$18 = 3x$, hence $x = 6$.

A7

a) $n(13 + t)$

b) $n = \dfrac{s}{13 + t}$

c) $n = \dfrac{198}{13 + 5} = 11$, hence 11 days before the 28th brings us to May 17th.

A8

a) i) $6x + 12$;
   ii) $6x + 12 = 3(x + 12)$
       $6x + 12 = 3x + 36$
       $3x = 24$
       $x = 8$
b) $(x - 1) = +\sqrt{3}$ or $-\sqrt{3}$
   $x = 1 + \sqrt{3}$ or $1 - \sqrt{3} = 1 + 1.73$ or $1 - 1.73 = 2.73$ or -0.73.

A9

5^4 is $5 \times 5 \times 5 \times 5$ which is 625, and 4^5 is $4 \times 4 \times 4 \times 4 \times 4$ which is 1024; so 4^5 is larger than 5^4.

A10

a) Multiply out left-hand side to give $2x^2 - x - 15 = 2x^2 + kx - 15$; hence $k = -1$.
b) $(x + 4)(x - 6) = 0$
   $x = -4$ and $x = 6$.

A11

a) $17 - (\frac{1}{2} \times 6) = 14$ hours   b) $17 - (\frac{1}{2} \times 0) = 17$ hours

A12

a) By substituting the known values of $v = 30$, $d = 75$, and $v = 50$, $d = 175$ into the relation $d = av + bv^2$, we get the pair of simultaneous equations:

   $175 = 50a + 2500b$ ... (1)
   $75 = 30a + 900b$ ... (2)

If we multiply equation (1) by 3 and equation (2) by 5 we get:
   $525 = 150a + 7500b$ ... (3)
   $375 = 150a + 4500b$ ... (4)

   We can now eliminate a by subtracting equation (4) from equation (3) to give:
   $150 = 3000b$
   Which solves to $b = 0.05$.

Now substitute this into the simplest equation (2) so that $75 = 30a + 45$, which solves to $30 = 30a$ or $a = 1$. So we have the answer $a = 1$, $b = 0.05$.

b) Put the found values a and b into the relation $d = av + bv^2$ to give $d = v + 0.05 \times v^2$. Now substitute $v = 70$ into this to give $d = 70 + 0.05 \times 4900$ and you will see that $d = 315$. Therefore the stopping distance for 70 mph will be 315 feet.

A13

$$M = \frac{150 \times 4}{5} = 120 \text{ grams}$$

A14

a) 4, 7, 12, 19, 28, 39
b) 10   FOR NUMBER = 1 TO 5
   20   PRINT NUMBER   2
   30   NEXT NUMBER   *
   40   END
   RUN

A15

a) $3x + 2y = 68$ where x = biros
   $2x + 3y = 62$ y = pens.

b) $9x + 6y = 204$
   $\underline{4x + 6y = 124}$

   $5x\quad\ \ = 80$
   $x\quad\ \ = 16p$

A16

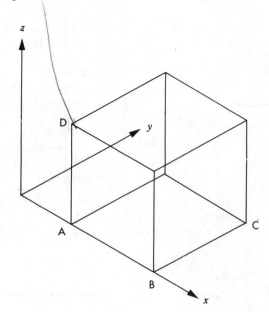

Fig. 8.8

b) $(6, 0, 2)$
   $(6, 3, 2)$
   $(1, 3, 0)$
   $(1, 3, 2)$
c) $(2\frac{1}{2}, 2\frac{1}{2}, 1)$

LEVEL CHECKLIST

For the level	You should be able to do the following.
4	Make general statements about patterns. Use simple formulae expressed in words.
5	Follow instructions to generate sequences. Understand and use formulae in symbols.
6	Solve simple equations.
7	Use algebra to express the rules of sequences. Use positive, integer indices. Solve simultaneous equations.
8	Manipulate formulae, equations or expressions. Solve inequalities.
9	Use ratio of indices for negative and fractional values.
10	Solve quadratic equations. Solve fractional equations.

A STUDENT'S ANSWER WITH EXAMINER'S COMMENTS

Question

1	2	3	4	5	6	7	8	9
10	11	12	13	14	15	16	17	18
19	20	21	22	23	24	25	26	27
28	29	30	31	32	33	34	35	36
37	38	39	40	41	42	43	44	45
46	47	48	49	50	51	52	53	54
55	56	57	58	59	60	61	62	63

The diagram shows a number grid with a T drawn on it. It is said to be *centred at 7* because the branches of the T meet at 7.

a) Find the total of the five numbers in the outline when it is *centred at 40*.

❝ A careless mistake. Should be 58. ❞

_____

_____

b) Complete the diagram below to show the five numbers in the T when it is *centred at x*

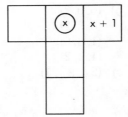

❝ Good answer ❞

c) Show that the five numbers in a T *centred at x* will total 5x + 27.

❝ Poor answer. Not shown from b) that these expressions add up to 5x + 27. Only used on one specific example. ❞

_____

_____

_____

d) Find the five numbers in the T that totals 247.

❝ Found the correct ones but no indication of *how*. ❞

_____

_____

_____

e) Explain why the total of the five numbers in the T could not be 240.

❝ Not a good attempt, since the equation 5x + 27 = 247 should have been solved. ❞

_____

_____

REVIEW SHEET

✎   _____ is the highest power of a linear equation whereas _____ is the highest power of a quadratic equation.

✎   Solve the following pairs of simultaneous equations using any method you wish.

a) $5x + y = 0$

$3x - 2y = 13$

b) $7x - 3y = 16$

$x + y = -2$

_____   _____

_____   _____

_____   _____

_____   _____

✎   Use simultaneous equations to solve this problem. Use a letter to represent each variable.
At a cafe, one order of 3 cups of tea and 3 cakes costs £3. Another order of 2 cups of tea and 5 cakes costs £3.05. How much will 4 cups of tea and 2 cakes cost?

_____

_____

_____

_____

✎   Expand the following and simplify where helpful.

a) $(4x - 5)(3x - 1)$ _____

b) $(2x + 3y)(3x + 2y)$ _____

c) $(3a + 4b)(2a + 2b)$ _____

d) $-p(2m + t) - t(3m - p)$ _____

✎   Solve the following quadratic equations by factorisation.

a) $6x^2 - 11x + 3 = 0$ _____

b) $4x^2 - 20x + 25 = 0$ _____

c) $8m^2 + 14m - 15 = 0$ _____

d) $25x^2 - 36y^2 = 0$ _____

✎   Make y the subject of the following formulae.

a) $x = 2(y - 1)$ _____

b) $x = y(b + 7)$ _____

c) $x = \dfrac{y + 1}{e + 1}$ _____

✎   Solve for x

a) $2^x \times 2^3 = 2^7$ _____

b) $3^x \div 3^4 = 3^3$ _____

c) $9^{-x} = \dfrac{1}{81}$ _____

d) $8^{-2} = \dfrac{1}{x}$ _____

e) $4^{\frac{3}{2}} = 8$ _____

f) $9^{\frac{x}{2}} = 729$ _____

✎   Where $f(x) = (x - 1)^2$ what is

a) $f(3)$ _____

b) $f(0)$ _____

c) $f(-3)$ _____

✎ Solve these quadratic equations by completing the square

a) $x^2 + 5x - 10 = 0$

_____

_____

_____

b) $5x^2 + 3x - 6 = 0$

_____

_____

_____

✎ Solve these quadratic equations using the formula method.

a) $3x^2 + 5x + 1 = 0$

_____

_____

_____

b) $x^2 - x - 10 = 0$

_____

_____

_____

✎ Tom ran the 42 km of a marathon race at an average speed of x km/h. Write down, in terms of x, an expression for the number of hours it took him to complete the race.

_____

✎ Charles ran the race at an average speed which was 2 km/h greater than Tom's speed. Write down, in terms of x, an expression for the number of hours that Charles took.

_____

✎ Given that the difference between the two times was 20 minutes, write down an equation in terms of x and show that it reduces to

$x^2 + 2x - 252 = 0$.

_____

_____

_____

✎ Solve the equation $x^2 + 2x - 252 = 0$ giving each answer correct to 1 decimal place. Hence find (in hours and minutes) the time it took Tom to complete the race.

_____

_____

_____

GRAPHS

GETTING STARTED

The importance of a *graph* is that it can be used to interpret information, giving a visual picture of the information or data. That picture may, for example, indicate a *trend* in the data, from which we might be able to make future predictions. The graph might also be used to approximate a *solution* to a particular situation.

All the graphs used are on what we call *rectangular co-ordinates*; that is, the axes are at right angles to each other. When reading from graphs, or drawing on them, the kind of accuracy looked for in the examination is usually no more than 1 mm out, although some Examination Boards will insist the error must be *less* than 1 mm. So be as accurate as you can in both reading from graphs and in drawing on them.

USEFUL DEFINITIONS

Linear A linear *equation* is one which involves no powers, other than 1 or 0, and no variables multiplied together, e.g. $x + y = 8$, or $3x = 4y - 2$.
A linear *graph* will be a straight line.

Quadratic A quadratic *equation* is one which has a square as the highest power, e.g. $x^2 + 3x - y = 5$.
A quadratic *curve* is a graph of a quadratic equation; it is a symmetrical **U** shape, or an upside-down **U**.

Cubic A cubic equation is one which has a cube as the highest power, e.g. $y^3 - 6x^2 + 3xy = 0$.

Gradient The *steepness* of a line, where the bigger the gradient the steeper the line *uphill*; a negative gradient will be a line sloping *downhill*.

Intercept Where a line crosses an axis; an intercept on the *x*-axis is where a line crosses the *x*-axis; similarly for the *y*-axis.

ESSENTIAL PRINCIPLES

1 > CO-ORDINATES

❝ Level 5 ❞

Co-ordinates are pairs of numbers that fix a particular position on a grid with reference to an origin.

The lines that go through the origin and have the numbers marked on them are called the *axes*; the horizontal one is called the *x*-axis, and the vertical one is called the *y*-axis. We always place the number representing the *horizontal* axis *before* that representing the *vertical* axis.

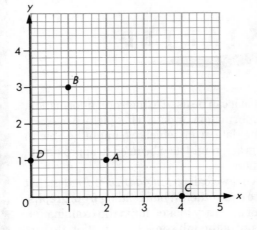

❝ Horizontal is *before* vertical in a co-ordinate ❞

Fig. 9.1

The origin in Fig. 9.1 is the zero co-ordinate (0, 0). The co-ordinate of point *A* is (2, 1) because to get from the origin to this point *A* you would move 2 along the *horizontal* axis then 1 up the *vertical* axis. The other points you see have co-ordinates *B* (1, 3), *C* (4, 0), *D* (0, 1).

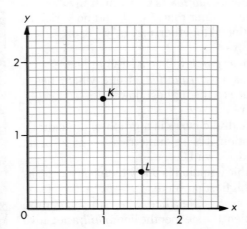

Fig. 9.2

Of course, sometimes we wish to find the co-ordinates of a point that is not exactly on the lines labelled. For example, in Fig. 9.2 the co-ordinates of *K* are $(1, 1\frac{1}{2})$ since *K* is 1 along the *x*-axis and $1\frac{1}{2}$ up the *y*-axis. In a similar way, the co-ordinates of *L* are $(1\frac{1}{2}, \frac{1}{2})$.

It is most important always to write and read co-ordinates in the correct way:
the *first* number is *how many along*, the *second* number is *how many up*.
One way to remember this is **OUT** (**O**ut and **U**p **T**o it).

EXERCISE 1

Plot the following co-ordinates on a grid, with both axes going from 0 to 8, and join the points up in the order given:
(1, 4), (3, 7), (7, 5), (5, 4), (7, 3), (1, 2)

NEGATIVE CO-ORDINATES

You are supposed to be able to read and plot co-ordinates within the full range of negative and positive numbers. For example, on the grid in Fig. 9.3 you should see that the co-ordinates of the points are:

$A(-2, -1)$, $B(-2, 0)$,
$C(0, -1)$, $D(1, -2)$.

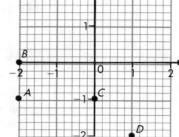

Fig. 9.3

| **2** | **DRAWING GRAPHS** |

One main use of co-ordinates is to help us draw graphs to assist us in sorting out information of one type or another. When we do this, the x and y axes are often labelled with other letters to help us see what the information is.

| **WORKED EXAMPLE 1** |

Using straight lines draw a graph from the information about the costs of transporting weights by Blue Star Parcel Deliveries, given in Table 9.1.

Weight (kg)	0	1	2	3	4	5
Cost (£)		1	2	3	6	7	8

Table 9.1

❝ Level 6 ❞

It is usual to draw graphs from tables like this with the top line giving you the horizontal axis. We can choose a simple scale of 1 cm per kg along the horizontal and 1 cm per £1 up the vertical. Plot the co-ordinates from the table $(0, 1)$, $(1, 2)$, $(2, 3)$ and so on to give the positions as shown in Fig. 9.4. Then join up each point.

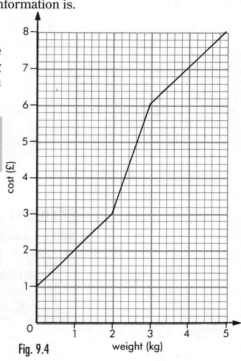

Fig. 9.4

READING THE GRAPH

Emphasis in graphical work is on the extraction and interpretation of information displayed by graphs of various kinds. We shall now consider some of those with which you should be familiar.

CONVERSION GRAPHS

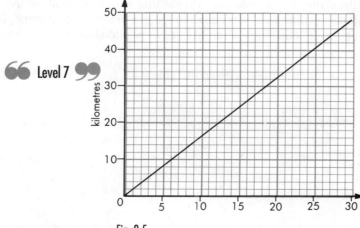

❝ Level 7 ❞

Fig. 9.5

To help convert from one unit to another it is often helpful to have a handy chart or graph, like the one in Fig. 9.5 which shows the conversion of miles to kilometres.

You can find the number of kilometres approximately equal to any number of miles up to 30. Take, for example, 25 miles. From the 25 mile mark follow the vertical line up to the graph and you will see it is 40 kilometres, hence 25 miles is approximately 40 kilometres.

We can also work the other way round. For example, take 30 kilometres. From the 30 kilometre mark, follow the horizontal line along to the graph, and where you meet it come down the vertical line to 19 miles. Hence 30 kilometres is approximately 19 miles. Notice too that each small line on the miles axis will represent a further mile since the 5 mile gap is divided into five equal parts, while on the kilometre axis each small line will represent 2 kilometres because the 10 kilometre gap is divided into five equal parts.

BRAKING DISTANCE

Another useful conversion graph is the braking distance graph. To help drivers realise that the faster they go the longer it takes to stop, the Ministry of Transport issued the graph, shown in Fig. 9.6.

From the graph in Fig. 9.6 you can see that each small horizontal line will represent 10 feet, while the vertical lines will represent 4 miles per hour. So, we can read from the graph that at 20 mph the stopping distance is approximately 30 feet, while at 70 mph (half way between the 60 and 80) the stopping distance will be approximately 165 feet.

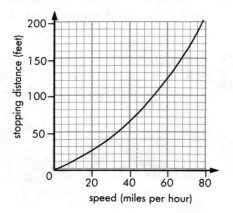

Fig. 9.6

EXERCISE 2

Table 9.2 shows the prices of different weights of new potatoes.

Weight (kg)	5	10	15	20	25
Cost (£)	1.20	2.40	3.60	4.80	6.00

Table 9.2

a) Plot the points on suitable axes to show this information on a graph.
b) Use your graph to find: i) the cost of 18 kg of new potatoes; ii) the weight of potatoes that can be bought for £2.

STRAIGHT LINES AND SMOOTH CURVES

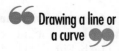
Drawing a line or a curve

You should be able to recognise when to draw a *straight line* through points or a *smooth curve*. Generally, if the information you are plotting is only a small sample of a lot of possible data that the graph will eventually show, e.g. a time/distance graph, then unless the points are in an obvious single straight line, we would always draw a smooth curve through them.

Draw a graph from the information given in Table 9.3.

Number of people	2	3	4	6
Hours to complete the job	6	4	3	2

Table 9.3

The points are *not* in a straight line, so we join them up with a smooth curve, see Fig. 9.7.

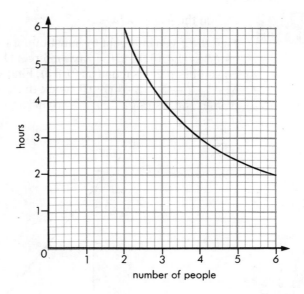

Fig. 9.7

Note

The straight line graphs are called *linear*, while the curved ones are *non-linear*.

CHOOSING SCALES

But do look to see if your question tells you which scale to use. Marks are usually lost for using your own scales instead.

When you are faced with information that needs to be put onto a graph, you have to decide what *scale* to use. You are always going to get a more accurate graph the bigger it is drawn, but there is a limit to the size of paper available. You need to look at the largest numbers needed for each axis, also if it needs to start at zero or not, then see how you can best fit this onto a scale that will fit the paper. Take care that you choose a scale where you can easily work out the position of in-between numbers.

For example, a scale going up in 3s and having five divisions between each 3 is going to be a useless scale for reading in-between numbers. Your scale should ideally be going up in 1's, or 2's, or 5's, or 10's, …

When you've decided upon your scales you must fully label each axis of the graph with the necessary numbers on each darker line of the graph paper together with a description of what that axis is for, e.g. velocity (mph) or time (seconds). Notice how the units are also written down, if there are any. Examples of this will be seen in the next section.

There are three main types of equation for which you should be able to draw graphs. But check carefully those that are needed at each level.

LINEAR EQUATIONS

A *linear equation* is of the form $y = mx + c$, where m and c are constants. A constant is a number that does not change at all, for example 3 or −5. This will always give a straight line. The minimum number of points to plot for a linear graph is three.

Draw the graph of $y = 4x - 3$ for x from −2 to 5.

We can see that the equation is linear, hence a straight line graph will be produced. We need at least three points to put in, so let's see what happens when $x = -2$, 0 and 5. A simple table of values can be made, see Table 9.4.

x	−2	0	5
$y = 4x - 3$	−11	−3	17

Table 9.4

From Table 9.4 you can see you will need 8 numbers on the x-axis, 5 to −2, which will fit best with 1 unit to 2 cm. You will need 29 numbers on the y-axis, 17 to −11, which will fit best with 1 unit to 1 cm. Draw these axes, label them, plot the three points (−2, −11), (0, −3) and (5, 17), and join them up with a straight line.

Sketch the graph of $5x + 2y = 7$.

Find the x axis intercept by substituting $y = 0$, which gives $5x = 7$, $x = 1.4$. So one point is found as $(1.4, 0)$. Find the y axis intercept by substituting $x = 0$, which gives $2y = 7$; $y = 3.5$. So another point is found as $(0, 3.5)$. Find another by substituting, say, $y = 2$, which gives $5x + 4 = 7 \rightarrow 5x = 3 \rightarrow x = 0.6$, hence the third point is found as $(0.6, 2)$. These can now be plotted and a straight line drawn through them, as shown in fig. 9.8.

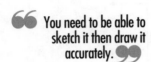

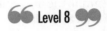 You need to be able to sketch it then draw it accurately.

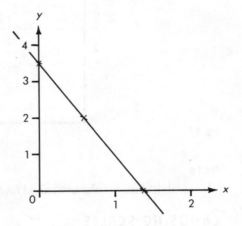

Fig. 9.8

QUADRATIC EQUATIONS

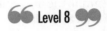 Level 8

A *quadratic equation* is of the form $y = ax^2 + bx + c$, where a, b and c are constants. This will always give you a curved graph, and the part that is usually asked for is the part that does a U turn. See Fig. 9.9 a) and b).

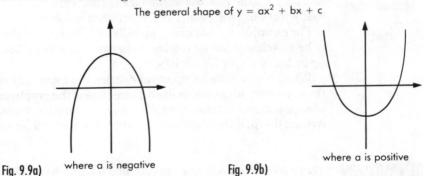

The general shape of $y = ax^2 + bx + c$

Fig. 9.9a)   where a is negative   Fig. 9.9b)   where a is positive

You need as many points as possible, especially round the *dip*.

Draw the graph of $y = x^2 - 2x + 1$ from $x = -2$ to 3.

You can see from the equation that the general shape is a **U**-shaped curve, hence you will need a table of values with x from -2 to 3. It is usually best to build up the value of y as indicated in the Table 9.5.

x	-2	-1	0	1	2	3
x^2	4	1	0	1	4	9
$-2x$	4	2	0	-2	-4	-6
$+1$	1	1	1	1	1	1
$y = x^2 - 2x + 1$	9	4	1	0	1	4

Table 9.5

From Table 9.5 you can see that you will need 6 numbers on the x-axis, 3 to -2, and this will fit best with 1 unit to 2 cm. You will need 10 numbers on the y-axis and no negative numbers, which will also fit best with 1 unit to 2 cm. Draw these axes, label them and plot the points $(-2, 9)$, $(-1, 4)$, $(0, 1)$, $(1, 0)$, $(2, 1)$ and $(3, 4)$, and join them up with a smooth curve.

WORKED
EXAMPLE 6

Neil, a bit of a mathematician, reckoned that when he played golf and teed off with a 'one

iron' then the path of the ball was given by the following equation: $y = \dfrac{3x(95 - x)}{200}$

where y is the vertical distance above the tee and x is the horizontal distance from the tee. With a 'one iron', Neil usually managed to hit the ball about 100 metres. Draw a graph of the path of the ball and find out its greatest height.

> Multiplying out will give an x^2 term, which is a quadratic

A table needs to be built up of values of x from 0 to 100. If we start with x going up in 20s to start with, we get the table in Table 9.6.

	x	0	20	40	60	80	100
	$3x$	0	60	120	180	240	300
	$95 - x$	95	75	55	35	15	−5
$y = \dfrac{3x(95-x)}{200}$		0	22.5	33	31.5	18	−7.5

Table 9.6

This now lets us plot the points as in Fig. 9.10

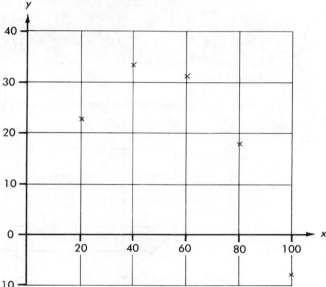

> Notice that I chose a scale that will fit the points on but not be too big.

Fig. 9.10

We could do with finding a few more points near the top of the hill. This seems around $x = 50$. Hence, find the y ordinate at $x = 42$, 45 and 48. Evaluating these gives us (42, 33.4), (45, 33.75), (50, 33.75). When we plot these points we get a much better picture of the solution and can now draw the graph as in Fig. 9.11, and the maximum height can be seen to be *33.8 metres*.

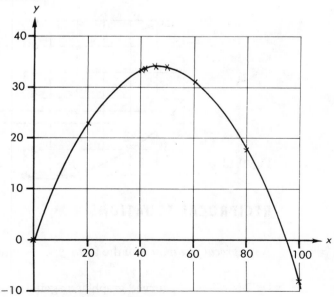

Fig. 9.11

EXERCISE 3

Draw the graph of $y = x^2 + 5x - 2$ from $x = -6$ to 2. Use the graph to solve the equation $x^2 + 5x - 2 = 0$.

Solutions to quadratic equations

These can be made from their graphs. For example, the solutions of $ax^2 + bx + c = 0$ will be where the graph of $y = ax^2 + bx + c$ cuts the x axis (i.e., where $y = 0$).

In general, the solution of $ax^2 + bx + c = d$ is where the graph of $y = ax^2 + bx + c$ cuts the line $y = d$.

WORKED EXAMPLE 7

Draw the graph of $y = x^2 + x - 4$ where $-3 \leqslant x \leqslant 3$ and hence find the solution to the equation $x^2 + x = 5$.

Construct the table of values for $-3 \leqslant x \leqslant 3$ as in Table 9.7.

x	-3	-2	-1	0	1	2	3
x^2	9	4	1	0	1	4	9
-4	-4	-4	-4	-4	-4	-4	-4
$y = x^2 + x - 4$	2	-2	-4	-4	-2	2	8

Table 9.7

This will give you the U-shaped curve as in Fig. 9.12.

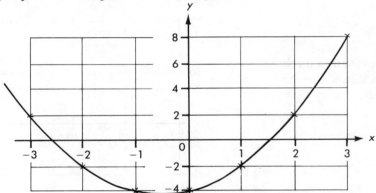

Fig. 9.12

The solution to $x^2 + x = 5$ is given by $x^2 + x - 4 = 1$. (Check that this is the same equation.) Hence our solutions are where the graph of $y = x^2 + x - 4$ crosses $y = 1$, as in Fig. 9.13. The solutions are where $x = -2.8$ and $x = 1.8$.

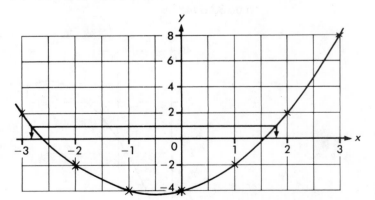

Fig. 9.13

RECIPROCAL EQUATIONS

A *reciprocal equation* is of the form $y = \dfrac{a}{x}$, where a is any integer and not equal to 0.

This will give a curved graph and again you need as many points given as possible.

WORKED EXAMPLE 8

Draw the graph of $y = \dfrac{12}{x}$ from $x = -12$ to 12 ($x \neq 0$).

Although we want as many points as possible, 24 points is excessive. Since the x is to be divided into 12, we could just choose numbers that divide exactly into 12, i.e. the factors of 12, positive and negative. Remember we do not consider $x = 0$. So the table of values will be as shown in Table 9.8.

x	−12	−6	−4	−3	−2	−1	1	2	3	4	6	12
$y = 12/x$	−1	−2	−3	−4	−6	−12	12	6	4	3	2	1

Table 9.8

From Table 9.8 you will see we need 25 numbers on the x-axis, which will fit best with five units to 2 cm. You will need 25 numbers on the y-axis also, and this will fit best with one unit to 1 cm. Draw these axes, plot the given points and join up with a smooth curve as shown in Fig. 9.14 (not to scale).

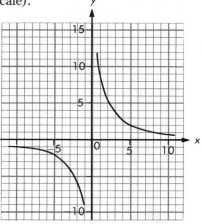

Fig. 9.14

Notice how you have two separate curves; they do not join, although it is interesting to speculate what happens at $x = 0$; study A level maths to find out!

GRADIENTS ON STRAIGHT LINES

4 ⟩ GRADIENTS

Gradient is the slope of a line

We will consider the *gradients of straight lines* first, then look at curves. The gradient of a *straight line* is a number and if the axes have any units on them, then the gradient will take its *units* from those two axes. The *number* for the gradient is found by taking two convenient points on the line as far apart as possible (but keeping the co-ordinates as round numbers if possible). If we say that the first point has co-ordinates (x_1, y_1) and the second point has co-ordinates (x_2, y_2), then the gradient will be equal to $\dfrac{y_2 - y_1}{x_2 - x_1}$, as shown in Fig. 9.15

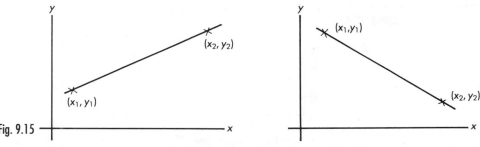

Fig. 9.15

Making sure your x_2 is always the biggest of the x co-ordinates will give you a *positive* denominator, so that when $y_2 > y_1$, your gradient is positive (uphill) and when $y_2 < y_1$, the gradient is negative (downhill). For instance, if your 2 points are (2, 6) and (4, 12) then the gradient will be:

$$\frac{12 - 6}{4 - 2} = \frac{6}{2} = +3$$

There will be a *positive* gradient (+3) in this case. (Change the co-ordinate values to find a *negative* gradient yourself!)

You will see on the distance/time graph in Fig. 9.16 that Paul drove from home 20 miles in the first hour when his average speed was 20 mph. In the next hour he drove a further 40 miles, hence his average speed was then 40 mph. During the last 2 hours he drove only 20 miles, which is 10 mph. We get an indication of the speed from how steep the lines are. The steeper the line, the greater the speed.

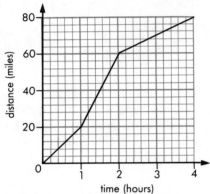

Fig. 9.16

For the line, we can calculate accurately, the *gradient*. As we have seen, this is a measure of how steep the line is. We measure the gradient of a straight line by calculating between any two points on the line the difference in their vertical co-ordinates divided by the difference in their horizontal co-ordinates. Further examples are given in Figs. 9.17, 9.18 and 9.19.

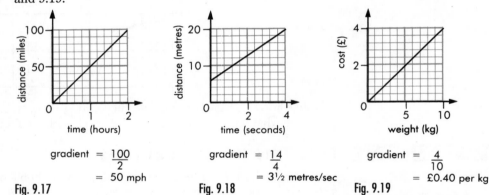

$$\text{gradient} = \frac{100}{2}$$
$$= 50 \text{ mph}$$
Fig. 9.17

$$\text{gradient} = \frac{14}{4}$$
$$= 3\frac{1}{2} \text{ metres/sec}$$
Fig. 9.18

$$\text{gradient} = \frac{4}{10}$$
$$= £0.40 \text{ per kg}$$
Fig. 9.19

Notice, too, how the units of the gradient come from the labels on the axes. On each of the examples, the whole line was used to find the gradient. This is as accurate as possible, but you can take a shorter part of the line to find the gradient if necessary. Try out these examples for yourself, using only *part* of the lines and calculating:
difference on vertical axis ÷ difference on horizontal axis.

❝ These practical situations need understanding and remembering, they will be asked in the exam. ❞

Look through the examples of axes, lines and gradients shown in Fig. 9.20 to gain the feel for changing axis units to gradient units.

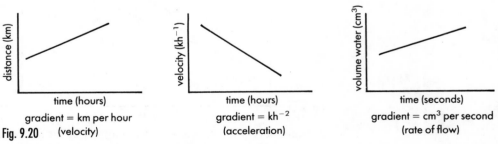

gradient = km per hour
(velocity)

gradient = kh^{-2}
(acceleration)

gradient = cm^3 per second
(rate of flow)

Fig. 9.20

The first two examples in Fig. 9.20 are the most common ones that you will meet in the examination, where the gradient of a time, distance graph is always the *velocity*, and the gradient of a time, velocity graph is always the *acceleration*.

❝ Formula for the gradient of a straight line ❞

The equation of the straight line can always be put into the form of $y = mx + c$ where m and c are some constants. The *coefficient of x*, namely m, will then always be equal to the *gradient* of the graph of that equation.

$$y = mx + c$$
where m = gradient
c = intercept (value of y when $x = 0$)

WORKED EXAMPLE 9

If you draw graphs from the following equations, all on the same axes, which will be the steepest line?

$$y = 3x + 7 \quad y = x - 5 \quad 3y = 6x + 7$$

The gradient of $y = 3x + 7$ is 3, the gradient of $y = x - 5$ is 1, and to find the gradient of $3y = 6x + 7$ we need to divide throughout by 3 to get $y = 2x + 7/3$. This gives a gradient of 2. Hence the first equation of $y = 3x + 7$ gives the steepest line.

EXERCISE 4

> Remember, to find the *gradient* of a time, velocity/ speed graph gives the *acceleration*. We return to this idea later in the chapter

The graph in Fig. 9.21 illustrates how Malcolm's velocity or speed changed on the motorway one morning. What was his acceleration at   i) 8.15;   ii) 8.30;   iii) 8.45?

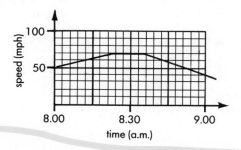

Fig. 9.21

GRADIENTS ON CURVES

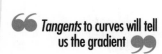
> Level 9

The *gradient on a curve* keeps changing! That is why the graph *is* a curve and not a straight line! So, to find the gradient on a curve you have to draw the straight line that *just* touches the curve at that point (the *tangent* to the curve at that point). Then the gradient of the curve at that point is the same as the gradient of that straight line, i.e. $y = mx + c$ where m is the gradient.

The sign of the value of m tells us whether the gradient is *uphill* or *downhill*.
If the m is positive then the graph will be *uphill*, see Fig. 9.22.
If the m is negative then the graph will be *downhill*, see Fig. 9.23.

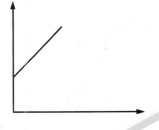

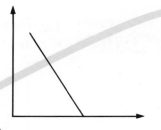

> *Tangents* to curves will tell us the gradient

Fig. 9.22   Fig. 9.23

Consider the distance/time graph shown in Fig. 9.24. This illustrates the speed of a ball thrown up to Michael at a window. He catches it and throws it back. While the ball is travelling up to Michael it will be slowing down, and this is illustrated on the curve between *A* and *B*. The curve starts steeply then slowly gets less steep. While Michael is holding the ball its speed is zero, hence the flat line *BC*. But when Michael throws the ball back its speed increases, or accelerates, as the graph shows the curve getting steeper, even if it is downhill.

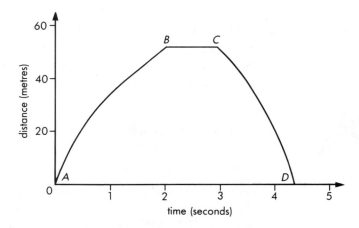

Fig. 9.24

So, on distance/time graphs, curves will be used to indicate gradual changes of speed as acceleration (getting quicker) or deceleration (getting slower). Below we shall look more closely as distance/time graphs.

5 › TRAVEL GRAPHS

Travel graphs are used to illustrate a journey of some sort. For example let's study the travel graph of Helen swimming shown in Fig. 9.25.

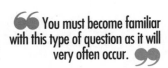

You must become familiar with this type of question as it will very often occur.

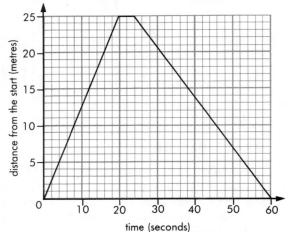

Fig. 9.25

Level 8

The graph shows Helen swimming the first length in 20 seconds, taking 4 seconds to turn around and set off back. Coming back she is much slower, probably because she is either tiring or doing a different stroke to the first length. We can work out how fast Helen swam the first length by seeing that 25 metres was swum in 20 seconds. This will give 75 metres per minute, which is $75 \times 60 = 4500$ metres per hour, or $4\frac{1}{2}$ kilometres per hour!

WORKED EXAMPLE 10

Fig. 9.26 is a travel graph of James's journey from home to town. He walked from home to a bus stop, waited, then caught the bus to town.

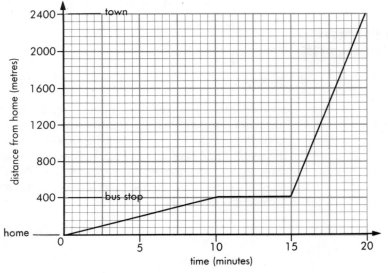

Fig. 9.26

a) How long did it take James to walk to the bus stop?
b) If he left home at 1.55 pm, at what time did he arrive in town?
c) What is the distance between the bus stop and town?
d) What was the average speed of the bus in kilometres per hour?

a) The bus stop is 400 metres away, and the graph is at 400 after 10 minutes.
b) It took James 20 minutes to get to town, and 20 minutes later than 5 minutes to 2 is 2.15 pm.
c) Town is 2400 metres away, the bus stop is 400 metres, and so the difference is 2000 metres.
d) The bus covers 2000 metres in 5 minutes, that is (2000 × 12) metres in an hour, which is 24000 metres. Hence the bus is travelling at an average speed of 24 kilometres per hour.

6 > DISTANCE/ TIME GRAPHS

66 Level 9 **99**

The graph in Fig. 9.27 represents a gradual slowing down of, maybe, a cyclist. But how do we find the speed at any particular time? We have seen that to find the speed, or velocity, at any given time we need to find the gradient at that point.

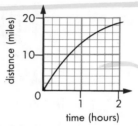

Fig. 9.27

WORKED EXAMPLE 11

From the distance/time graph shown in Fig. 9.28, find the velocity after 30 minutes.

66 The tangent as you see is the line that just touches the curve and once only. **99**

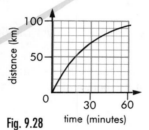

Fig. 9.28

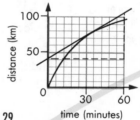

Fig. 9.29

You need to draw the tangent to the curve where time is 30 minutes as shown in Fig. 9.29.

From the drawn tangent, calculate its gradient from the largest convenient triangle as shown. Here it is 60 km along the vertical divided by 1 hour along the horizontal, giving a gradient which is the velocity of 60 km/h.

WORKED EXAMPLE 12

The graph in Fig. 9.30 illustrates how Helen has swum in a 100 m freestyle race. Find her velocity after i) 5 seconds; ii) 15 seconds.

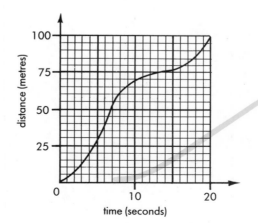

Fig. 9.30

We need to draw the tangent to the curve at each point and find its gradient.

i) In Fig. 9.31, after 5 seconds we see that the gradient of the tangent at the curve is given by $\dfrac{65m}{8s} = 8.1\text{ms}^{-1}$ or 8.1 m/s

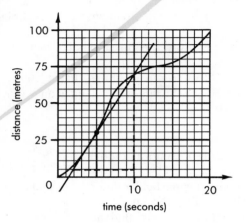

Fig. 9.31

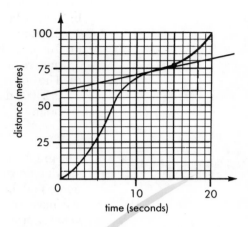

Fig. 9.32

ii) In Fig. 9.32, after 15 seconds the tangent to the curve does cut the curve later on but at the point, 15 seconds, it is touching the curve and *not* cutting through it. Here the gradient of the tangent is given by $\dfrac{20m}{18s} = 1.1\text{ms}^{-1}$ or 1.1 m/s.

EXERCISE 5

The velocity, v ms^{-1} of a ball after a time, t sec, over the first 4 seconds, is given by the equation $v = 4t - t^2$.

i) find the acceleration of the ball after 3 seconds, and
ii) what is the greatest velocity of the ball, and what is its acceleration at that time?

EXERCISE 6

The graph in Fig. 9.33 shows the speeds of three different cars when being driven away from a standing start over a time of 25 seconds.

a) From the graph, what is the speed of the Rover after 12 seconds?
b) How long does it take each car to reach the speed of 40 km/h?

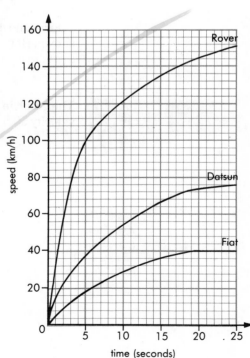

Fig. 9.33

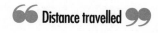

The graph in Fig. 9.34 shows a steady increase of speed from 0 to 40 mph over the first hour, then a steady 40 mph for the next hour. As we have seen the increase in speed is the *acceleration*, and is measured by the gradient of the line.

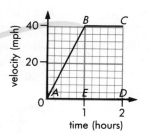

Fig. 9.34

From this type of graph we can also find the *distance travelled*, by finding the area under the line. So, in this example, the distance travelled in the first hour is given by the area of the triangle *ABE*. The total distance travelled with be given by the area of the trapezium *ABCD*.

Straight line graphs

Consider first the area under a *straight line graph*. Work through the following two examples:

" A more accurate method "

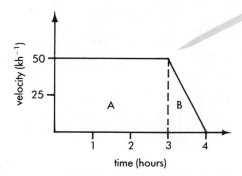

Fig. 9.35

> **WORKED EXAMPLE 13**

In Fig. 9.35 the horizontal line indicates a steady speed of 50 km per hour for 3 hours. This will cover a distance of $50 \times 3 = 150$ km. The area, A, under this line is also 50×3 (using the units on the scale), indicating that the area under the graph on a velocity/time graph indicates the distance travelled. Now, consider the area B under the line, which indicates the velocity dropping steadily from 50 km per hour to a standstill. The area underneath is the area of the triangle $\frac{1}{2} \times 1 \times 50 = 25$ km. Hence the total distance covered here will be $150 + 25 = 175$ km.

> **WORKED EXAMPLE 14**

In Fig. 9.36 the graph indicates the water flow through a pipe, steadily for the first 20 minutes then slowing down to nothing after 30 minutes. The horizontal line indicates the steady flow of 40 litres per minute for 20 minutes, which will be a total flow of $40 \times 20 = 800$ litres, also found by the corresponding area A under the line. Similarly the area B under the sloping graph indicates the amount of water flowing through the pipe over the last 10 minutes, which is $\frac{1}{2} \times 10 \times 40 = 200$ litres. So the total volume of water that flowed through the pipe was $800 + 200 = 1000$ litres.

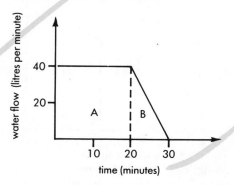

Fig. 9.36

Area under curves

The previous idea is continued under *curves*, where the area will represent some quantity defined by the axes. The problem with curves of course is calculating the area. There are two common methods; one is *counting squares* to approximate the area, (although strictly speaking we do not have to use squares and in practice rectangles are very often used just as effectively) and another is *splitting the shape up into estimated trapeziums* and calculating the area of each to give us an estimated total. (The most accurate way is with *calculus* and you will discover this neat way when you study for your A level.)

Counting squares

The graph in Fig. 9.37 illustrates the flow of water through a pump. The area under the curve tells us exactly how much water was pumped in 3 seconds. The shaded area represents 20 litres of water. Hence in this case approximately 60 litres should have been pumped in the 3 seconds, as the whole area is approximately three times the shaded area.

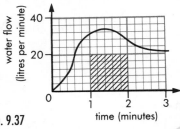

Fig. 9.37

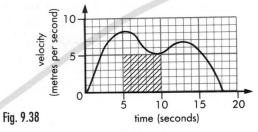

Fig. 9.38

The graph in Fig. 9.38 illustrates a runner in a race. To tell how far he ran we need the area under the curve. The shaded area represents 25 metres, and the total area under the curve is approximately four of these squares. Hence the runner ran for 25×4, which is 100 metres.

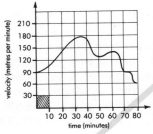

Fig. 9.39

The graph in Fig. 9.39 indicates the speed of Kirsty while jogging round a sponsored run. To estimate the total distance Kirsty covered, count the number of squares under the curve. This, I estimate as 34 squares. Now consider one square. Look at the bottom left hand square next to the origin. This represents 30 m per minute for 10 minutes, which is a distance of $30 \times 10 = 300$ metres. Hence the total distance Kirsty covered was 34×300 metres = 10200 metres, which is 10.2 km.

It is very important to find what the area of each square actually stands for, and the one at the bottom left hand corner next to the origin is usually the easiest one to help you to work this out (where this is a *complete* square).

Trapezoidal method

This is useful where there are perhaps too many squares to reasonably count and you want an easier rule of thumb method. Follow the example in Fig. 9.40 to show you how this method can work quite effectively.

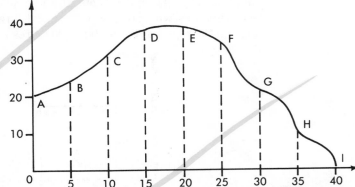

Fig. 9.40

The area of a trapezium is found by the average of the lengths of the two parallel sides multiplied by the distance between them. So in the above shape, split into eight trapeziums, where the length of the parallel sides (the vertical sides) are of lengths A, B, C … I, respectively, and all are a distance of 5 units from each other, the total area would be found by:

$$\text{Area} = \frac{5(A + B)}{2} + \frac{5(B + C)}{2} + \frac{5(C + D)}{2} \ldots + \frac{5(G + H)}{2} + \frac{5(H + I)}{2}$$

$$= \frac{5}{2}\Big[(A+B) + (B+C) + (C+D) + \ldots + (G+H) + (H+I)\Big]$$

$$\text{Total area} = \frac{5}{2}\{A + 2(B+C+D+E+F+G+H) + I\}$$

This give us a good rule of thumb to work with to estimate the area under the curve, i.e.

i) Split into as many strips as you wish, width of each, d.
ii) Add up first and last length.
iii) Add up all those in between and double.
iv) Add these last two results together, i.e. ii) + iii).
v) Now multiply by d and halve.
vi) You have your estimated total area!

WORKED EXAMPLE 15

During a thunderstorm the rainfall down a particular road was measured and graphed as illustrated in Fig. 9.41. Estimate the total rainwater that flowed down the road that day.

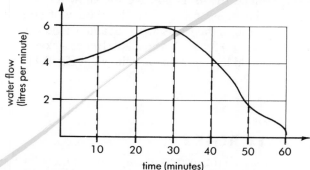

Fig. 9.41

Draw on the diagram strips to form the parallel sides of the trapeziums.
The width of each strip is 10.
The end lengths are 4 and 0, giving a total of 4.
The middle lengths add up to 4.4 + 5.4 + 5.8 + 4.4 + 1.6 = 21.6, which when doubled and added to 4 gives (21.6 × 2) + 4 = 47.2.
Multiply this by 10, divide by 2, to give 236

i.e. total = $\dfrac{10}{2}$ {4 + 2 (4.4 + 5.4 + 5.8 + 4.4 + 1.6) + 0} = 236

The unit *square* we have been using is 1 litre per minute × 1 minute = 1 litre. Hence the total water flow would be 236 litres.

EXERCISE 7

From the velocity/time graph shown in Fig. 9.42:
a) Calculate the speed after $1\frac{1}{2}$ minutes;
b) Calculate the total distance travelled;
c) Suggest what event is taking place.

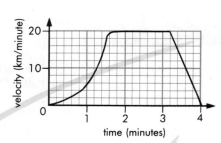

Fig. 9.42

8 **SKETCH GRAPHS**

It is always helpful to be able to sketch the graph you are going to draw, but at the higher level of GCSE it is essential that you can sketch graphs reasonably accurately.

LINEAR EQUATIONS

 **Level 7**

You should already know that the shape of the graph from a *linear equation* $y = mx + c$ is a straight line with m the gradient and c the y-axis intercept, where the line crosses the y-axis. Hence you can sketch the graph from a linear equation quite easily.

WORKED EXAMPLE 16

Sketch the graph of $y + 2x = 10$.

Rewrite the equation to make y the subject: $y = 10 - 2x$ or $y = -2x + 10$, when we see that the gradient is -2, hence *downhill* and that the graph cuts through the y-axis at $y = 10$. So your sketch could look like the one shown in Fig. 9.43.

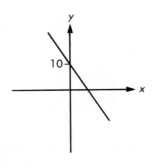

Fig. 9.43

QUADRATIC EQUATIONS

 Level 8

If the equation is of a quadratic nature i.e. $y = ax^2 + bx = c$, then it will be a U-shaped curve if a is positive, and a $\cap$-shaped curve if a is negative. The value of c is again the y-axis intercept. See what happens when $x = 1$. This should then give sufficient information for a rough sketch.

WORKED EXAMPLE 17

Make a sketch of the graph of

$y = 3x^2 + 2x - 1$.

Since the 'a' is positive we know it's a U shape, since the 'c' is -1 we know it cuts through the y-axis at $y = -1$, and when $x = 1$, then $y = 3 + 2 - 1$ which is 4. Hence a sketch could look like the one shown in Fig. 9.44.

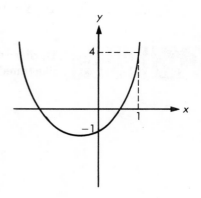

Fig. 9.44

EXERCISE 8

Sketch the graphs of $x + y = 10$, and $3x + 2 = y$ and so obtain an estimate of their solution.

9 > INEQUALITIES

When considering graphing an inequality such as $y < 3x$ we need to indicate all the points on the grid where this is true. You will soon see that you have a lot of points and *not* all in a straight line but all to one side of a straight line. The line in this case will be $y = 3x$. Now if we were graphing the inequality $y \leqslant 3x$ the solution would include the points on the line $y = 3x$ whereas the solution of $y < 3x$ will not include the points on this line. So to sketch a region given by, say, $y > 4x$, we need first to draw the line $y = 4x$ then find which side of that line we want. One way to do this is to choose any convenient point that is *not* on the line itself and see if it is in the region or not. If it is, then shade in that region; if not, then shade the other region.

WORKED EXAMPLE 18

Shade on suitable axes the region

$x + 2y > 6$.

Consider the line $x + 2y = 6$. It's a straight line and can be rewritten as $y = 3 - \frac{1}{2}x$.

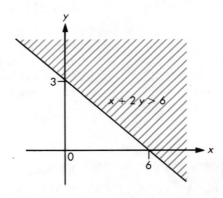

Fig. 9.45

From this we can draw the line and then consider a point *not* on it. The point $(0, 0)$ is the easiest to consider, so substitute into $x + 2y > 6$ the values $x = 0$, $y = 0$, and see if it fits. However this gives $0 > 6$, which is false, so $(0, 0)$ is *not* in the region and we should shade the other side of the line, as shown in Fig. 9.45, to give us the region we require.

SOLUTION SETS

When we have to find a solution set from a number of inequalities, it is easier to *shade out* the regions we do not want, leaving unshaded the solution set.

WORKED EXAMPLE 19

Illustrate the set of points that is satisfied by the inequalities: $y \geqslant 0$, $x \geqslant 0$, $x + y < 5$, $x + 2y > 6$.

$y \geqslant 0$ and $x \geqslant 0$ indicates to us that we only need the region where both x and y are positive. Then, shading out the other two regions, as shown in Fig. 9.46, gives us the points we are looking for.

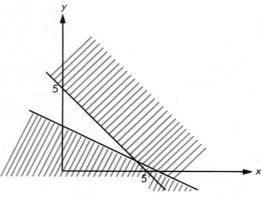

Fig. 9.46

Note

You always need to be aware of the inequality sign and to notice whether it is $>$ or $\geqslant$. In the latter case you *do* need to include the points on the line in your solution sets.

WORKED EXAMPLE 20

The Carterknowle housing development wish to buy 5600 m² of land on which they intend to build x houses and y bungalows.

a) Each house uses 400 m² of land and each bungalow uses 700 m² of land. Write down an inequality between x and y.

b) A house cost £84 000 to build and a bungalow cost £60 000 to build. £840 000 has been set aside for building costs. Write down and simplify an equation for this.

c) Represent these inequalities graphically.

d) Research shows that the developer can make a profit of £18 000 on a house and £15 000 on a bungalow. How many of each type of building should he build to obtain the maximum profit. What is this profit?

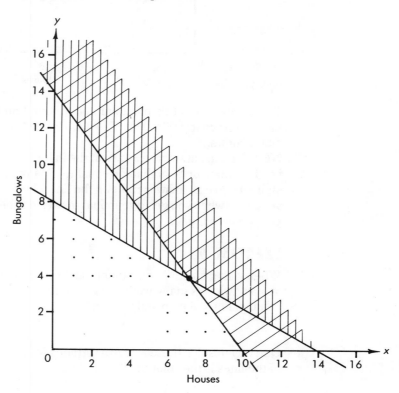

Fig. 9.47

a) From the original question we can say that $400x + 700y \leqslant 5600$. This will simplify to $4x + 7y \leqslant 56$.

b) This will be $84\,000x + 60\,000y \leqslant 840\,000$, which will simplify to $84x + 60y \leqslant 840$, which simplifies even further to $7x + 5y \leqslant 70$.

c) The graph should look like that in Fig. 9.47, the unshaded area representing the possible solution set. The dots represent the actual possible solutions, i.e. *whole* numbers of houses and bungalows. Care needs to be taken to identify those points possible on or near to the lines.

d) Profit $\propto (18\,000x + 15\,000y) \rightarrow$ Profit $\propto (18x + 15y)$
$\rightarrow$ Profit $\propto (6x + 5y)$.

So we need to draw a line for Profit $= 6x + 5y$ and find where this maximum point is. In Fig. 9.48, the dashed line shows the graph of $6x + 5y = 30$, so the maximum Profit $= 6x + 5y$ is on a line parallel to this and furthest out from the origin. In other words we want a dot (whole number of houses and bungalows) which is *in* the solution set but on a profit line ($6x + 5y$) of highest value, i.e. furthest from the origin.

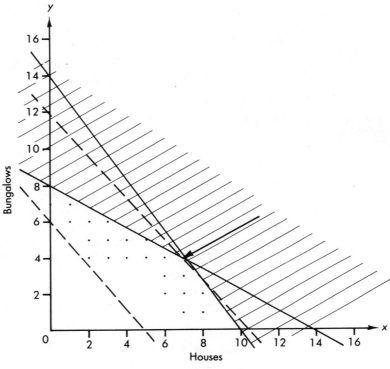

Fig. 9.48

The arrow shows this maximum point found on the line where $x = 7$ and $y = 4$. So the maximum profit is $(£18\,000 \times 7) + (£15\,000 \times 4) = £186\,000$. This is building 7 houses and 4 bungalows.

NB. You must always be aware of the inequality sign you are working with, is it $<$ or $\leqslant$, i.e. 'less than' or 'less than or equal to'. Many marks are lost in examinations because students give an answer right on the line where $\leqslant$ holds yet the line is really $<$ (or vice versa). So when you get to your final answer, do check it out, to see that it fits the inequality you are working to.

EXERCISE 9

When taking bookings for a tour of, at the most, 14 people, a tour operator insists on taking at least twice as many women as men. Illustrate on a graph the solution set of possible combinations of men and women.

One way to solve these is to draw graphs from both equations. The point of intersection of the lines is the solution.

WORKED EXAMPLE 21

❝ But only solve this way if you're told to in the question, because the method is not as accurate as algebra. ❞

❝ Level 9 ❞

Find the points that satisfy both these equations: $y = x^2 - x - 2$ and $y = 2x$.
Draw the graph of both equations on the same axes as shown in Fig. 9.49. The graphs intersect at the points $(-\frac{1}{2}, -1)$, and $(3\frac{1}{2}, 7)$. Hence the solutions are $x = -\frac{1}{2}$, $y = -1$ and $x = 3\frac{1}{2}$, $y = 7$.

EXERCISE 10

The product of two numbers less than 8 is 12. One of the numbers is 1 less than the square of the other. By drawing suitable graphs, find the two numbers.

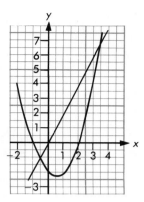

Fig. 9.49

SOLUTIONS TO EXERCISES

S1

You should obtain an answer looking like Fig. 9.50.

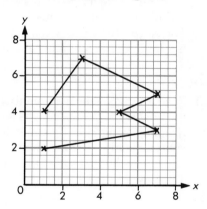

Fig. 9.50

S2

a) Your result should be like the graph shown in Fig. 9.51.

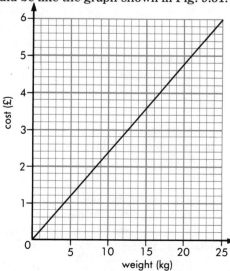

Fig. 9.51

b) Read from *your* graph, but if your graph is like the one shown in Fig. 9.51 then you should have answers very close to: i) £4.30;   and ii) 8.5 kg.

S3

You should have a table of values as shown in Table 9.9 which gives a U shape.

x	-6	-5	-4	-3	-2	-1	0	1	2
x^2	36	25	16	9	4	1	0	1	4
$5x$	-30	-25	-20	-15	-10	-5	0	5	10
-2	-2	-2	-2	-2	-2	-2	-2	-2	-2
y	4	-2	-6	-8	-8	-6	-2	4	12

Table 9.9

The solution to $x^2 + 5x - 2 = 0$ is the points on the graph where $y = 0$, these points are where the graph cuts the x-axis and you should have answers of approximately -5.4 and 0.4.

S4

i) Gradient of the line gives 57 mh^{-2}.
ii) Gradient of the line is zero, hence no acceleration.
iii) Gradient is negative, indicating deceleration of 75 mh^{-2} (or acceleration of -75 mh^{-2}).

S5

Draw the graph of $v = 4t - t^2$
i) Find the gradient at $t = 3$; this will mean drawing the tangent to the curve at that point giving a gradient of -2 ms^{-2}.
ii) The largest the velocity can get up to is the top of the hill which is where the velocity is 4 ms^{-2}. The acceleration at this point is the gradient of the tangent which is zero.

S6

a) Read from 12 on the horizontal axis up to the Rover graph, where taking a straight line horizontally to the speed axis it reads around 130 km/h.
b) Reading along the 40 km/h line we initially come to the Rover line which is approximately 1 second, then comes the Datsun line which is just above 5 seconds, and finally the Fiat which first reaches 40 km/h after almost 20 seconds.

S7

a) By drawing a tangent to the curve at time equal to $1\frac{1}{2}$ minutes you obtain a straight line with gradient of $25 \div 1.6$, which rounds off to 16 km/minute.
b) The total distance travelled will be given by the area under the whole graph. This can be estimated at just under five squares, each representing 10 kilometres, hence the total distance will be approximately 50 km.
c) The maximum speed is 20 km per minute which is 1200 km/h. This is very close to the speed of sound or of a very fast aircraft. The event could possibly be a short flight by a jet plane.

S8

They are both linear, hence two straight lines are wanted. A simple sketch should reveal the intersection to give $x = 2$, $y = 8$.

S9

If we use m for the men, and w for the women, then we can obtain two inequations, $m + w \leqslant 14$ and $w \geqslant 2m$. If we draw graphs of these two and shade out the regions we do not want, we obtain the diagram shown in Fig. 9.52. The unshaded part represents all the possible combinations of men and women.

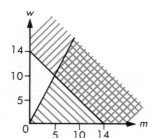

Fig. 9.52

S10

Let the two numbers be x and y, and we then have two equations: $xy = 12$ and $y = x^2 - 1$. Neither is linear, so both give curves. Remembering that each number is less than 8, the possible tables of values of each equation could be as shown in Tables 9.10 and 9.11.

x	6	4	3	2
$y = 12/x$	2	3	4	6

Table 9.10

x	3	2	1	0
x^2	9	4	1	0
$y = x^2 - 1$	8	3	0	–1

Table 9.11

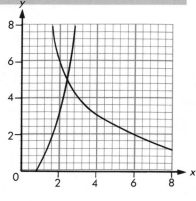

Fig. 9.53

These you can plot on a graph, see Fig. 9.53. Join up both lines with smooth curves, and you should get an answer like the graph shown which gives a solution approximately equal to $x = 2.4$, $y = 5$. So the two numbers are approximately 2.4 and 5.

EXAM TYPE QUESTIONS

Q1

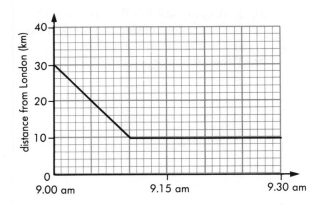

Fig. 9.54

The graph in Fig. 9.54 shows the distance of a train from London in km. Find the speed of the train in km/h at:
a) 9.05 am; b) 9.15 am.   (MEG)

Q 2

The conversion graph in Fig. 9.55 has been drawn to show the rate of exchange from English £ to German Marks in 1985.

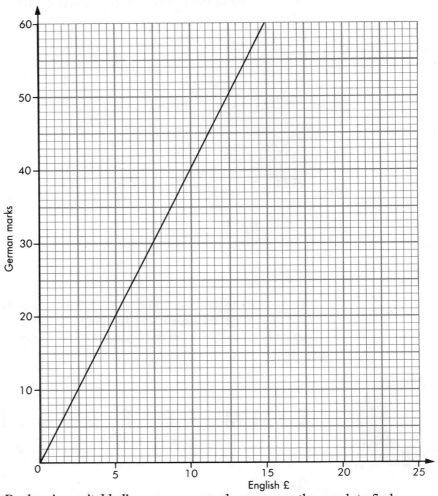

Fig. 9.55

a) By drawing suitable lines on your graph paper, use the graph to find:
   i) the number of German Marks equivalent to £10
   ii) the cost in £ of a watch bought in Germany for 50 Marks.
b) A new exchange rate gives £1 = 3.75 Marks. On the graph draw a *new line* to represent this.

Q3

The travel graph in Fig. 9.56 shows the journey of two men, Albert (A) and Brian (B) who both set off at 1200 noon one day to meet at a cafe. Brian starts 8 km nearer the cafe than Albert, and walks steadily for 3 hours with no rests. Albert runs for 1 hour, then rests for an hour, before running to the cafe.

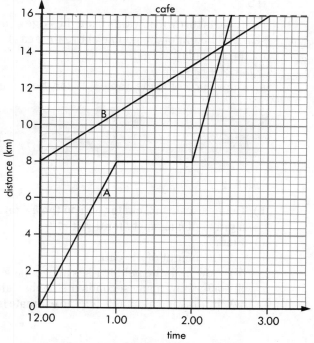

Fig. 9.56

a) What was   i) Albert's speed before his rest?   ii) Brian's speed?
b) At what time did Albert overtake Brian?
c) How long did Albert have to wait at the cafe for Brian to arrive?   (MEG)

Q4

The speed of a car is observed at regular intervals of time. The velocity/time graph shown in Fig. 9.57 has been derived from these observations.

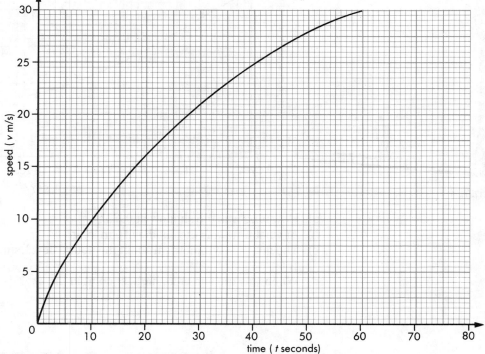

Fig. 9.57

i) Use the graph to estimate the car's acceleration at $t = 20$.
ii) State briefly how the acceleration of the car changes over the 60 seconds for which the graph is drawn.

iii) Use the graph to estimate how far the car travels in the first minute.
iv) At $t = 60$ the driver applies the brakes to produce a constant retardation of 2 m/s². Extend the graph to show this retardation and state the value of t when the car comes to a stop.
(NEAB)

Q5

A pebble is thrown upwards from the edge of a sea-side cliff and eventually falls into the sea. The height of the pebble above the sea after t seconds is h metres, where h is given by the formula:

$h = 24 + 8t - 2t^2$

a) Copy and complete Table 9.12 for the values of h.

t	0	1	2	3	4	5	6
h							

Table 9.12

b) Using a scale of 2 cm for 5 m on the h-axis and 2 cm for 1 second on the t-axis, draw a graph of h against t for $0 \leqslant t \leqslant 6$.
c) Find:
   i) the height of the cliff;
   ii) how high the pebble rises above the level of the cliff-top;
   iii) after how many seconds the pebble lands in the sea;
   iv) by drawing a suitable line, an estimate for the speed of the pebble after 5 seconds.
(ULEAC)

Q6

The lamp-post shown in Fig. 9.58 casts a shadow on the ground. The length of the shadow alters with the time of day. The graph in Fig. 9.59 shows the length of the shadow from 0900 to 1400 hours.

Fig. 9.58

Fig. 9.59

a) How long was the shadow at 0930?
b) At what time was the shadow 16 m long?
c) The graph is symmetrical about the dotted line. Estimate the length of the shadow at 1500.
d) When was the sun at its highest point in the sky?
(MEG)

Q7

Fig. 9.60 shows vertical cross-sections of two cylindrical containers, *A* and *B*, and of two containers, *C* and *D*, each of which is part of a cone.

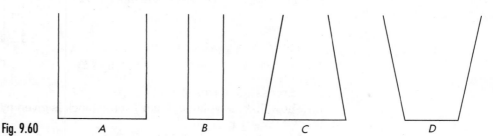

Fig. 9.60   *A*   *B*   *C*   *D*

Each container is filled from a tap from which water is flowing at a constant rate. The graphs below show the depth of water measured against time in each of three of the containers.

Identify the container to which each graph in Fig. 9.61 refers.

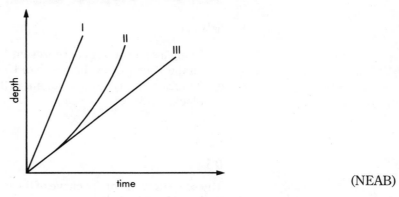

Fig. 9.61   (NEAB)

Q8

The distance/time graph in Fig. 9.62 illustrates two cyclists, Vijay and Neil, in a race. Describe what happened in the race.

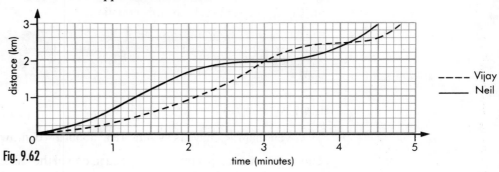

Fig. 9.62

Q9

a) Given that $y = 4x^2 - x^3$, copy and complete the Table 9.13.

x	0	0.5	1	1.5	2	2.5	3	3.5	4
y	0		3		8	9.375		6.125	0

Table 9.13

Using a scale of 4 cm to represent 1 unit on the *x*-axis and 2 cm to represent 1 unit on the *y*-axis, draw the graph of $y = 4x^2 - x^3$ for values of *x* from 0 to 4 inclusive.

b) By drawing appropriate straight lines on your graph:
  i) estimate the gradient of the curve $y = 4x^2 - x^3$ at the point (3.5, 6.125);
  ii) find two solutions of the equation $4x^2 - x^3 = x + 2$.

(MEG)

Q10

A rectangular block shown in Fig. 9.63 has a square base of side x cm and a height of h cm. The total surface area of the block is 72 cm^2.

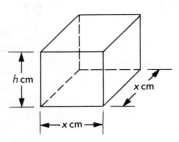

Fig. 9.63

a) Express h in terms of x.
b) Show that the volume, V cm^3, of the block is given by
$V = 18x - \frac{1}{2} x^3$
c) Copy and complete Table 9.14 to show corresponding values of x and V

x	0	1	2	3	4	5	6
V	0			40.5	40		0

Table 9.14

d) Using a scale of 2 cm to represent 1 unit on the x-axis and 2 cm to represent 10 units on the V-axis, draw the graph of $V = 18x - \frac{1}{2} x^3$ for values of x from 0 to 6 inclusive.
e) A block of this type has a volume of 30 cm^3. Given that $h > x$, find the dimensions of the block. (MEG)

Q11

The scale drawing of the curve of the two supporting cables of a steel suspension bridge is given by the equation:

$$y = \frac{x^2}{8} - \frac{3x}{2} + 7$$

a) Complete Table 9.15 for this equation.

z	0	1	2	3	4	5	6
y		5.625				2.625	

Table 9.15

b) Given that the curve is symmetrical about $x = 6$, draw its graph.

The bridge has supporting pillars at each end of the cables. These ends are 350 m above the water level and 600 m apart.

c) State the scale used. *Answer* _____
d) Taking the x axis as the water level, draw on your graph the horizontal road across the bridge, which is 120 m above the water level.
e) Vertical supports are placed at 75 m intervals along the road to join it to the cables. Find from your graph, the length of steel required to place these supports along the total length of BOTH sides of this section of the bridge.
f) A girder, whose equation on the scale drawing is $y = x + 4$, is placed from a point on a pillar to a point on one of the cables.
   i) Find how far, horizontally, along the bridge, this girder would meet the cable.
   ii) Without substituting a value for x show that the x co-ordinate of the point on the curve satisfies the equation:
   $x^2 - 20x + 24 = 0$. (NISEAC)

Q12

a) Write down the values of n, where n is a whole number, such that
   $-6 < 2n \leqslant 10$

   Answer a) _____

b) The number x is such that $x^2 \leqslant 4$.
   Represent all the possible values of x on the number line below.

c) The region R is defined by the three inequalities
   $x \geqslant -1, \quad y \geqslant 2x - 7, \quad x + 2y < 2.$
   On the grid below, shade the region R.   (MEG)

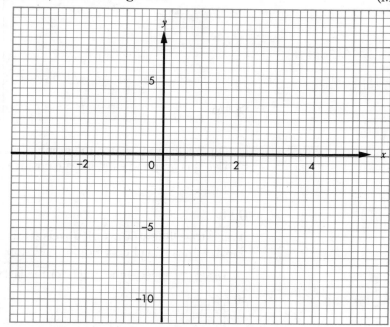

Fig. 9.64

Q13

Alison takes part in a 10 mile charity run. When the event starts she sets off at a steady speed of 8 miles per hour. She runs at this speed for 45 minutes. She then gets tired and gradually slows down until she has to stop. She has a rest for 10 minutes after which she feels a lot better and then takes 20 minutes to complete the remainder of the run.

Draw a possible travel graph of her run.

(SEG)

Q14

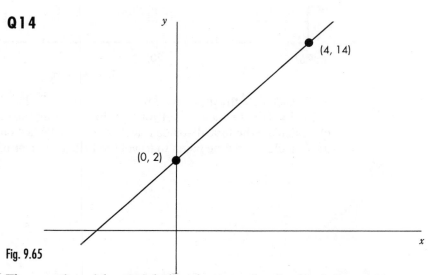

Fig. 9.65

The equation of the straight line drawn on the above axis is $y = mx + c$
a) Find the values of c and m.
b) Give the co-ordinates of the point where the line $y = 3x - 4$ crosses the y axis.

(ULEAC)

Q15

The diagram shows a sketch of the graph $y = x^3$.

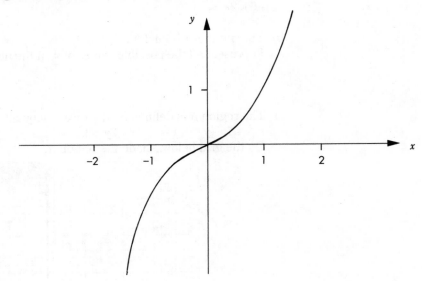

Fig. 9.66

a) On the diagram sketch the graph of $y = 3 - x^2$.
b) Use this graph to estimate the positive solution of the equation $3 - x^2 = x^3$.

(ULEAC)

Q16

A car is travelling at 50 m/s. It travels at this speed for a further 20 seconds and then slows down, with constant deceleration and stops after a further 45 seconds.

a) Draw the speed–time graph for the last 65 seconds of the car's journey.

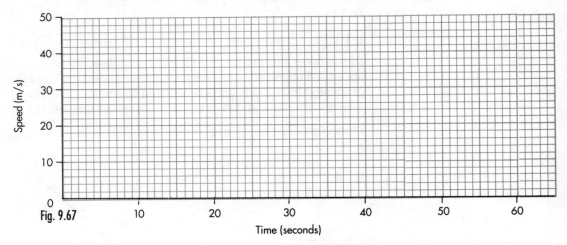

Fig. 9.67

b) i) Calculate the gradient of the graph during the last 45 seconds.
   ii) Explain the meaning of your gradient, stating the units.
c) Calculate the total distance travelled during the last 65 seconds of the car's journey.
d) Calculate the time taken to travel the FIRST quarter of the distance.

OUTLINE ANSWERS TO EXAM QUESTIONS

A1

a) Speed is the gradient of the sloping line, which is 20 km in 10 min, hence 120 km/h.
b) At 9.15 the train is not moving, hence speed is 0 km/h.

A2

a) i) £10 = 40 Marks;
   ii) 50 Marks = £12.50.
b) Line joined through (0, 0), (10, 37.5), or equivalent.

A3

a) i) Albert covered 8 km in 1 hour, hence his speed was 8 km/h;
   ii) Brian travelled 8 km in 3 hours, an average of $8 \div 3 = 2\frac{2}{3}$ km/h. It is likely that an answer in between $2\frac{1}{2}$ and 3 km per hour, inclusive, would be acceptable.
b) This happens where the two lines cross. Since there are 10 divisions represented by the lines between each hour, each one will represent 6 minutes. The lines cross over at 4 small lines past 2.00, which will be 24 minutes past 2. It would be quite acceptable to give any answer between, and including, 21 minutes and 27 minutes past 2.
c) When the lines reach the 16 km line, that is the cafe. So the time waited is the difference of the time shown by the two ends on the cafe line, this is 30 minutes.

A4

i) Tangent at $t = 20$ has gradient of approximately 0.6 m/s²
ii) The acceleration is getting smaller.
iii)
   Area under the curve, approximately 1000 m (1 km).
iv) Should be a straight line from (60, 30) to (75, 0), i.e. $t = 75$.

A5

a)

t	0	1	2	3	4	5	6
h	24	30	32	30	24	14	0

Table 9.16

b) See the graph in Fig. 9.68 (the scale is half that requested)

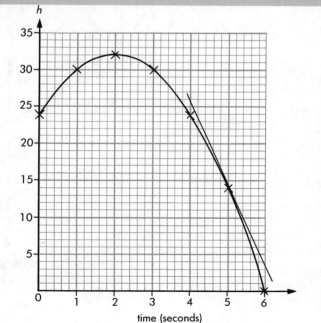

Fig. 9.68

c) i) 24 m, the starting height.
   ii) $32 - 24 = 8$ m.
   iii) 6 seconds, when $h = 0$.
   iv) Draw the tangent to the curve at $t = 5$, to give a line of gradient which, when dividing vertical distance by horizontal distance, should give 12. Hence 12 m/s.

A6

a) 19.5 m; b) 10.08; c) same as 11.00, which is 11.5 m; d) when the shadow was shortest, that is 13.00.

A7

Graph I fills the quickest and at a steady rate, hence is container B.
Graph II gradually fills more quickly, hence is smaller at top and so is container C.
Graph III fills steadily but the slowest, hence is container A.

A8

Your description should be written in sentences, i.e. good English, and not in note form. It should include the following details: Neil takes the lead then gradually slows down to a standstill. Vijay overtakes Neil after 3 minutes but then slows down himself and Neil overtakes him. Neil then goes on to win the race after $4\frac{2}{3}$ minutes.

A9

a) The missing values in the table are 0.875, 5.625 and 9.
b) i) By drawing a tangent at $x = 3.5$, the gradient is about -8.75;
   ii) By drawing the line $y = x + 2$ and finding the points of intersection, you find the solutions to be $x = -0.6$, 1 or 3.6.

A10

a) Total surface area is given by $2(hx + hx + x^2) = 72$ hence from $4hx + 2x^2 = 72$ we can get

$$h = \frac{72 - 2x^2}{4x} \quad \text{or} \quad \frac{36 - x^2}{2x}$$

b) Volume = base area × height $= x^2 \times \dfrac{72 - 2x^2}{4x} = \dfrac{72x - 2x^3}{4} = 18x - \frac{1}{2}x^3$

c)

x	0	1	2	3	4	5	6
V	0	17.5	32	40.5	40	27.5	0

d) See Fig. 9.69 (not to scale)

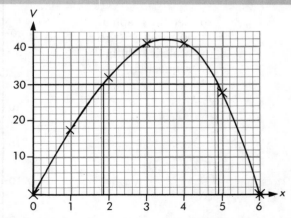

Fig. 9.69

e) Find the points on the graph where $V = 30$; these are at $x = 1.85$ and 4.85
   If $h > x$ then we need the smaller, which is $x = 1.85$ cm
   $h = 8.8$ cm

A11

a)

x	0	1	2	3	4	5	6
y	7	5.625	4.5	3.75	3	2.625	2.5

b) See Fig. 9.70, the curve.

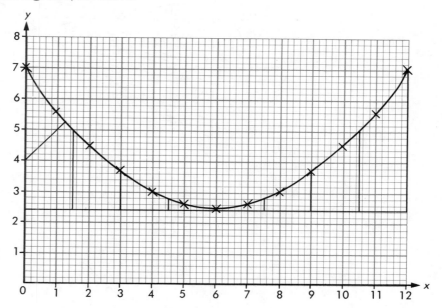

Fig. 9.70

c) This will depend on the scale you used for your graph.
   A scale of 1 cm to 1 unit, will have a scale of 1 : 5000,
   A scale of 2 cm to 1 unit, will have a scale of 1 : 2500 etc.
d) The road is shown by the line $y = 2.4$.
e) The 7 supports are shown on the graph, being a total of
   $2.5 + 1.35 + 0.4 + 0.1 + 0.4 + 1.35 + 2.5 = 8.6$ units which gives 8.6×50 m = 430 m.
   (Double for both sides, ie 860 m)
f) i) This girder is drawn from (0, 4) to (1.3, 5.3).
      Hence the horizontal distance = 1.3×50 m = 65 m.

   ii) This point is where $y = \dfrac{x^2}{8} - \dfrac{3x}{2} + 7 = x + 4$ hence $\dfrac{x^2}{8} - \dfrac{5x}{2} + 3 = 0$
       multiply through by 8 to give $x^2 - 20x + 24 = 0$.

A12

a) $-3 < n \leqslant 5$,   possible n ... $-2, -1, 1, 2, 3, 4, 5$
b) See Fig. 9.71, $0 \leqslant x \leqslant 2$

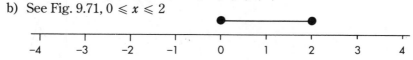

Fig. 9.71

c) See Fig. 9.72

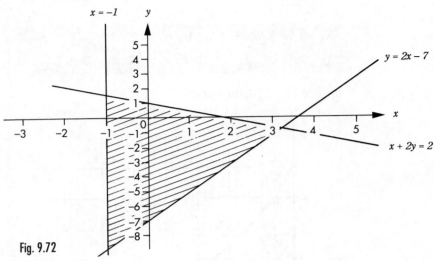

Fig. 9.72

A13

See Fig. 9.73

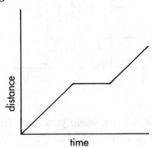

Fig. 9.73

A14

a) $m = \text{gradient} = \dfrac{14 - 2}{4 - 0} = \dfrac{12}{4} = 3$

$c = y$ axis intercept $= 2$
i.e. $c = 2$, $m = 3$

b) it cuts the y axis where $x = 0$
i.e. $y = -4$

A15

a) See Fig. 9.74

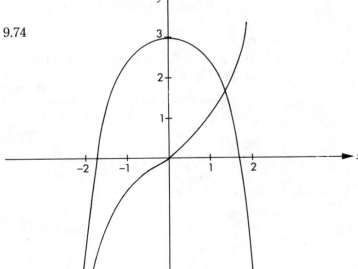

Fig. 9.74

b) Your answers must be the x ordinates of the intersection of the two graphs.

A16

a) Your graph should have a horizontal line at 50 m/s from $t = 0$ to 20, then a straight line down to $(65, 0)$

b) i) $\dfrac{-10}{9}$ or -1.1 ii) deceleration, m/s^2

c) Area under the graph $= 50 \times 20 + \frac{2}{3} \times 50 \times 45 = 2125$ m

d) $\dfrac{2125}{4} = 531$ m approx, (in the 50 m/s part), $531 \div 50 = 10.5$ seconds approx.

LEVEL CHECKLIST

For the level	You should be able to do the following
5	Use co-ordinates in the first quadrant.
6	Plot and draw simple graphs of simple situations.
7	Solve simultaneous equations by drawing graphs. Draw and interpret linear graphs.
8	Interpret and use m and c in $y = mx + c$ Interpret quadratic, cubic, reciprocal graphs. Interpret graphs which describe real-life situations.
9	Solve difficult equations by drawing graphs. Find gradients of graphs by constructing tangents. Sketch graphs of trigonometrical functions.
10	Find the area between a curve and the horizontal axis between two limits, and interpret the results. Sketch and compare graphs of functions. Understand linear programming.

A STUDENT'S ANSWER
WITH EXAMINER'S COMMENTS

Question

The graph shown is that of the function f which is defined by $f(x) = 10 - \dfrac{5}{x}$

    i)   From the graph, find the value of x for which $f(x) = 4$.

    ii)   g is the function: $g(x) = 2x$

           Draw the graph of the function g for $0 \leqslant x \leqslant 5$.

    iii)   Use your graphs to solve the equation:

$$2x = 10 - \frac{5}{x}.$$

Give your solutions correct to one decimal place.

66 Graph slightly out here,
but good enough to
get full marks. 99

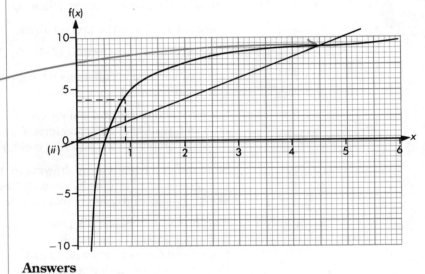

Answers

66 Good — correct
answers 99

_____

_____

R E V I E W   S H E E T

✎   Pairs of numbers fixing a position on graph paper are called _____. In brackets, the first number represents distance _____ axis and the second number distance _____ axis.

✎   Referring back to Figure 9.1 in this chapter, write down the co-ordinate for each new point

   a) one unit along (to the right) and one unit *up* from point D   (,).

   b) one unit along (to the right) and one unit *up* from point A   (,).

   c) two units along (to the right) and two units *down* from point B   (,)

   d) one unit along (to the right) and two units *up* from point C   (,).

✎   Plot these points on Figure 9.2.

   a) $(1\frac{1}{2}, 2)$ b) $(\frac{1}{2}, 1\frac{1}{2})$ c) $(2, 1\frac{1}{2})$ d) $(1, \frac{1}{2})$

✎   Plot these points on Figure 9.3.

   a) $(-1, 1)$ b) $(1, -1)$ c) $(-2, -2)$ d) $(2, -1)$

✎   From Fig. 9.5, convert the following:

   a) 10 miles = _____ km   b)   20 miles = _____ km

   c) 30 km = _____ miles   d)   40 km = _____ miles

✎   From Fig. 9.6, convert the following:

   a) 40 m.p.h. = _____ feet stopping distance.

   b) 150 feet stopping distance = _____ m.p.h.

✎   An equation of the form $y = mx + c$ is a _____ equation.

   An equation of the form $y = ax^2 + bx + c$ is a _____ equation.

✎   If a is negative in a quadratic equation the curve will look like this

✎   The value of c will give you the intercept on the _____ axis, telling you the value of _____ when _____ is zero.

✎   An equation of the form $y = \dfrac{a}{x}$ is called a _____ equation.

✎   Write down the gradient of a *straight line* joining each of the following pairs of points

   a) (2, 3), (4, 6)   b) (3, 6), (4, 2)

   c) (4, 2), (5, 1)   d) (3, 3), (2, 4)

✎   A straight line which just touches a curve at a single point is called a _____.

✎   The gradient of a distance/time graph will tell us the _____ of travel at a certain time.

✎   The gradient of a velocity/time graph will tell us the _____ at a certain time. If the gradient is negative, we call this _____.

✎   In Fig. 9.28 find the approximate velocity (speed) after 48 minutes (draw a tangent) _____ km/hr.

✎ In Fig. 9.34 find the acceleration

a) at 30 minutes _____ miles/hour^2

b) at 90 minutes _____ miles/hour^2.

✎ Again, using Fig. 9.34 estimate the area *under* the curve, i.e. the distance travelled; _____ miles.

✎ Estimate the distance travelled after 25 seconds in the earlier Fig. 9.33 for:

a) the Fiat _____ km

b) the Datsun _____ km

c) the Rover _____ km

(remember to change km/hr into metres/second)

✎ If the inequality is ⩽ we would _____ all points on the line, but _____ them if the inequality is <.

✎ In Fig. 9.45 write down the inequality expression for all points on the line $x + 2y = 6$ or below it.

_____

✎ On Fig. 9.45 draw a line and shade the region for $x + 2y \leqslant 4$

✎ On the travel graph in Fig. 9.56, find:

a) the total distance travelled by Albert (A) after $2\frac{1}{2}$ hours (i.e. by 2.30 pm) _____ km

b) the total distance travelled by Brian (B) after 3 hours (i.e. by 3.00 pm). _____ km

✎ On the velocity/time graph in Fig. 9.57, find the car's acceleration at:

a) t = 10 seconds _____ m/s^2

b) t = 40 seconds _____ m/s^2

GEOMETRY

GETTING STARTED

Geometry can be defined as the science of properties and relations of magnitudes (as lines, surfaces and solids in space). The emphasis in the examinations will be on the well-established geometrical properties and relationships, and on how these can be used to convey information and to solve problems. As a result, this topic often appears as an important part of questions on *drawings, bearings* and even *algebra*, as well as in questions devoted *solely to geometry.* Many facts that you should learn and be familiar with are given in this chapter, so that when they arise within questions you can recognise the situation and apply the facts with confidence.

USEFUL DEFINITIONS

Angle	The amount of turn, measured in degrees.
Transversal	A line that crosses through at least two parallel lines.
Diagonal	A line joining two corners of a geometric shape.
Subset	A part of a larger set.
Circumference	The perimeter of a circle.
Semi-circle	Half of a circle.
Vertex	A point where two lines, or edges, meet.
Included angle	The angle in between two lines of defined length.
Edge	The line where two faces meet.
Face	Surface of a solid shape bounded by edges.
Cross section	The plane shape revealed by cutting a solid shape at right angles to its length, or height.

E S S E N T I A L   P R I N C I P L E S

1 > ANGLES

Every angle can be described by its size, and depending on this it falls into one of four main categories

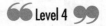
Level 4

- *Acute angles* – angles less than 90°
- *Right angles* – angles that equal 90°
- *Obtuse angles* – angles that are bigger than 90° but less than 180°.
- *Reflex angles* – angles that are bigger than 180° but less than 360°.

There are situations that you should be familiar with and they are illustrated here:

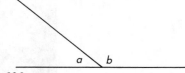

Fig. 10.1

Fig. 10.2

Angles on a line, as *a* and *b* shown in Fig. 10.1, will always add up to 180°.

Angles around a point, as *a*, *b* and *c* shown in Fig. 10.2, will always add up to 360°.

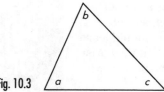

Fig. 10.3

Fig. 10.4

The three angles inside a triangle, as *a*, *b* and *c* shown in Fig. 10.3 will always add up to 180°.

A right angle is usually written as a box in the angle, as shown in Fig. 10.4. Any two lines that are at right angles to each other are said to be *perpendicular*.

2 > PARALLEL

Two lines are said to be parallel if the perpendicular distance between them is always the same, as shown in Fig. 10.5.

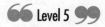

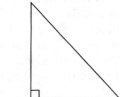

Fig. 10.5

Fig. 10.6

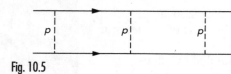
Level 5

As you will see in Fig. 10.6, parallel lines are not necessarily straight, but in most situations if you are told two lines are parallel you should assume that they are straight lines unless you have a very good reason not to.

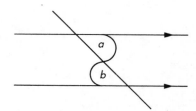

Fig. 10.7

Fig. 10.7 shows a pair of parallel lines and a *transversal* cutting them. The angles marked *a* and *b*, which are called *alternate angles*, are always equal to each other.

3 > PLANE FIGURES

You should recognise, be able to name and know the facts about each shape shown here.

ISOSCELES TRIANGLE

Fig. 10.8

An *isosceles triangle* has two of its sides the same and two angles the same, as indicated in Fig. 10.8. Sides of the same length are marked.
Equal angles are marked with

RIGHT-ANGLED TRIANGLE

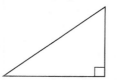

Fig. 10.10

A *right-angled triangle* is one that contains a right angle, see Fig. 10.10

RECTANGLE

Fig. 10.12

A *rectangle* has four sides and its opposite sides are equal, as shown in Fig. 10.2, and all its angles are right angles.

KITE

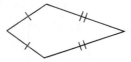

Fig. 10.14

A *kite*, recognisable as a kite shape, has four sides, as shown, the top two sides with the same length and the bottom two sides with the same length, see Fig. 10.14.

RHOMBUS

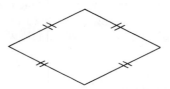

Fig. 10.17

A *rhombus* is a parallelogram that has all its sides the same length, see Fig. 10.17. The *diagonals* of a rhombus are *perpendicular*. This last fact will often be needed in examinations and should be learnt.

EQUILATERAL TRIANGLE

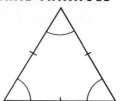

Fig. 10.9

An *equilateral triangle*, as shown in Fig. 10.9, has all its three sides the same length and all its angles are 60°.

QUADRILATERAL

Fig. 10.11

A *quadrilateral* has four sides, and the four angles it contains will add up to 360°, see Fig. 10.11.

SQUARE

Fig. 10.13

A *square* has all its four sides equal and all its angles are right angles, see Fig. 10.13.

PARALLELOGRAM

fig. 10.15

A *parallelogram* has four sides and the opposite sides are of equal length as shown in Fig. 10.15. The opposite sides are parallel. In a parallelogram the angles next to each other will always all add up to 180°.

For example, $a + b = b + c = c + d = d + a = 180°$. Also, the angles opposite each other will be equal, for example, $a = c, b = d$.

TRAPEZIUM

Fig. 10.16

A *trapezium* is a quadrilateral that has two parallel sides, the pairs of angles between each parallel side add up to 180°. For example, in the trapezium in Fig. 10.16 $(a + b) = 180°$ and $(d + c) = 180°$.

This one fact is so often forgotten or ignored in exams. Do learn it.

SETS

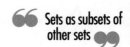
Sets as subsets of other sets

It is useful to remember that:
{square} ⊂ {rhombus} ⊂ {kite} ⊂ {quadrilateral}
{square} ⊂ {rectangle} ⊂ {parallelogram} ⊂ {trapezium} ⊂ {quadrilateral}
It is a useful exercise to put the above sets into a Venn diagram.

4 > POLYGONS

66 Level 6 99

You ought to be familiar with the names of the polygons mentioned below. *Polygons* are *many-sided two-dimensional shapes*.

- *Triangle* 3 sides - *Quadrilateral* 4 sides - *Pentagon* 5 sides
- *Hexagon* 6 sides - *Septagon* 7 sides - *Octagon* 8 sides
- *Nonagon* 9 sides - *Decagon* 10 sides

Polygons have two main types of angles. There are *interior* angles (inside) and *exterior* angles (outside) as shown in Fig. 10.18.

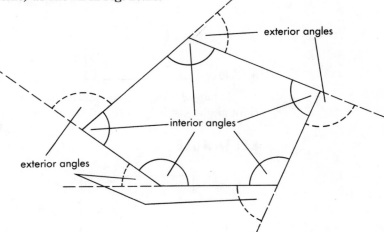

Fig. 10.18

A polygon will have as many interior as exterior angles, which will be the same as the number of sides of the polygon. You should know the following facts about these angles:

- All the *exterior angles* of any polygon always add up to 360°.
- All the *interior angles* of any N-sided polygon always add up to $180(N-2)°$.

Properties of a regular polygon

A *regular polygon* is one that has all its sides the same length and where each exterior angle is equal.

Then: the size of each exterior angle is given by $\dfrac{360°}{N}$

the size of each interior angle is given by $180° - \dfrac{360°}{N}$

WORKED EXAMPLE 1

Calculate the size of the exterior and interior angles of a regular decagon.

There will be 10 equal exterior angles, all adding up to 360°, hence the size of each one will be 360 ÷ 10 which is 36°. You should be able to see from the diagram above that the exterior angle and the interior angle add up to 180°. Hence, if we've just calculated the exterior angle to be 36°, then the interior angle will be 180° − 36°, which is 144°.

EXERCISE 1

Calculate the interior angle of a regular octagon.

5 > CIRCLES

66 Level 10 99

Any straight line drawn from the centre of a circle to the edge of that circle (the *circumference*) is called a *radius*, see Fig. 10.19. In any circle you can draw, if you wish to, hundreds of radii (plural of radius) all of which would be the same length. A straight line drawn from one side of a circle to the other side, passing through the centre, is called a *diameter*. Again, any circle will have hundreds of diameters all of the same length.

Any straight line drawn in a circle from one part of the circumference to another, as shown in Fig. 10.20, is called a *chord*. The two parts of this circle have been split into *segments*; the smaller one is called the minor segment and the larger one is called the major segment.

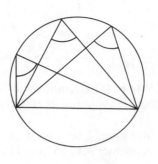

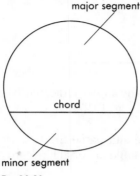

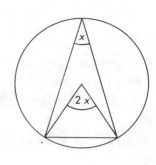

Fig. 10.19   Fig. 10.20   Fig. 10.21   Fig. 10.22

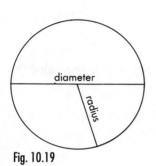

There are a number of interesting facts about angles in a circle that you should know. You can test all of them for yourself by drawing your own examples.

From any chord; in a circle there are many triangles that can be formed in the same sector that touch the circumference, as shown in Fig. 10.21. All these angles opposite the chord will be *equal*.

From any chord in a circle there is only one triangle that can be drawn to the centre of the circle, and this angle will be *double* any angle drawn to the circumference in the same sector as the centre. For example, in Fig. 10.22 the angle at the centre is $2x°$ and at the circumference it will be $x°$.

Any quadrilateral drawn so that its four vertices touch the circumference of a circle is said to be *cyclic*. Its opposite angles will add up to 180°. For example, in Fig. 10.23 $(a + c)$ = $(b + d)$ = 180°. It is also true that any quadrilateral that has opposite angles adding up to 180° is cyclic and hence a circle can be drawn around the vertices.

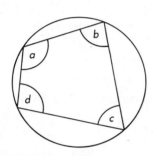

Fig. 10.23

SEMI-CIRCLE

If you draw any triangle in a semi-circle where one side is the diameter, as shown in Fig.10.24, then the angle made at the circumference will always be a *right* angle.

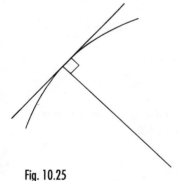

Fig. 10.24

TANGENTS

A *tangent* to a curve, or a circle, is a line that will touch the curve or circle at only one point. If drawn on a circle this tangent will be perpendicular to a radius, see Fig. 10.25.

There are therefore two ways to draw a tangent on a circle at a particular point. One is to put your ruler on that point and simply draw the line that only touches the circle there. The other way is to construct a right angle at that point on the radius and hence draw in the tangent, see Chapter 12.

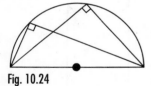

Fig. 10.25

EXERCISE 2

In Fig. 10.26 *D* and *C* are the centres of the two circles. *A* and *B* are the points where the common tangent touches the circles.

  i) What is the full name of the quadrilateral *ABCD*?

  ii) When will *ABCD* be cyclic?

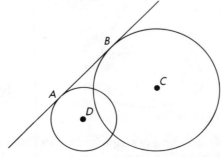

Fig. 10.26

ALTERNATE SEGMENT THEOREM

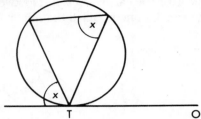

Fig. 10.27

Now see how many of these facts you've remembered; go on, test yourself.

Where OT is a tangent at T, then the angles indicated (*x*) are equal, this being called the 'alternate segment' theorem (see Fig. 10.27).

6 > SOLID SHAPES

You should be able to recognise and name the following *solid shapes* and be able to construct some of them from suitable material like card or straws.

CUBE

A *cube* has all its sides the same length, see Fig. 10.28.

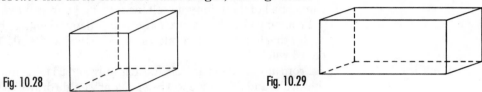

Fig. 10.28

Fig. 10.29

RECTANGULAR BLOCK

A *rectangular block*, or *cuboid* has each opposite side the same length, see Fig. 10.29.

SPHERE

A *sphere* is just like a football or a tennis ball, see Fig. 10.30.

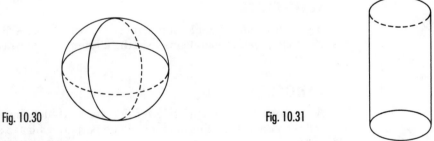

Fig. 10.30

Fig. 10.31

CYLINDER

A *cylinder* is like a cocoa tin or a drain pipe, with circular ends, see Fig. 10.31.

CONE

A *cone* is like an upside down Cornetto, with a circle for the base and a smooth curved surface rising to a point at the top, like a witch's hat. See Fig. 10.32.

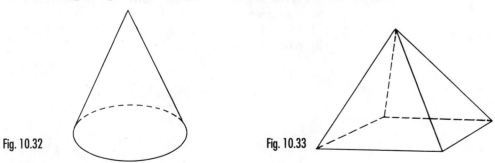

Fig. 10.32

Fig. 10.33

PYRAMID

A *pyramid* can have any shape for its base, but then from each side of the base the sides of the pyramid will meet at a point as shown in Fig. 10.33. This shape would be called a *square based pyramid* since the base is a square. When the vertex is perpendicularly above the centre of the base the correct name is a *right pyramid*.

PRISMS

Any three-dimensional shape with the *same cross section through its length or height* is called a *prism*.

For example, consider the shapes in Fig. 10.34. They are all prisms, since they are shapes you could *slice* up in such a way that each cross section would be identical.

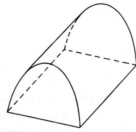

Fig. 10.34

 Level 6 You should be familiar with the words used to describe the different features of solids (see Chapter 8). These are:

- *Face*, the flat surfaces of solid shapes.
- *Edge*, lines where faces join together.
- *Vertex*, a point where edges join.

VIEWS

When looking at solid shapes you get different views from different positions. Two important views are *plans* and *elevations*.

Plans

The *plan* of a shape is the view you get when looking down from directly above the shape.

Elevation

The *end elevation* of a shape is the view you get when looking at the *end* of the shape. The *front elevation* of a shape is the view you get when you look directly at the *front* of the shape.

WORKED EXAMPLE 2 Fig. 10.35 represents one of the great Pyramids. Draw a sketch of the view you would get of this pyramid when:

a) looking directly from one side (end elevation):
b) looking down from above (plan).

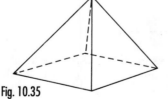

Fig. 10.35

Fig. 10.36

Fig. 10.37

The end elevation will be as shown in Fig. 10.36.
The plan will be as shown in Fig. 10.37.

NETS

A *net* is a flat shape that can be folded up to create a solid shape.

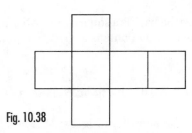

Fig. 10.38

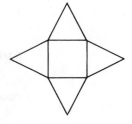

Fig. 10.39

This net would fold up to make a *cube*.

This net would fold up to make a *square based pyramid*.

You need to be able to recognise what shape a net will fold into, and also to draw a net for yourself for any given shape. There is usually more than one possible net that will give any shape.

For example, try to find at least two more nets that will make up the cube. But, do beware; when actually making a real net you would put *tabs* onto a number of sides so that you could glue the shape together, whereas an examination question (as the figures here) will not usually have them shown, or will expect you to put them onto the shape when drawing them.

EXERCISE 3

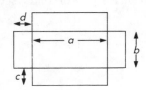

Fig. 10.40

Fig. 10.40 shows the net of an open box. The box will be 20 cm long, 10 cm wide and 5 cm high.
  i) If this net was the right size for the box described, what would be the lengths of *a*, *b*, *c*, and *d*?
  ii) What are the dimensions of the smallest rectangular piece of card that could be used to cut out this net?

7 > SIMILARITY

66 Level 8 99

Any two shapes are said to be *similar* if all the angles that could be drawn and measured in the shapes are the same, and if one shape is the same as the other but a different size. See the reference to Similarity in Chapter 7.

The two triangles in Fig. 10.41 are similar because all their angles are the same. It is true to say that if any two triangles have exactly the same angles as each other they will be similar.

Fig. 10.41

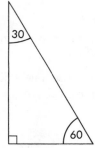

As well as looking at angles in other shapes we shall need to see if one shape can be enlarged to be the same as the other. You will meet this idea later in transformation geometry.

WORKED EXAMPLE 3

A builder built a garage with a floor similar to the rectangle in Fig. 10.42. The garage was built with a width of 2 metres. How long was it?
Since the two shapes are similar, then the enlargements of the sides will be the same. The width has gone from 1 cm, if you measure it, to 2 metres. That is 200 times larger, so the length will go from 3 cm, if you measure it, to 3 × 200, which is 600 cm. So the garage was 6 metres long.

Fig. 10.42

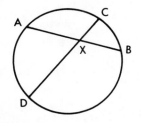

8 > INTERSECTING CHORD THEOREM

This can quite easily be shown by drawing and measuring, and will probably have been part of your coursework.

INTERNAL INTERSECTING

In Fig. 10.43, chords AB and CD intersect each other at X, then AX.XB = CX.XD.

Fig. 10.43

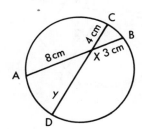

Fig. 10.44

WORKED EXAMPLE 4

In Fig. 10.44, find y.
We can use the intersecting chord theorem to say AX.XB = CX.XD,

hence $8 \times 3 = 4 \times y$

$\rightarrow \dfrac{8 \times 3}{4} = y = 6$ cm.

EXTERNAL INTERSECTING

 Level 9

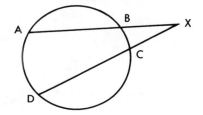

Fig. 10.45

In Fig. 10.45, the **same** rule works also, i.e. AX.XB = CX.XD

WORKED EXAMPLE 5

In Fig. 10.46, find y.
Using the theorem AX.XB = CX.XD, then $(5 + 2) \times 2 = 3 \times (y + 3)$

$\rightarrow 14 = 3y + 9$

$14 - 9 = 3y = 5$

$y = \dfrac{5}{3}$ cm.

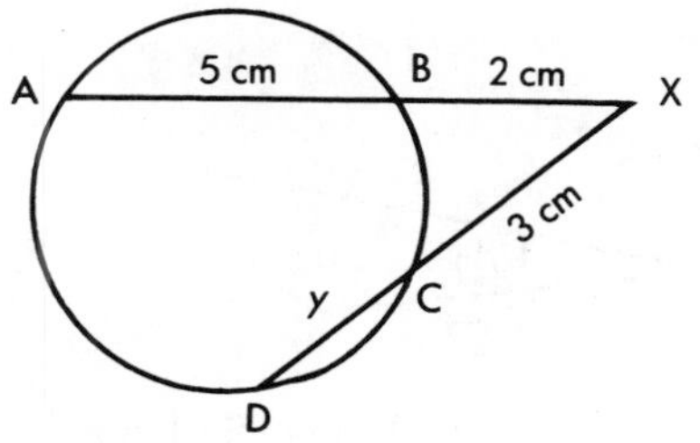

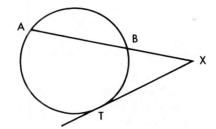

Fig. 10.46

TANGENTS

Where XT is a *tangent* to the circle at T when the intersecting chord theorem is AX.XB = XT^2.

Fig. 10.47

EXERCISE 4

Where TC is the tangent to the circle, find
the lengths of   i) *p*,   ii) *q*.

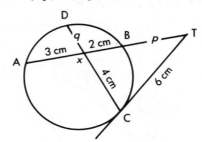

Fig. 10.48

Congruent shapes are exactly the same in size and shape (although one shape may well
be a reflection of the other).

In mathematics examinations it is usual for this to be tested within triangles where
certain minimum pieces of information can tell us that the two triangles are congruent.
These pieces of information are:

■ SSS → all three sides equal in length.

Figure 10.49 shows △ ABC congruent to △ XYZ.

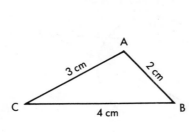

Fig. 10.49

■ AAS or ASA → two angles the same (which is the same as all
three angles the same!), and a corresponding side equal.
Figure 10.50 shows △ ABC congruent to △ PQR.

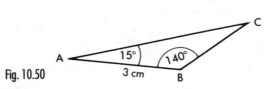

Fig. 10.50

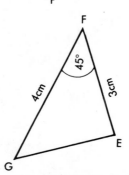

■ SAS → Two sides and the included angle equal.
Figure 10.51 shows △ ABC congruent to △ FEG.

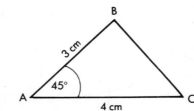

Fig. 10.51

NB. Notice how each letter must correspond exactly to its angle, e.g. if ABC is congruent
to XYZ, then A = X, B = Y, C = Z
and AB = XY, BC = YZ, CA = ZX.

EXERCISE 5

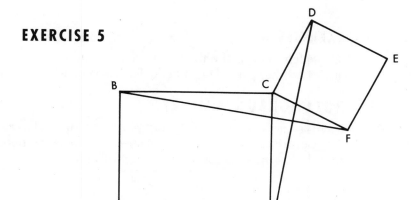

Fig. 10.52

a) In Fig. 10.52, ABCG and CDEF are both squares. Find a pair of congruent triangles.
b) State two triangles in Fig. 10.53 that are:
  i) congruent;
  ii) similar but not congruent.

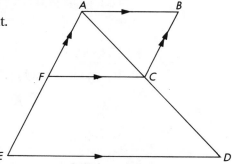

Fig. 10.53

Note

It is worth noticing that shapes that are congruent are obviously *similar*, but similar shapes are only congruent when *identical*.

10 SYMMETRY

There are two particular types of symmetry to be familiar with, *line* symmetry and *rotational* symmetry.

LINE SYMMETRY

If you can fold a shape over so that one half fits exactly on top of the other half, then the line over which you have folded is called a *line of symmetry*. The examples in Fig. 10.54 will illustrate this. The dotted lines are the lines of symmetry.

Level 5

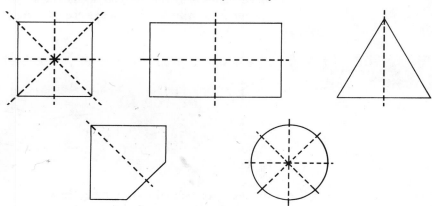

Fig. 10.54

The square has four lines of symmetry, the rectangle two, the isosceles triangle and the pentagon just one, while the circle has thousands and thousands of lines of symmetry; there are too many for us to count so we call this an *infinite* number.

Often, of course, you cannot fold over a shape that you are looking at, so you either have to imagine it being folded or trace it on tracing paper and then fold it. In most examinations you would be allowed to trace the shape and fold it over to find lines of symmetry.

EXERCISE 6

i) Sketch a hexagon with only one line of symmetry.

ii) What other possible number of lines of symmetry can a hexagon be drawn with?

ROTATIONAL SYMMETRY

This is sometimes also called *point symmetry*. A square has *rotational* symmetry of order 4, because if you turn it round its centre there are four different positions that it can take that all look the same, as shown in Fig. 10.55

Fig. 10.55

Try this out with a rectangle (use this book) and you should find that the rectangle has rotational symmetry of order 2.

Any shape that has what we would call *no rotational symmetry*, such as an elephant shape or an L shape, has rotational symmetry of order 1, since there is only one position where it looks the same! By the way, a circle will have rotational symmetry of an infinite order.

EXERCISE 7

a) In each letter in Fig. 10.56 draw, if any, all the lines of symmetry.

Fig. 10.56

b) Which of the above letters have rotational symmetry of order 2?

POLYGON SYMMETRY

All regular polygons will have the same number of lines of symmetry as the order of rotational symmetry, which is the same as the number of sides. Look at a square or at any regular polygon and check this out for yourself.

3D SYMMETRY

Level 6

The symmetry of 3D shapes is of two types, as in 2D shapes.

PLANES OF SYMMETRY

These are similar to lines of symmetry in 2D. A shape has a *plane of symmetry* if you can *slice* the shape into two matching pieces, one the exact mirror image of the other. To find these planes of symmetry you need to be able to visualise the shape being cut and to see in your mind whether the pieces are matching mirror images or not.

WORKED EXAMPLE 6

Find how many planes of symmetry the cuboid shown in Fig. 10.57 has.

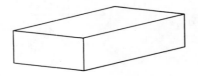

Fig. 10.57

Consider the cuboid shown in Fig. 10.57. We can cut it into two exact halves in the three ways shown in Fig. 10.58. Hence the shape has three planes of symmetry.

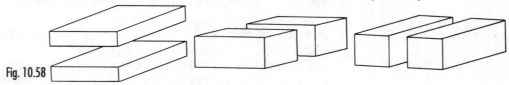

Fig. 10.58

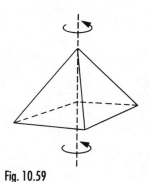

Fig. 10.59

EXERCISE 8

Find how many planes of symmetry a rectangular based right pyramid has.

AXES OF SYMMETRY

An *axis of symmetry* is a line around which the shape may rotate and yet still occupy the same space.

For example, in the square-based pyramid shown in Fig. 10.59 there is an axis of symmetry along the line through the vertex and the centre of the base. Around this axis the shape has rotational symmetry of order 4, since it can occupy four different positions within the same space.

EXERCISE 9

What are the symmetries of: i) a teacup;   ii) a bar of chocolate?

OUTLINE SOLUTIONS TO EXERCISES

S1

There will be 8 exterior angles each measuring $360 \div 8 = 45°$. Hence the interior angle will be $180 - 45 = 135°$.

S2

Since A and B are both points of circles where there is a tangent, there is a radius from each point to the respective centres. Since these radii arc to tangents they will both be perpendicular to the line AB, hence AD and BC are parallel.

i)   So $ABCD$ is a trapezium.
ii) Since the two right angles must remain right angles, the only time the opposite angles will add up to 180 is when all four are right angles – hence, when $ABCD$ is a rectangle; that is, when the circles are the same size.

S3

i)   You should now consider the full size box to give: $a = 20$ cm, $b = 10$ cm, $c = 5$ cm and $d = 5$ cm. The correct units here are important.
ii) Smallest rectangle which you would need would have to be $(20 + 5 + 5)$ by $(10 + 5 + 5)$ or 30 cm by 20 cm.

S4

i)   To find p, use AT.TB = TC² $\rightarrow (5 + p) \times p = 36$
    $\rightarrow 5p + p^2 = 36$ $\rightarrow p^2 + 5p - 36 = 0$
which solves to give $p = 4$ and $p = -9$, the negative answer here has no use to us, so we take the solution $p = 4$.
ii) To find q, use AX.XB = XC.XD $\rightarrow 3 \times 2 = 4 \times q$

$$\rightarrow 6 = 4q \rightarrow q = \frac{3}{2}$$

S5

a)   By identifying which line is equal to which, and which angles are the same, you should have found that BCF and GCD are congruent.
b)   Since the opposite sides of a parallelogram are equal, then the triangles ABC and AFC will have all three sides the same as each other to give congruent triangles ABC and CFA, since angle BAC is equal to angle ACF.
Similar triangles will be AFC and AED.

S6

i) A possible answer could be as shown in Fig. 10.60

ii) You will find that you can draw hexagons with 2, 3 and 6 lines of symmetry, but not 4 or 5. In other words, the factors of 6 can be used.

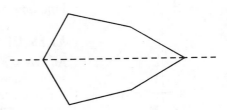

Fig. 10.60

S7

a) Your lines of symmetry should be drawn to look like Fig. 10.61.

Fig. 10.61

You would lose marks for putting too many lines in, or missing lines.

b) The only two letters are H and S.

S8

It will have just two. Both cutting the shape through the vertex and bisecting the opposite sides of the base.

S9

i) Teacup has one plane of symmetry only.

ii) Chocolate will have two planes of symmetry and one axis of symmetry.

EXAM TYPE QUESTIONS

Q1

The net in Fig. 10.62 can be folded to make a triangular prism. Which letter will point *J* join?

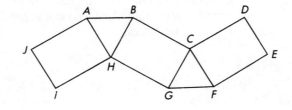

Fig. 10.62

(SEG)

Q2

One angle of a cyclic quadrilateral is 50°.

a) Write down one set of possible sizes of the other three angles.

b) Could these angles also be the angles of a trapezium?

> **Remember, a diagram will very often help you here.**

Q3

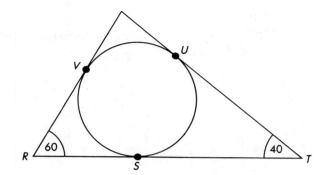

Fig. 10.63

In Fig. 10.63, *RST*, *RV* and *TU* are tangents to the circle at *S*, *V*, and *U* respectively. Calculate the size of angle *VSU*.   (SEG)

Q4

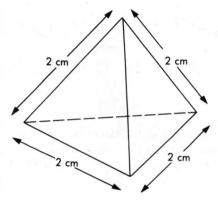

Fig. 10.64

Fig. 10.64 shows a triangular pyramid (tetrahedron) each of whose faces is an equilateral triangle of side 2 cm. Sketch two nets of the tetrahedron which are not congruent.

(ULEAC)

Q5

Karen has joined some of the vertices in a regular polygon and formed three triangles.

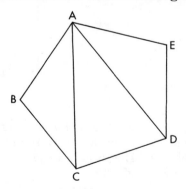

Fig. 10.65

a) Calculate the size of the angle ABC.
b) Name a triangle congruent to the triangle ABC which has been formed by the lines drawn in the polygon.   (SEG)

Q6

i) Describe the symmetries of the wallpaper pattern in Fig. 10.66 with reference to points *A*, *B* and *C*.

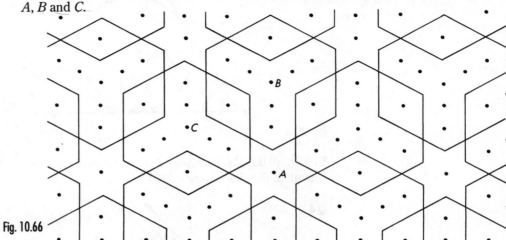

Fig. 10.66

ii) Shade a rhombus already outlined in Fig. 10.66 and state the size of each of its angles.
(NEAB)

Q7

O is the centre of the circle in Fig. 10.67.
Calculate the size of the angle *OBC*.
(ULEAC)

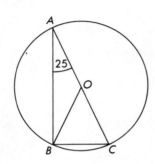

Fig. 10.67

Q8

Fig. 10.68 shows a symmetrical design for an Italian herb garden.

a) State the order of rotational symmetry of this diagram.
b) Draw on the diagram all the lines of symmetry. (NEAB)

Fig. 10.68

Q9

Fig. 10.69 is a design for a *big wheel* at a fun fair. The framework is made from two regular 9-sided polygons. The corners are joined to the centre by straight struts.

Calculate the angle *a* and the angle *b*.
Do not try to measure the drawing
(MEG)

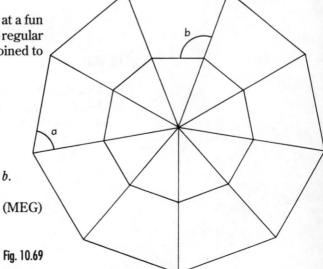

Fig. 10.69

Q10

Ian has some regular hexagonal paving stones and some square paving stones, each with 30 cm sides, see Fig. 10.70. He needs to fit paving stones together to completely cover an area of garden.

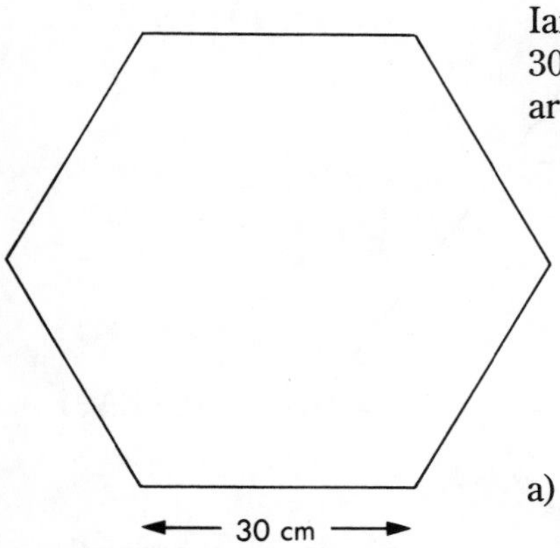

Fig. 10.70

a) What is the size of one interior angle of:
   i) the square stone;
   ii) the hexagonal stone?
b) Explain why Ian cannot fit a combination of square and hexagonal stones together to cover the area of garden.
c) Ian thinks he might make his own *regular-shaped* stone to fit with one square and one hexagonal stone.
   i) What would be the size of each angle of his stone?
   ii) How many sides would his stone have?
d) Ian decides his stone would be too large and cuts some of his hexagonal stones into equilateral triangular stones.
   i) Show in a sketch how he can now fit together two squares, one hexagon and one equilateral triangle at any one point.
   ii) Calculate the height of each equilateral triangle stone (not the thickness of the stone).
   iii) Calculate the area covered by the arrangement in part d) i).

Q11

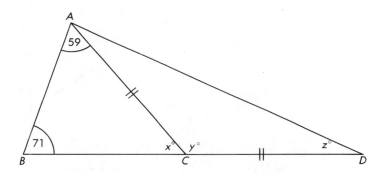

Fig. 10.71

In the framework in Fig. 10.71, the lengths AC and CD are equal. Angle $ABC = 71°$, angle $BAC = 59°$.
Calculate the angles marked $x°$, $y°$, $z°$. (MEG)

Q12

The net in Fig. 10.72 is folded along the dotted lines to form a solid. How many edges has the solid?

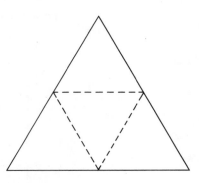

Fig. 10.72

(NEAB)

(NEAB)Q13

In Fig. 10.73 $\angle ABE = \angle ACD = 90°$.
$AC = 4.00$ m, $BC = 2.50$ m,
$CD = 3.00$ m.
Calculate BE.

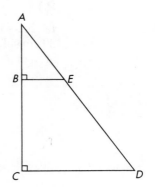

Fig. 10.73

(ULEAC)

Q14

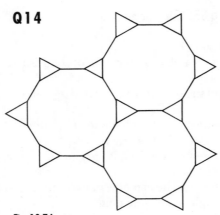

Fig. 10.74 shows part of a floor covered with two kinds of tiles. All the tiles are regular polygons.

a) Find the sizes of the angles of the triangular tiles.

b) Find the sizes of the angles of the remaining tiles.   (MEG)

Fig. 10.74

Q15

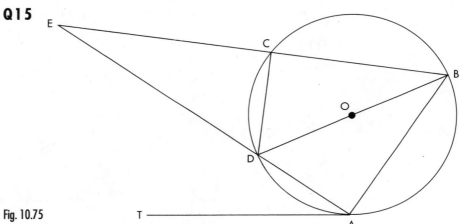

Fig. 10.75

(Diagram not accurately drawn.)

In the diagram, BD is a diameter of the circle ABCD with the centre at O.
TA is the tangent at A to the circle.
BCE and ADE are straight lines.
Angle DAT = 47° and angle DEC = 18°.

Find the size of angle CBD.   (ULEAC)

OUTLINE ANSWERS TO
EXAM QUESTIONS

A1

F

A2

a) One of the angles you must give must be 180 – 50, which is 130°; the other two must add up to 180°. So, possibly, the three angles could be 130°, 110°, 70°. There are lots more possibilities.

b) Yes, the pairs of angles between each parallel side of a trapezium add up to 180°, so you could have, for example, 50°, 130°, 50°, 130°, which would give a trapezium.

A3

Since *RV* = *RS*, then ∠ *VSR* = ∠ *SVR* = (180 – 60) ÷ 2 = 60°.
Similarly ∠ *UST* = 70° and hence ∠ *VSU* = 180 – (60 + 70) = 50°.

A4

Fig. 10.76

One answer is shown in Fig. 10.76, but there are other possible ways to do this.

A5

a) Calculate an interior angle, i.e. ∠ ABC, as $180 - \dfrac{360}{5} = 108°$

b) Triangle AED.

A6

i) There are two lines of symmetry, one line being *AB*, the other being perpendicular to *AB* at point *A*. The shape has rotational symmetry of order 3 about the point *A*, or the point *B* or point *C*.

ii) Your rhombus will have each side the length represented by 3 dots, and the angles will be 120°, 60°, 120° and 60°.

A7

Either 90 – 25 or (180 – 50) ÷ 2 to give 65°.

A8

a) 4

b)

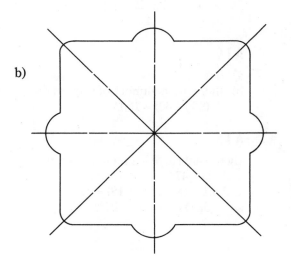

Fig. 10.77

A9

The angle at the centre will be $360 \div 9 = 40°$.
Hence angle a will be $\frac{1}{2}(180 - 40) = 70°$. Angle b will be $180 - 70 = 110°$.

A10

a) i) Size of one angle of square = $90°$.
    ii) Size of one angle of hexagon = $180 - (360/6) = 120°$.
b) At any point total angle = $360°$.
   Squares cannot meet hexagons since no combination of 90 and 120 gives 360.
c) i) Angle = $360 - 90 - 120 = 150°$.
    ii) Exterior angle = $180 - 150 = 30°$.
       Number of sides = $360/30 = 12$.
d) i)

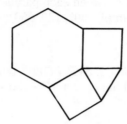

Fig. 10.78a)

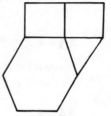

Fig. 10.78b)

ii) Height = $30 \sin 60 = 26$ cm.
iii) Area of triangle = $\frac{1}{2} \times 30 \times 26 = 390$
Area of hexagon = $6 \times 390 = 2\,340$
Area of square = $30 \times 30 = 900$
Total area = $3\,630$ cm^2

A11

$x = 180 - (71 + 59) = 50$

$y = 180 - 50 = 130°$; $z = \frac{1}{2}(180 - 130) = 25$

A12

6

A13

AB will be $4 - 2.5 = 1.5$ m
ABE and ACD are two similar triangles in the ratio 1.5 to 4.

Hence $BE = \dfrac{1.5 \times 3}{4} = 1.125$ m.

A14

a) $60°$;
b) there are a number of ways of doing this, but the simplest way is
    $\frac{1}{2}(360 - 60) = 150°$.

A15

By the alternate segment theorem,
$\angle ABD = 47°$
$\angle ABE = 180 - (90 + 18) = 72°$
so $\angle CBD = 72 - 47 = 25°$.

LEVEL CHECKLIST

For the level	You should be able to do the following
4	Know the language of 2-D and 3-D shapes. Recognise line and rotational symmetry.
5	Use properties associated with intersecting and parallel lines. Know basic facts about triangles. Identify the symmetries of various shapes.
6	Classify and define types of quadrilaterals. Know and use angle properties of polygons.
8	Understand the conditions for similar shapes. Know the intersecting chord theorem.
9	Understand the conditions for congruent triangles.
10	Know and use tangent properties of circles. Know and use angle properties of circles.

A STUDENT'S ANSWER WITH EXAMINER'S COMMENTS

Question

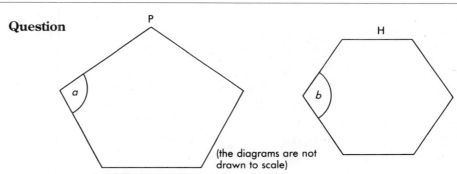

(the diagrams are not drawn to scale)

The drawings show two different tiles P and H.

Tile P is in the shape of a regular 5-sided polygon.
Tile H is in the shape of a regular 6-sided polygon.
  i) Calculate the size of the angles marked 'a' and 'b'.
 ii) Explain why tiles in the shape of a 6-sided regular polygon will fit together on a floor without any gaps between them whereas tiles in the shape of a 5-sided regular polygon will not.

A poor, thoughtless answer. The *exterior* angle has been calculated in each case instead of the *interior*.

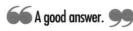
A good answer.

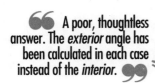
A shame that this candidate would have lost a lot of marks because of not knowing what the interior and exterior angles were.

Answer

i) Angle a = 360° (Sum of internal angles) ÷ 5 (No. of regular angles in P) = 72°

   Angle b = 360° (Sum of internal angles) ÷ 6 (No. of regular angles in H) = 60°

ii) The 5-sided regular polygon will not fit together on a floor without any gaps because the inside angles (108°) will not divide into 360° precisely (to 2 sign. Fig.) whereas the six-sided regular polygon's inside angles (120°) will.

R E V I E W   S H E E T

✎ Write down the name of each angle

    a) less than 90° _____   b) > 90° < 180° _____

    c) > 180° < 360° _____   d) equal 90° _____

✎ If two lines are at right angles to each other they are said to be _____

✎ Draw, and write down what you know about the properties of each shape.

    a) Isosceles triangle _____

    _____

    _____

    b) Equilateral triangle _____

    _____

    _____

    c) Parallelogram _____

    _____

    _____

    d) Trapezium _____

    _____

    _____

✎ How many sides does each *polygon* have?

    a) Hexagon _____   b) Nonagon _____   c) Octagon _____

    d) Pentagon _____   e) Septagon _____   f) Decagon _____

✎ A _____ polygon has all its sides the same length and each exterior angle is equal.

✎ Write down the formula for a *regular* polygon of N sides

    a) exterior angle = [   ]   b) interior angle = [   ]

✎ The _____ of a circle is any straight line drawn from the centre to the edge. A straight line drawn from one side of the circle to the other, passing through the centre, is called the _____.

✎ Describe the relationship between each marked angle in the following diagrams

    a) _____   b) _____   c) _____   d) _____   e) _____

✎ We call the quadrilateral in diagram c) above a _____ quadrilateral

What solid shape could be made from each of these nets?

a) _____   b) _____

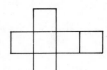

 Two shapes are **similar** if _____

_____

 Two shapes are **congruent** if _____

_____

 Use the intersecting chord theorem to calculate the following:

a) length DX = _____   b) length DC = _____

          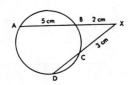

c) length XT = _____

 Draw in some *lines of symmetry* for each of these shapes (one shape has none!).

a) _____ b) _____ c) _____ d) _____ e) _____ f) _____

(has none)

 Write down the order of *rotational symmetry* for each of these shapes.

a) _____ b) _____ c) _____ d) _____ e) _____

GETTING STARTED

This chapter is all about *measuring* length, area and volume from given facts. There are a lot of formulae involved that you need to learn. You need to be *familiar* with the formulae and to be confident in *using* them. Learn a formula and it will help to make you quicker and more confident in what you are doing. The chapter brings together many ideas you will already have met in number, algebra and approximation. Although this is a small chapter many questions will be set on this topic in the examination.

USEFUL DEFINITIONS

Perimeter	Length round all the outside of a flat shape.
Area	Flat space included in a boundary, measured in squares.
Arc	Part of the circumference of a circle.
Volume	Space inside a three-dimensional shape, measured in cubes.
Hypotenuse	The longest side of a right-angled triangle.
Opposite	The side of a triangle opposite to the angle concerned.
Adjacent	The side of a triangle next to the angle concerned and the right angle.
Elevation, angle of	The angle measured above the horizon.
Depression, angle of	The angle measured below the horizon.

E S S E N T I A L   P R I N C I P L E S

1 ▷ PERIMETER

Level 4

The *perimeter* is the total outside length of any flat shape.
The perimeter of a *rectangle*, can be found by the formula

$$2 \times (\text{length} + \text{breadth})$$

The perimeter of a *circle*, known as the *circumference*, can be found by the formula:

$$\text{circumference} = \pi \text{ multiplied by the diameter}$$

where π can be taken to be 3, or 3.1 or 3.14, or found more accurately by pressing the π button on a calculator.

WORKED EXAMPLE 1

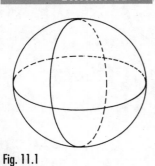

Fig. 11.1

Which has the longer perimeter; a rectangle measuring 6 cm by 2 cm or a circle of diameter 5 cm?

The perimeter of the rectangle will be $6 + 2 + 6 + 2 = 16$ cm.
The perimeter (circumference) of the circle is approximately $3.14 \times 5 = 15.7$ cm, so the perimeter of the rectangle is the longer.

EXERCISE 1

The diameter of the earth, as shown in Fig. 11.1, is approximately 7900 miles.

a) Freda went half way round the world to visit her aunt. How far has she travelled?
b) Mr Graves travelled round the world in 80 days. How many miles would he average a day?

2 ▷ AREA

Level 5

Area is the amount of space inside a flat 2-D shape, and is measured in squares, eg. square centimetres or square yards.

The area of a *rectangle*, as shown in Fig. 11.2, can be found with the formula:

$$\text{area} = \text{length} \times \text{breadth}.$$

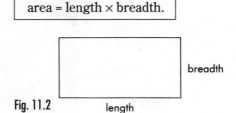

breadth

Fig. 11.2 length

height

Fig. 11.3 base

The area of a *triangle*, as shown in Fig. 11.3, can be found with the formula:

$$\text{area} = \tfrac{1}{2} \text{ of base length} \times \text{height}.$$

WORKED EXAMPLE 2

Find the total surface area of the cuboid in Fig. 11.4.

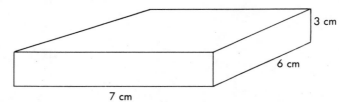

3 cm

6 cm

Fig. 11.4 7 cm

Each face is a rectangle, and the opposite faces are equal. So there will be a total surface area of:

$$2 \times [(7 \times 6) + (7 \times 3) + (6 \times 3)]$$
$$= 2 \times (42 + 21 + 18), \text{ which is } 2 \times 81, \text{ or 162 square centimetres,}$$
written as 162 cm^2

UNUSUAL SHAPES

For awkward shapes we can calculate the area by placing a suitable squared grid over the shape and counting the whole squares and estimating what the bits add up to.

Here is a map of Lake Riverlin, which has a scale of 1 square unit to 1 square kilometre. What is the surface area of Lake Riverlin?

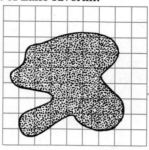

Fig. 11.5

Lake Riverlin

Count the whole squares, you should get 20. Now go through the smaller bits and estimate how many whole squares they would add up to. This should be close to 12, giving a total of 32 square units. Hence Lake Riverlin will have a surface area of 32 square kilometres.

PARALLELOGRAM

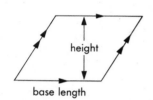

Fig. 11.6

The area of a *parallelogram*, as shown in Fig. 11.6 is found by the formula:

> area = base length × height.

TRAPEZIUM

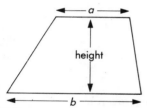

Fig. 11.7

The area of a *trapezium* as shown in Fig. 11.7, is found by multiplying the height (*h*) by the average length of the parallel sides. This is often written as:

$$\text{area} = \frac{h}{2}(a + b) \text{ or } h\,\frac{a + b}{2} \text{ both of which are the same formula.}$$

Which of the two shapes in Figs. 11.8 and 11.9 has the larger area?

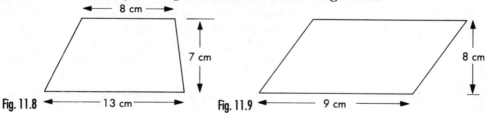

Fig. 11.8   **Fig. 11.9**

Fig. 11.8 is a trapezium with an area of $\frac{7}{2}(8 + 13) = 73.5$ cm².
Fig. 11.9 is a parallelogram with an area of $8 \times 9 = 72$ cm².
Hence the trapezium has the larger area.

CIRCLE

Level 6

The area of a *circle* is found by the formula:

> area = π × (radius)²

You should use the π on your calculator.

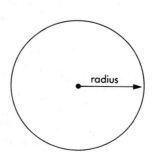

Fig. 11.10

EXERCISE 2

A triangle, parallelogram and circle all have the same height of 6 cm, and the same area. What are the base lengths of: i) the triangle; ii) the parallelogram.
Give answers to one decimal place.

SECTOR

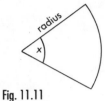

Fig. 11.11

The area of a *sector* of angle x is found by finding the fraction $\dfrac{x}{360}$ of the whole circle area,

i.e.

$$\text{sector area} = \frac{x}{360} \times \pi \times (\text{radius})^2$$

WORKED EXAMPLE 5

VACMAN as shown below, starts as a sector of a circle with a radius of 3 cm; each smaller circle is 1 cm in radius. Each time VACMAN eats a circle he increases in area by the same area as that of the circle he eats.

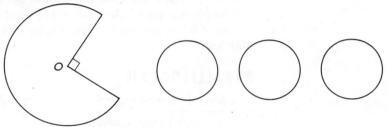

Fig. 11.12

vacman

a) Calculate the area of VACMAN before he starts eating.
b) Calculate the area of one small circle.
c) After VACMAN has eaten 14 small circles, calculate
   i) his new area;
   ii) his new radius assuming he stays a similar shape.

> 66 A typical easy error here is to think of the sector angle as 90°, so be careful 99

a) This is a sector of angle 270° and radius 3 cm, so its area is given by:

$$\frac{270}{360} \times \pi r^2 = \frac{270}{360} \times \pi \times 9$$

which rounds to 21.2 cm² giving the area of VACMAN

b) One small circle area will be πr^2 where $r = 1$, hence each is 3.1 cm² (or π cm²).

c) i) VACMAN's new area will be his old area + 14π, so being as accurate as possible you should use 21.20575 + (14 × π), which is 65.2 cm² (rounded off).

   ii) If the new area is 65.2, then where r is the radius we shall have the equation:

$$65.2 = \frac{270}{360} \times \pi r^2, \quad \text{rearranged to give} \quad r^2 = \frac{65.2 \times 360}{270 \times \pi}$$

So, using the accurate area of 65.2 (before it was rounded off) this will give $r^2 = 27.66$ … (do not round off yet) which will give $r = 5.3$ cm (rounded off) as VACMAN's new radius.

3 > ARC LENGTH

It also follows that a *length of arc*, as seen in Fig. 11.13, is found by the fraction $\dfrac{x}{360}$ of the whole circumference.

Hence, the arc length of a sector of angle x is given by:

$$\text{arc length} = \frac{x}{360} \times \pi \times \text{diameter}.$$

Since, the diameter is 2 × radius, it follows that:

$$\text{arc length} = \frac{x}{360} \times 2\pi r.$$

Fig. 11.13

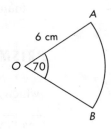

WORKED EXAMPLE 6

Find the arc length *AB* in the sector *AOB*.

Arc length is given by:

$$\frac{70}{360} \times 2\pi \times 6 = 7.3 \text{ cm (rounded of)}.$$

6 cm

O 70

A

B

Fig. 11.14

EXERCISE 3

A pendulum swings through an angle of 40°. How much further does the end of a 30 cm pendulum move, than a point half way down it?

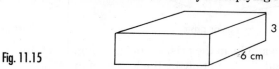

$$\frac{40}{360} \times 2\pi \times 30 = 20.94$$

10.47

4 ⟩ VOLUME

66 Level 5 99

Volume is the amount of space inside a 3D shape, and is measured in cubes, e.g. cubic millimetres and cubic metres.

The volume of a cuboid is found by multiplying length by breadth by height.

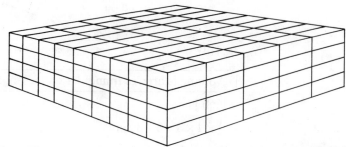

Fig. 11.15

3 cm

6 cm

7 cm

For example, the volume of the cuboid in Fig. 11.15 is $7 \times 6 \times 3$, which is 126 cubic centimetres, written as 126 cm³.

WORKED EXAMPLE 7

a) How many boxes are in the pile in Fig. 11.16?

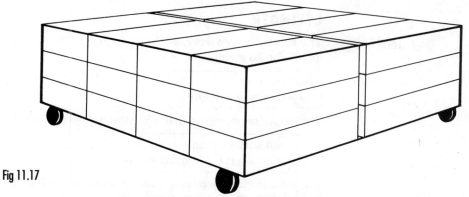

Fig. 11.16

b) Fred put some of the boxes from the pile into this trolley. How many of the boxes altogether will fit into the trolley shown in Fig. 11.17?

Fig 11.17

c) Fred was told to move all the boxes in the pile, using the trolley. How many times must he fill the trolley in order to move them all?

a) The number of boxes will be found by finding how many boxes there are along the length, breadth and height of this pile and multiplying together to give $9 \times 5 \times 4$, which gives a total of 180 boxes in the pile.

b) Using the same method as before to see how many boxes will fit into length, breadth and height, you should get $4 \times 2 \times 3$, which is 24 boxes which Fred can fit into his trolley.

c) The number of journeys Fred had to make to move all the boxes in the pile will be found by dividing 180 by 24, which gives 7.5. So your answer should be 8 journeys, or 7 full loads and a small one. Writing 7.5 on its own would not get full marks.

PRISMS

The *volume* of any *prism* is found by multiplying the area of the regular cross section (which is the same as the end!) by the length of the shape.

volume = area of regular cross section × length

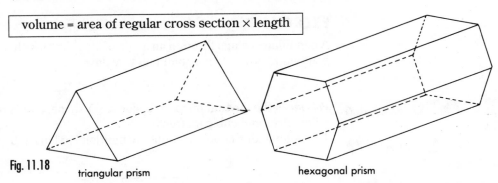

Fig. 11.18   triangular prism   hexagonal prism

So, for example, in the prisms shown in Fig. 11.18, the first thing to calculate is the area of the end, then multiply by the length of the shape.

WORKED EXAMPLE 8

Calculate the volume of the prism.

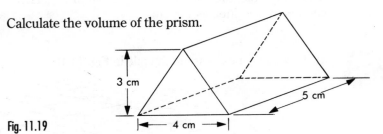

Fig. 11.19

Volume is area of triangular end × length

which is:

$\frac{1}{2} \times 4 \times 3 \times 5 = 30$ cm³.

5 ▷ MEASURING SOLIDS

You should be familiar with the following solid shapes and their mensuration.

CYLINDER

The *volume* of a *cylinder*, as shown in Fig. 11.20, is found by multiplying its base area by its height, so giving:

volume = $\pi r^2 h$ (r = radius; h = height)

The *curved surface area*, that is just the curved part of the cylinder, is found by the formula;

Curved surface area = $\pi D h$ (D = diameter; h = height)

The *total surface area* of a cylinder then, will be found by:

total surface area = $\pi D h + 2\pi r^2$

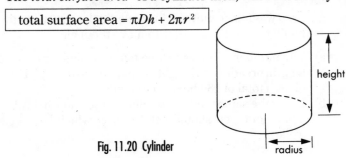

Fig. 11.20 Cylinder

SPHERE

The *surface area* of a *sphere*, as shown in Fig. 11.21, of radius r is given by the formula:

$$\text{surface area} = 4\pi r^2$$

The *volume* is given by:

$$\text{volume} = \tfrac{4}{3}\pi r^3$$

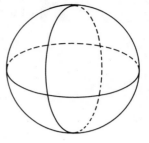

Fig. 11.21 Sphere

  ## PYRAMID

The *volume* of a *pyramid*, as shown in Fig. 11.22, is found by multiplying its base area by one-third of its height:

$$\text{volume} = \frac{h}{3} \times \text{base area}$$
where h = height.

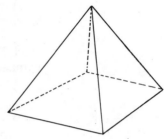

Fig. 11.22

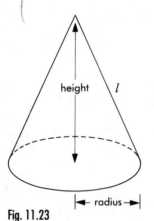

Fig. 11.23

CONE

Where a *cone* of height h has a base radius r and a slant height of l, then:

$$\text{curved surface area} = \pi r l$$

The *volume* is given by:

$$\text{volume} = \tfrac{1}{3}\pi r^2 h.$$

EXERCISE 4

A gold sphere of radius 10 cm was melted down and made into a cone whose height is the same as the sphere's diameter. What is the radius of the base of the cone?

6 ▷ SOLUTION OF TRIANGLES

PYTHAGORAS

You ought to know the rule of Pythagoras, which says that:

In a right-angled triangle the squares of the two smaller sides add up to the same as the square of the longest side (the hypotenuse).

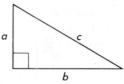

Fig. 11.24

The formula to express this rule, referring to Fig. 11.24, is:

$$a^2 + b^2 = c^2.$$

You will need to use this rule in two ways as illustrated in worked example, 9.

Kate has a ladder that will reach 12 feet up the wall when the bottom is 5 feet away from the wall.

Fig. 11.25

a) How long is the ladder?
b) How far up the wall will this ladder reach when its bottom is 4 feet away from the wall?

Since Fig. 11.25 illustrates that we have a right-angled triangle, we can use the rule of Pythagoras.

a) In the triangle made with the ladder, the wall and the floor, the two small sides are 5 and 12. Hence, if the hypotenuse is called x then $x^2 = 5^2 + 12^2 = 25 + 144 = 169$. Hence $x = \sqrt{169} = 13$, so the ladder is 13 feet long.

b) In this part we know the hypotenuse and need to find a small side. Using the same rule and calling the unknown small side y;

 **Be careful to round off properly, not doing so throws marks away.**

we have	$4^2 + y^2 = 13^2$
that is	$16 + y^2 = 169$
giving	$y^2 = 169 - 16 = 153$
hence	$y = \sqrt{153} = 12.4$ (rounded off).

EXERCISE 5

In a right-angle triangle two sides are known to be 4 cm and 7cm. What two possible areas could the triangle have?

7 ⟩ TRIGONOMETRY

You have probably spent quite a lot of time on trigonometry already, but here are the main facts that you ought to be familiar with. In any right-angled triangle we call the long side, which is always opposite the right angle, the *hypotenuse*. Then, depending on which angle of the triangle we are finding or going to use, we name the other two sides. The side opposite the angle we call *opposite* and the one next to both the angle under consideration and the right angle, we call the *adjacent*, as shown in Fig. 11.26.
Then, for the given angle x

 Level 8

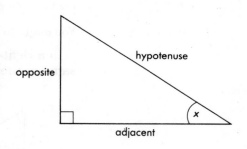

Fig. 11.26

$$\text{tangent} = \frac{\text{opposite}}{\text{adjacent}} \qquad \text{sine} = \frac{\text{opposite}}{\text{hypotenuse}} \qquad \text{cosine} = \frac{\text{adjacent}}{\text{hypotenuse}}$$

You may well be given this information on a formula sheet in the examination but not every Examination Board does this, so check it out for yourself. But in any case it's useful to remember this information, and one way of doing it is to learn a sentence to help.

For example, we can abbreviate the formulae to T = O/A, S = O/H, C = A/H, which can be put into a sentence such as 'Tommy On A Ship Of His Caught All Herring'. Of course, you can make up one of your own that *you* find easier to remember.

Help in remembering

This information is used in two ways; firstly, to find the size of angles, and, secondly, to calculate lengths of triangles.

TO FIND ANGLES

If you are finding an *angle* in a right-angled triangle and you know all three sides, then you have the choice of three ways to find the size of the angle. However, usually you will only know two sides, and therefore only one way is suitable. Look at the following examples, where in each right-angled triangle we are calculating the size of the angle x.

WORKED EXAMPLE 10

We look first to see which sides we know. In Fig. 11.27 these are the *opposite* and the *adjacent*, hence we need to calculate *tangent*. Using the previous information:

$$\text{tangent } x = \frac{\text{opposite}}{\text{adjacent}} = \frac{7}{5} = 1.4$$

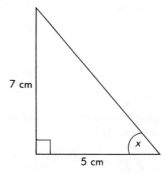

Fig. 11.27

We now need the angle that has a *tan* of 1.4. It is best to do this on the calculator by obtaining 1.4 in the display, finding and pressing the $\tan^{-1}$ button (often by pressing *INV* first then *tan*) and hence obtaining an answer that will round off to 54.5°.

WORKED EXAMPLE 11

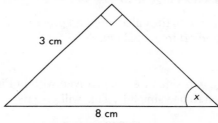

Fig. 11.28

In Fig. 11.28 we have *opposite* and *hypotenuse* which leads us to sine. Hence we can say:

$$\text{sine } x = \frac{\text{opposite}}{\text{hypotenuse}} = \frac{3}{8} = 0.375$$

and again find $\sin^{-1}$ to press on the calculator, giving 22.0°.

WORKED EXAMPLE 12

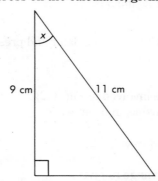

Fig. 11.29

In Fig. 11.29 we are given the *adjacent* and the *hypotenuse* which leads us to cosine. We can say:

$$\text{cosine } x = \frac{\text{adjacent}}{\text{hypotenuse}} = \frac{9}{11} = 0.81818 \ldots$$

Leave it all in the calculator.
Press $\cos^{-1}$ to obtain 35.1°.

Note

If you do not possess a calculator with trigonometrical functions, then you will have to use trigonometrical tables to find these figures, which will be a serious disadvantage to you.

TO FIND LENGTHS

In a right-angled triangle, once you are told one of the other angles, say 25°, then you are in a position to find the other angle. Here it will be 90 – 25 which is 65°. So really again you often have a choice of methods to use to find a missing *length*, but as far as possible always try to use the information given to you in the first place, it is more likely to be correct! Look at these examples of finding missing lengths.

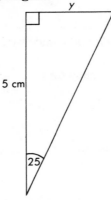

Fig. 11.30

WORKED EXAMPLE 13

In Fig. 11.30 the given side is *adjacent*, and the side we are finding, *y*, is the *opposite*, so we shall use tangent 25° to give:

$$\text{tangent } 25° = \frac{\text{opposite}}{\text{adjacent}} = \frac{y}{5}$$

So, rearrange to give

$$y = 5 \times \text{tangent } 25°.$$

Put 25 into the calculator and press *tan* to find the tangent of 25°. Now multiply by 5 and round off to get 2.3 cm.

WORKED EXAMPLE 14

The two sides we are involved with in Fig. 11.31 are *opposite* and *hypotenuse*, hence we need to use sine 36°. This will give us:

$$\text{sine } 36° = \frac{\text{opposite}}{\text{hypotenuse}} = \frac{y}{8}$$

So, rearrange to give

$$y = 8 \times \text{sine } 36°.$$

Fig. 11.31

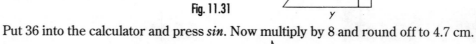

Put 36 into the calculator and press *sin*. Now multiply by 8 and round off to 4.7 cm.

WORKED EXAMPLE 15

We are involved in Fig. 11.32 with cosine, and can write:

$$\text{cosine } 65° = \frac{y}{15}$$

rearrange to give

$$y = 15 \times \text{cosine } 65°,$$

which gives us *y* = 6.3 cm.

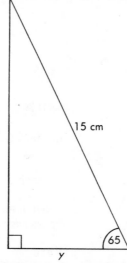

Fig. 11.32

Note

It it's the *hypotenuse* we are being asked to find, then we have to be careful. Look at the worked example 16.

WORKED
EXAMPLE 16

We can recognise the sine situation in
Fig. 11.33 and write down:

$$\text{sine } 57° = \frac{\text{opposite}}{\text{hypotenuse}} = \frac{8}{y}$$

which will rearrange to give:

$$y = \frac{8}{\text{sine } 57°}$$

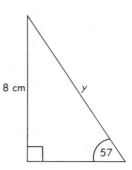

Fig. 11.33

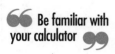 **Be familiar with
your calculator**

This is where you need to be specially careful, for different calculators can do this in many
different ways. One way that will work on all scientific calculators is to put 57 into the
display, press *sin* and put the result into memory, then put 8 into the display and divide
this by the *memory recall* to give a rounded answer of 9.5 cm. But do look to see how *your*
calculator can do this as simply as possible.

3D SITUATIONS

 **Level 9**

At the higher levels of GCSE you will be expected to be able to use the trigonometry you
have learned to solve three-dimensional problems. This will often involve what we call
dropping perpendiculars, that is to say, if something was to fall to the ground from any point
above the ground, it would fall in a vertical line, perpendicular to the horizontal.

In any 3-D situation that you are required to work with, it is vital that you are able to *see*
the right angles and use them.

WORKED
EXAMPLE 17

Fig. 11.34 illustrates a prisoner's escape hole just on the edge of the perimeter fence.
There was one lookout on a tower 8 yards high due north, and another lookout on a tower
10 yards high due west. Both lookouts were 18 yards away. The prisoner tried to escape
one night when visibility was 20 yards.

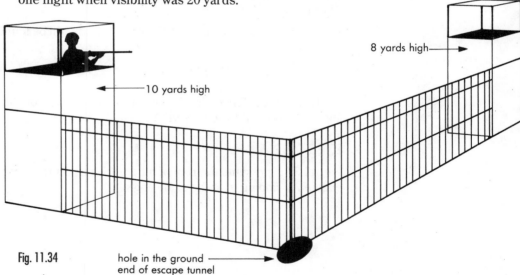

Fig. 11.34   hole in the ground ——
end of escape tunnel

a) Which of the two lookouts could see the prisoner escape?
b) What visibility would you need for one lookout just to be able to see the other?

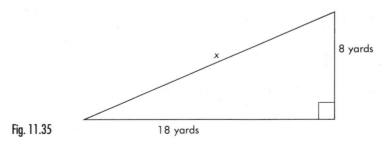

Fig. 11.35   18 yards

a) Looking at the situation of the northern lookout we have the triangle shown in Fig.
11.35. The distance from the lookout to the prisoner's hole is the hypotenuse, which
is found by the rule of Pythagoras:

$$x^2 = 18^2 + 8^2 = 388,$$

hence $x = 19.7$ yards. This distance is less than 20 yards, so the guard in this lookout tower can see the escape hole. A similar situation from the viewpoint of the other lookout gives a right-angled triangle with a solution of:

$$x^2 = 18^2 + 10^2 = 424$$

hence $x = 20.6$ yards. This distance is greater than 20 yards, so the guard in this lookout tower cannot see the escape hole.

b) Drawing a line from one lookout to the other gives us Fig. 11.36.

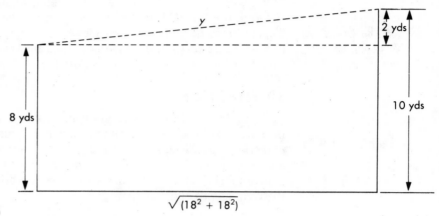

Fig. 11.36

The distance between the lookouts is found by considering the right-angled triangle formed between the foot of each lookout tower and the escape hole to give:

$$\sqrt{(18^2 + 18^2)}.$$

So the actual distance between the two lookouts will be found by the rule of Pythagoras:

$$y^2 = \left(\sqrt{(18^2 + 18^2)}\right)^2 + 2^2$$

which is 652. Hence y is $\sqrt{652}$ which is 25.53. Therefore a visibility of 26 yards will just allow one lookout to see the other.

EXERCISE 6

Fig. 11.37 represents the roof of a barn with a rectangular base and *isosceles triangular* ends both sloping in at the same angle.

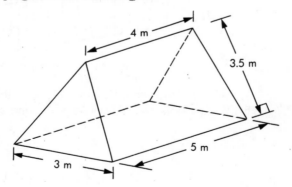

Fig. 11.37

Calculate the slope made with the horizontal of: i) the rectangular faces of the roof; ii) the triangular faces of the roof.

8 ▷TRIGONOMETRICAL GRAPHS

You need to be able to recognise the special features about the graph of each trig function, so that you can sketch them when necessary.

THE SINE CURVE

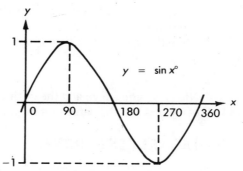

Fig. 11.38

In Fig. 11.38, see how the sine of angles between 0 and 180 are positive, and the sine of angles between 180 and 360 are negative.

Solve the equation $\sin x = 0.5$ $(0 < x < 180)$.
Using $\sin^{-1}x$ on the calculator gives $x = 30°$, but look at the graph and you will see that there are two angles with a sine of 0.5. One is 30° (check with the calculator). Now, from the symmetry of the graph you can see that the other angle will be $(180 - 30)$ which is 150°.

Hence $x = 30°$ and $x = 150°$.

Check then from the graph that:

for $0 < x \leqslant 180$ $\sin (180 - x) = \sin x$.
for $180 < x \leqslant 360$ $\sin (180 + x) = -\sin x$.

 Useful facts to learn Play about with these two facts on your calculator and show to yourself that they are true. They are difficult facts to learn, but if you learn the shape of the sine curve and its main points then you can always work them out again for yourself.

WORKED EXAMPLE 19

Sketch the graph of $y = \sin 3x$ $0 < x < 180$
A table of values can be built as in Table 11.1

x	0	30	60	90	120	150	180
$3x$	0	90	180	270	360	450	540
$y = \sin 3x$	0	1	0	−1	0	1	0

Table 11.1

Sketched smoothly this gives Fig. 11.39

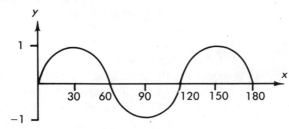

Fig. 11.39

EXERCISE 7

Sketch the graph of $y = 3 \sin x$.

Similar facts and statements can be made about cos and tan. Follow through them now.

THE COSINE CURVE

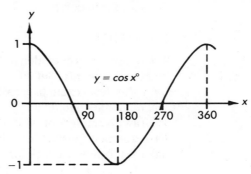

Fig. 11.40

In Fig. 11.40, see how the cosine of angles between 0 and 90, or 270 and 360 are positive, and of angles between 90 and 270 are negative.

From the symmetry of the graph:
$$\cos (180 - x) = - \cos x$$
$$\cos (180 + x) = - \cos x$$
$$\cos (360 - x) = \cos x$$

NB. The sine curve and the cosine curve are exactly the same shape, where the graph of $\cos x$ is just the same as $\sin x$ moved down $90°$.

THE TANGENT CURVES

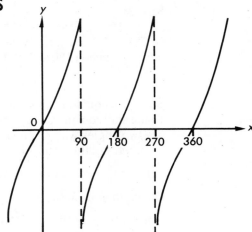

Fig. 11.41

Notice that Fig. 11.41 is a series of parallel curves with what we call 'asymptotes' at $x = 90$ and 270. (But more of that at A level.) It is quite different from the sin and cos curves, yet it still has symmetry to enable us to see that
$$\tan (180 - x) = - \tan x$$
$$\tan (180 + x) = \tan x.$$

EXERCISE 8

Sketch the graphs of $y = \cos 2x$ and $y = \tan x$ to estimate a solution to $\cos 2x = \tan x.$ $0 < x < 180.$

ANGLES BIGGER THAN 90°

To find the trig ratio of angles bigger than $90°$ just press the correct buttons on your calculator, but when given a ratio and you are asked for possible angles, then most calculators will not tell you. You need either to remember the above rules or sketch the graph to remind you.

WORKED EXAMPLE 20

Solve the equation $\cos x = 0.8.$ $(0 < x < 360)$
On the calculator $\cos^{-1} 0.8 = 36.9°.$
Also, $\cos (360 - x) = \cos x$, hence where $x = 36.9°$; another solution is $(360 - 36.9)$, which is $323.1°$. So $x = 36.9°$ and $323.1°$.
(You can always easily check the solutions by the use of cos on the calculator.)

EXERCISE 9

Solve the equation $\tan x = 2$ $(0 < x < 360)$

SINE RULE

 Level 10

Trigonometry is extended to solve non-right-angled triangles with the use of the *sine rule* and the *cosine rule*. But do check to see if this is necessary for you, since it only appears on higher level exam papers. However, it could be interesting to look at the topic even if you do not need to do it.

Draw a triangle (obtuse if you wish), and label it as in the diagram. Notice how the small letters come opposite the capital letters. Then measure each angle and the length of each side. You can now check for yourself the *sine rule*, which will work for **any** triangle.

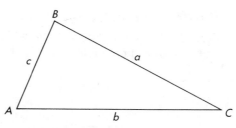

Fig. 11.42

The Sine Rule

$$\frac{a}{\sin A} = \frac{b}{\sin B} = \frac{c}{\sin C} \quad \text{or} \quad \frac{\sin A}{a} = \frac{\sin B}{b} = \frac{\sin C}{c}$$

WORKED EXAMPLE 21

Find the marked length x.
We can apply the sine rule to give:

$$\frac{x}{\sin 110} = \frac{8}{\sin 40}$$

which gives:

$$x = \frac{8 \sin 110}{\sin 40} = 11.7 \text{ cm.}$$

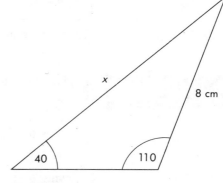

Fig. 11.43

WORKED EXAMPLE 22

Find the marked angle θ.
We apply the sine rule to give

$$\frac{\sin \theta}{3} = \frac{\sin 130}{5},$$

which gives:

$$\sin \theta = \frac{3 \sin 130}{5} = 0.4596(\ldots)$$

giving $\theta = 27.4°$

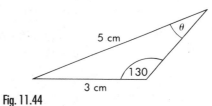

Fig. 11.44

WORKED EXAMPLE 23

In Fig. 11.45 find $x°$.

We cannot go straight to x here but to the other unknown angle, let's call it y, then apply

the sine rule: $\dfrac{\sin y}{5} = \dfrac{\sin 60}{10}$ Fig. 11.45

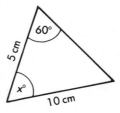

$$\rightarrow \sin y = \frac{5 \sin 60}{10} = 0.4330$$
$$\rightarrow y = 25.7 \text{ or } (180 - 25.7) = 154.3$$

Since one angle is already given as 60°, then another angle cannot be 154.3, since 60 + 154.3 > 180.
hence $y = 25.7$ and so $x = 180 - (60 + 25.7)$
$x = 94.3°$.

COSINE RULE (1)

This is used when we know all three sides of a triangle and we wish to find an angle.

If we wish to find angle A in Fig. 11.46,
then

$$\cos A = \frac{b^2 + c^2 - a^2}{2bc}$$

Note which side comes last.
For angle B:

$$\cos B = \frac{a^2 + c^2 - b^2}{2ac}$$

Try to write the rule for angle C yourself.

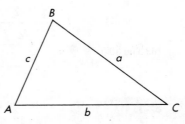

Fig. 11.46

WORKED EXAMPLE 24

Find angle θ, in Fig. 11.47.
We apply the cosine rule to give?

$$\cos \theta = \frac{5^2 + 7^2 - 6^2}{2 \times 5 \times 7} = 0.5428(\ldots)$$

giving $\theta = 57.1°$.

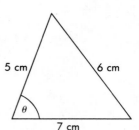

Fig. 11.47

WORKED EXAMPLE 25

In Fig. 11.48, find x.
Use the cosine rule as

$$x = \sqrt{(3^2 + 5^2 - 2 \times 3 \times 5 \times \cos 115)}$$

$$= \sqrt{(46.678548)}$$

$x = 6.8$ cm

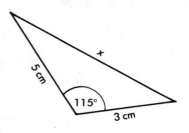

Fig. 11.48

(Note the cos 115 was negative, but should have caused no problems.)

EXERCISE 10

In Fig. 11.49, find x.

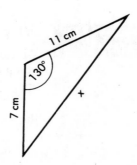

Fig. 11.49

COSINE RULE (2)

If we are given the information about two sides and the included angle, then we can find another side by turning the cosine rule round to give:

$$a = \sqrt{(b^2 + c^2 - 2bc \cos A)} \quad \text{OR} \quad b = \sqrt{(a^2 + c^2 - 2ac \cos B)}$$

Try to write the rule for c yourself.

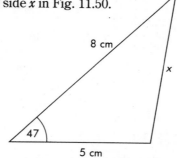

WORKED EXAMPLE 26

Find the marked side x in Fig. 11.50.

8 cm

x

47

5 cm

Fig. 11.50

We apply the cosine rule to give:

$$x = \sqrt{(5^2 + 8^2 - 2 \times 5 \times 8 \cos 47)}$$
$$= 5.9 \text{ cm}.$$

WORKED EXAMPLE 27

In Fig. 11.51, find the size of angle B.

Use the Cosine Rule to give $\cos B = \dfrac{9^2 + 8^2 - 15^2}{2 \times 9 \times 8} = -0.5556$

giving $B = 123.7° = 124°$.

(Note that if the cosine works out to be negative, the angle will be obtuse.)

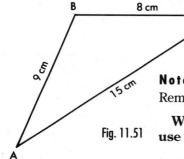

B   8 cm   C

9 cm

15 cm

A

Fig. 11.51

Note

Remember when to use each one by a simple rule:

    When two sides involved make the angle cosy, use the cosine rule, otherwise use the sine rule.

EXERCISE 11

In the triangle ABC in Fig. 11.52 calculate the size of the
i) smallest angle   ii) largest angle.

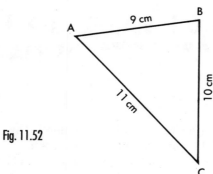

A   9 cm   B

11 cm

10 cm

C

Fig. 11.52

AREA

A simple way to find the *area of a triangle*, if you know two sides as in Fig. 11.53 and the included angle, is to use:

> Area = $\frac{1}{2}\, ab \sin C$, or
> Area = $\frac{1}{2}\, bc \sin A$.

Try to write the rule if it is angle B which you are given.

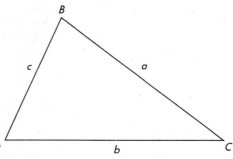

B

c a

A b C

Fig. 11.53

<table>
<tr><td>

**WORKED
EXAMPLE 28**

</td><td>

In Fig. 11.54, find the area of triangle ABC.
Use the sine rule as:
Area = $\frac{1}{2} \times 4 \times 5 \times \sin 120$ = 8.7 cm².

</td></tr>
</table>

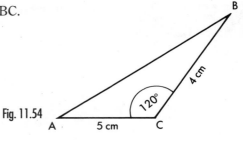

Fig. 11.54

EXERCISE 12

Find the area of the triangle ABC in Fig. 11.55.

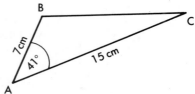

Fig. 11.55

<table>
<tr><td>

**WORKED
EXAMPLE 29**

</td><td>

Find the area of the triangle, in Fig. 11.56

Use the area sine formula:

$\quad$ Area = $\frac{1}{2} \times 7 \times 9 \times \sin 63$
$\qquad$ = 28 cm²

</td></tr>
</table>

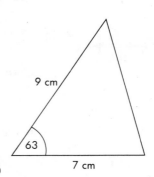

Fig. 11.56

ELEVATION AND DEPRESSION

You may come across an angle defined as an
angle of depression, which is like angle *A* in
Fig. 11.57, an angle made with a line below
the horizontal. Or you may come across an
angle of elevation which is like angle *B* in Fig.
11.57, an angle made with a line above the
horizontal.

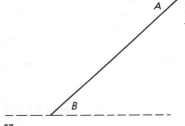

Fig. 11.57

SOLUTIONS TO EXERCISES

S1

a) The circumference of the world will be π multiplied by the diameter of the world, which
will be π × 7900. Do this on your calculator and round off to 24 800 miles. Hence
halfway round the world will be approximately half of 24 800 miles, which is 12 400
miles.

b) Divide the most accurate figure you had for the circumference around the world by
80, then round off to 310, giving the average day's journey by Mr Graves to be 310
miles.

S2

Area of circle = $\pi r^2 = \pi \times 3^2 = \pi \times 9 = 28.27(\ldots)$. Put this accurate calculator display into
the memory, and we'll use it rather than the 28.27.

i) From area of triangle = $\frac{1}{2}$ base length × height, we get the equation

$\quad$ 28.27(...) = $\frac{1}{2}$ × length × 6, which rearranges to give:

$$\text{length} = \frac{2 \times 28.27(\ldots)}{6} = 9.4 \text{ cm (rounded off)}.$$

ii) From area of parallelogram = base length × height we get the equation:

28.27(…) = length × 6, which solves to give:

$$\text{length} = \frac{28.27(\ldots)}{6} = 4.7 \text{ (rounded off)}.$$

S3

Arc length of the end of the pendulum in Fig. 11.58 is given by:

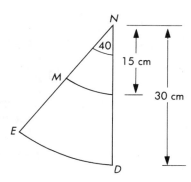

$$ED = \frac{40}{360} \times 2\pi \times 30 = 20.94.$$

Length of the arc in the middle is given by:

$$MN = \frac{40}{360} \times 2\pi \times 15 = 10.47.$$

The answer is that the pendulum moves 10.5 cm more (rounded off).

Fig. 11.58

S4

Calculate the volume of the sphere, given by $\frac{4}{3}\pi r^3$ where $r = 10$, and this will be 4189 (rounded, but keep the accurate value in the memory of your calculator to use later). The volume of a cone is given by $\frac{1}{3}\pi r^2 h$, so when the volume is as above and the height equal to 20 cm, we have $4189 = \frac{1}{3}\pi r^2 \times 20$ which can be rearranged to give

$$r^2 = \frac{4189 \times 3}{\pi \times 20} = 200$$

(using the accurate value of 4189). Hence $r = \sqrt{200}$, so the radius of the base of the gold cone will be 14.1 cm.

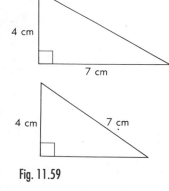

Fig. 11.59

S5

The two possible triangles are shown in Fig. 11.59.
The upper triangle has an area of $\frac{1}{2} \times 4 \times 7 = 14$ cm². We need to find the smaller missing side in the lower triangle. This length is given by $\sqrt{(7^2 - 4^2)} = \sqrt{33} = 5.7(\ldots)$.
The area of this triangle is:

$$\tfrac{1}{2} \times 4 \times 5.7 \,(\ldots) = 11.5 \text{ cm}^2 \text{ (rounded off)}.$$

So, the possible areas are 14 cm² and 11.5 cm².

S6

i) From any point along the 4 m edge of the rooftop in Fig. 11.60, imagine a perpendicular dropped to the base of the roof and a line drawn perpendicular to the 5 m edge. This gives a right-angled triangle as shown, with x the angle we are asked for.

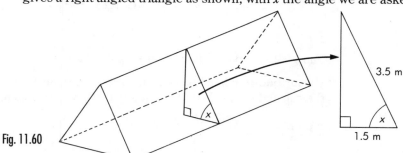

Fig. 11.60

This is found with cosine $x = \dfrac{1.5}{3.5}$, hence x is 64.6° rounded to one decimal place.

ii) From the triangle in i), you can calculate the height of the roof by the rule of Pythagoras:

Height² = 3.5² – 1.5² = 10, hence height is √10 (no need to calculate yet). Now, from the very edge of the 4 m roof line, drop a perpendicular to the roof base, and imagine a line drawn perpendicular to the 3 m edge to give the right-angled triangle seen in Fig. 11.61.

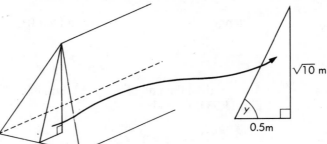

Fig. 11.61

The base is 0.5 m since the difference between the top line and bottom line is 1 metre, so there is 0.5 m to come in at each end. This gives the angle *y* as:

tangent $y = \dfrac{\sqrt{10}}{0.5}$ so *y* will be 81.0°.

S7

See Fig.11.62.

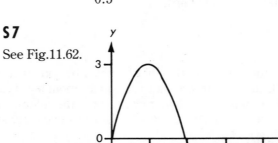

Fig. 11.62

S8

See Fig. 11.63. The intersection will be the solution of approximately *x* = 20°.

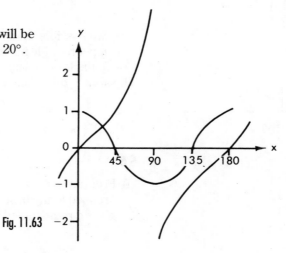

Fig. 11.63

S9

Tan *x* = 2   *x* = 63.4   and   180 + 63.4 = 243.4.

(In any question like this you can always test your answers by finding their tangents on the calculator and checking that indeed they are equal to what you started with.)

S10

Use cosine rule to give $x = \sqrt{(11^2 + 7^2 - 2 \times 11 \times 7 \times \cos 130}$

$$= \sqrt{(121 + 49 + 99)} = \sqrt{269}$$

$$x = 16.4 \text{ cm.}$$

(The most common mistake is to forget to square root, but if you are in the correct habit of checking that your answers are sensible then you will spot that error.)

S11

The smallest angle is always opposite the smallest length and similarly, the largest angle is opposite the largest length. Hence smallest angle is opposite the smallest side of 9, hence C. This is found by the cosine rule as:

$$\cos C = \frac{a^2 + b^2 - c^2}{2ab} \rightarrow \cos C = \frac{10^2 + 11^2 - 9^2}{2 \times 10 \times 11} = 0.6364$$
$$\rightarrow C = 50.5°.$$

The largest angle is opposite 11, the largest side, hence B. This also is found by the cosine rule to give B = 70.5°.

S12

Area = $\frac{1}{2} \times 7 \times 15 \times \sin 41 = 34.4$ cm².

EXAM TYPE QUESTIONS

Q1

In Fig. 11.64 are some solids made from centimetre cubes.

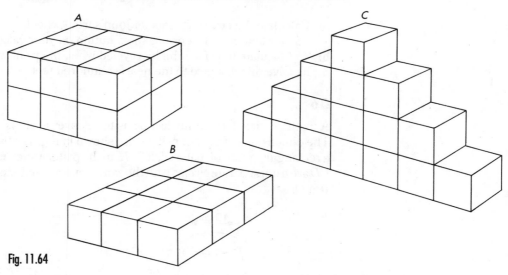

Fig. 11.64

Find the total surface area of each solid.   (NEAB)

Q2

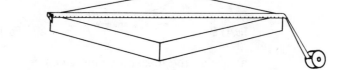

Fig. 11.65

The instructions for erecting a greenhouse say: 'First make a rectangular base 2 m by 3.5 m. To check that it is rectangular measure the diagonal. It should be about 4 m.' Using Pythagoras' theorem, explain why the diagonal in Fig. 11.65 should be about 4 m.

(SEG)

Q3

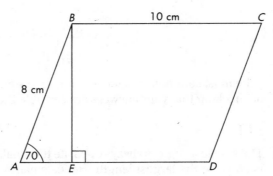

Fig. 11.66

In Fig. 11.66, the parallelogram *ABCD*, *BE* is perpendicular to *AD*, angle *A* = 70°, *AB* = 8 cm and *BC* = 10 cm.
Calculate, giving your answers correct to two significant figures:

a) the length of *BE*;
b) the area of the parallelogram *ABCD*.   (MEG)

Q4

The square in Fig. 11.67 has area 2500 cm².
What is the length of each side of the square?

2500 cm²

Fig. 11.67

Q5

John's cycle in Fig. 11.68 has wheels of radius 1 ft.

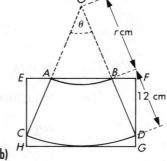

Fig. 11.68

1 ft

a) Calculate the circumference of John's front wheel.
    (Either take π as 3.14 or use the π button on your calculator.)
b) i) Calculate how far John has cycled when the front wheel has rotated 70 times.
    ii) Give this distance to the nearest hundred feet.   (SEG)

Q6

A mathematical DIY enthusiast plans to re-cover a lampshade of circular cross-section. The dimensions of the lampshade are shown in Fig. 11.69a). The fabric is to be cut from a rectangular piece of material, *EFGH*, to the pattern shown in Figure b). The arcs *AB* and *CD* are from separate circles with the same centre *O* and each arc subtends the same angle θ at *O*.

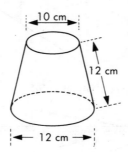

Fig. 11.69a)

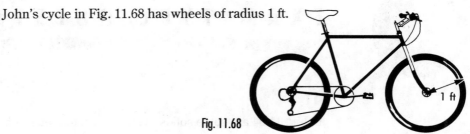

Fig. 11.69b)

a) Using the measurements given in Fig. 11.69a) write down, as a multiple of π, the lengths of: i) arc *AB*; ii) arc *CD*.
b) Using the measurements given in Fig. 11.69b), write down, in terms of *r*, θ and π, the lengths of i) arc *AB*; ii) arc *CD*.
c) Use the results of a) and b) to find i) *r*, ii) θ.   (ULEAC)

Q7

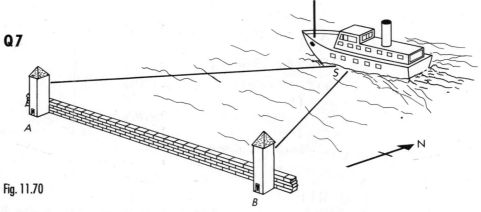

Fig. 11.70

In Fig. 11.70 two lookout posts, A and B on a straight coastline running east-west sight a ship, S, on a bearing 067° from A and 337° from B.

a) Explain why angle ASB is 90°
   The distance from A to B is 5 kilometres.
b) Calculate the distance of the ship from A.
c) Calculate the distance of the ship from B.
   The ship sails on a course such that angle ASB is always 90°.
d) Describe the path the ship must take.
e) What is the bearing of the ship from A, to the nearest degree, when it is 3 kilometres from it? (SEG)

Q8

Fig. 11.71 represents two fields ABD and BCD in a horizontal plane $ABCD$.
AB = 270 m, BD = 250 m, angle ABD = 57°, angle BCD = 37° and angle CBD = 93°.

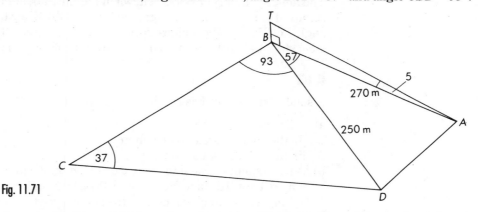

Fig. 11.71

A vertical radio mast BT stands at the corner B of the fields and the angle of elevation of T from A is 5°. Calculate, correct to three significant figures:

a) the height of the radio mast;
b) the length of AD;
c) the length of BC;
d) the area, in hectares, of the triangular field ABD (1 hectare = 10^4 square metres). (MEG)

Q9

A, B and C are three points on the map in Fig. 11.72. They all lie on the 10 metre contour line but are separated by the river estuary as shown. The map surveyor measured the straight line distance from A to B as 120 m and the angles BAC and ABC were found to be 54° and 90° respectively.

Calculate the straight line distances BC and AC.

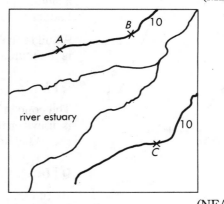

Fig. 11.72

(NEAB)

Q10

From Fig. 11.73:

a) Write down an expression for *BD* in terms of *h*.

b) Write down an expression for *DC* in terms of *h*.

c) Hence calculate *h*.

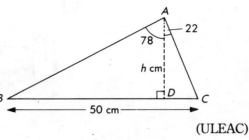

Fig. 11.73   (ULEAC)

Q11

AB is a chord of a circle and *AC* is a diameter. The length of *AB* is 14 cm and the radius of the circle is 25 cm. Calculate the length of the chord *BC*.

(MEG)

Q12

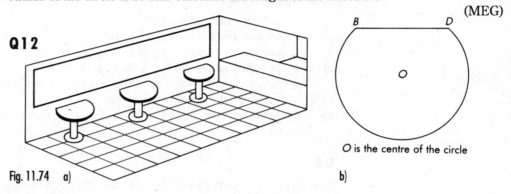

Fig. 11.74   a)   b)

O is the centre of the circle

The tables in a Burger Bar, as shown in Fig. 11.74a), are circular, with a minor segment removed to form a straight edge, see Fig. 11.74b). They have a diameter of 1 metre, and angle *BOD* is 90°. The tops are covered with formica and the perimeter is bound with thin steel strip. Calculate the area of the table top and the length of strip required.   (SEG)

Q13

A solid silver sphere has a radius of 0.7 cm.

a) Calculate:
   i) the surface area of the sphere;
   ii) the volume of the sphere;

b) A silversmith is asked to make a solid pyramid with a vertical height of 25 cm and a square base. To make the pyramid, the silversmith has to melt down 1000 of the silver spheres. Assuming that none of the silver is wasted, calculate the total surface area of the pyramid.   (MEG)

Q14

These instructions are issued by the British Decorating Association.

Working at Heights

If a ladder is used as a means of access, it should rise to a height of 3 ft 6 in (1.074 m) above a landing place.

Ladders should be set at 75° to the horizontal.

A builder has a contract to resurface a flat roof which is 7.5 m above ground level. What is the minimum length of ladder that should be issued to the workers?   (NEAB)

Q15

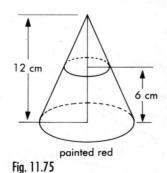

12 cm

6 cm

painted red

Fig. 11.75

The cone in Fig. 11.75 has a base radius of 5 cm and a vertical height of 12 cm. A circle is drawn on the surface at a vertical height of 6 cm. The surface below the circle is painted red. What area, in cm², is painted red? Take π = 3.14.   (MEG)

Q16

i) In Fig. 11.76 *a* = 7 and *b* = 24.
   Calculate the value of *c*.

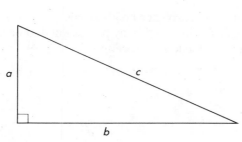

Fig. 11.76

a	b	c
3	4	5
5	12	13
7	24	
9	40	41
11	60	61
13	84	85
15		113
17		

Table 11.2

ii) Use your answer to part i) to complete the third row in the table.

iii) By considering the patterns in the rows and the columns of Table 11.2, complete the remaining rows. (NEAB)

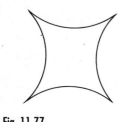

Fig. 11.77

Q17

The shape in Fig. 11.77 shows the plan of a flower-bed. It is formed from four quarter circles, each radius 5 m. Calculate the perimeter of the flower-bed, taking $\pi = 3.1$.

Q18

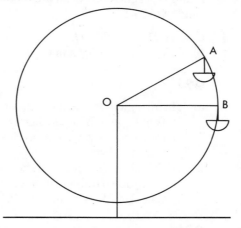

Fig. 11.78

The Big Wheel in a fairground, see Fig. 11.78, has two chairs shown. The horizontal radius OB is 11 m and the vertical height of A above OB is 5.5m.

a) Show that the angle AOB is 30°.

b) Calculate the distance travelled by a chair when the Big Wheel rotates through 30°. (NISEAC)

Q19

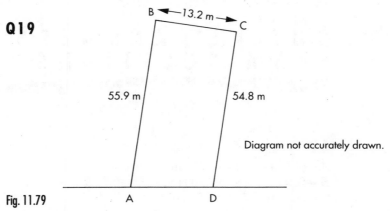

Fig. 11.79

The diagram represents the Leaning Tower of Pisa.

AB = 55.9 m,   BC = 13.2 m   and CD = 54.8 m.
AD is horizontal.
Angles B and C are right angles.

a) Calculate the angle the tower makes with AD.

b) Find the length of AD. (ULEAC)

Q20

A space station, S, is in orbit at a height of 4000 km above the Earth's surface. The Earth may be assumed to be a sphere of a radius 6400 km, with centre O.

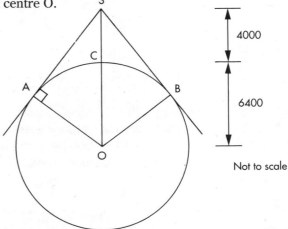

Not to scale

Fig. 11.80

A and B are the ends of an arc on the surface of the Earth, just visible from the satellite. Angle $OAS = 90°$

a) Calculate angle AOS.
b) Calculate the length of the arc ACB. (SEG)

Q21

a) The distance between the point $P(3, 4, 0)$ and the point $Q(3, 4, 12)$ is 12 units.
   i) Write down the coordinates of three other points which are 12 units from Q.
   ii) Describe fully the geometrical figure formed by the set of points which are 12 units from Q.
b) i) Calculate the length of the line from the origin $O(0, 0, 0)$ to the point $Q(3, 4, 12)$.
   ii) Write down the coordinates of the point R on the positive z-axis such that $RQ = OQ$.
   iii) Calculate the size of angle OQR. (MEG)

Q22

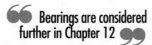
Bearings are considered further in Chapter 12

Two lightships, A and B are 30 km apart. The bearing of A from B is 120°. A yachtsman at Y finds that the bearing of A is 140°, and the bearing of B is 246°. Calculate the distance of Y from A. (SEG)

OUTLINE ANSWERS TO EXAM QUESTIONS

A1

$A = (4 \times 6) + (2 \times 4) = 32$ cm².
$B = (2 \times 9) + (4 \times 3) = 30$ cm².
$C = (2 \times 16) + 7 + 15 = 54$ cm².

A2

Because $\sqrt{(2^2 + 3.5^2)} = \sqrt{(16.25)} = 4.03$, to two significant figure accuracy, the answer is 4.0, or 4 m.

A3

a) $BE = 8 \sin 70 = 7.5$ cm,
b) Area $= 10 \times 7.5 = 75$ cm².

A4

$\sqrt{2500} = 50$ cm.

A5

a) Circumstance = $\pi D = \pi \times 2 = 6.28$ ft.
b) i) $70 \times \pi \times 2 = 440$ ft (rounded off)   ii) 400 ft.

A6

a) i) arc $AB = \pi D = 10\pi$;   ii) arc $CD = \pi D = 12\pi$

b) i) arc $AB = \dfrac{\theta}{360} \times 2 \times \pi \times r$;   ii) arc $CD = \dfrac{\theta}{360} \times 2 \times \pi \times (r + 12)$.

c) i) From $AB = 10\pi = \dfrac{\theta}{360} \times 2\pi r$; and $CD = 12\pi = \dfrac{\theta}{360} \times 2\pi(r + 12)$

$$\frac{10\pi}{2\pi r} = \frac{\theta}{360} = \frac{5}{r} \qquad \frac{12\pi}{2\pi(r + 12)} = \frac{\theta}{360} = \frac{6}{r + 12}$$

hence $\dfrac{\theta}{360} = \dfrac{5}{r} = \dfrac{6}{r + 12}$

hence $5r + 60 = 6r$; giving $r = 60$ cm.

ii) Substitute back into one of the equations to get $\theta = 30°$.

A7

a) There are many ways to explain this. One of them is:
   A is on a bearing of $(180 + 067) = 247°$ from S.
   B is on a bearing of $(180 + 337) - 360 = 157°$ from S.
   Hence the difference between A and B is $247 - 157 = 90°$.

b) from $\triangle ABS$, in Fig. 11.81
   $AS = 5 \cos 23 = 4.6$ m.

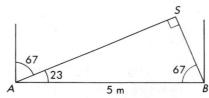

Fig. 11.81

c) $SB = 5 \cos 67 = 2.0$ m.
d) The ship will sail in a circle of diameter AB.

e) $\angle SAB = \cos^{-1} \frac{3}{5} = 53°$ (to nearest degree) so the bearing will be $90 - 53° = 37°$.

A8

a) $TB = 270 \tan 5 = 23.6$ m.
b) Use cosine rule to give

$$AD = \sqrt{(270^2 + 250^2 - 2 \times 270 \times 250 \times \cos 57)} = 249 \text{ m.}$$

c) Use sine rule to give $BC = \dfrac{250 \times \sin(180 - 37 - 93)}{\sin 37} = 318$ m.
d) Use sine rule to give $A = \frac{1}{2} \times 250 \times 270 \times \sin 57 = 28\,300$ m² = 2.83 hectares.

A9

From Fig. 11.82

$BC = 120 \tan 54° = 165$ m

$AC = \dfrac{120}{\cos 54} = 204$ m.

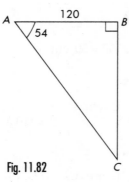

Fig. 11.82

A10

a) $h \tan 78$ or $h \times 4.7(\ldots)$.
b) $h \tan 22$ or $h \times 0.404(\ldots)$.
c) $h \times 4.7(\ldots) + h \times 0.404(\ldots) = 50 = h \times 5.108(\ldots)$,
   $h = 50 \div 5.108(\ldots) = 9.787(\ldots)$
   round off to 9.8 cm.

A11

You should have sketched a semi-circle with a right-angled triangle ABC.

Hence $BC = \sqrt{50^2 - 14^2} = 48$ cm

A12

From Fig. 11.83:

Area of sector $= \dfrac{270}{360} \times \pi \times (0.5)^2$
$= 0.589$ m²
Area of triangle $= \frac{1}{2}(0.5) \times 0.5$
$= 0.125$ m²
Total area of table $= 0.714$ m² or 7140 cm²

Arc length $BD = \dfrac{270}{360} \times \pi \times 1$
$= 2.356$ m.
Straight length

$BD = \sqrt{(0.5^2 + 0.5^2)} = 0.707$ m.
Total strip needed $= 3.06$ m or 306 cm.

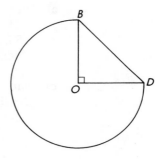

Fig. 11.83

A13

a) i) $4\pi r^2 = 4 \times \pi \times (0.7)^2 = 6.16$ cm²   ii) $\frac{4}{3}\pi r^3 = \frac{4}{3} \times \pi \times (0.7)^3 = 1.44$ cm³
b) Volume of pyramid = 1436.755, using the accurate answer in calculator for part a) ii).

Base of pyramid $= \dfrac{1436.755 \times 3}{25}$ (from volume $= \frac{1}{3}$ base $\times$ height)
$= 172.4106$.

Length of base $= \sqrt{172.(\ldots)} = 13.1$ cm
Area of one triangle face of pyramid $= \frac{1}{2} \times 13.1 \times l$ (l = slant height).

Slant height $= \sqrt{\left(25^2 + \left(\dfrac{13.1}{2}\right)^2\right)} = 25.8(\ldots)$.

Area of one triangle face = 169.3 cm²
Total surface area $= (4 \times 169.3) + 172.4106 = 850$ cm².

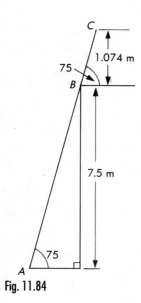

Fig. 11.84

A14

In Fig. 11.84, the length of the ladder up to the top of the building is given by:

$$AB = \frac{7.5}{\sin 75} = 7.76(\ldots).$$

Ladder length above landing place is given by:

$$BC = \frac{1.074}{\sin 75} = 1.11(\ldots).$$

Total ladder minimum
$= AB + BC = 8.88$ m.

A15

Original surface area given by $\pi r l = \pi \times 5 \times 13 = 204.(\ldots)$.
 Top cut off surface area given by $\pi \times 2.5 \times 6.5 = 51.(\ldots)$.
 Hence painted area = 153 cm².

A16

 i) $c = \sqrt{(7^2 + 24^2)} = 25$
 ii) Table 11.3 is filled in as:

a	b	c
3	4	5
5	12	13
7	24	25
9	40	41
11	60	61
13	84	85
15	112	113
17	144	145

Table 11.3

The c is always one more than the b. The b numbers have differences of 4, 8, 12, 16 … .

A17

The four quarter circles give the same perimeter as a full circle of radius 5 m, which gives a perimeter of $\pi \times 2 \times 5 = 31$ m.

A18

a) From Fig. 11.85: $\sin x = \dfrac{5.5}{11} = 0.5$
    inv sin (sin⁻¹) gives $x = 30°$

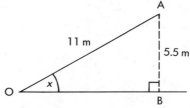

Fig. 11.85

b) The arc length AB is given by $\dfrac{30}{360} \times \pi \times 22 = 5.76$ m.

A19

a) $\tan x = \dfrac{13.2}{(55.9 - 54.8)} = \dfrac{13.2}{1.1}$

    $x = 85.2°$

b) $\sqrt{(1.1^2 + 13.2^2)} = 13.24$ m

A20

a) OS = 4000 + 6400 = 10400
   OA = 6400

   $\cos AOS = \dfrac{6400}{10400}, \quad AOS = 52°$

b) $\dfrac{104}{360} \times 2\pi \times 6400 = 11600$ km $(104 = 2 \times 52°)$

A21

a) i) Some possible answers are (3, 4, 24), (15, 4, 12), (3, 16, 12)
    ii) a sphere of radius 12 units with centre (3, 4, 12)

b) i) $\sqrt{(3^2 + 4^2 + 12^2)} = 13$ units
    ii) (0, 0, 24)
    iii) Use the cosine rule, $\cos OQR = \dfrac{13^2 + 13^2 - 24^2}{2.13.13}$

               OQR = 134.8°

A22

By considering the bearings, see fig. 11.86.
The angles in BAY can be found.
BAY = 180 − (106 + 54) = 20°

Use sine rule $\dfrac{BY}{\sin 20} = \dfrac{30}{\sin 106}$

$BY = \dfrac{30 \times \sin 20}{\sin 106} = 10.7$ m.

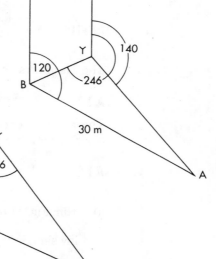

Fig. 11.86

LEVEL CHECKLIST

For the level	You should be able to do the following
4	Understand perimeter.
5	Find areas of simple shapes. Find volumes of simple solids.
6	Understand and use bearings. Find the areas of circles.
7	Use co-ordinates to locate positions in 3-D. Understand and apply Pythagoras theorem. Calculate lengths in plane and solid shapes.
8	Use trigonometry in right angled triangles.
9	Calculate with trigonometry in 3-D situations. Use the relationships between similar shapes of length, area and volume. Calculate lengths and areas in sectors. Calculate areas and volumes in cylinders, spheres, and cones. Find the trig ratios for all angles.
10	Use the sine and cosine rules to solve problems.

A STUDENT'S ANSWER WITH EXAMINER'S COMMENTS

Question
The circle shown has centre O and radius 6 cm.
PB has length 8 cm.

Calculate a) the size of the angle PAB
b) the length of AP.

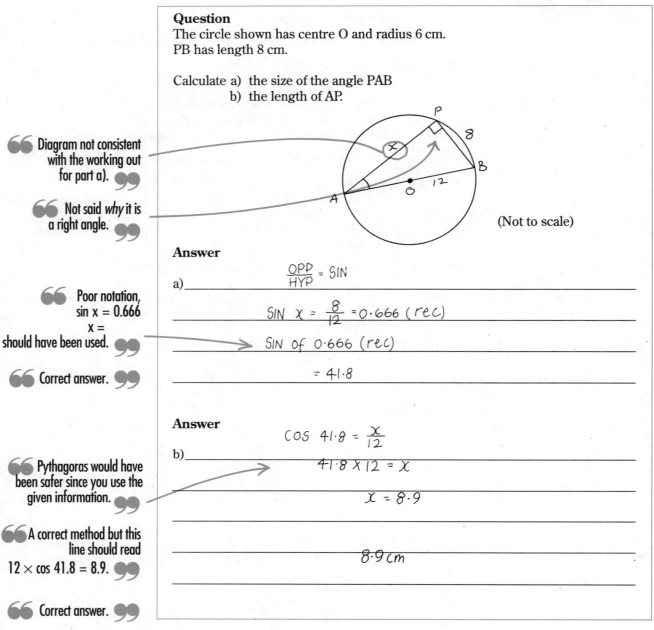

(Not to scale)

66 Diagram not consistent with the working out for part a). 99

66 Not said *why* it is a right angle. 99

Answer

a)
$$\frac{OPP}{HYP} = SIN$$

$$SIN \ x = \frac{8}{12} = 0.666 \ (rec)$$

$$SIN \ of \ 0.666 \ (rec)$$

$$= 41.8$$

66 Poor notation, sin x = 0.666 x = should have been used. 99

66 Correct answer. 99

Answer

b)
$$COS \ 41.8 = \frac{x}{12}$$

$$41.8 \times 12 = x$$

$$x = 8.9$$

$$8.9 \ cm$$

66 Pythagoras would have been safer since you use the given information. 99

66 A correct method but this line should read
$12 \times \cos 41.8 = 8.9$. 99

66 Correct answer. 99

R E V I E W   S H E E T

✏ Complete the following table for each rectangle (all units are in cm or cm²).

	Length	Breadth	Perimeter	Area
a)	6	4		
b)	10	8		
c)	10			30
d)		3		21

✏ Complete the following table for each triangle. (All units are in cm or cm².)

	Area	Base	Vertical Height
a)		6	8
b)	36		3
c)	108	36	
d)		3	63

✏ Complete the following table for each parallelogram. (All units are in cm or cm².)

	Base	Vertical Height	Area
a)	6	4	
b)	9		27
c)		13	65
d)	3.5	2.5	

✏ Complete the following table for each trapezium. (All units are in cm or cm².)

	Vertical Height	Parallel Side 1	Parallel Side 2	Area
a)	8	5	6	
b)		8	4	36
c)	6		11	54
d)	10	4		90

✏ Complete the table for each circle

	Radius	Diameter	Circumference	Area
a)	7 cm			
b)	10 m			
c)		28 mm		
d)		8.4 cm		
e)			88 cm	
f)			220 m	

Calculate the total surface areas and volumes of the following shapes:

a)

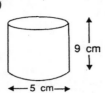

b)

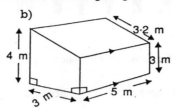

 Find the volumes of the following shapes:

a) Pyramid with square base of length 7 cm and height of 12 cm

b) Cone with a base radius of 4 cm and a height of 15 cm

 Find the surface areas of the following solids:

a)

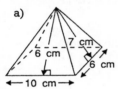

b)

 Find the volume and the surface area of:

a) a sphere with radius 5 cm

b) a hemisphere with diameter 12 cm

 In each triangle below, calculate the marked length:

 In each triangle below, calculate the marked angle:

DRAWING

TRIANGLES
RECTANGLES
QUADRILATERALS
CONSTRUCTIONS
LOCI
BEARINGS

GETTING STARTED

The National Curriculum includes drawing, in particular geometrical type drawing. It is the intention of all GCSE examinations to test the use of geometry in conveying information and solving problems, often by means of drawing and measuring. So you do need to be able to draw certain shapes, and accurately!

You need to be able to use a *protractor* (sometimes called an angle measurer) to measure and draw acute, obtuse and even reflex angles. You must be able to use a pair of *compasses* to draw a circle or to measure a given distance. It is important that you can use a *set square* both to draw a right angle and to draw parallel lines. Of course you also need to be able to draw accurate lines and measure with a ruler. Be careful to use the *centre* of the marks on the ruler when you are using it to measure, or else you could be inaccurate.

When asked to draw or to construct a diagram, a common accuracy that is looked for is to be no more than 1 mm out on lengths of lines, and no more than 1 or 2 degrees out on angles. So be warned; be accurate, or you will certainly lose marks.

Only when you are confident that you can use these items of equipment can you be confident in your ability to draw accurately when necessary.

USEFUL DEFINITIONS

Right angle	An angle that measures 90°.
Acute angle	One that is less than 90°.
Obtuse angle	One that is between 90° and 180°.
Reflex angle	One that is between 180° and 360°.
∠	Shorthand for angle.
Quadrilateral	A shape with only four straight sides.
Trapezium	A quadrilateral with a pair of opposite sides parallel.
Parallelogram	A quadrilateral with both pairs of opposite sides parallel.
Polygon	A flat shape with many straight sides.
Pentagon	A polygon with five sides.
Hexagon	A polygon with six sides.
Octagon	A polygon with eight sides.
Vertex	The *sharp bit* of an angle.
Perpendicular	At right angles to.

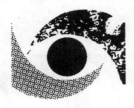

ESSENTIAL PRINCIPLES

You can be given certain information about a *triangle* and be expected to draw it accurately

ALL ANGLES KNOWN AND A SIDE GIVEN

66 Level 4 99

You should already know that the three angles of a triangle add up to 180°. So, if you are told two of the angles the other one is easily worked out. If one angle is 40° and another 60°, then the third angle must be 80° (i.e. 180 − (40 + 60)). It is usually best to try and draw the triangle so that the side *given* is the *base* of what you are to draw and then to draw lines at the angles specified.

WORKED EXAMPLE 1

Draw a triangle *ABC* where ∠*A* = 60°, ∠*B* = 40° and *AB* = 7 cm. It is helpful to *sketch* the triangle *ABC* first. This will help you to see exactly what you need to draw.

Start by drawing the 7 cm line with a ruler. This is the side *given* and you should draw it as the *base* of the triangle. Then use a *protractor* to draw a faint line at 60° from the left-hand end of the base line, and a faint line at 40° from the right-hand end. Draw these faint lines so that they cross over. When you know *where* they cross you can draw the lines more heavily up to that point, see Fig. 12.1.

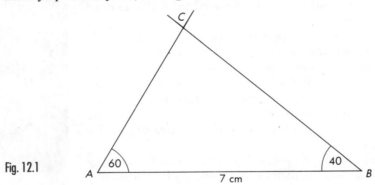

Fig. 12.1

TWO SIDES AND THE INCLUDED ANGLE

This is where you are told one angle and the length of each side next to the angle. It is common to draw the *longest side* as the *base*. Then draw a line at one end of the base at the required angle and to the required length. Now join up to complete the triangle.

WORKED EXAMPLE 2

Draw a triangle *ABC* where ∠ *A* = 50°, *AB* = 4 cm and *AC* = 6 cm.

Start by drawing the *longest side* as the *base* of the triangle, bottom side. Draw this as accurately as possible with a ruler, then use a *protractor* to draw a faint line at 50° at the left-hand end. Measure accurately 4 cm up this line and draw more heavily. You can then join this end to the right-hand end of the 6 cm base line. See Fig. 12.2.

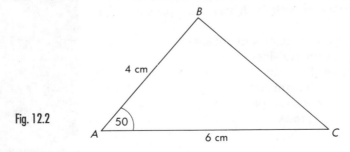

Fig. 12.2

ALL THREE SIDES GIVEN (NO ANGLES)

Again you would usually start by drawing the *longest side* as the *base* of the triangle. Then use a pair of *compasses* to *arc* each of the other two lengths.

Draw a triangle *ABC* where *AB* = 2 cm, *BC* = 4 cm and *AC* = 3.5 cm.
Start by drawing the base length of 4 cm as accurately as possible with your ruler. Now, you need your pair of compasses. Make the distance between the sharp end and the pencil end 3.5 cm.

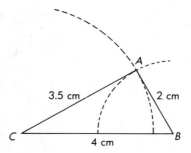

Fig. 12.3

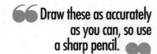

Then, with the sharp end positioned at the left-hand end of the base line draw a faint *quarter circle* above the base line, as shown by the dotted line in Fig. 12.3; we call this *arcing*. Repeat this for the distance of 2 cm from the other end. Where these two arcs *cross* is the point to which you draw the other two lines, giving you all three sides of the triangle.

EXERCISE 1

Draw the triangle *ABC* where:

> i) $\angle A$ = 70°, $\angle B$ = 30°, *BC* = 6 cm;
> ii) $\angle B$ = 60°, *AB* = 4.7 cm, *BC* = 5.6 cm;
> iii) *AB* = 4 cm, *BC* = 7 cm, *AC* = 5 cm.

2 > RECTANGLES

To construct a *rectangle*, all you need to be told is its *length* and *breadth*.
For example, to draw a rectangle that measures 8 cm by 4 cm you would start by drawing the *base length* of 8 cm. Then faintly draw the angles of 90° at each end, either by *set square* or *protractor*. Measure 4 cm up each line, then join the tops to give you the rectangle.

3 > QUADRILATERALS

You could be asked to construct a *quadrilateral* to some particular size. You would be given sufficient information to allow you to start with a *base* line and angles on either side, like drawing a triangle with two angles and a side given. The length of at least one other side would be given. This can be drawn in *after* faint lines have been drawn from each end of the base line at the appropriate angles.

EXERCISE 2

Construct the quadrilateral *ABCD* where *AB* = 4 cm, *AD* = 10 cm, *CD* = 7 cm, $\angle A$ = 70°, $\angle D$ = 80°. Measure the length of *BC*.

4 > CONSTRUCTIONS

Level 6

When asked to *construct*, you need to show *how* you have constructed the line or shape, otherwise the examiner will assume that you have guessed or used a protractor and you will lose marks.
The constructions given here are the ones expected to be used in the examination. Of course other suitable alternative *constructions* will always gain full marks also.

LINE BISECTOR

Fig. 12.4 illustrates how to cut the line *AB* *exactly in half*, in other words to *bisect* it. Set your compasses to about three-quarters of the length of the line *AB*, and with the sharp point at one end draw a faint semi-circle; then repeat from the other end keeping the compass arc the same. You need to find out where the two semi-circles cross over. The straight line between these points will give the *line bisector*.

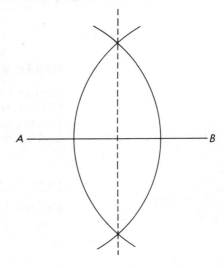

Fig. 12.4

> An example of *arcing*

> Draw these as accurately as you can, so use a sharp pencil.

ANGLE BISECTOR

Fig. 12.5 illustrates how to bisect the angle *PQR*. With your compasses set at about 2 cm, put the sharp end at the vertex of the angle, *Q*, and arc the angle as shown with a faint line. At both points where this arc cuts the *sides* of the angle, and using the sharp end of the compasses, draw another faint arc across the angle as shown. Where these *cross*, join to the vertex at *Q*. The resulting line is the line that bisects the angle, i.e. cuts it in half.

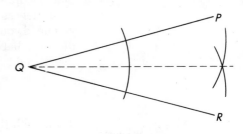

Fig. 12.5

A RIGHT ANGLE

Often associated with a *perpendicular* line, a right angle can always be drawn with a set square, or more accurately with ruler and compasses, as shown in Fig. 12.6.

To construct a right angle at the point *D* on the line shown, you need two marks at *equal distances* on either side of the point (the line may well need extending to do this).

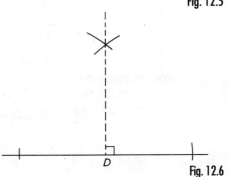

Fig. 12.6

The marks are made usually by compasses and simply arced through at either side. Then repeat what you would normally do to bisect a line but this time use the *two arcs* you've just made on the horizontal line for the sharp point of your compasses. You don't need to draw full semi-circles as we are only interested in *one side* of the line – that side on which we want to construct the right angle. Find where the arcs you have drawn cross over. Join up with the point *D* and you have your right angle.

A 60° ANGLE

To construct an angle of 60° at point *E* on the line *EF* shown in Fig. 12.7, you can set your compasses to any distance you like. Then with the sharp end at point *E* draw faintly the quarter circle that arcs through *EF*. Where this has cut *EF*, put the sharp end of the compasses (keep it the same distance again!) and draw the arc faintly that goes from *E* and cuts through the first arc. Where these *cross* you can draw a straight line to point *E* and you have your angle of 60°.

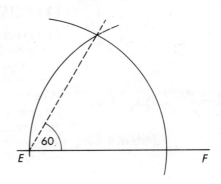

Fig. 12.7

OTHER ANGLES

You can now construct many more angles. If you bisect a right angle you can make 45°, and you can bisect again to make $22\frac{1}{2}°$, or you can bisect 60° to make 30°, and bisect again to make 15°. If you really wish to (it is fun to try!) you can put these together to create angles like 75°, (45+30) or (60+15).

EXERCISE 3

Construct angles of: i) 30°;   and   ii) 75°.

A PERPENDICULAR LINE FROM A POINT

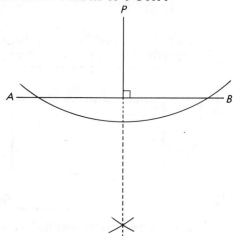

Fig. 12.8

In the diagram shown here, there is a line *AB*. We are going to construct the *perpendicular line* from point *P* to this line. Use your compasses to draw as wide an arc as you can cutting *AB* at two points, with *P* as the centre of that arc. Then from *each point on AB that you have arced*, and using the same compass opening, make an arc *under* the line *AB* as shown. The two arcs will cross, giving you the point from which to draw the perpendicular line from *P* to the line *AB*.

---

5 ›   LOCI

Loci are the paths of moving points that usually have some pattern to them. You are quite likely to be asked to find the locus of a point, but there are some locus situations that you ought to know to start off with.

> Singular *Locus* plural *Loci*

The *locus* of a point moving so that it is a *constant distance* from:

1   a point A; is a circle (see Fig. 12.9).

> Level 7

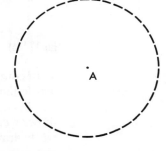

Fig. 12.9

2   two fixed points, A and B; is the perpendicular bisector of the line joining those two points (see Fig. 12.10).

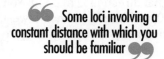

Fig. 12.10

3   a line AB; is a 'racetrack' shape, made up of two parallel lines and two semi-circles (see Fig. 12.11).

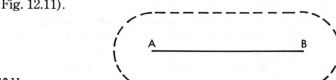

Fig. 12.11

4   two lines AB and DC; is the angle bisector of the angle that both lines subtend to (see Fig. 12.12).

> Some loci involving a constant distance with which you should be familiar

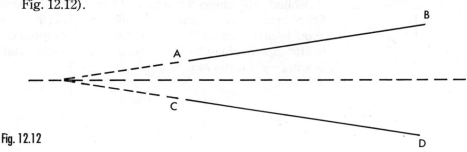

Fig. 12.12

WORKED EXAMPLE 4

Draw the locus of the point P which is always 1 cm away from the rectangle ABCD in Fig. 12.13.

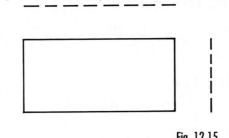

Fig. 12.13

You can see from Fig. 12.14 that the distances easily worked out are those vertically perpendicular 1 cm from the straight edges.

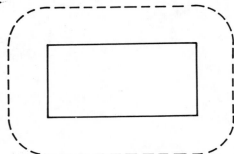

Fig. 12.14

Fig. 12.15

We then need to consider the point, P, 1 cm away from each vertex A, B, C and D. These will be *quarter circles* joining the given straight lengths already to give the final locus as in Fig. 12.15.

WORKED EXAMPLE 5

Two pegs A and B are fixed in the ground a distance of 5 metres apart. A rope is tied to each peg leaving 6 metres of rope loose. A peg is put into the ground at a point P so that this 6 metres of rope is taut, as shown in Fig. 12.16a). Sketch, using 1 cm to 1 m, the locus of this point P.

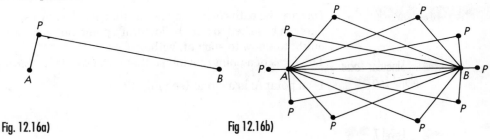

Fig. 12.16a)   Fig 12.16b)

With compasses we can find various positions of P as shown in Fig. 12.16b). Each point was found by finding the *vertex* of a triangle which has its base between the two pegs A and B, and where the top two sides add up to 6 cm. We can now see a pattern and could draw an *oval shape* going through each point P. This is then the *locus* of the point P when we've drawn that shape in.

EXERCISE 4

Construct an equilateral triangle of side 4 cm, then draw the locus of the point, P, which is 1 cm away from the triangle (and not inside it).

6 > BEARINGS

 Level 6

Fig. 12.17

If you have ever been out walking on the hilltops when the mist has come down you will realise how important it is to be able to read a *compass*, as shown in Fig. 12.17. On a compass the magnetic needle moves round to point towards the North Pole (not to the north on your compass). The compass then needs to be rotated so that the needle *does* point towards the N on the compass. Then, by moving your map around so that it too is pointing to the north (there should be an arrow on the map indicating north), you can tell which way you should be walking, or sailing or even flying!

Around your compass you may well see other numbers like 005, 080, 260. These are 3 figure bearings and represent the angle from north which that direction is making. You should see the east will be 090, south-east is 135, south is 180, west is 270 and north-west is 315°. You ought to be able to put any of the eight main compass points into a 3-figure bearing – see if you can.

WORKED EXAMPLE 6

If you found yourself right in the middle of Whitwell wood, see Fig. 12.18, where all eight paths meet:

a)   Which path would you take to get to Firbeck Common? What is its bearing?
b)   Where do you come to if you take the north-west path?

a)   From the centre of the wood, draw or imagine a north line. Put your protractor on this to measure the angle between north and the path to Firbeck Common, you should read about 60°. Hence the path to Firbeck Common is the one on a bearing of 060°.
b)   The north-west path is the top left-hand corner one that leads to Bondhay Farm.

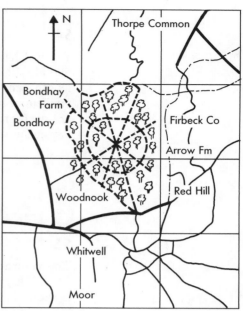

Fig. 12.18

BEARING BACK

If we know the bearing of a point *B* from a point *A*, then we can always find the bearing of *A* from *B* by adding on 180°.

WORKED EXAMPLE 7

James and John were out on a hill walk when James fell into a pothole! John walked on a bearing of 075° to find help. When he found help, on what bearing should he walk back in order to find the pothole that James had fallen down?

The bearing back again will be 180+75, which is 255°.

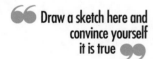 Draw a sketch here and convince yourself it is true

EXERCISE 5

Swinton is on a bearing of 160° from Wath. What is the bearing of Wath from Swinton? If Swinton is 1 km east of Wath, how far north is Wath from Swinton?

SOLUTIONS TO EXERCISES

S2

If you started with *AD* as the *base*, then drew *AB* at 70° and *DC* at 80°, you should have ended up with *BC* measuring 8 cm. However, if you are no more than 2 mm out, you have done well.

S3

i) You should have constructed 60° then bisected it.
ii) The simplest way would have been to construct 60°, then another angle of 60° on the first (to give 120°). Bisect, then bisect the angle again, to leave a 15° on top of a 60°, giving 75°. See Fig. 12.19.

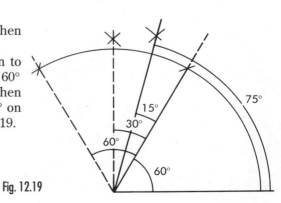

Fig. 12.19

S4

You will have a shape looking something like Fig. 12.20. With three straight sides of length 4 cm, each parallel to one side of the equilateral triangle, then the curved parts are each arcs of circles with radius 1 cm having the centres the vertices of the triangle.

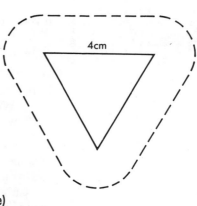

Fig. 12.20
(not to scale)

S5

The return bearing is 180+160, which is 340°. A diagram to help us with the next part is shown in Fig. 12.21. The angle marked is 20°, since 360–340 is 20°. You can either draw this accurately and measure the length *x*, or use trigonometry. Either way you should get an answer of 2.7 km.

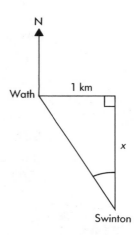

Fig. 12.21

EXAMINATION TYPE QUESTIONS

Q1

A girl, whose eyes are $1\frac{1}{2}$ metres above the ground, stands 12 metres away from a tall chimney. She has to raise her eyes 35° upwards from the horizontal to look directly at the top of the chimney.

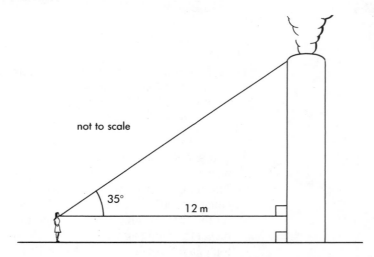

Fig. 12.22

not to scale

35°

12 m

Using a scale of 1 cm to represent 1 metre, find the height of the chimney by scale drawing.

(MEG)

Q2

A ship leaving port sails on a bearing of 060° for 100 km. It then sails due south for 120 km and then due east for a further 135 km.

a) Use a scale drawing (scale 1 cm : 20 km) to find:
   i) the overall distance travelled due east;
   ii) the overall distance travelled due south;
   iii) the bearing of the ship from its starting point.
b) Use trigonometry to calculate the answers for i), ii), iii) above.
c) Explain briefly any differences in the answers to a) and b).   (NISEAC)

Q3

a) You are facing due west and you turn clockwise to face north-east. Through how many degrees do you turn?
b) State two directions which are at right angles to south-west.

Q4

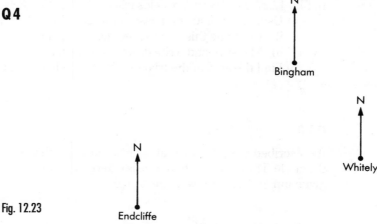

Fig. 12.23

From the sketch map in Fig. 12.23, with a scale 1 cm to 2 km:

a) find the bearing of Bingham from Endcliffe;
b) find the distance from Endcliffe to Whitely.   (NEAB)

Q5

A plane left an airport on a bearing of 060° flying a distance of 120 kilometres, landing at an airport to pick up vital medical supplies. The plane then flew for 250 kilometres on a bearing of 150°. What single journey must the plane now fly to return to its starting point?

Q6

A *mayday* call is heard by the three boats marked on Fig. 12.24 by dots: H, M and S. They can tell by the reception that the mayday call is nearer to ship M than it is to ship H, and the call is less than 3 km from ship S.

Draw an accurate plan of the position of the ships, using 1 cm to 1 km, and indicate all the possible positions of the mayday call.

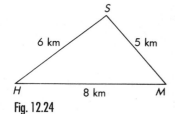

Fig. 12.24

Q7

At an exhibition, one of the buildings is in the shape of a pyramid with a square base, see Fig. 12.25.

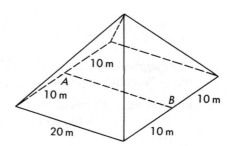

Fig. 12.25

The height is 8 m.
A vertical wall 3 m high is to be built up from *AB*. It touches the sloping sides. Make an accurate drawing of this wall. Use a scale of 1 cm to 2 m. (MEG)

Q8

Draw a rectangle with the same area as the trapezium in Fig. 12.26. Explain your answer.

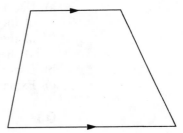

Fig. 12.26

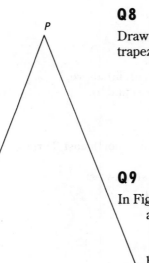

Fig. 12.27

Q9

In Fig. 12.27, *PQR* is an isosceles triangle with *PQ* = *PR*.
   a) Using ruler and compasses only, construct the bisector of angle *P*.
      i)   Continue this line to meet *QR* at a point *X*
      ii) Measure and write down the length of the line *PX*.
   b) Find the area of the triangle *PQR*, clearly indicating the method you have used. (NEAB)

Q10

An inscribed circle is one that is drawn inside a triangle where each side is a tangent to the circle. The centre of this circle is where the angle bisectors all intersect. In the triangle given in Fig. 12.28, draw an inscribed circle.

Fig. 12.28

Q11

Draw a circle radius 4 cm and construct a tangent to the circle at any point.

Q12

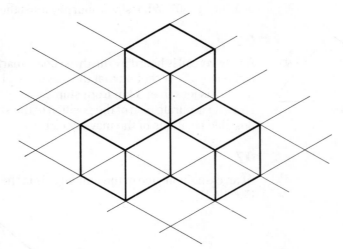

Fig. 12.29

The diagram above represents an arrangement of four equal cubes. There are three cubes on the bottom layer.

a) How many planes of symmetry has this arrangement?
b) The cube at the top is moved so that it is directly above a different cube in the bottom layer. (MEG)

On the isometric paper below, draw a diagram to show the four cubes in the new position.

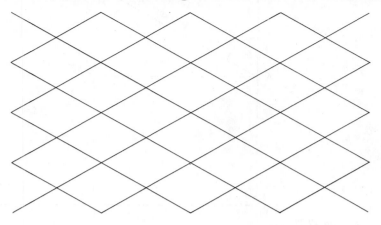

Fig. 12.30

Q13

A goat is tied to a rope 3 m long.

At the other end of the rope is a ring which can slide along a straight wire, PQ, which is 7 m long.

The goat is able to move along both sides of the wire and around both ends.

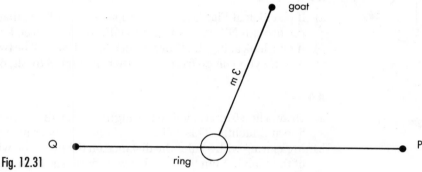

Fig. 12.31

Make a sketch to show the area of ground that the goat can reach.   (ULEAC)

OUTLINE ANSWERS TO EXAM QUESTIONS

A1

You can draw this picture quite accurately, then you can measure the height of the chimney as 9.9 m. Don't forget the girl's height of 1.5 m.

A2

a) Your diagram will look like that in Fig. 12.32.

Giving answers around:

 i) 222 km
 ii) 70 km
iii) 288°

b) i) Length AC = 100 cos 30 = 86.6
        Total east = 86.6+135 = 221.6 km
    ii) Length BC = 100 sin 30 = 50 km
        Total due south = 120–50 = 70 km.

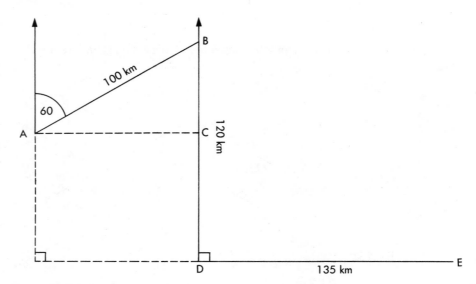

Fig. 12.32

iii) Angle AED given by $\tan^{-1} \frac{70}{2216} = 17.5°$
hence bearing = 270+17.5 = 287.5°

c) Any differences are due to drawing errors, and unavoidable. The most accurate ought to be from part b) the trigonometry.

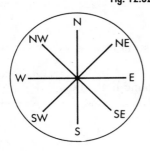

Fig. 12.33

A3

a) If you look at Fig. 12.33 or a compass, you will see that from due west clockwise you go through NW and N to get to NE, which is three lots of 45°, hence 135°.

b) Again, look at Fig. 12.33 or a compass, and 90° will be two compass points round either way. So you will go from SW either through S to SE, or through W onto NW.

A4

a) Draw a line from Endcliffe to Bingham, then measure the angle made from the north line at Endcliffe. This will be 45°, hence the bearing will be either 045° or north-east.

b) Measuring with a ruler the distance on the map, you will get 6 cm, and since the scale of the map is 1 cm to 2 km this will represent 12 km.

A5

If you draw this out to a suitable scale, you will end up with a drawing as shown in Fig. 12.34. The dotted line indicates the return journey which will be approximately 270 km on a bearing of 306°.

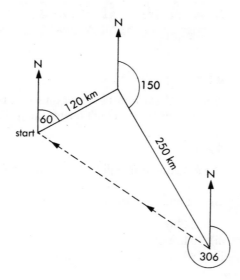

Fig. 12.34

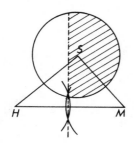

Fig. 12.35

A6

You can draw a triangle to the scale suggested and get a triangle the same shape (but larger) than the one shown in Fig. 12.35. If the call is nearer to *M* than *H*, then we need a bisector drawn between *H* and *M*, as we have done before, and the call is shown to be to the right of this line. As the call is less than 3 km from *S*, there will be a circle around *S* of radius 3 km in which the mayday call will lie. Hence we obtained the shaded part which is both nearer *M* than *H* and less than 3 km from *S*.

A7

You will need to construct the sloping sides by finding the apex of the pyramid first. Your diagram will be like that in Fig. 12.36.

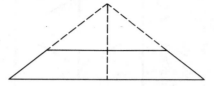

Fig. 12.36

The dotted line represents the construction lines to help you and as such should be very faint.

A8

One way is simply to measure the dimensions, calculate the areas and then draw a suitable rectangle! Another way is to find the halfway mark on each sloping side, and use this to mark the sides of the rectangle as in Fig. 12.37. Either way is acceptable as long as it is carefully explained.

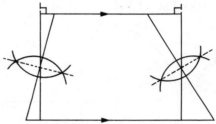

Fig. 12.37

A9

a) Construct the bisector and measure its length from *P* to *X*; this is 6.6 cm.
b) the area is found by $\frac{1}{2} \times$ base $\times$ height. The base measures 5 cm, hence
    area $= \frac{1}{2} \times 5 \times 6.6 = 16.5$ cm^2

A10

Bisect each angle carefully, and although only two bisectors are necessary, the third one acts as a check on the other two. Where they cross is the centre, then simply draw the circle.

A11

Draw the circle, choose a point on the circumference, then draw in, faintly, the radius to this point. Construct a line perpendicular to the radius at this point which can be extended to give the tangent.

A12

a) 3 planes of symmetry
b) See Fig. 12.38

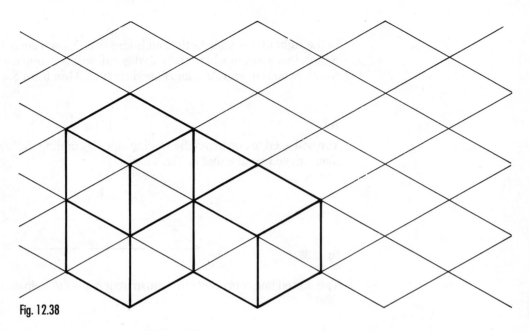

Fig. 12.38

This is one of two possible answers.

A13

See Fig. 12.39 (not to scale)

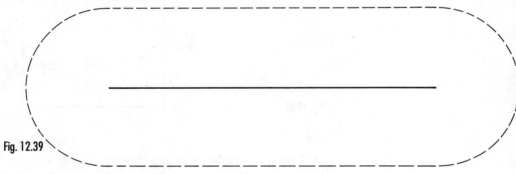

Fig. 12.39

LEVEL CHECKLIST

For the level	You should be able to do the following
4	Know that the angles of a triangle add up to 180°.
5	Measure and draw angles to the nearest degree.
6	Use 2D representation of 3D objects. Construct bisectors, right angles, 60° and perpendicular lines.
7	Determine the locus of a point which is moving subject to a rule.

A STUDENT'S ANSWER WITH EXAMINER'S COMMENTS

Question

i) In the rectangle shown, draw accurately the sets:
   $P = \{X : XA = XB\}$ and $Q = \{Y : YA = 4.5 \text{ cm}\}$

ii) Given that $P \cap Q = \{H, K\}$, draw the circle that passes through B, H, and K.

iii) Find the area of triangle BHK in two different ways, stating clearly the methods you have used.

Comment on the degrees of accuracy of your answers.

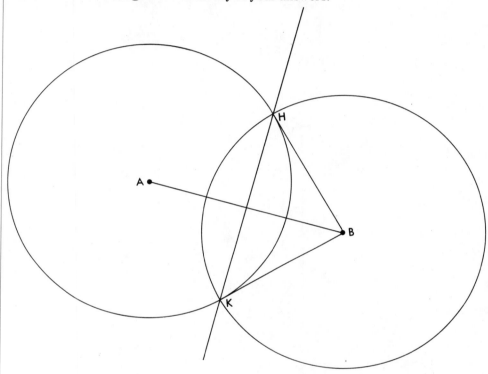

> **Good answer for i)**

> **Wrong answer for ii)**

> **Good. Two different ways used**

> **Would have been better to have *identified* the lengths used on the diagram.**

> **Comment too vague. Your answer should have stated that accuracy of one decimal place only is sufficient.**

Area of BHK = $\frac{1}{2}$ Base × perpendicular height
 = $\frac{1}{2}$ × $5\frac{1}{2}$ × 3.65
 = 10.04 cm²

Area of triangle (BHK) = $\frac{1}{2}$ × 4.4 × 4.4
  = 9.68 cm²

My degrees of accuracy in my answers are not too precise as the diagram has to be drawn precise to work totally properly, mine wasn't that precise.

R E V I E W   S H E E T

✎   Draw a triangle ABC where ∠ A = 60°,   ∠ B = 40° and AB = 7 cm

○

✎   Draw a triangle ABC where ∠ A = 50°, AB = 4 cm and AC = 6 cm

○

✎   Draw a triangle ABC, where AB = 2 cm, BC = 4 cm and AC = 3.5 cm

✎   Draw the *line bisector* to **AB**

A_____B

✎ Draw the *angle bisector* to angle PQR

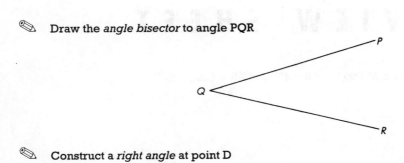

✎ Construct a *right angle* at point D

D

✎ Construct a 60° angle at point E

E   F

✎ Construct a perpendicular line from the point P to line AB

+ P

A

B

✎ Construct both triangles shown
(You may need to use separate paper)

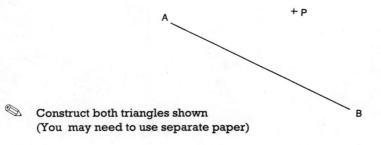 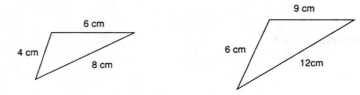

TRANSFORMATION GEOMETRY

GETTING STARTED

You will need to look carefully at exactly which parts of this chapter are in *your* syllabus. You will need to consider the *level* of the examination you are sitting. Only the *higher* levels will include *matrix transformations*, and its related parts.

The essence of *transformation geometry* is looking at how shapes change position and size according to certain rules. You will not be required to prove anything, but you will need to *describe* how a shape has changed, or to *actually change* the shape itself to the rules given.

There are some definite links in this chapter with the ideas of *symmetry* you met in Chapters 7 and 10. This connection is often used in actual examination questions.

USEFUL DEFINITIONS

Transformation	A change of position.
Reflection	A mirror image the other side of a line.
Rotation	A turn around some fixed point.
Translation	A slide *without* any turning.
Enlargement	A change in size (in mathematics an enlargement can be smaller!) to create a similar shape.
Matrix	A collection of numbers in some specific order.
Vector	A single list in a particular order.
Tessellation	A regular pattern created from shapes that leave no spaces at all.

ESSENTIAL PRINCIPLES

1 ▷ REFLECTIONS

Level 4

Tracing can be helpful

When you are asked to *reflect* a shape in a given line, then there are two ways of doing it.

For example, if you were asked to reflect the rectangle in the line *AB* shown in Fig. 13.1, you could trace it, then flip the tracing paper over so that the reflection appears under the line with the tracing of line *AB* exactly on top of the original (especially *A* on top of *A* and *B* on top of *B*). Then, with a pencil, press down on each corner of the tracing to make a *dint* in the paper underneath. Take the tracing away, join up the dots and this will give you the reflection. If you do this carefully it is the easiest way.

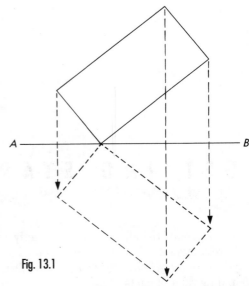

Fig. 13.1

The other way is to draw faint lines from each vertex of the rectangle perpendicular to the line *AB*, then measure the distance from each point to the line, and its reflection is exactly the same distance away from *AB* the other side of *AB* along this faint perpendicular line you've just drawn. Put a dot at this position. Do this for *each vertex* then join up the dots. On squared paper particularly this method is the most accurate.

Sometimes called the mirror line

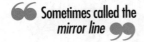

When you have completed a reflection, by either method, you can check it by making sure that the line you reflected on (sometimes called the mirror line) is a line of symmetry for your drawing, and hence the reflected shape will have all its dimensions and angles the same as before – it's just the position that is different.

2 ▷ ROTATIONS

You need to be able to *rotate* any given shape through 90°, either way, and through 180°.

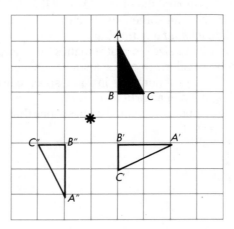

Fig. 13.2

For example, Fig. 13.2 shows the triangle *ABC* has been rotated about the centre of rotation *, through 90° clockwise, (S turn) to position *A'B'C'*, then another 90° clockwise, which is equivalent to a rotation of 180° to *A"B"C"*.

Level 4

Again tracing may help

One way to do the 90° rotation is again to use tracing paper and trace the shape you are to rotate with the centre of rotation marked with a suitable + (following the lines of the grid). Then with your pencil point on the centre of rotation, turn the tracing paper until you can see the + back on top of itself having turned 90°. How you can press on each vertex of the triangle, take off the tracing paper and join up the dots. Remember that if you are working on squared paper the shape will end up with the vertices on the corners of the squares and that each line of the new triangle will have turned through 90° also. The resultant shape should be the same size, have the same angles, but just be in a different position. To do the 180° rotation you would DO the same, but of course turn through 180°.

The other way to rotate 90° is to, again, look at the position of the vertex from the centre of rotation and, for example, if *A* is 3 up and 1 to the right, then it rotates to 3 to the right and 1 down from the centre of rotation. This works for all points, and then join them up. To rotate the 180°, point *A* this time will change to 3 down and 1 to the left, and so on for the other points. When you've practised and mastered it, this last technique is by far the easiest and quickest!

The idea of an *enlargement* is to make a shape larger and in a specific place. Hence you will be given a *scale factor* which tells you how many times bigger each line will be, and a *centre of enlargement* which will determine where the enlargement ends up!
For example, to enlarge the shaded square in Fig. 13.3a) with a scale factor of 2 from the centre of enlargement *, the distance from the centre of enlargement to each vertex in the shape is multiplied by 2, i.e. doubled.

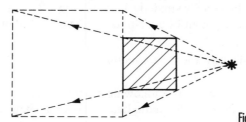

Fig. 13.3 a)

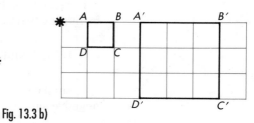

Fig. 13.3 b)

This is shown on Fig. 13.3a) by the faint dotted lines. The enlarged shape will have all its dimensions multiplied by the scale factor, but keep all its angles the same. In other words it is a *similar* shape.

Enlargements will tend to be more accurate if done on squared paper when you can use the lines instead of measuring.

For example, in Fig. 13.3b) we see a square being enlarged from * with a scale factor of 3.

Since *A* is one square along from *, then its new position *A'* will be $1 \times 3 = 3$ squares along. Since *C* is 2 along and 1 down, its new position *C'* will be $2 \times 3 = 6$ along and $1 \times 3 = 3$ down.

You can use either way for any positive scale factor, even $1\frac{1}{2}$, when you simply multiply distances from the centre of enlargement by $1\frac{1}{2}$. However, if you are asked to do an enlargement by $\frac{1}{2}$, then the procedure is the same, only this time you will end up with a shape only half its size.

For example, if, in Fig. 13.3b) we were asked to enlarge the shape *A'B'C'D'* from centre of enlargement * with a scale factor of $\frac{1}{3}$, then the result would be the drawing of square *ABCD* as shown.

NEGATIVE ENLARGEMENT

This is the most difficult one, and is often done badly. So go carefully.

You have seen how to transform a shape with a positive enlargement. However, you could be given a *negative* scale factor. In that case we draw the lines back through the centre of the enlargement and then enlarge as shown in Fig. 13.4 in an enlargement of the small triangle through * with an enlargement of – 2. Notice how, with a negative scale factor, the enlarged shape has ended up *upside down* but still a similar shape.

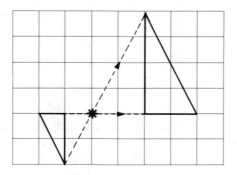

Fig. 13.4

4 ⟩TRANSLATIONS

A *translation* is a movement along the plane without any rotating, reflecting or enlarging. It is described by a movement horizontally and a movement vertically which we put together as a *vector*.

Level 8

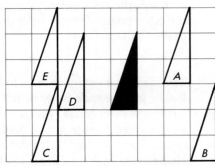

Fig. 13.5

For example, the heavily shaded triangle in Fig. 13.5 has been translated to position A by moving 2 to the right and 1 up. Notice that every point on the triangle has moved this way. We write this movement as a vector $\begin{pmatrix} 2 \\ 1 \end{pmatrix}$

In a similar way we write the following translations. Notice how and when we use a negative sign. Each one is from the heavily shaded triangle.

To B we move 3 to the right and 2 down $= \begin{pmatrix} 3 \\ -2 \end{pmatrix}$.

To C we move 3 to the left and 2 down $= \begin{pmatrix} -3 \\ -2 \end{pmatrix}$.

To D we move 2 to the left only $= \begin{pmatrix} -2 \\ 0 \end{pmatrix}$.

To E we move 3 to the left and 1 up $= \begin{pmatrix} -3 \\ 1 \end{pmatrix}$.

EXERCISE 1

On a grid with x from -5 to 8, and y from -6 to 9 draw the triangle with vertices (corners) $A(1, 1)$, $B(1, 3)$, $C(2, 1)$. On this triangle *do* the following transformations:

i) reflection in the x-axis ($y = 0$);
ii) rotation, around $(0, 0)$, of 90° anticlockwise;

iii) translation of $\begin{pmatrix} 3 \\ -4 \end{pmatrix}$;

iv) enlargement scale factor 3 from centre of enlargement $(3, 0)$;
v) enlargement scale factor -2 from centre of enlargement $(0, 0)$;

None of your answers should be overlapping another!

5 ⟩ COMBINATION OF TRANSFORMATIONS

If we *combine* two transformations, say a rotation of 90° clockwise around the origin and a reflection in the y-axis, then the *order* in which we do this will make a difference.

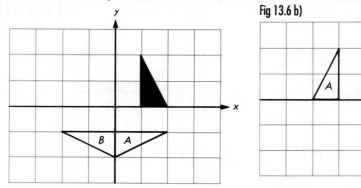

Fig. 13.6 a)

Fig 13.6 b)

For example, this rotation and enlargement have been combined to give the following situations on the same triangle. Fig. 13.6a) shows the rotation of shaded triangle to A followed by the reflection to give B. Fig. 13.6b) shows the reflection to A followed by the rotation to give B. The same transformations, when combined in a different way, give different results, hence the *order* in which you combine transformations is important. However, this is not always so; see if you can find some combinations that make no difference to what is done first.

6 ⟩ TESSELLATIONS

Not really a transformation at all, but a pattern. A *tessellation* is a regular pattern with *one* shape that could cover a larger area without leaving gaps, except at the very edge. Below are some examples of tessellations.

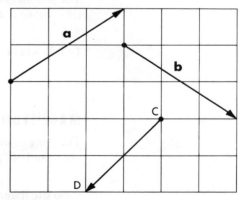

Fig. 13.7

Each tessellation is made from one plane shape and could continue its pattern to fill in a large area leaving no gaps. It is true to say, and you can test it out for yourself, that every triangle and every quadrilateral will tessellate!

7 ⟩ VECTOR

A *vector* is a given displacement or movement. It has direction and a specific magnitude (size). Two vectors that are equal do not have to be in the same place, but they will be parallel.

VECTOR NOTATION

- Often a vector is referred to by a bold small case letter, e.g. **a**.
- Sometimes because of printing difficulties you will find a vector written with a squiggle underneath as **a̰**.
- Sometimes a vector is defined on a diagram as being the vector from a point A to a point B, hence the vector can be labelled $\overrightarrow{AB}$ or $-\overrightarrow{BA}$.
- Vectors are often referred to as *column vectors*, as on the grid, by use of horizontal displacement and vertical displacement.

> **The *top* number is movement horizontally, the *bottom* number is movement vertically**

For example, in Fig. 13.8:

$$\mathbf{a} = \begin{pmatrix} 3 \\ 2 \end{pmatrix} \quad \mathbf{b} = \begin{pmatrix} 3 \\ -2 \end{pmatrix}$$

$$\overrightarrow{CD} = \begin{pmatrix} -2 \\ -2 \end{pmatrix}$$

The *top* number in each column represents movement *horizontally*; + to the right and – to the left. The *bottom* number in each column represents movement *vertically*; + upwards and – downwards.

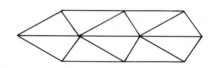

Fig. 13.8

VECTOR ADDITION AND SUBTRACTION

Look at Fig. 13.9 and note that **a** + **b** = **c**. If you look at the 'column vectors', then

where $\mathbf{a} = \begin{pmatrix} 1 \\ -2 \end{pmatrix}$ $\mathbf{b} = \begin{pmatrix} 2 \\ 3 \end{pmatrix}$, $\mathbf{a} + \mathbf{b} = \begin{pmatrix} 1 \\ -2 \end{pmatrix} + \begin{pmatrix} 2 \\ 3 \end{pmatrix} = \begin{pmatrix} 3 \\ 1 \end{pmatrix}$

which is **c**, hence this illustrates **a** + **b** = **c**

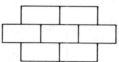

Fig. 13.9

Similarly if we looked at $\mathbf{a} - \mathbf{b} = \mathbf{d}$

then $\begin{pmatrix} 1 \\ -2 \end{pmatrix} - \begin{pmatrix} 2 \\ 3 \end{pmatrix} = \begin{pmatrix} -1 \\ -5 \end{pmatrix} = \mathbf{d}$

Notice on the grid in Fig. 13.10 how $-\mathbf{b}$ is the same size as $\mathbf{b}$ but the opposite direction.

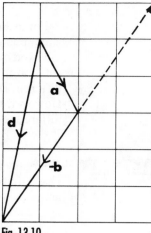

Fig. 13.10

VECTOR MULTIPLICATION

Where $\mathbf{a} = \begin{pmatrix} 3 \\ 1 \end{pmatrix}$ then $2\mathbf{a} = \begin{pmatrix} 6 \\ 2 \end{pmatrix}$ etc.

$2\mathbf{a} = \mathbf{a} + \mathbf{a}$ (See Fig. 13.11).

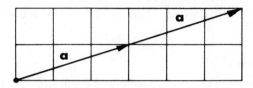

Fig. 13.11

POSITION VECTORS

The *position vector* of any point A, is the vector from some given reference point (usually the origin) to that given point A. It follows that the position vector of the co-ordinate

$(-1,3)$ will be $\begin{pmatrix} -1 \\ 3 \end{pmatrix}$

MAGNITUDE

The *magnitude* of a vector can be represented by a length in a given diagram. The magnitude of any column vector can be found by Pythagoras' theorem.

So the magnitude of the vector $\begin{pmatrix} x \\ y \end{pmatrix}$ is given by

$| \mathbf{a} | = \sqrt{(x^2 + y^2)}.$

$| \mathbf{a} |$ is often used as notation for the magnitude of vector $\mathbf{a}$.

EXERCISE 2

Where $\mathbf{x} = \begin{pmatrix} 3 \\ 4 \end{pmatrix}$ $\mathbf{y} = \begin{pmatrix} -4 \\ -1 \end{pmatrix}$ $\mathbf{z} = \begin{pmatrix} 2 \\ 7 \end{pmatrix}$

i) Calculate the magnitude of the vector $\mathbf{x} + \mathbf{y}$, i.e. $|\mathbf{x} + \mathbf{y}|$

ii) What is special about the vectors $\mathbf{x} + \mathbf{y}$ and $\mathbf{z} - \mathbf{x}$?

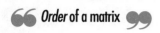

8 ⟩ MATRICES

A *matrix* is a collection of information in a specific order.

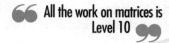
Order of a matrix

Eg. $\begin{pmatrix} 3 & 0 & 1 \\ 1 & 5 & 2 \end{pmatrix}$ is a 2 by 3 or (2×3) matrix, since it has 2 rows and 3 columns. This is called the *order* of the matrix.

ARITHMETIC

You may only *add* or *subtract* matrices with the same order, and then by combining corresponding positioned numbers.

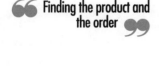
All the work on matrices is Level 10

Example: $\begin{pmatrix} 3 & 0 & 1 \\ 1 & 5 & 2 \end{pmatrix} + \begin{pmatrix} 4 & 2 & 7 \\ 0 & 1 & 3 \end{pmatrix} = \begin{pmatrix} 7 & 2 & 8 \\ 1 & 6 & 5 \end{pmatrix}$

Example: $\begin{pmatrix} 3 & 0 & 1 \\ 1 & 5 & 2 \end{pmatrix} - \begin{pmatrix} 4 & 2 & 7 \\ 0 & 1 & 3 \end{pmatrix} = \begin{pmatrix} -1 & -2 & -6 \\ 1 & 4 & -1 \end{pmatrix}$

To *multiply* two matrices you need first to consider their orders.

Example: Where $A = \begin{pmatrix} 1 & 2 & 3 & 4 \\ 5 & 6 & 7 & 8 \end{pmatrix}$ and $B = \begin{pmatrix} 0 & 3 & 7 \\ 9 & 1 & 0 \\ 2 & 6 & 3 \\ 5 & 4 & 6 \end{pmatrix}$

the order of A is (2×4) and the order of B is (4×3).

Finding the product and the order

You can evaluate the product AB since $(2 \times 4)(4 \times 3)$ has the middle two numbers the same, the end two numbers give the order of the answer, i.e. (2×3).

You then multiply the matrices by the 'diving board' technique (see Fig. 13.12). '*Go along then down*'. Find the product of *EACH ROW* with *EACH COLUMN* starting at the top and right. The final product of a row with a column is found by summing the individual products as you go along and down.

Fig. 13.12
'go along'   then   'down'

Example (see Fig. 13.13): To start multiplying A to B (i.e. AB) in the matrices above, the first row in A and the first column in B, combine to give

$(1 \times 0) + (2 \times 9) + (3 \times 2) + (4 \times 5)$
$= 0 + 18 + 6 + 20$
$= 44$

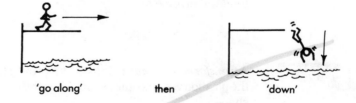

Multiplying first row and first column in respective matrices

Fig. 13.13

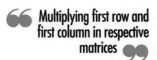

Since this is the product of first row with first column, its position in the answer matrix is first row, first column. You can now check out yourself, by continuing this process, that

the final answer to AB is given by $\begin{pmatrix} 44 & 39 & 40 \\ 108 & 95 & 104 \end{pmatrix}$

If you then tried to evaluate BA, consider the orders $(4 \times 3)(2 \times 4)$ you will see the middle two numbers are not the same and so this product cannot be done.

Identity matrix

The *identity matrix* is the one that multiplies to any other and leaves it unaltered.

It is $\begin{pmatrix} 1 & 0 \\ 0 & 1 \end{pmatrix}$ for a 2×2 matrix.

Inverse matrices

A matrix and its *inverse* will multiply together to give the identity matrix.

This is a complicated formula and one of those always given on the formula sheet if you have it in your syllabus.

It is defined as:

The inverse matrix of $\begin{pmatrix} a & b \\ c & d \end{pmatrix}$ is given by $\dfrac{1}{(ab - bc)}\begin{pmatrix} d & -b \\ -c & a \end{pmatrix}$

The bracket $(ad - bc)$ is often referred to as the *determinant*. If the determinant of a matrix is zero, then there is no inverse of that matrix.

WORKED EXAMPLE 1

Find the inverse of the matrix $\begin{pmatrix} 4 & 1 \\ 3 & 2 \end{pmatrix}$

Use the formula where $a = 4$, $b = 1$, $c = 3$ and $d = 2$

then the inverse is $\dfrac{1}{(4 \times 2 - 1 \times 3)}\begin{pmatrix} 2 & -1 \\ -3 & 4 \end{pmatrix} = \dfrac{1}{5}\begin{pmatrix} 2 & -1 \\ -3 & 4 \end{pmatrix} = \begin{pmatrix} 0.4 & -0.2 \\ -0.6 & 0.8 \end{pmatrix}$.

EXERCISE 3

Find the inverse of $\begin{pmatrix} 6 & 2 \\ 4 & 3 \end{pmatrix}$

9 ＞TRANSFORMATION MATRICES

A *transformation matrix* is usually a (2 by 2) matrix. If it is multiplied to a matrix containing the position vectors of any shape, then the resulting product will determine the transformed shape.

WORKED EXAMPLE 2

A transformation T is defined as

$$\text{T:}\begin{pmatrix} x \\ y \end{pmatrix} \rightarrow \begin{pmatrix} 1 & 0 \\ 0 & -1 \end{pmatrix}\begin{pmatrix} x \\ y \end{pmatrix}.$$

> 66 Exam questions are often phrased this way, do be familiar with it. 99

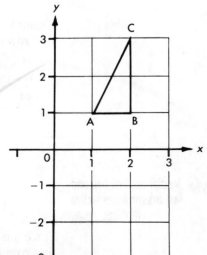

Fig. 13.14

Use this to transform the triangle in Fig. 13.14, then fully describe the transformation T.
By putting the position vectors of the triangle ABC into a matrix we can evaluate

$$
\begin{matrix} A & B & C \end{matrix} \qquad \begin{matrix} A' & B' & C' \end{matrix}
$$

$$
\begin{pmatrix} 1 & 0 \\ 0 & -1 \end{pmatrix}\begin{pmatrix} 1 & 2 & 2 \\ 1 & 1 & 3 \end{pmatrix} = \begin{pmatrix} 1 & 2 & 2 \\ -1 & -1 & -3 \end{pmatrix}
$$

Then plotting the transformed shape onto a diagram (see Fig. 13.15) gives us,

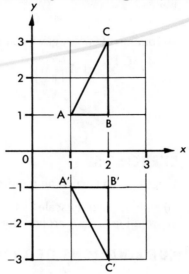

Fig. 13.15

which illustrates that T is a reflection in the X axis.

EXERCISE 4

By use of the triangle ABC in the worked example 1, fully describe transformations represented by the matrices

i) $\begin{pmatrix} 0 & 1 \\ 1 & 0 \end{pmatrix}$ ii) $\begin{pmatrix} 0 & -1 \\ 1 & 0 \end{pmatrix}$ iii) $\begin{pmatrix} 2 & 0 \\ 0 & 2 \end{pmatrix}$

BASE VECTORS

Base vectors, often called *unit vectors*, can be used to define very quickly a matrix transformation, or even to help evaluate that transformation. For example, where T:

$$
T: \begin{pmatrix} x \\ y \end{pmatrix} \rightarrow \begin{pmatrix} 0 & -1 \\ -1 & 0 \end{pmatrix}\begin{pmatrix} x \\ y \end{pmatrix}
$$

then consider how the unit matrix, $\begin{pmatrix} 1 & 0 \\ 0 & 1 \end{pmatrix}$ transforms to $\begin{pmatrix} 0 & -1 \\ -1 & 0 \end{pmatrix}$ where the columns of

the matrices are position vectors.

Then it can be seen in Fig. 13.16 what happens to them.

see that $\begin{pmatrix} 1 \\ 0 \end{pmatrix} \rightarrow \begin{pmatrix} 0 \\ -1 \end{pmatrix}$

$$
\begin{pmatrix} 0 \\ 1 \end{pmatrix} \rightarrow \begin{pmatrix} -1 \\ 0 \end{pmatrix}
$$

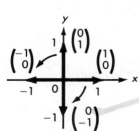

Fig. 13.16

The transformation can now be seen as 'reflection in the line y = –x'. Try this technique out on the matrices in Exercise 4 to see how much simpler it is to define the matrix in this way.

Find the transformation matrix that describes a rotation of 90° clockwise around the origin (see Fig. 13.17).
Consider the base vectors, then

$$\begin{pmatrix} 1 \\ 0 \end{pmatrix} \rightarrow \begin{pmatrix} 0 \\ -1 \end{pmatrix} \text{ and } \begin{pmatrix} 0 \\ 1 \end{pmatrix} \rightarrow \begin{pmatrix} 1 \\ 0 \end{pmatrix} \text{ (see Fig. 13.17)}$$

hence $\begin{pmatrix} 1 & 0 \\ 0 & 1 \end{pmatrix} \rightarrow \begin{pmatrix} 0 & 1 \\ -1 & 0 \end{pmatrix}$

so rotation of 90° clockwise around the origin is defined as

$$\text{T:} \begin{pmatrix} x \\ y \end{pmatrix} \rightarrow \begin{pmatrix} 0 & 1 \\ -1 & 0 \end{pmatrix} \begin{pmatrix} x \\ y \end{pmatrix}$$

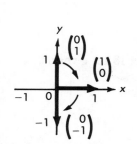

Fig. 13.17

EXERCISE 5

Find the transformation matrices that represent

 i) enlargement of scale factor –3, centre of enlargement is the origin
ii) rotation of 180° around the origin.

COMBINATIONS OF TRANSFORMATIONS

Two or more matrices can quite easily be combined by finding the product of their transformation matrices.

A transformation is defined as 'reflect in the Y axis, then rotate through 90° anti-clockwise (around the origin)'. What single transformation will this represent?
Find the transformation matrix for each transformation.

Reflect in Y axis (see Fig. 13.18):

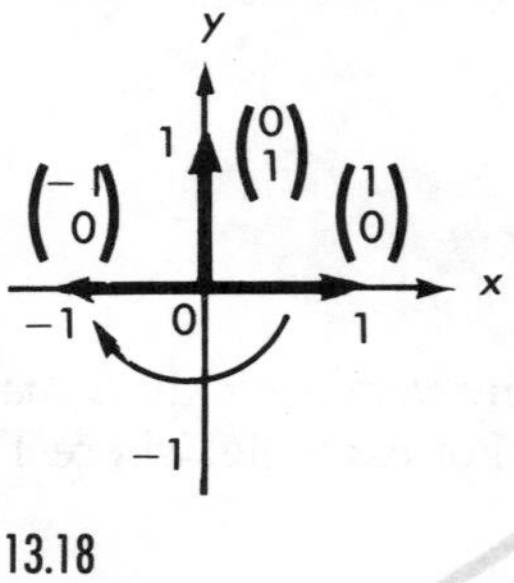

$$\begin{pmatrix} 1 \\ 0 \end{pmatrix} \rightarrow \begin{pmatrix} -1 \\ 0 \end{pmatrix} \text{ and } \begin{pmatrix} 0 \\ 1 \end{pmatrix} \rightarrow \begin{pmatrix} 0 \\ 1 \end{pmatrix}$$

hence $\begin{pmatrix} 1 & 0 \\ 0 & 1 \end{pmatrix} \rightarrow \begin{pmatrix} -1 & 0 \\ 0 & 1 \end{pmatrix}$

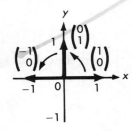

Fig. 13.18

Rotate anticlockwise 90° (see Fig. 13.19):

$$\begin{pmatrix} 1 \\ 0 \end{pmatrix} \rightarrow \begin{pmatrix} 0 \\ 1 \end{pmatrix} \text{ and } \begin{pmatrix} 0 \\ 1 \end{pmatrix} \rightarrow \begin{pmatrix} -1 \\ 0 \end{pmatrix}$$

hence $\begin{pmatrix} 1 & 0 \\ 0 & 1 \end{pmatrix} \rightarrow \begin{pmatrix} 0 & -1 \\ 1 & 0 \end{pmatrix}$

Fig. 13.19

Hence the *combined* transformation will be:

$$\begin{pmatrix} x \\ y \end{pmatrix} \rightarrow \begin{pmatrix} 0 & -1 \\ 1 & 0 \end{pmatrix} \begin{pmatrix} -1 & 0 \\ 0 & 1 \end{pmatrix} \begin{pmatrix} x \\ y \end{pmatrix}$$

(note how the first transformation performed needs to be on the right),

i.e. $\begin{pmatrix} x \\ y \end{pmatrix} \rightarrow \begin{pmatrix} 0 & -1 \\ -1 & 0 \end{pmatrix} \begin{pmatrix} x \\ y \end{pmatrix}$

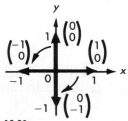

Fig. 13.20

which is $\begin{pmatrix} 1 \\ 0 \end{pmatrix} \rightarrow \begin{pmatrix} 0 \\ -1 \end{pmatrix}$ and $\begin{pmatrix} 0 \\ 1 \end{pmatrix} \rightarrow \begin{pmatrix} -1 \\ 0 \end{pmatrix}$

seen as Fig. 13.20. Hence a reflection in the line $y = -x$.

EXERCISE 6

Remember, give the answer as a single transformation; it's wrong if you state two transformations.

Find the combination of the transformations:

i) rotate 90° clockwise around the origin then reflect in the x axis.

ii) reflect in the x axis and then rotate 90° clockwise around the origin.

INVERSE TRANSFORMATIONS

The *inverse* of a transformation is that transformation which moves a shape back to where it started. For example:

the inverse of 'rotation of 90° clockwise around the origin' is …

a 'rotation of 90° anticlockwise around the origin.'

Or, the inverse of 'an enlargement of scale factor 3, centre of enlargement (0,0)', is an enlargement of scale factor D, centre of enlargement (0,0)'. *Self inverses* are those that are the inverses of themselves; all reflections are self inverses. For example, the inverse of

'reflection in the x-axis' is 'reflection in the x-axis'.

The matrix representing the inverse of a transformation T, will be the inverse matrix of the matrix representing T.

WORKED EXAMPLE 5

Find the matrix defining the inverse of the transformation T, where

$$T: \begin{pmatrix} x \\ y \end{pmatrix} \rightarrow \begin{pmatrix} 2 & 3 \\ 1 & 2 \end{pmatrix} \begin{pmatrix} x \\ y \end{pmatrix},$$ and hence find the point P that has the image under T of (3,1).

Inverse matrix of $\begin{pmatrix} 2 & 3 \\ 1 & 2 \end{pmatrix}$ is given by $\dfrac{1}{ad - bc} \begin{pmatrix} d & -b \\ -c & a \end{pmatrix}$

where $a = 2$, $b = 3$, $c = 1$ and $d = 2$.

Hence inverse matrix is $\dfrac{1}{(4-3)} \begin{pmatrix} 2 & -3 \\ -1 & 2 \end{pmatrix} = \begin{pmatrix} 2 & -3 \\ -1 & 2 \end{pmatrix}$

So the point P will be $\begin{pmatrix} 2 & -3 \\ -1 & 2 \end{pmatrix} \begin{pmatrix} 3 \\ 1 \end{pmatrix} = \begin{pmatrix} 3 \\ -1 \end{pmatrix}$

INVARIANCE

Most transformations have a point or a line of points that do not alter under the transformation. These are called 'invariant points' or the 'invariant line'. For example: in the transformation 'rotation of 90° clockwise about (0,0)' the point (0,0) is the invariant point (see Fig. 13.21).

NB. The centre of rotation will always be the point of invariance of a rotation.

As in any reflection, the line of reflection is the invariant line.

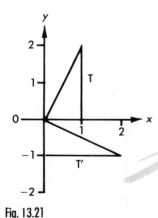

Fig. 13.21

EXERCISE 7

Write down the invariant point(s) of the transformation represented by:

i) $\begin{pmatrix} 0 & -1 \\ -1 & 0 \end{pmatrix}$ ii) $\begin{pmatrix} 2 & 0 \\ 0 & 1 \end{pmatrix}$

FURTHER TRANSFORMATIONS

There are a number of transformations that are only likely to be examined at the highest level of GCSE mathematics (if they are on your syllabus). These are *one way stretches* and *shears*.

One-way stretch

A *one way stretch* is an enlargement in one direction only. The transformation matrix of a one way stretch is of the type:

$$\begin{pmatrix} K & 0 \\ 0 & 1 \end{pmatrix}$$: a one way stretch of scale factor K with *y* axis invariant.

$$\begin{pmatrix} 1 & 0 \\ 0 & K \end{pmatrix}$$: a one way stretch of scale factor K with *x* axis invariant.

Shear

A *shear* is a 'push over'. It has an invariant line and any point, P, moves in a direction parallel to the invariant line, and a distance given by (perpendicular distance from the invariant line) multiplied by the (shear factor).

WORKED EXAMPLE 6

On the diagram in Fig. 13.22, construct the image of A'B'C' of ABC under the shear which has invariant line *l* and maps A onto A'.

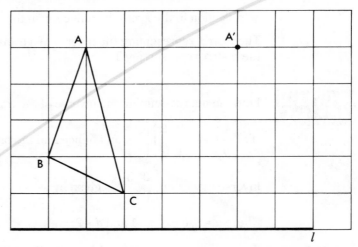

Fig. 13.22

As the shear is a 'push over' with *l* invariant, draw the lines from A through each of the points B and C to the invariant points, X and Y respectively. Then from X and Y draw in the 'push over' to XA' and YA'. Each point moves parallel to the invariant line, hence follow B and C along their lines of parallel to the lines XA' and YA' respectively to find B' and C'.

Hence join up A'B'C' as in Fig. 13.23. (The shear factor here is $\dfrac{4}{5}$, since point A, 5 units from the invariant line, has only moved 4 units.)

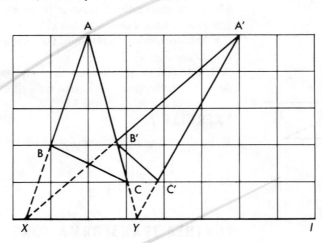

Fig. 13.23

SOLUTIONS TO EXERCISES

S1

Your solution should be as in Fig. 13.24 with no shapes overlapping.

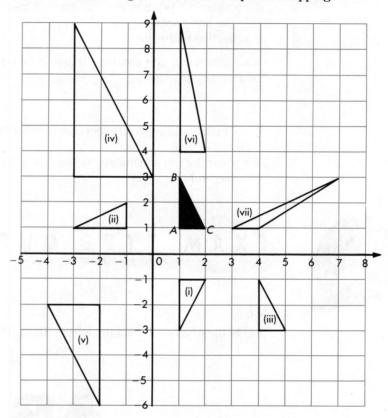

Fig. 13.24

S2

i) $\quad \mathbf{x} + \mathbf{y} = \begin{pmatrix} 3 + -4 \\ 4 + -1 \end{pmatrix} = \begin{pmatrix} -1 \\ 3 \end{pmatrix}$

magnitude $= \sqrt{((-1)^2 + 3^2)} = \sqrt{(10)} = 3.2$

ii) $\mathbf{z} - \mathbf{x} = \begin{pmatrix} 2-3 \\ 7-4 \end{pmatrix} = \begin{pmatrix} -1 \\ 3 \end{pmatrix}$ which is equal to $\mathbf{x} + \mathbf{y}$.

The vectors $(\mathbf{x} + \mathbf{y})$ and $(\mathbf{z} - \mathbf{x})$ are equal.

S3

$\dfrac{1}{10} \begin{pmatrix} 3 & -2 \\ -4 & 6 \end{pmatrix}$

S4

i) reflection in the line $y = x$
ii) rotation of 90° anticlockwise around the origin.
iii) enlargement, scale factor 2, centre of enlargement the origin.

S5

i) $\begin{pmatrix} -3 & 0 \\ 0 & -3 \end{pmatrix}$ ii) $\begin{pmatrix} -1 & 0 \\ 0 & -1 \end{pmatrix}$

S6

i) combine the two transformations with base vectors or otherwise to give a 'reflection in the line $y = x$'

ii) reflection in the line $y = -x$.

(Note that when you combine transformations in different orders, you usually get a different result.)

S7

i) the matrix can be seen to represent a reflection in the line $y = -x$, which is the invariant line.

ii) try out the transformation to see that it 'stretches' out from the y axis, which is the invariant line.

EXAM TYPE QUESTIONS

Q1

a) On the diagram reflect the letters AB in i) the x-axis, ii) the y-axis.

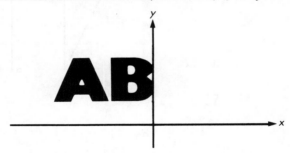

Fig. 13.25

b) Complete the diagram so that it has rotational symmetry of order 2. (NEAB)

Q2

Blank crosswords often have two lines of symmetry, from each corner to corner diagonally. Complete the blank crossword in Fig. 13.26 in this way.

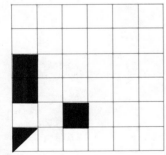

Fig. 13.26

Q3

a) On Fig. 13.27, enlarge the rectangle

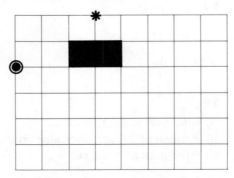

Fig. 13.27

i) from * with scale factor 3,
ii) from ⊚ with scale factor 2.
b) What do you notice about the increase in area in each case?

Q4

Show how the shape given will tessellate in a regular pattern. Show at least 8 shapes.

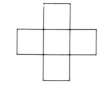

Fig. 13.28

Q5

Describe fully two different single transformations which will map the right hand A on to the left hand A in Fig. 13.29.

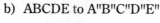

Fig. 13.29

(NISEAC)

Q6

Describe, fully, the single transformation that maps, in Fig. 13.30:

a) ABCDE to A'B'C'D'E',
b) ABCDE to A"B"C"D"E"

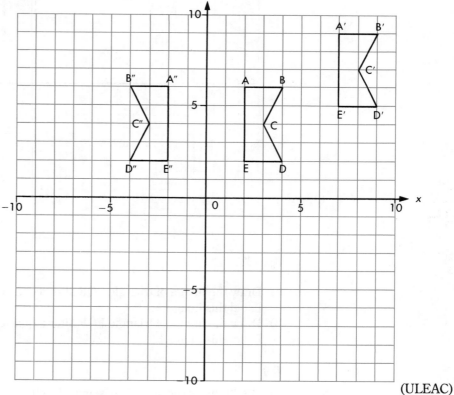

Fig. 13.30

(ULEAC)

Q7

In a video game in Fig. 13.31, the screen is 100 units by 100 units. The player has to enter a vector to give the direction the ball will travel. The ball starts at O (0,0). John enters the vector $\begin{pmatrix} 1 \\ 2 \end{pmatrix}$ and the ball moves, making an angle $a°$ with OR.

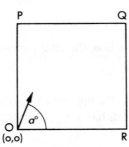

Fig. 13.31

a) What is the value of a?
b) The position of the ball as it moves to the top of the screen, PQ, can be written as

K $\begin{pmatrix} 1 \\ 2 \end{pmatrix}$. What is the value of K when the ball reaches PQ?

c) What are the co-ordinates of the point where the ball hits PQ?
d) When the ball hits PQ it rebounds so that the 'new' path is at 90° to the 'old' path. Which vector describes the ball's direction after it rebounds from PQ?
e) What are the co-ordinates of the point where the ball hits QR? (WJEC)

Q8

From Fig. 13.32:

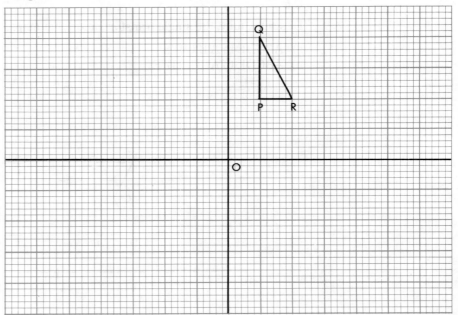

Fig. 13.32

a) Draw the image of triangle PQR after a quarter turn, anticlockwise about P. Label this image A.
b) Draw the image of triangle PQR after a quarter turn, clockwise about O. Label this image B. (ULEAC)

Q9

Fig. 13.33 shows the map of an island (the shaded region) drawn on a square grid. A boat is to sail from A to D.

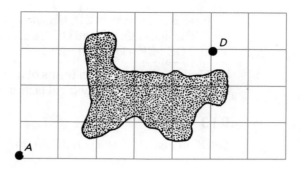

Fig. 13.33

a) On Fig. 13.33, label two grid points (corners of squares) B and C so that the route A to B to C to D (consisting of three straight line segments) does not cross the shaded region.

b) Write down the column vector for:

i) $\overrightarrow{AB}$ ii) $\overrightarrow{BC}$ iii) $\overrightarrow{CD}$.

c) Add together the three column vectors for $\overrightarrow{AB}$, $\overrightarrow{BC}$ and $\overrightarrow{CD}$.

d) Explain how to check your answer to part c) by using the vector $\overrightarrow{AD}$.

(NEAB)

Q10

a) On a grid with values from 0 to 6 on both axes draw the rectangle with vertices $O(0, 0)$, $A(3, 0)$, $B(3, 2)$ and $C(0, 2)$.

b) i) Draw the image of the rectangle $OABC$ after the transformation where the transformation matrix is R when $R = \begin{pmatrix} 1 & 1 \\ 0 & 1 \end{pmatrix}$.

ii) What has happened to the area of the transformed shape?

c) Write down the matrix of the inverse transformation of R.

Q11

a) On a grid with values from −4 to 4 on both axes, draw the triangle with vertices $A(0, 1)$, $B(1, 1)$ and $C(2, 0)$.

b) Draw the image of the triangle ABC after the transformation defined by E,

where E: $\begin{pmatrix} x \\ y \end{pmatrix} \rightarrow \begin{pmatrix} -2 & 0 \\ 0 & -2 \end{pmatrix} \begin{pmatrix} x \\ y \end{pmatrix}$.

c) Describe fully this transformation.

(NEAB)

Q12

In Fig. 13.34, OABC is a plane quadrilateral with $\overrightarrow{OA} = 4\mathbf{a}$, $\overrightarrow{OB} = 2\mathbf{a} + 2\mathbf{c}$, $\overrightarrow{OC} = 3\mathbf{c}$.

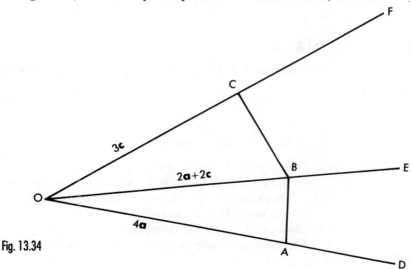

Fig. 13.34

a) Express the vectors $\overrightarrow{CO}$, $\overrightarrow{CB}$ and $\overrightarrow{AB}$ in terms of **a** or **c** or **a**. and **c**.

The lines OA, OB and OC are produced to D, E and F respectively, where OC = CF and OB : BE = OA : AD = 2 : 1.

b) Find $\overrightarrow{FC}$, $\overrightarrow{FE}$ and $\overrightarrow{DE}$ in terms of **a** or **c** or **a** and **c**.

c) Write down two geometrical facts about the points D, E and F. (ULEAC)

Q13

OABC in Fig. 13.35 is a parallelogram.

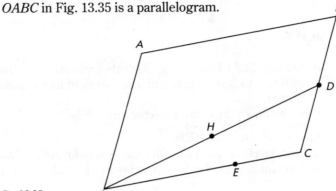

Fig. 13.35

D is the midpoint of *CB*.
H is the midpoint of *OD*.
$\overrightarrow{OE} = \frac{2}{3} \overrightarrow{OC}$.
Vector $\overrightarrow{OA}$ = **a** and vector $\overrightarrow{OC}$ = **c**.

a) Express, in terms of **a** and **c**:

　i) $\overrightarrow{OD}$　　ii) $\overrightarrow{AE}$　iii) $\overrightarrow{HE}$.

b) Show that $\overrightarrow{AE} = 4\overrightarrow{HE}$ and explain what this proves about the points *A*, *H* and *E*.

(NEAB)

Q14

The transformation *T* consists of a reflection in the *x*-axis followed by an enlargement with centre (0, 0) and scale factor 2. Find:

a) the image of $\begin{pmatrix} 1 \\ 0 \end{pmatrix}$ and $\begin{pmatrix} 0 \\ 1 \end{pmatrix}$ under *T*;

b) the matrix associated with *T*;

c) the image of $\begin{pmatrix} 2 \\ 3 \end{pmatrix}$ under *T*. (NEAB)

Q15

a) Describe fully the transformations represented by the matrices.

　i) $S = \begin{pmatrix} -1 & 0 \\ 0 & 1 \end{pmatrix}$　　　　ii) $T = \begin{pmatrix} 1 & 0 \\ 0 & -1 \end{pmatrix}$

b) If *M* = *ST*, calculate the matrix *M*

The triangle U has been drawn on the grid.
V is the image of U under the transformation represented by M.

c) i) Work out the co-ordinates of the vertices of V.
　ii) On the grid, draw and label V.

d) Describe fully the single transformation represented by M.

e) Describe as simply as possible the transformation represented by M^2.

(ULEAC)

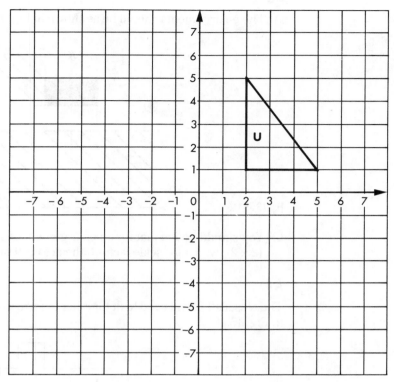

Fig. 13.36

OUTLINE ANSWERS TO EXAM QUESTIONS

A1

a) You should end up with a diagram looking like Fig. 13.37 (but not with the dotted AB).

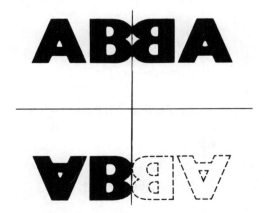

Fig. 13.37

b) Then fit the last AB into the bottom right-hand corner as we've illustrated with the dotted AB in Fig. 13.37.

You would have found the question easier if you had used tracing paper.

A2

Draw in the diagonal lines of symmetry, then complete the crossword for one line of symmetry first then the other, to end up with Fig. 13.38. Here it is easiest to use the squares to help.

Fig. 13.38

A3

a) The enlargements should be as shown in Fig. 13.39. Use the lines on the grid to help you.

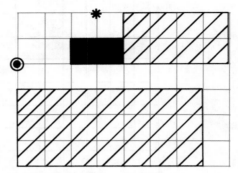

Fig. 13.39

b) You should notice that for an enlargement of scale factor 2 the area is 4 times as big (2×2), whilst for scale factor 3 the area is 9 times as big (3×3).

A4

The tessellation will need to fit together to form a regular pattern and leave no spaces, as in Fig. 13.40.

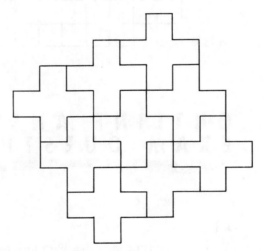

Fig. 13.40

A5

a) A translation of $\begin{pmatrix} 5 \\ 0 \end{pmatrix}$.

b) A reflection in the line $x = 0.5$.

A6

a) A translation of $\begin{pmatrix} 5 \\ 3 \end{pmatrix}$.

b) A reflection in the y-axis.

A7

a) $a = \tan^{-1} \dfrac{2}{1}$, giving $a = 63.4°$. See Fig. 13.41

b) At the top of the screen, the y ordinate will be 100, hence K will be 50 as $2 \times 50 = 100$.

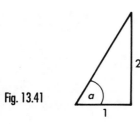

Fig. 13.41

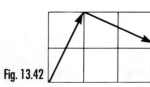

Fig. 13.42

c) $50 \begin{pmatrix} 1 \\ 2 \end{pmatrix} = \begin{pmatrix} 50 \\ 100 \end{pmatrix}$, hence co-ordinate is (50,100).

d) As in Fig. 13.42, the vector perpendicular to $\begin{pmatrix} 1 \\ 2 \end{pmatrix}$ will be $\begin{pmatrix} 2 \\ -1 \end{pmatrix}$.

e) The ball needs to go 50 units to the right, hence the ball will move

$$25 \begin{pmatrix} 2 \\ -1 \end{pmatrix} = \begin{pmatrix} 50 \\ -25 \end{pmatrix}.$$

25 units down from the top is 75 on the y axis, and QR is $x = 100$, so the co-ordinate where QR is hit is (100,75).

A8

See Fig. 13.43.

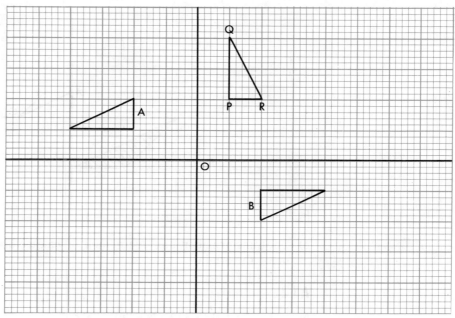

Fig. 13.43

A9

See Fig. 13.44

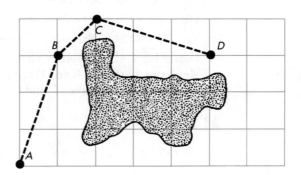

Fig. 13.44

a) Your points B and C will be similar to those here, but there are a lot of other possible correct answers.

b) These answers will depend on your points B and C for Fig. 13.44

i) $\overrightarrow{AB} = \begin{pmatrix} 1 \\ 3 \end{pmatrix}$; ii) $\overrightarrow{BC} = \begin{pmatrix} 1 \\ 1 \end{pmatrix}$; iii) $\overrightarrow{CD} = \begin{pmatrix} 3 \\ -1 \end{pmatrix}$.

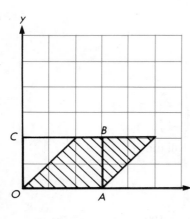

Fig. 13.45

c) $\begin{pmatrix} 1 \\ 3 \end{pmatrix} + \begin{pmatrix} 1 \\ 1 \end{pmatrix} + \begin{pmatrix} 3 \\ -1 \end{pmatrix} = \begin{pmatrix} 5 \\ 3 \end{pmatrix}$

d) By finding the single vector $\overrightarrow{AD}$, this should be the same.

A10

Fig. 13.45 is the diagram you should have for a) and b) i).

b) ii) The area remains the same, since the area of a parallelogram is base × height, which is 6, the same as the rectangle.

c) Using the formula for an inverse matrix given in the text, when $a = 1$, $b = 1$, $c = 0$ and

$d = 1$, we get: the inverse matrix $= \dfrac{1}{(1 - 0)} \begin{pmatrix} 1 & -1 \\ 0 & 1 \end{pmatrix}$ which is $\begin{pmatrix} 1 & -1 \\ 0 & 1 \end{pmatrix}$

A11

Fig. 13.46 is the diagram you should have for a) and b).

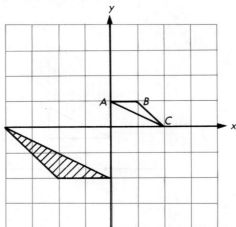

Fig. 13.46

c) The transformation is an enlargement of scale factor −2, with the centre of enlargement being the origin.

A12

a) $\overrightarrow{CO} = -3\mathbf{c}$, $\overrightarrow{CB} = -3\mathbf{c} + (2\mathbf{a} + 2\mathbf{c}) = 2\mathbf{a}-\mathbf{c}$

$\overrightarrow{AB} = -4\mathbf{a} + 2\mathbf{a} + 2\mathbf{c} = 2\mathbf{c} - 2\mathbf{a}$

b) $\overrightarrow{FC} = -3\mathbf{c}$, $\overrightarrow{BE} = \frac{1}{2}(2\mathbf{a} + 2\mathbf{c}) = \mathbf{a} + \mathbf{c}$

$\overrightarrow{FE} = -6\mathbf{c} + (3\mathbf{a} + 3\mathbf{c}) = 3\mathbf{a} - 3\mathbf{c}$

$\overrightarrow{DE} = -6\mathbf{a} + (3\mathbf{a} + 3\mathbf{c}) = 3\mathbf{c} - 3\mathbf{a}$

c) $\overrightarrow{FE} = 3\mathbf{a} - 3\mathbf{c}$ and $\overrightarrow{DE} = -3\mathbf{a} + 3\mathbf{c} = -(3\mathbf{a} - 3\mathbf{c})$

Hence $\overrightarrow{FE} = -\overrightarrow{DE}$ or rather $\overrightarrow{FE} = \overrightarrow{ED}$.

Hence we see that F, E and D are co-linear (all in the same straight line) and that E is exactly halfway between F and D.

A13

a)   i) $\overrightarrow{OD} = \mathbf{c} + \frac{1}{2}\mathbf{a}$;   ii) $\overrightarrow{AE} = \frac{2}{3}\mathbf{c} - \mathbf{a}$ (or $-\mathbf{a} + \frac{2}{3}\mathbf{c}$)

   iii) $-\frac{1}{2}(\mathbf{c} + \frac{1}{2}\mathbf{a}) + \frac{2}{3}\mathbf{c} = \frac{1}{6}\mathbf{c} - \frac{1}{4}\mathbf{a}$

b) $\overrightarrow{AE} = \frac{2}{3}\mathbf{c} - \mathbf{a}$

$4\overrightarrow{HE} = 4(\frac{1}{6}\mathbf{c} - \frac{1}{4}\mathbf{a}) = \frac{2}{3}\mathbf{c} - \mathbf{a} = \overrightarrow{AE}$ hence $\overrightarrow{AE} = 4\overrightarrow{HE}$.

A14

a) By possibly drawing on a grid these base vectors, we can see that:

$$\begin{pmatrix} 0 \\ 1 \end{pmatrix} \rightarrow \begin{pmatrix} 2 \\ 0 \end{pmatrix} \text{ and } \begin{pmatrix} 0 \\ 1 \end{pmatrix} \rightarrow \begin{pmatrix} 0 \\ -2 \end{pmatrix}.$$

b) Hence the matrix will be $\begin{pmatrix} 2 & 0 \\ 0 & -2 \end{pmatrix}$.

c) $\begin{pmatrix} 2 & 0 \\ 0 & -2 \end{pmatrix} \begin{pmatrix} 2 \\ 3 \end{pmatrix} = \begin{pmatrix} 4 \\ -6 \end{pmatrix}$.

A15

a) By considering base vectors you will find
      i) reflection in the y axis
      ii) reflection in the x axis

b) $\begin{pmatrix} -1 & 0 \\ 0 & -1 \end{pmatrix}$

c) $\begin{pmatrix} -1 & 0 \\ 0 & -1 \end{pmatrix} \begin{pmatrix} 2 & 5 & 2 \\ 1 & 1 & 5 \end{pmatrix} = \begin{pmatrix} -2 & -5 & -2 \\ -1 & -1 & -5 \end{pmatrix}$

d) A rotation of 180° about (0, 0)

e) M^2 is M followed by M, and since M is a reflection, then M^2 is the identity transformation.

LEVEL CHECKLIST

For the level	You should be able to do the following.
4	Understand and draw reflections and simple rotations.
6	Enlarge shapes with a given scale factor.
7	Understand what tessellations are.
8	Understand and use vector notation. Understand translations.
9	Understand and use the laws of addition and subtraction of vectors.
10	Understand how transformations are related by combinations and inverses. Use matrices to define transformations in 2D.

A STUDENT'S ANSWER WITH EXAMINER'S COMMENTS

Question
On the graph paper provided draw the triangle ABC, where A, B, C are the points (1,3), (2,3), (2,5) respectively.

The transformation P is a reflection in the line x = –1.
The transformation Q is a reflection in the line y = 1.

R is the translation $\begin{pmatrix} 2 \\ -2 \end{pmatrix}$.

a) Triangle ABC is mapped onto triangle $A_1B_1C_1$ by P
   Triangle $A_1B_1C_1$ is mapped onto triangle $A_2B_2C_2$ by Q.
   Triangle $A_2B_2C_2$ is mapped onto triangle $A_3B_3C_3$ by R.

Draw these triangles on your diagram and label them clearly.

b) Describe the single transformation which maps triangle ABC onto triangle $A_3B_3C_3$.

> Not a bad attempt. Yet because $A_3 B_3 C_3$ is wrong, there can be few marks gained here.

Answer _An enlarged reflection in the line x = –2½_

c) A further transformation T is an enlargement, centre the origin, scale factor $\frac{1}{2}$.

   Draw the image of triangle ABC under T.

d) If the area of a triangle is x square units, state the area of the image of this triangle under T.

> The correct answer of $\frac{1}{4}$x is badly written here, and would score few marks.

Answer _1/4X_

> Confused here. An enlargement has been drawn instead of a translation.

> Good.

> Good enlargement of scale factor $\frac{1}{2}$.

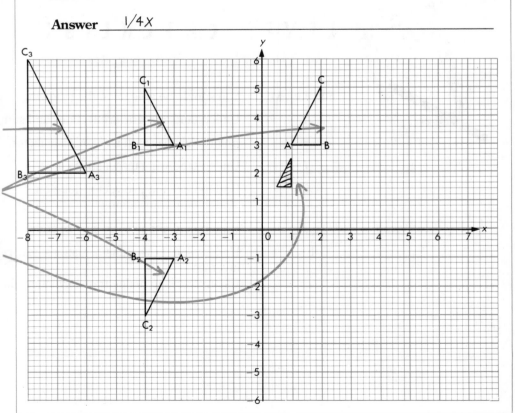

REVIEW SHEET

 Use pencil to solve each of these questions on the grid. Erase your drawings after each solution.

   a) Draw the triangle that has vertices A(1, 1), B(2, 1), C(1, 3).

   b) Reflect ABC in the *x*-axis and label it T_b.

   c) Reflect ABC in the *y*-axis and label it T_c.

   d) Draw on your grid the line that joins (1, −1) to (−1, 1) then reflect ABC in this line and label it T_d.

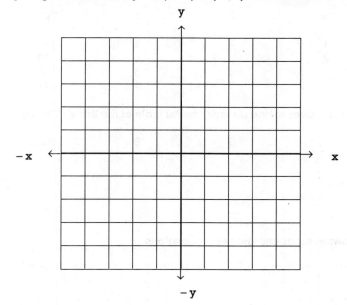

 a) Draw the triangle that has vertices A(2, 1), B(2, 3), C(1, 3).

   B) Rotate ABC 90° clockwise about (0, 0) and label it T_b.

   c) Rotate ABC 90° anticlockwise about (0, 0) and label it T_c.

   d) Rotate ABC 180° about (0, 0) and label it T_d.

 a) Draw the triangle that has vertices A(1, 1), B(3, 1), C(3, 2).

   b) Enlarge ABC from the origin with scale factor 3 and label it T_b.

   c) Enlarge ABC from (2, 2) with scale factor 2 and label it T_c.

   d) Enlarge ABC from (−5, −5) with scale factor $\frac{1}{2}$ and label it T_d.

 a) Draw the triangle that has vertices A(1, 1), B(1, 3), C(2, 3).

   b) Translate ABC 3 units in the *x* direction, label this T_b.

   c) Translate ABC 4 units in the *x* direction and 3 units in the *y* direction, label this T_c.

✎ At the beginning of the last day of the British Games the top of the medals table was shown here:

	G	S	B	Total
England	23	14	18	55
Wales	19	21	16	56
N. Ireland	16	21	18	55
Scotland	16	18	22	56

The medals won during the last day were:

	G	S	B	Total
England	4	3	2	9
Wales	3	3	4	10
N. Ireland	4	2	3	9
Scotland	2	5	4	11

Add together these matrices to find the final medal table of the British Games that year.

	G	S	B	Total
England				
Wales				
N. Ireland				
Scotland				

✎ Complete the following diagrams and vector notations

a)

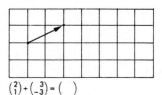

$$\begin{pmatrix} 2 \\ 1 \end{pmatrix} + \begin{pmatrix} 3 \\ -3 \end{pmatrix} = \begin{pmatrix} \ \ \\ \ \ \end{pmatrix}$$

b)

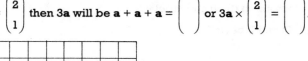

$$\begin{pmatrix} 5 \\ 2 \end{pmatrix} - \begin{pmatrix} 3 \\ 4 \end{pmatrix} = \begin{pmatrix} \ \ \\ \ \ \end{pmatrix}$$

c) If $\mathbf{a} = \begin{pmatrix} 2 \\ 1 \end{pmatrix}$ then 3**a** will be $\mathbf{a} + \mathbf{a} + \mathbf{a} = \begin{pmatrix} \ \ \\ \ \ \end{pmatrix}$ or $3\mathbf{a} \times \begin{pmatrix} 2 \\ 1 \end{pmatrix} = \begin{pmatrix} \ \ \\ \ \ \end{pmatrix}$.

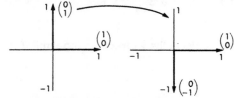

$3\mathbf{a} = \mathbf{a} + \mathbf{a} + \mathbf{a} = \begin{pmatrix} \ \ \\ \ \ \end{pmatrix}$

✎ Find the matrix which will describe this rotation of 90° clockwise around the origin.

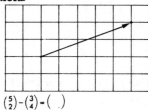

✎ Complete the matrices under b) and c) below

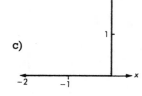

a)

base vectors

$\begin{pmatrix} 1 & 0 \\ 0 & 1 \end{pmatrix}$

b)

after reflecting in the *y* axis they become

$\begin{pmatrix} \ \ & \ \ \\ \ \ & \ \ \end{pmatrix}$

c)

after enlarging from the origin with a scale factor of 2, they become

$\begin{pmatrix} \ \ & \ \ \\ \ \ & \ \ \end{pmatrix}$

GETTING STARTED

Statistics are all around us. They are used on television and in the papers, and sport is littered with them. However, the term *statistics* used here refers to more than pieces of data or information. It refers to the various *methods* of organising data, or of displaying data so that they make more sense.

You must be able to read the statistics as presented and to display that information in a way that highlights the major points or trends. The vast majority of examination questions will leave you in little doubt as to exactly what type of display you should use. You might also be asked for an interpretation or a conclusion to be drawn from the statistics.

The *probability* ideas you will meet are at a simple level and usually quite predictable. Do be careful of your notation. Many Examination Boards do not allow probability answers to be shown as anything but fractions, either vulgar or decimal.

USEFUL DEFINITIONS

Mode	The most frequently occurring value in a set of data.
Median	The middle of a set of data in numeric order.
Mean	A type of average calculated from all relevant data.
Frequency	The number of times some defined event occurs.
Pictogram	A display of information using pictures to represent the frequency.
Bar chart	A display of information using bars of different lengths to represent the information.
Pie chart	A circular picture divided in the ratio of the frequencies of the different events occurring.
Histogram	Like a bar chart, with the area of the bars being directly proportional to the frequency. Often the widths to the bars will be different.
Cumulative	Increasing by successive additions.
Ogive	The line representing cumulative frequency on a graph.
Dice	Often referred to as a die. Unless told otherwise, any reference in a question to dice or die will mean a cube marked on each face from one to six spots, or the numbers.
Sample	A selection of items from a 'population'.
Standard deviation	A measure of dispersion; i.e. of how widely the data varies around the average.

ESSENTIAL PRINCIPLES

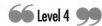 **AVERAGE**

What people usually mean by average is the m*iddle thing*, or the thing that most people do or have. But when we say that the average number of children in a family is 1.8, there is no family at all that has this number of children! So, let's look carefully at averages. There are three different types of average, and you should know the difference between them.

MODE

66 Level 4 99

This is what m*ost* people have or do. From a survey in which people were asked what their favourite evening drink was, the following information was gained:

Tea, 28: Coffee, 115; Cocoa, 136; Other 9

The most common choice was cocoa, hence we would say the *modal* drink was cocoa, or in this situation that the average evening drink was cocoa. What is the average evening drink in your house?

MEDIAN

This is the m*iddle*, once the information has been put into a specific order.
For example, if you have seven people and wanted to find their median height you would put them into the order of their height and whoever was in the middle would be of median height, or average height.

WORKED EXAMPLE 1

Here are 15 test results, what is the median score?

81, 63, 59, 71, 36, 99, 56, 31, 5, 65, 46, 83, 71, 53, 15

Put the marks into order, i.e. 5, 15, 31, 36, 46, 53, 56, 59, 63, 65, 71, 71, 81, 83, 99. Now find the middle one, which is 59. So the median score is 59.
If there is no single middle number then there will be two middle numbers, and the median in this case is halfway between the two middle numbers.
An easy way to work out where the middle is, is to put the numbers into order, count how many you've got, call this n, add 1 and divide by 2, i.e. $(n+1)/2$. This will tell you how many to count along for your median.

WORKED EXAMPLE 2

Find the median of 1, 3, 4, 4, 6, 8, 8, 9, 10, 13

Count the numbers, there are ten of them. Add one and divide by 2, giving $5\frac{1}{2}$, so count along five numbers and you come to the 6. Now you need halfway between this and the 8, which is 7, so the median of this list is 7.

MEAN

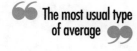 *66 The most usual type of average 99*

This is often known as the *arithmetic mean* and is perhaps the average that most people are familiar with and really intend by the word *average*. It is found by adding up all the data and dividing by how many items of data you had. So, for example, the mean test score from Example 1, is found by adding together all the scores and dividing by the total number of scores, which was 15. This will give us a mean of $834 \div 15$, which is 55.6.

WORKED EXAMPLE 3

G. Boycott scored the following number of runs in five test matches one year: 250, 85, 175, 110, 215. What was the mean number of runs scored in these matches?

Add up each score to give 835, divide this by 5 to give 167, which will be the mean number of runs scored per test match.

EXERCISE 1

From the numbers 2, 5, 1, 7, 1, 1, 4, state: a) the mode; b) the median; c) the mean.

RANGE

The *range* of a set of data is simply the difference between the highest and the lowest; for example, in G. Boycott's test scores in the above example, his range is 250–85, which is 165

2 > FREQUENCY DISTRIBUTION

Frequency is the number of times a certain event has happened, and is often found by means of a *tally chart*.

For example, if you were doing a road survey and wished to count how many cars, buses, vans and lorries went past a particular spot during an interval of time it would be tedious and quite hard to count them all, so we use a tally chart.

	Tally	f
Cars	₶₶ ₶₶ ₶₶ ₶₶ ₶₶ ₶₶ ₶₶ ₶₶ ₶₶ ₶₶ |||	53
Buses	₶₶ ₶₶ ||	12
Vans	₶₶ ₶₶ ₶₶ ₶₶ ₶₶ ||||	29
Lorries	₶₶ ₶₶ ₶₶		16
	Total	110

Fig. 14.1

Fig. 14.1 shows an example of a tally made outside a school in a half-hour period one Friday morning. Each time a vehicle came by one person shouted out what it was, say, *car*, and someone else with the tally chart put a little mark, or tally, in the correct space beside the type of vehicle. Every fifth tally was put through the previous four, as you can see. This was to make counting up easier and the figures were more likely to be accurate. Finally the frequency was found by adding up all the tally marks for each type of vehicle and putting this total in the end column marked, *f*, for frequency. These are then added up to give the total number of vehicles passing. This way of collecting information, or data, is widely used in surveys for all sorts of things.

Once you have collected the frequencies, or been given them, you need to decide how to display this information. If the information is such that you can draw nice pictures of it, and you do not need to be all that accurate, then you can display the information on a pictogram, otherwise use a bar chart. However, in an examination situation you are most likely to be told which to do. In that case you simply need to decide upon a suitable scale for the frequency, since neither the pictogram nor the bar chart wants to be too large or too small.

Visual display is important

PICTOGRAMS

Level 4

Fig. 14.2 shows a *pictogram*; it displays information with pictures. Here it is displaying information about a poll taken shortly before an election in a town. Note that a whole person represents 100 votes, and so we can use half a person (see the LOONY party) to represent 50 votes. Here you see displayed LAB with 300 votes and CONS with 350.

DEM	𝅘 𝅘 𝅘 𝅘 𝅘 𝅘
CONS	𝅘 𝅘 𝅘 𝅘
LAB	𝅘 𝅘 𝅘
LOONY	𝅘

Fig. 14.2   𝅘 represents 100 votes

Notice how a pictogram must have what is called a *key*, which tells us how many the individual *pictures* stand for, and also that each *picture* (here it is of a man) is of the same size.

This kind of display can be *animated* i.e. *come alive*, on the TV where changing information can be shown to walk about from one poll to the next.

BAR CHARTS

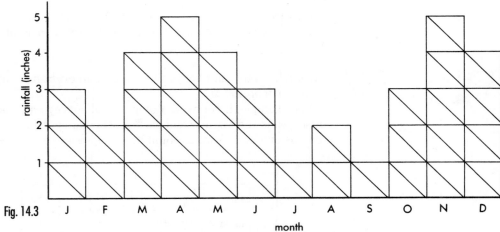

Fig. 14.3

Fig. 14.3 shows a *bar chart*, each bar representing a piece of information so it can be more accurate than a pictogram since the scale can be made to have much smaller units. Often a bar chart will have gaps between the bars, but not necessarily. This bar chart displays how much rain fell each month, to the nearest inch, during one year at a holiday resort. The wettest months are April and November, both with 5 inches of rain. You should be able to pick out from this bar chart when the *summer* was! Note how this bar chart has both axes fully labelled just like a normal graph. This is an important part of any bar chart as it helps us to interpret the displayed information.

Level 5

PIE CHART

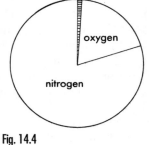

Fig. 14.4

Fig. 14.4 shows a *pie chart*, so called since it has the appearance of a pie and is cut into slices to illustrate the different *ingredients* of the pie. This pie chart illustrates the gases in our air. The actual information is difficult to read accurately, but it does show us how the vast majority of the air is made up from nitrogen, only about a fifth being oxygen. The small shaded sector represents about 1% of what are called inert gases.

You are likely to be asked to show in an examination that you can extract some precise information from a pie chart.

WORKED EXAMPLE 4

The pie chart in Fig. 14.5 represents the ingredients of 500 ml of a drink. There are 250 ml of lemonade and 25 ml of ginger

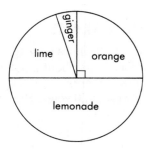

Fig. 14.5

a) How much: i) orange; ii) lime is there?
b) What angle represents ginger?

a) The orange is represented by an angle of $90°$, that is $\dfrac{90}{360}$ of a circle, which is $\frac{1}{4}$; hence the orange is $\frac{1}{4}$ of 500 ml, which is 125 ml. The lime and ginger together form a right angle, and so are the same quantity as the orange, which is 125 ml. Since the ginger accounts for 25 ml the lime will be 125–25, or 100 ml.
b) The angle for ginger will be a fraction of $360°$.

This fraction will be $\dfrac{25}{500}$.

So on the calculator, calculate $\dfrac{25}{500} \times 360$, which is 18°.

CONSTRUCTION OF PIE CHARTS

To *construct a pie chart* there is a set way to go about it once you have gathered your information.

TV viewing figures	
Channel	Number
BBC1	3000
BBC2	1000
ITV3	500
ITV4	7500

Table 14.1

For example, say we found the information in Table 14.1. Now we need to find the angle of the sector that each channel will be. We do this by finding what fraction of the whole data each channel is, and using this to find the same fraction of a complete circle or of 360°.

Channel	Frequency	Angle
BBC1	3000	$\dfrac{3000}{12000} \times 360 = 90°$
BBC2	1000	$\dfrac{1000}{12000} \times 360 = 30°$
ITV3	500	$\dfrac{500}{12000} \times 360 = 15°$
ITV4	7500	$\dfrac{7500}{12000} \times 360 = 225°$
	12000	360°

Table 14.2

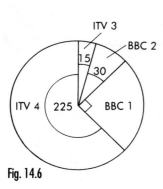

Fig. 14.6

Table 14.2 illustrates what we have done and Fig. 14.6 the completed pie chart. Note how, when the pie chart was being drawn, the very first angle to be put in would have been the smallest, then the next smallest and so on, so that the last angle should be the largest, hence any slight error is not so noticeable. The pie chart has also been fully labelled with the description of each sector and its angle.

Note

Although the pie charts you see in everyday use will probably not have their sector angles labelled, it is usually expected in an examination situation where you are trying to show that you know what the angle should be.

EXERCISE 2

A school survey was done on 90 pet owners with the following numbers being the favourite pets:

Rabbit, 20;   Cat, 27;   Dog, 34;   Bird, 9.

Represent this information on: a) a bar chart, and; b) a pie chart.

3 > GROUPED DATA

Height (cm)	Frequency
100–109	12
110–119	19
120–129	35
130–139	32
140–149	21
150–159	10
160–169	2

Table 14.3

Quite often we are faced with non-precise information, as in the following example. A survey was carried out to find the average height of pupils in a school, and Table 14.3 represents the results. The data have been *grouped* to make the information easier to read, and the raw data will have been rounded off.

For example, if someone had a height of 109.8 cm, then it seems that he or she does not appear on the chart, but 109.8 will have been rounded off to give 110 cm and put into that particular group.

It is an essential feature of a grouped frequency such as this that we know what the group *boundaries* are. Here, for example, the first group will really take in heights from 99.5 to 109.499 … Note that 109.5 would be rounded to 110, but in the table it is more convenient to show the heights in the way we have done. Care must be taken that we do not have any confusion at group boundaries.

For example, if we had groups here of 100–110, 110–120, 120–130, etc., then it is not at all clear what happens at 110, 120, 130, etc., so this type of grouping must be avoided, although you'll see it in the Press and on TV.

USES OF GROUPED DATA: ESTIMATION OF THE MEAN

This kind of information can be put to good use by giving us nice compartments in which to draw up a histogram or pie chart if we so wish. One main use of this kind of information is to estimate what the *mean* is. To do this we find the halfway mark of each group and estimate all frequencies in that group to have the same mark.

 Level 5

For example, using the information in Table 14.3 to estimate the mean we would extend the table as shown in Table 14.4.

66 Level 7 99

Height (cm)	Halfway (m)	f	m × f
100–109	104.5	12	1254
110–119	114.5	19	2175.5
120–129	124.5	35	4357.5
130–139	134.5	32	4304
140–149	144.5	21	3034.5
150–159	154.5	10	1545
160–169	164.5	2	329
	Totals	131	16999.5

Table 14.4.

66 Students often make silly errors in calculating these mid-values. Take great care 99

The halfway point was found by calculating the mean of the group boundaries. Then the final column is the estimated total height of people in that group, found by multiplying halfway by frequency. Then we divide the total estimated height by the total frequency to give 16 999.5 ÷ 131, which will round off to 130 cm. It must be remembered that this is an *estimated mean* height and therefore has been rounded to three significant figures.

EXERCISE 3

Mark	Mid-value (m)	Frequency (f)	m × f
0–20		60	
21–50		680	
51–80		1160	
81–100		200	

Table 14.5

The grouped frequency table, Table 14.5, shows the number of candidates obtaining various ranges of marks in an examination. Complete this table and hence estimate the mean mark per candidate (give your answer to the nearest integer).

HISTOGRAM

There are two types of data that we need to be able to distinguish between: *discrete* and *continuous*.

Discrete data

66 Discrete data and continuous data 99

These are data that *can* be identified by a single number; for example, the number of goals scored by teams, the number of people in a car or the marks given for a test.

Continuous data

These are data that *cannot* be measured exactly and are usually given to a rounded off amount; for example, the height of a number of people, or weight, a length of time or a person's age.

When we use continuous data we generally replace bar charts with histograms, which definitely do not have any gaps in them because of the continuous nature of the data included.

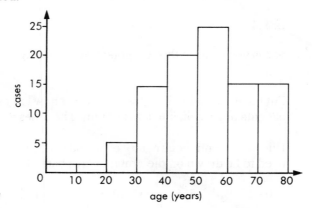

Fig. 14.7

The histogram in Fig. 14.7 illustrates the age incidence of duodenal ulcers found during a survey in a city hospital. Note a difference from the bar chart in the way the horizontal axis is labelled. Since each item of data is continuous, each *bar* has not been labelled as such, although its end points have.

In a histogram it is strictly the *area* of the bars (rectangles) that should distinguish the frequencies. However, at all but the highest level examination, your bars will all be of equal width and hence the heights will still be used to determine the frequencies, as in Fig. 14.7.

UNEQUAL WIDTH HISTOGRAMS

66 Note the idea of frequency density 99

Remember that it is the area of the rectangles in a histogram that represent the data. This is used when we consider *unequal interval histograms* with, now, the vertical axis being *frequency density* instead (often abbreviated to f.d.), so that the reading of the frequency density multiplied by the width of the rectangle will give the actual frequency which that particular rectangle is representing.

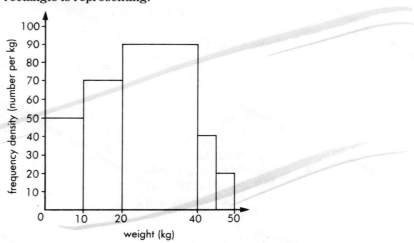

Fig. 14.8

For example, in the histogram in Fig. 14.8, the weight of an *average* sized box handled by a book delivery service is between 20 and 40 kg. The histogram illustrates the number of boxes handled in one particular week. Notice how, since the vast majority of the boxes are of average weight, they have been *lumped* together and the smaller number of heavier weights have been made such that we can see the difference between just above average and beyond. So from this histogram the groupings are as shown in Table 14.6.

Box weights	f.d. × width	Frequency
0–10	50 × 10	= 500
11–20	70 × 10	= 700
21–40	90 × 20	= 1800
41–45	40 × 5	= 200
46–50	20 × 5	= 100

Table 14.6

So, as you can see this is a good way to display information that is quite varied.

WORKED EXAMPLE 5

Put the information in Table 14.7, about how long Dr. K. Speed took over examining his patients one week, into a histogram. The times are to the nearest minute.

Due to the continuous nature of the data and the size of the numbers, then the groups will need to be drawn on the graph to give bars of the following widths;

0 –2.5, 2.5 –5.5, 5.5 –10.5, 10.5 –20 with widths of:
  2.5 ,   3 ,   5 ,   9.5

Since the area of the bars represents the frequency, then the height of each bar is given in Table 14.8.

Time taken (minutes)	Frequency
0– 2	8
3– 5	15
6–10	36
11–20	57

Table 14.7

Group	Width	Frequency	Height
0–2	2.5	8	8 ÷ 2.5 = 3.2
3–5	3	15	15 ÷ 3 = 5.0
6–10	5	36	36 ÷ 5 = 7.2
10–20	9.5	57	57 ÷ 9.5 = 6.0

Table 14.8

So the accurate histogram will be as in Fig. 14.9.

EXERCISE 4

The weekly take-home wages of a firm's employees were given in Table 14.9 to show the spread of wages.

Wage per week	Number of employees
Under £50	8
Between £51 and £200	36
Between £201 and £225	4
Between £226 and £250	1

Table 14.9

Draw a suitable histogram to illustrate this distribution.

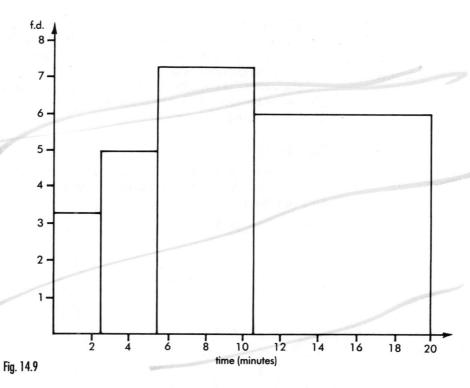

Fig. 14.9

4 > CUMULATIVE FREQUENCY

Sometimes known as running total graphs. They can be quite useful to show a spread of marks and to find the median as well as quartiles.

For example, the examination results for mathematics in one particular college one year were summarised as shown in Table 14.10.

Marks	Frequency	Cumulative frequency
0–20	50	50
21–30	50	100
31–40	95	195
41–50	120	315
51–60	80	395
61–70	55	450
71–80	30	480
81–100	20	500

Table 14.10

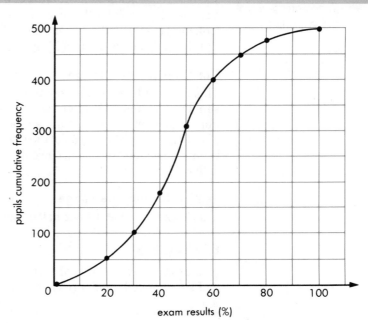

Fig. 14.10

Notice how the *cumulative frequency* is a running total of the frequency given. On its own, this information is not particularly useful but it can be when we graph it on what we would call a *cumulative frequency curve*. This example graphs as shown in Fig. 14.10. The cumulative frequency is always put on the vertical scale, and we plot the groups near the boundary with the cumulative frequency, so that we can draw in the curve as shown. It is known as the *ogive*. It has a distinctive shape as here, and from this type of curve we can find quartiles and the interquartile range.

QUARTILES

As the name suggests, *quartiles* are found by dividing the cumulative frequency, c.f., into four quarters. The points on a c.f. that give us the quartiles can be found by dividing the total into four equal groups.

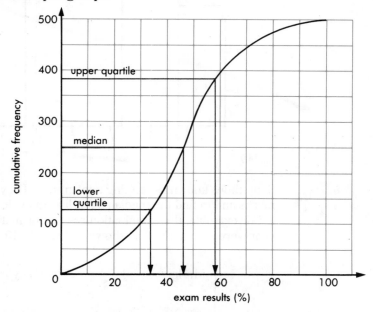

Fig. 14.11

For example, imagine the graph in Fig. 14.10 split into 4. Since we have 500 pupils, the halfway mark is 250 (O.K. it actually is $250\frac{1}{2}$ but can you really tell the difference?). This will give us the median mark, in our case about 44%. If we then halve the frequency again, or find one-quarter of the total frequency, it will give us 125. This is the quarter mark, or, as it is called, the *lower quartile*. In the same way find three-quarters of the way up the c.f., here it will be 375, and you find the *upper quartile*, which here is 56%. This can be seen in Fig. 14.11.

Careful, though; although this method works well for large frequencies, if you have smaller frequencies then you will need to be more precise. To find the exact median from a c.f. of n, you look for the mark of the $\frac{1}{2}(n+1)$ on the c.f. To find the lower quartile you look for $\frac{1}{4}(n+1)$ on the c.f., and so the upper quartile will be the $\frac{3}{4}(n+1)$ mark on the c.f. But this only needs doing if it's going to make a significant difference on your ogive.

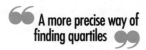

The interquartile range

This is the difference between the upper and lower quartiles, and should be expressed simply as the number difference on the horizontal axis.

For instance in our previous example the interquartile range will be 56%–33%, which is 23%. This tells us the spread of the middle half of the given population. This spread of 23% is not a very good one at all since it means that only 23% separates half the pupils at this college!

Semi-interquartile range

This is exactly what it says: half of the interquartile range.

EXERCISE 5

A café owner kept records of the number of meals served each week over a period of time and summarised the figures in a cumulative frequency table, Table 14.11.

Number of meals served per week	Number of weeks
Less than 100	20
Less than 200	90
Less than 300	240
Less than 400	370
Less than 500	435
Less than 600	470
Less than 700	490
Less than 800	500

Table 14.11

a) Draw the ogive from this information.
b) Use your ogive to estimate:
   i) the median number of meals served per week;
   ii) the interquartile range.
c) The café runs at a loss if less than 180 meals are served in a week. For how many weeks did the café run at a loss?

5 > SCATTER DIAGRAMS

A *scatter diagram* is used to test for any relationships that may be present in your statistics. For example, we have *scattered* the information about some children's heights and weights.

 Level 6

Name	cm	kg
James	135	47
John	105	26
Joseph	60	11
Paul	101	25
Michael	85	20
Jenny	74	16
Robert	120	32
Helen	130	45
Neil	130	42
Kirsty	95	18
Gary	180	57
Mark	145	55

Table 14.12

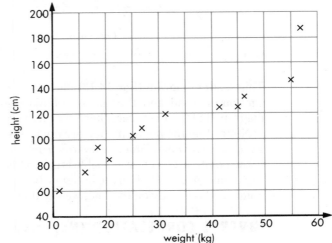

Fig. 14.12

You can draw a line on the diagram that represents the line of best fit. This will help you to see what the connection is.

Each cross represents an individual child by plotting a co-ordinate found from weight and height. From the chart we can easily deduce that the taller a child is the more likely he/she is to weigh more than a smaller child! You can use this scatter diagram to suggest very roughly the expected weight of a child of height 140 cm. You will see from the diagram that the child is likely to weigh more than 35 kg and less than 55 kg, not a very good estimation, but it can be used as a guide.

The use of scatter diagrams is one way of examining data to check if there is any type of connection between two properties of the same person, or whatever, in which case the points would lie in some line, as above. It is a practice in common use within examinations to see whether any one examination can be described as much too hard or easy compared with other subjects in which the same people are being examined.

6 > CORRELATION

The *scatter diagram* is a good way of seeing whether there is a connection between two sets of data. If there *is* a connection, we say we have a *correlation*. There are two main types of correlation: *direct* (or positive) correlation and *inverse* (or negative) correlation.

DIRECT CORRELATION (Positive Correlation)

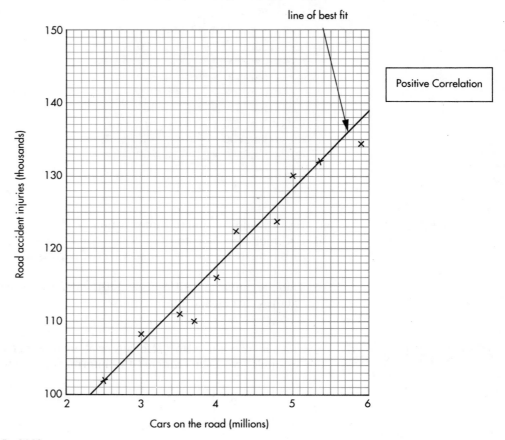

Fig. 14.13

This scatter diagram (Fig. 14.13) illustrates a *direct* correlation between 'the number of cars on the road' and 'the number of injuries from car accidents'. We can see from the diagram that the more cars there are on the road, the more road accident injuries occur.

Notice that the points plotted are not all on the same line. However they do mostly lie along a narrow band going upwards from left to right. A straight line which is drawn to fit the points as closely as possible is called 'the line of best fit'. The closer most points are to this line of 'best fit' then the better is the correlation between the two sets of data. If the points all lie exactly on the line, we say there is 'perfect correlation'.

INVERSE CORRELATION (Negative Correlation)

The scatter diagram (Fig. 14.14) shows an *inverse* correlation between the number of video recorders sold and the number of people going to cinemas. We can see from the diagram that the more video recorders are sold, the fewer the number of people going to cinemas. This inverse correlation is sometimes called negative or indirect correlation.

Again, notice that the points are not all on the line of best fit. However, the points do mostly lie along a narrow band going downwards from left to right, so there is a high degree of inverse correlation between the two sets of data.

EXERCISE 6

Draw scatter diagrams for the following sets of data and state the type of correlation, if any.

a) Some examination results from students are as follows.

Maths	68	28	81	85	86	50	58	38	63	99
Music	80	45	87	89	90	62	68	51	67	100

b) Batting and bowling averages for the all-rounders of a cricket team are given in the following tables.

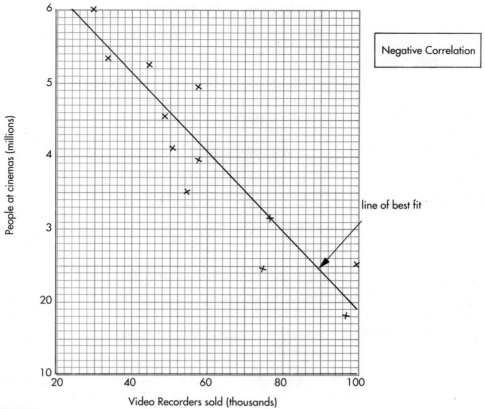

Fig. 14.14

Batting	9	12	19	27	28	42	45	48
Bowling	35	12	24	32	15	26	10	36

7 › PROBABILITY

> It's no use understanding this if you can't do fractions! I hope you can.

> Level 4

Or chance; this is finding out whether an event is likely or unlikely to happen, or whether one event has more chance of occurring than another. We calculate the probability of an event happening as a fraction given by:

$$\frac{\text{the number of ways the event can happen}}{\text{the total number of ways that equally likely events can happen}}$$

For example, the probability of rolling a die and getting a number 5 is $\frac{1}{6}$ since there is only one 5 on the die and six numbers altogether. Another example is the probability of cutting a pack of cards and obtaining an ace. The probability of this is 4/52 since there are four aces and 52 cards to choose from.

There are three important chances to know. An event that we may say has an *even* chance or a *50–50* chance is one like tossing a coin and getting a head; the probability is $\frac{1}{2}$. The probability of something impossible is 0, for example the probability of rolling a die and getting a 7 is $\frac{0}{6}$ which is 0. The probability of a certainty is 1, for example, the probability of rolling a die and getting a number less than 7 is $\frac{6}{6}$ which is 1.

Hence, any probability will be in between 0 and 1; the closer to nought then the more unlikely the event is to happen; the closer to 1 then the more likely the event is to happen.

WORKED EXAMPLE 5

In two bags of sweets, the larger one had 14 toffees and 6 mints, and the smaller one had 11 toffees and 4 mints. Being given a sweet out of a bag at random, which bag has a bigger probability of giving you a toffee?

The probabilities of getting toffees are: from the big bag $\frac{14}{20}$ and from the small bag $\frac{11}{15}$. We need to know which is the bigger fraction, and the easiest way to do this is to convert each fraction to a decimal number. $\frac{14}{20}$ is $14 \div 20$ which is 0.7, and $\frac{11}{15}$ is $11 \div 15$ which is 0.7333 ..., so $\frac{11}{15}$ is bigger than $\frac{14}{20}$. Therefore the small bag gives the best chance of getting a toffee.

EQUALLY LIKELY EVENTS

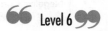 Level 6

When you roll a die, any number from 1 to 6 has just as much chance of coming up as any other, i.e. $\frac{1}{6}$.

When you toss a coin, you have an equal chance of getting a head or a tail, i.e. $\frac{1}{2}$.

So when we are considering more than one event, it can be helpful to consider *all* the equally likely events. For example:

i) tossing two coins gives the events

HH	TH
HT	TT

So the probability of each event is $\frac{1}{4}$

ii) tossing three coins gives the events

H	H	H		T	H	H
H	H	T		T	H	T
H	T	H		T	T	H
H	T	T		T	T	T

So the probability of each event is $\frac{1}{8}$.

 A tree diagram can be helpful

Notice the pattern made in the tables. This pattern should help you to write down all 16 *equally likely* events when you toss *four* coins. Try this for yourself now.

When creating lists like this, *tree diagrams* can help (we look at these in more detail later in the chapter).

For example, tossing three coins could have been illustrated as in this tree diagram.

1st	2nd	3rd	Events

```
                         H      H H H
                    H <
                         T      H H T
               H <
                         H      H T H
                    T <
                         T      H T T

                         H      T H H
                    H <
                         T      T H T
               T <
                         H      T T H
                    T <
                         T      T T T
```

A Tree Diagram for three tosses of a coin

Fig. 14.15

Sometimes you can show all the possible outcomes by drawing up a *table*. For example, when rolling two six sided dice, the following outcomes could occur.

		2nd dice					
		1	2	3	4	5	6
	1	(1,1)	(1,2)	(1,3)	(1,4)	(1,5)	(1,6)
	2	(2,1)	(2,2)	(2,3)	(2,4)	(2,5)	(2,6)
	3	(3,1)	(3,2)	(3,3)	(3,4)	(3,5)	(3,6)
1st	4	(4,1)	(4,2)	(4,3)	(4,4)	(4,5)	(4,6)
dice	5	(5,1)	(5,2)	(5,3)	(5,4)	(5,5)	(5,6)
	6	(6,1)	(6,2)	(6,3)	(6,4)	(6,5)	(6,6)

We can see that there are 36 equally likely events from rolling two dices.

EXPECTATION

If, for example, we know that the probability of rolling a 3 on a dice is $\frac{1}{6}$, then if the dice was rolled 100 times, how many times would we *expect* it to be a 3?

The answer is found by multiplying the number of times you do it by the probability, so here it is $100 \times \frac{1}{6} = 16.66\ldots$, which will be rounded to 17. Hence, you would expect to get around 17 threes if you rolled the dice 100 times. Try it, you'll not be far out.

Level 7

WORKED EXAMPLE 6

A firework being dud has a probability of $\frac{3}{100}$. Out of a big box of 450, how many duds would you expect?

Just multiply 450 by $\frac{3}{100}$ to get 13.5, which you would round to 14. So 14 dud fireworks would be expected.

EXERCISE 7

A doctor did a check on 140 patients chosen at random, and found that 42 of them had back trouble.
a) State as a fraction in its simplest form the probability of any one of his patients having back trouble.
b) The doctor had 900 patients. How many of them would he expect to have back trouble?

COMBINED EVENTS

When we want to find the probability of a *combined event*, that is, where two or more events are happening at the same time, then we need to be clear about whether we want two events to happen at the same time or whether either event can happen but not necessarily at the same time as the other. These two fall into different types that can be described as AND and OR.

Level 7

AND

AND is the type where both events happen at the same time. To find this combined probability we *multiply* the probabilities of each single event.

WORKED EXAMPLE 7

When rolling a dice and tossing a coin, what is the probability that you will roll a 4 and toss a head at the same time?

The probability of rolling a four is $\frac{1}{6}$, the probability of tossing a head is $\frac{1}{2}$; hence, the combined probability of a four AND a head will be $\frac{1}{6} \times \frac{1}{2} = \frac{1}{12}$.

WORKED EXAMPLE 8

Find the probability of tossing a head AND then a head AND then a head, and so on for four times. Hence, the probability will be $\frac{1}{2} \times \frac{1}{2} \times \frac{1}{2} \times \frac{1}{2}$, which is $\frac{1}{16}$.

OR

OR is the type when either one event or the other can happen but *not both at the same time*. To find this combined probability we *add* the probability of each event.

WORKED EXAMPLE 9

To finish a game a boy needed to throw a 6 or a 4. What was his chance of finishing on the next throw?

Each event has a probability of $\frac{1}{6}$ so for either event the probability will be $\frac{1}{6} + \frac{1}{6}$ which is $\frac{2}{6}$ or $\frac{1}{3}$.

WORKED EXAMPLE 10

On any day in February the weather probabilities are given as rain $\frac{1}{10}$, snow $\frac{1}{3}$. What is the probability of a day in February being either rainy or snowy? We assume it cannot be both.

Since we want the probability of either rain OR snow, then we add the probabilities of $\frac{1}{10}$ and $\frac{1}{3}$ to get $\frac{13}{30}$.

AND and OR

This is how many of your examination problems are going to come, in situations where you need a combination of AND and OR.

The probability of Paul getting to school on time is 0.95. The probability of Michael being late for school is 0.1. What is the probability on any one day that either Paul or Michael (or both) are late for school?

The events that we can have are:

A: Paul late AND Michael not late.
B: Paul not late AND Michael late.
C: Paul late AND Michael late.

As the probability of Paul not being late is 0.95, the probability that he is late is $(1-0.95)$ = 0.05.
As the probability of Michael being late is 0.1, the probability that he is not late is $(1-0.1)$ = 0.9.

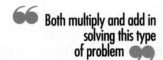
Both multiply and add in solving this type of problem

Hence the P(A) = 0.05×0.9 = 0.045
     P(B) = 0.95×0.1 = 0.095
     P(C) = 0.05×0.1 = 0.005

As we can have A OR B OR C, then add the probabilities to give

  P(A) + P(B) + P(C) = 0.145.

Note: The last worked example illustrated the way in which AND and OR can be combined together, but for that example there is a quicker way of getting to the final answer. That is to first find the probabilities of neither being late, i.e. Paul is on time AND Michael is on time. This is 0.95×0.9 = 0.855.

The probability that one or the other is late = 1 – the probability of both not being late = 1 – 0.855 = 0.145.
As you see, this way is much quicker – if you spot it.

Tree diagrams are, as we have seen, a very useful way of looking at all the possibilities of a given situation and help us to find various probabilities. A Tree diagram can use both the ideas of AND and OR that we have just met.

Level 8

For example, when travelling down from Sheffield to Cornwall on the motorways there is a $\frac{1}{10}$ chance of being held up on the M1, and a $\frac{1}{5}$ chance of being held up on the M5. What are the chances of being held up, or not, on the total journey?

We can illustrate the possibilities with a tree diagram, as shown in Fig. 14.16.

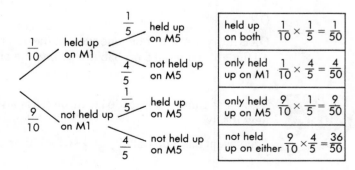

Fig. 14.16

Notice how the individual probabilities have been put on the *branches* of the tree diagram, with each *pair* adding up to 1, since in each pair one of the branches *must* happen. Then to find the probabilities of the combined events, you just multiply along the branches as shown.

But, beware of the following type of situation.

WORKED EXAMPLE 12

I have a bag of sweets containing 5 toffees, 3 mints and 2 jellies. What are the probabilities of taking two of the same sweets out to eat?

You must consider taking out first one sweet, then the other, but when you take out the second sweet there are fewer sweets in the bag, so look carefully at the probabilities this situation gives us; see Fig. 14.17.

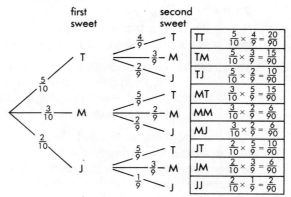

Fig. 14.17

Notice again that each set of branches from the same point will all add up to 1. Look at the second sweet branches. There are only 9 sweets left in the bag and when the toffee was the first sweet out there were only 4 toffees left, or in the case where the mint was the first sweet out there were 5 toffees and 2 jellies but only 2 mints. Also if you add up the final probabilities they should add up to 1.

WORKED EXAMPLE 13

Caroline has 30 cassettes, of which 15 are *heavy metal*, 10 are *rock* and 5 are *pop*. She is late for a party and asks her Mum: 'Oh, get me any two, Mum!!' Draw a tree diagram to help you find the probability that both cassettes are of the same type.

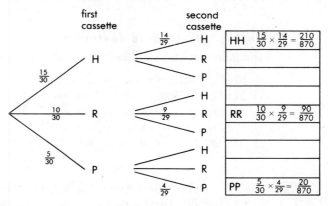

Fig. 14.18

We shall not need all the probabilities for this particular question, so we shall only put the relevant probabilities on the tree diagram, but just test yourself that you could do it all if asked. Notice in Fig. 14.18, that by not cancelling down it keeps all the fractions the same type which helps when it comes to adding them together. So the probability of either both being heavy metal OR both being rock, OR both being pop will be:

$$\frac{210}{870} + \frac{90}{870} + \frac{20}{870} \text{ which is } \frac{230}{870} \text{ (not far off a D chance)}.$$

9 ▷ SAMPLING

Level 9

The idea of estimating the features of a population by taking *samples*, is widely used in statistical research. For example, during General Elections, Polls are regularly taken by asking a few thousand people how they would vote. This information is then used to estimate how the whole population would vote if this sample were typical of the population.

Another example of the use of samples is in quality control, such as in the production of light bulbs. Samples of light bulbs are taken and the average length of life of each sample is worked out to help test whether the reliability of *all* the bulbs is meeting a certain target figure.

When taking a sample, it is important to try to take a sample which is truly representative of the whole 'population', and is not biased in any way.

Random Sampling

A *random sample* is one in which every member of the population has an equal chance of being selected for the sample. Sometimes 'random number tables' are used to help you select a random sample.

Quota Sampling

Different types of sampling can be used for different applications

Here each person taking a sample will have been given a quota of people (say 40) to interview. Further the *type* of person to include in the quota will have been stated:

For example: 5 men over 40, 5 men between 20 and 40
5 women over 50, 5 women between 30 and 50
5 men dressed in a suit, 5 smokers
5 women with children, 5 women without children, etc.

The aim of giving so detailed a list in quota sampling is to try to get a balance of people in the sample which is representative of the population as a whole, their sex, ages, appearance, habits, family grouping, etc. A lot of interviewers might select their sample at the same time of day and then telephone or fax their results into a central office for the results to be noted and classified.

Generally speaking, the larger the size of the sample, the more accurate a sample result is likely to be in making a prediction about the population as a whole.

10 STANDARD DEVIATION

The *standard deviation* is widely used as a measure of *dispersion*; i.e. how much the data varies around the average (mean).

Many calculators have the ability to help you calculate the standard deviation of data you have entered. However, in an examination you will be expected to show *how* you calculated the standard deviation. Of course you can always *check* your result on the calculator.

Finding the standard deviation

The following steps will help you to find the standard deviation.

a) Find the mean for the given data.
b) Find the deviations from the mean for each piece of data.
c) Square each of the deviations.
d) Find the mean of these squares.
e) The square root of this mean is the standard deviation.

WORKED EXAMPLE 14

Find the standard deviation of the weights of a sample of ten boxes of chocolate, all sold as 1 kg weight. Their actual weights were found to be: 998g, 1001g, 999g, 998g, 1001g, 1000g, 1001g, 999g, 997g, 1002g.

The standard deviation of the weights is found as follows

a) Find the mean of the ten boxes as 999.6g.

Put the rest of the information into a table as follows. We can use this table to help with the other steps in the calculation.

Weight (g)	deviation from mean (d)	square of deviation (d^2)
998	− 1.6	2.56
1001	1.4	1.96
999	− 0.6	0.36
998	− 1.6	2.56
1001	1.4	1.96
1000	0.4	0.16
1001	1.4	1.96
999	− 0.6	0.36
997	− 2.6	6.76
1002	2.4	5.76
		$\Sigma d^2 = 24.40$

The *minus* values in the deviations from the mean should exactly equal the *plus* values

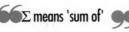
Σ means 'sum of'

$$\text{Standard deviation} = \sqrt{\frac{\Sigma d^2}{n}} = \sqrt{\left(\frac{24.4}{10}\right)} = 1.56 \text{ g}$$

EXERCISE 8

Find the standard deviation of the ages of the 11 members of a football team:
32, 32, 29, 23, 24, 28, 29, 32, 31, 27, 32.

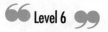

CRITICAL PATH ANALYSIS

66 Level 6 99

A *critical path* is a sequence of operations that should be followed in order to reach a conclusion.

This type of problem can come in a number of forms, the two most common being:

i) networks and shortest routes to be found.
ii) lists of tasks and times, then the shortest time for the completed tasks to be found.

i) NETWORKS

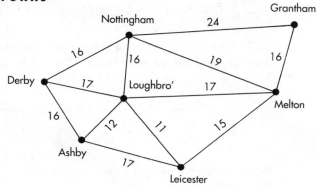

Fig. 14.19

The diagram shows the distances in miles between a network of towns and cities.

A computer firm wants to connect all the towns and cities together with cable, either directly or indirectly. Find the least amount of cable needed to connect the towns.

The problem is a relatively simple one and can be solved by trial and error, selecting different places to put the cable. It is usual to try to use the shorter distances while avoiding the longer distances.

After some trials you will arrive at a network, giving a minimum length of 86 miles.

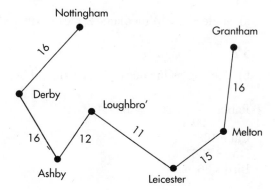

Fig. 14.20

Note that the cable could also have been laid from Nottingham to Loughbro' in place of Derby to Ashby.

ii) COMBINING TASKS

Level 10

This involves looking for the best way to combine or separate tasks, in order to complete the whole task. If you can be doing more than one task *at the same time*, then you may be using time and resources in the best way possible.

Example. Tasks needed to put up a Christmas Tree.

	Activity	Time	Preceding Activity
A	Buy the tree	30 min	–
B	Find and clean the tub	15 min	–
C	Find stones to put in tub	10 min	–
D	Cut the tree to length	5 min	A
E	Stand tree in the tub	5 min	D
F	Put stones in tub, steady tree	5 min	E
G	Find and test the lights	15 min	–
H	Put lights on the tree	15 min	F
I	Find decorations for tree	20 min	–
J	Put decorations on tree	20 min	H

To find the shortest time for two people to do the whole job, we have to separate out jobs that can be done *simultaneously.* This can be illustrated by a critical path diagram, as below.

$$\text{Start} \quad * \underset{B \xrightarrow{15} C \xrightarrow{10} G \xrightarrow{15} I \xrightarrow{\quad 20 \quad} *}{\underset{}{\overset{A \xrightarrow{30} D \xrightarrow{5} E \xrightarrow{5} F \xrightarrow{5} H \xrightarrow{15} J \xrightarrow{20} *}{}}} \quad \text{Finish}$$

So the shortest time will be governed by the top line of the critical path, which is 1 hour 20 minutes.

Care needs to be taken to make sure that the preceding activities have all been completed for each specific task.

SOLUTIONS TO EXERCISES

S1

a) Mode = 1;   b) median = 2;   c) mean = 21 ÷ 7 = 3.

S2

b) The angles in your pie chart should be:

Rabbit $\dfrac{20}{90} \times 360 = 80°$;

Cat = 108°
Dog = 136°
Bird = 36°

S3

Care was needed with the mid-values, but then the estimated mean is:

118 820 ÷ 2100 = 56.58

To the nearest integer then, this is 57.

Mark	Mid-value (*m*)		Frequency (*f*)	*m* × *f*
0– 20	10		60	600
21– 50	35.5		680	24.140
51– 80	65.5		1160	75 980
81–100	90.5		200	18 100
		Totals	2100	118 820

S4

Be careful with units and frequency density units, but you should have an answer like the one shown, in Fig. 14.21.

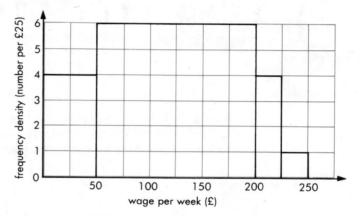

Fig. 14.21

Notice how 1 *square* represents 1 *person* hence the frequency density is 1 unit per £25, since the width of a square representing 1 person is £25. An alternative scale to the graph would be to have said 1 square represents 1 person.

S5

a) When you graph this it should look something like Fig. 14.22. You should, of course, use a larger scale to that shown here, to make your answer more accurate.

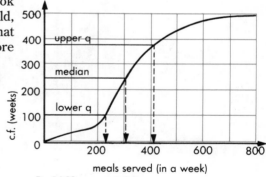

Fig. 14.22

b) i) Read from your graph, the median is at 250 on the cumulative frequency, which is about 313 meals served.
   ii) The interquartile range is the difference of the upper and lower quartiles which should be around 407–223, which is about 184. *Note* that in the examination you will be marked from *your* graph.

c) You need to read off from where meals served are 180, and read along the ogive to the c.f. This will give around 70 weeks that the café ran at a loss.

S6

a) Direct correlation
b) No correlation at all

S7

a) $\dfrac{42}{140}$ cancels down to $\dfrac{3}{10}$ or 0.3.   b) $900 \times \dfrac{3}{10} = 270$

S8

Standard deviation = $\sqrt{\dfrac{106}{11}}$ = 3.1 years

EXAM TYPE QUESTIONS

Q1

It is known that flash bulbs reach their maximum brightness very quickly, as the aluminium they contain burns. A test was done on 100 flash bulbs to find how long each bulb took to reach maximum brightness. The results are summarised in the Table below.

Fig. 14.23

Time (seconds)	0–0.01	–0.02	–0.03	–0.04	–0.05	–0.06	–0.07	–0.08	–0.09	–0.10
Number of flash bulbs	6	15	29	24	14	6	2	2	1	1

a) Draw a histogram on the grid below to represent the information in the table.

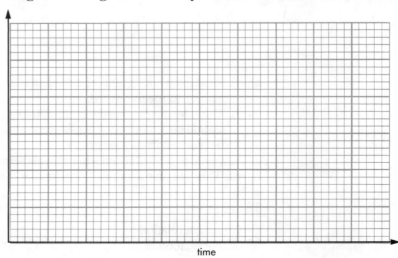

Fig. 14.24

time

b) How long does it usually take for a flashbulb to reach its maximum brightness?

(NEAB)

Q2

Samantha and Teresa both did ten Mathematics homeworks. Here are their marks out of ten.

Samantha	10	10	7	4	9	8	5	2	9	8
Teresa	5	7	6	8	6	8	7	8	7	6

a) Work out the mean mark for each of them.
b) Work out the range for each of them.
q) Say who you think was better at Maths. Give a reason for your answer.

(MEG)

Q3

The pie-chart below is published by Dr Barnardo's in Northern Ireland to show how they spend each £1. If a school raised £2680 for Dr Barnardo's, work out:

a) How much of that money would go directly to child care?
b) How much would be spent on education and appeals?

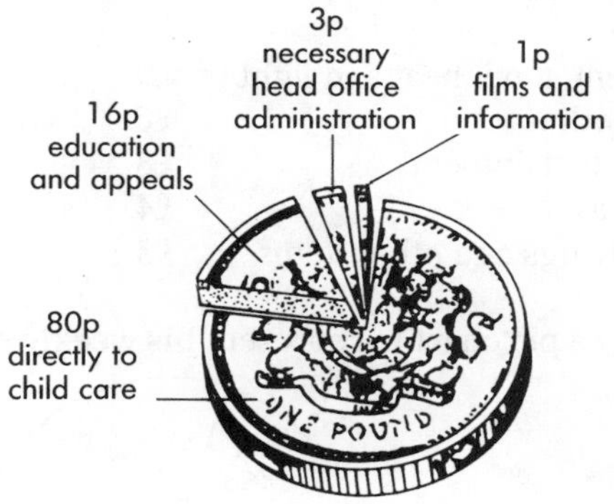

Fig. 14.25

(NISEAC)

Q4

A survey in a hospital was carried out to see how long it took to give patients a check-up. The results are summarised in the Table below.

a) By suitably extending the table, calculate the estimated mean time taken to give one patient a check-up. Give your answer to the nearest minute.

Time taken to the nearest minute	Frequency
11–15	18
16–20	27
21–25	12
26–30	3
Total	60

b) A doctor is available to do check-ups on one afternoon for 4 hours. Using the average time per patient that you found in part a), estimate how many patients the doctor can see during this time.
c) Using the average time per patient as before, estimate how many doctors the hospital would need in order to give 83 patients a check-up during a 3 hour morning session.
(NEAB)

Q5

The probability of a train arriving early at a station is $\frac{1}{10}$. The probability of a train arriving late at a station is $\frac{2}{5}$.

a) If 400 trains are expected at a station during the day, how many of them are likely to arrive at the correct time?

b) What is the probability that both the trains arriving at the station from Exeter are late? (SEG)

Q6

Pop stars often say they do not get a fair share of the selling price of the LP records they make. For example, for a record selling at £5.40: £1.50 goes to the shop, 90p goes to the government in tax, 54p is the cost of materials, £1.80 goes to the record company, and the rest goes to the pop star.

a) How much of the £5.40 goes to the pop star?

b) How many records must be sold for the pop star to be paid £1000?

c) Draw a suitable pie chart to show how the money paid for an LP record is distributed.

Q7

a) In 1985, an apprentice electrician's *take home* pay was £30 per week. His weekly budget was as follows:

Rent, food, heat and light	£9
Clothes	£6
Entertainment	£8
Travel	£4
Savings and other items	£3

Draw a pie chart to represent his weekly budget.

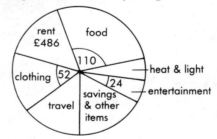

Fig. 14.26

b) The pie chart in Fig. 14.26 represents the *average family* budget in 1985. The *average family's* net income in 1985 was £3240. Calculate:
   i) how much was spent on food;
   ii) what angle is represented by rent;
   iii) what percentage of the family's net income was spent on entertainment.

c) By comparing the two pie charts, comment briefly on the major differences between the *average family* budget and the *apprentice's* budget. (SEG)

Q8

In a game to select a winner from three friends Arshad, Belinda and Connie, Arshad and Belinda both roll a normal die. If Arshad scores a number greater than 2 *and* Belinda throws an odd number, then Arshad is the winner. Otherwise Arshad is eliminated and Connie then rolls the die. If the die shows an odd number Connie is the winner, otherwise Belinda is the winner.

Calculate the probability (P) that:

a) Arshad will be the winner;

b) Connie will roll the die;

c) Connie will be the winner. (ULEAC)

Q9

The table below shows the prices of some paperback novels and the number of pages in them.

Price	85p	£1.00	95p	£1.25	£1.50	£1.65	95p	£1.00	£1.35	65p	75p
Pages	224	254	170	236	330	380	210	190	320	136	150

On graph paper construct a scatter diagram for this information. Use scales of 2 cm to represent 50 pages and 2 cm to represent 20p.

a) Draw a line of best fit.
b) Use your line to estimate the cost of a book with 300 pages.   (NEAB)

Q10

To be an advanced motor mower driver you must pass three tests, and the following are the probabilities of passing these individual tests:

Ability to walk in a straight line $\frac{3}{5}$.

Ability to swerve out of the way of stray animals $\frac{1}{5}$.

Ability to talk constantly while driving $\frac{9}{10}$.

Each test is taken in the order given above.
a) Draw a tree diagram to illustrate the ways in which you can fail and hence find the probabilities that
   i) you will fail only one test.
   ii) you fail to become an advanced motor mower driver.
b) If 100 people were tested, how many would you expect to pass?

Q11

James tosses a coin and then rolls a die. The diagram shows the result (Tail, 5).

 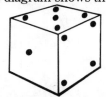

Two other possible results are (Head, 3) and (Tail, 4). List all the other possible results.
(SEG)

Q12

The table below shows the distribution of the working life of 400 'Betta' projector bulbs.

Working life (x hours)	$2 < x \leqslant 4$	$4 < x \leqslant 5$	$5 < x \leqslant 6$	$6 < x \leqslant 7$	$7 < x \leqslant 8$	$8 < x \leqslant 10$
Number of bulbs	30	106	140	50	36	38

a) Using mid-interval values, calculate an estimate of the mean of this distribution.
b) On the grid below, draw a histogram to represent this distribution.   (MEG)

Q13

60% of the pupils taught by the 'Arrow' School of Motoring pass their driving test at the first attempt.
Each time a pupil retakes the test, the pupil's chance of passing improves by 10%, i.e. a 70% chance of passing after one failure etc.

a) i) On the tree diagram, write the missing probabilities on the dotted lines.

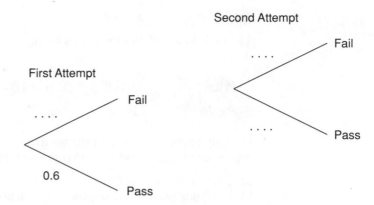

ii) Calculate the probability that an 'Arrow' pupil chosen at random will pass at the second attempt.

b) Calculate the probability that an 'Arrow' pupil chosen at random will pass at the third attempt. (ULEAC)

Q14

Karen is keen to improve her scores at darts. She always aims to hit the bull (at the centre of the darts board) and her last twelve scores were

32,   25,   56,   52,   23,   60,   19,   36,   36,   20,   56,   20.

a) Calculate the mean and standard deviation of these scores.

Karen decides to change her tactics and to aim to hit treble twenty (towards the top of the board). It is found that the mean of her next twelve scores is 33.75 and their standard deviation is 21.4.

b) Karen is unfamiliar with statistical terms. What advice would you give her about her tactics and what explanation would you give?

(MEG)

Q15

The activities involved when two workers replace a broken window pane, and the times taken for each activity, are given in the table below.

	Activity	Duration in minutes	Preceding activity
A	Remove broken pane	20	–
B	Measure size of pane	15	–
C	Purchase glass and putty	25	B
D	Put putty in frame	10	A, C
E	Put in new pane of glass	5	D
F	Putty outside and smooth	10	E
G	Sweep up broken glass	5	A
H	Clean up	5	F, G

Using a critical path diagram, or otherwise, find how the two workers should share the activities to complete the replacement of the broken window pane in the minimum possible time.

State this minimum time. (ULEAC)

OUTLINE ANSWERS TO EXAM QUESTIONS

A1

a) See Fig. 14.27. The vertical axis could also be described (it is more correct!) with frequency density of 1000, 2000, 3000.

b) Between 0.02 and 0.04 seconds.

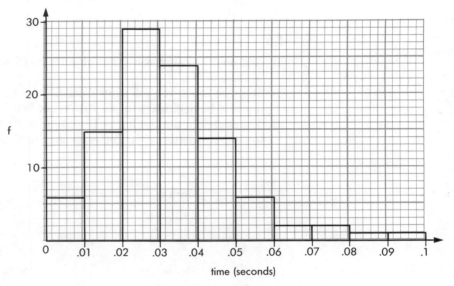

Fig. 14.27

A2

a) Samantha's mean = 72 ÷ 10 = 7.2
Teresa's mean = 68 ÷ 10 = 6.8

b) Samantha's range = 2 to 10
Teresa's range = 5 to 8

c) You could argue for *either* being better; it is your reason that is being marked. For example, Samantha, since she has the better average score; or Teresa, since she is more reliable and has a better all round knowledge.

A3

a) $£2680 \times \dfrac{80}{100} = £2144$

b) $£2680 \times \dfrac{16}{100} = £428.80$

A4

You need a halfway mark then a $m \times f$ column, so the table should be extended as shown in the Table.

Time taken	Halfway (m)	f	$m \times f$
11–15	13	18	234
16–20	18	27	486
21–25	23	12	276
26–30	28	3	84
	Totals	60	1080

a) Hence the estimated mean will be $1080 \div 60$, which is 18 minutes.

b) 4 hours is 4×60 minutes, which is 240. So the doctor sees $240 \div 18$, which is 13.33; hence he will only have time for 13 check-ups.

c) 83 patients at 18 minutes each means 1494 *patient minutes* to be checked in $3 \times 60 = 180$ minutes. The hospital will therefore need $1494 \div 180$ doctors, which is 8.3; so to see all the patients this needs to be rounded off to 9 doctors.

A5

a) The probability of the train arriving early OR late is $\frac{1}{10} + \frac{2}{5} = \frac{5}{10}$; hence, the probability that it is on time is $1 - \frac{5}{10} = \frac{5}{10}$; hence, you would expect $400 \times \frac{5}{10} = 200$ to arrive on time.

b) $\frac{2}{5} \times \frac{2}{5} = \frac{4}{25}$

A6

a) Add up the totals given and subtract from £5.40, and you will get £5.40 – £4.74, which is £0.66 or 66p.

b) To make £1000 you will need to sell £1000 ÷ £0.66 records which is 1515.15 …, hence it would be necessary to sell 1516 records to be sure of £1000.

c) The angles for the pie chart will be found by the following: change everything to pence to simplify matters then find each as a fraction of 360°.

Money		Angle		
Shop	150	$\frac{150}{540} \times 360$	$= 100°$
Tax	90	$\frac{90}{540} \times 360$	$= 60°$
Materials	54	$\frac{54}{540} \times 360$	$= 36°$
Company	180	$\frac{180}{540} \times 360$	$= 120°$
Pop star	66	$\frac{66}{540} \times 360$	$= 44°$
Total....................	540			$360°$

Then the accuracy of the actual pie chart is up to you, but you should put the angles in starting with the smallest angle of 36° first and going up in order to 120°. Do not forget to label angles and sectors.

A7

a) Rent, etc .... $\frac{9}{30} \times 360 = 108°$

Clothes .... $\frac{6}{30} \times 360 = 72°$

Entertainment .... $\frac{8}{30} \times 360 = 96°$

Travel .... $\frac{4}{30} \times 360 = 48°$

Savings, etc. .... $\frac{3}{30} \times 360 = 36°$

b) i) $\dfrac{110}{360} \times 3240 = £990$ ii) $\dfrac{x}{360} \times 3240 = 486$ iii) $\dfrac{24}{360} \times 100 = 6.67\%$

$$x = \dfrac{486 \times 360}{3240} = 54°$$

c) Apprentices spend more on entertainment and clothes and much less on rent, food, heat and light.

A8

a) $P(\text{A no.} > 2) = \dfrac{4}{6}$ or equivalent   b) $P(\text{C rolls die}) = 1 - \text{part a)} = \dfrac{2}{3}$

$P(\text{B odd no.}) = \dfrac{1}{2}$ c) $P(\text{C odd no.}) = \dfrac{1}{2}$

$P(\text{both above}) = \dfrac{2}{3} \times \dfrac{1}{2}$ $P(\text{C winner}) = \dfrac{2}{3} \times \dfrac{1}{2} = \dfrac{1}{3}$

$P(\text{A winner}) = \dfrac{1}{3}$

A9

The answer to part b) is taken from *your* line of best fit. But the answer should be between £1.25 and £1.40.

A10

You've been asked to draw a tree diagram, so you might lose marks if you tried the question without one! The tree diagram should look like the one in Fig. 14.28. Only the final probabilities that would be needed for the answers have been inserted, see if you can fill in the rest for yourself.

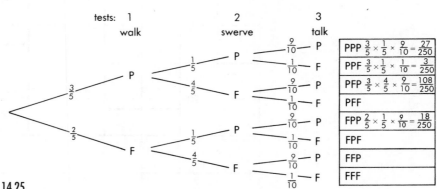

Fig. 14.25

a) i) Only failing one test can be done in the 3 ways; PPF, PFP or FPP, add together their probabilities to get

$\frac{3}{250} + \frac{108}{250} + \frac{18}{250}$, which is $\frac{219}{250}$.

ii) You fail to become a proper driver only if you do not pass all three tests, hence the probability is $1 - \frac{27}{250}$ which is $\frac{223}{250}$.

b) If 100 people take the tests, then since the probability of passing all three is $\frac{27}{250}$, we would expect to see $100 \times \frac{27}{250}$ pass, which rounds to 11 people.

A11

(Head, 1)   (Tail, 1)
(Head, 2)   (Tail, 2)

(Head, 4)   (Tail, 3)
(Head, 5)   (Tail, 6)
(Head, 6)

These are the ones not already given.

A12

a) $(3 \times 30) + (4.5 \times 106) + (5.5 \times 140) + (6.5 \times 50) \times (7.5 \times 36) \times (9 \times 38) \div 400$
    $= 5.685$ $= 5.7$ hours

b) Since we have unequal widths we need a frequency
    density as vertical axis with heights as:

width	height
2–4	$30 \div 2 = 15$
4–5	$106 \div 1 = 106$
5–6	$140 \div 1 = 140$
6–7	$50 \div 1 = 50$
7–8	$36 \div 1 = 36$
8–10	$38 \div 2 = 19$

Giving the histogram as shown in Fig. 14.29.

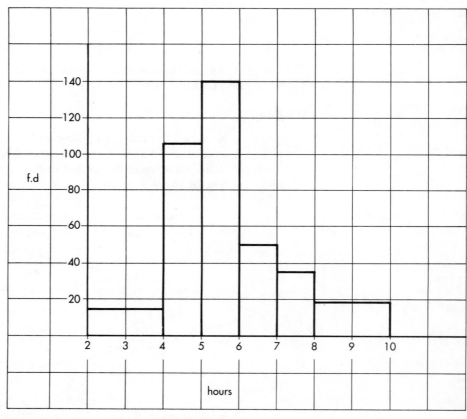

Fig. 14.29

A13

a) i) the missing probabilities are 0.4, 0.3 and 0.7
    ii) $0.4 \times 0.7 = 0.28$
b) Fail × Fail × Pass
    $0.4 \times 0.3 \times 0.8 = 0.096$

A14

a) i) mean $= \dfrac{435}{12} = 36.25$

ii)

Score	d	d² (rounded)
32	4.25	18.06
25	11.25	126.56
56	19.75	390.06
52	15.75	248.06
23	13.25	175.56
60	23.75	564.06
19	17.25	297.56
36	0.25	0.06
36	0.25	0.06
20	16.25	264.06
56	19.75	390.06
20	16.25	264.06

$$sd = \sqrt{\frac{\Sigma d^2}{12}}$$

$$= \sqrt{(228.185}$$

$$= 15.1$$

b) She scored higher and more consistently by going for the bull. Stick to going for the bull.

A15

A and G can be done by one worker, while the other does B, C, D, E, and F; H will be done by both.

Hence   A, G   gives   20 + 5 = 25 min
         B, C, D, E, F, H   gives   15 + 25 + 10 + 5 + 10 + 5 = 70 min
         minimum time 70 mins.

LEVEL CHECKLIST

For the level	You should be able to do the following
4	Tally data and create a frequency table. Understand and use median and mode. Construct and interpret frequency diagrams. Calculate the mean of a set of data. Understand and use the probability scale 0 to 1. List all possible outcomes of an event.
5.	Construct and interpret pie charts. Calculate the expectation of a particular experiment.
6	Create scatter graphs, and understand correlation. Identify all the outcomes of combining two independent events.
7	Calculate the mean from grouped data. Compare the mean, median, mode and range of frequency distributions. Draw frequency polygons. Draw lines of best fit on scatter diagrams. Calculate the probability of combined events.
8	Construct and interpret a cumulative frequency diagram. Understand and calculate quartiles and inter-quartile range.
9	Construct histograms with unequal width bases. Use sampling techniques.
10	Calculate standard deviation. Understand the idea of a normal distribution.

A STUDENT'S ANSWER WITH EXAMINER'S COMMENTS

Question

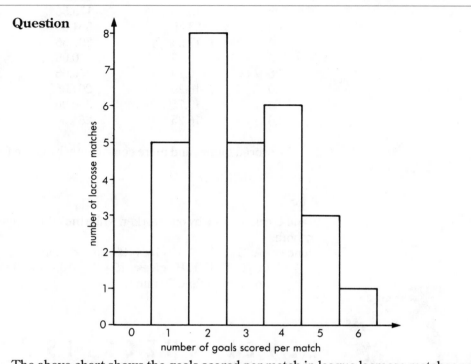

number of lacrosse matches

number of goals scored per match

The above chart shows the goals scored per match in league lacrosse matches on a certain Saturday.

i) Write down the number of matches in which 2 goals were scored.

Calculate:

ii) the number of matches played;

iii) the number of goals scored altogether;

iv) the mean number of goals scored per match.

Answers:

66 Good. **99**

i) 8 matches

ii) 1 match   (6 goals)

~~2 matches~~

3 matches   (5 goals)

5×2 match   = 30 matches

66 Although the answer is correct the method shown is incomplete, and marks will be lost. **99**

66 Correct and method shown **99**

iii) 0 × 2 = 0   4 × 6 = 24

1 × 5 = 5   5 × 3 = 15

2 × 8 = 16   1 × 6

3 × 5 = 15   = 81 goals

iv) $\frac{81}{30}$ goals = 2·7

R E V I E W   S H E E T

✎ Name each *type* of average

a) most frequent item _____

b) middle value when arranged in order _____

c) total value divided by number of items _____

✎ Write down a list of 5 numbers that:

a) has a mode of 3 _____

b) has a median of 4 _____

c) has a mean of 5 _____

✎ Look again at the *pictogram* in Fig. 14.2. Represent the same information as a *pie chart*, using the 4 political parties (fill in the circle below).

✎ Look again at the information given in Table 14.3. Represent the same information as a *histogram*.

✎ Look again at the *cumulative frequency curve* in Fig. 14.10. Use the curve there to draw, and estimate:

a) The lower quartile _____

b) The median _____

c) The upper quartile _____

✎ Look again at the *scatter diagram* in Fig. 14.12. Draw the 'line of best fit' on the diagram. What is your estimate for height when:

a) weight is 40 kg: _____ cm

b) weight is 50 kg; _____ cm?

✎ What *type of correlation* is there between weight and height? _____ correlation.

✎ If, when one variable increases, the other decreases, we say there is _____ correlation.

✎ Complete the following *tree diagram* probabilities involving a journey.

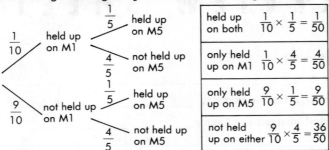

held up on both	$\frac{1}{10} \times \frac{1}{5} = \frac{1}{50}$
only held up on M1	$\frac{1}{10} \times \frac{4}{5} = \frac{4}{50}$
only held up on M5	$\frac{9}{10} \times \frac{1}{5} = \frac{9}{50}$
not held up on either	$\frac{9}{10} \times \frac{4}{5} = \frac{36}{50}$

✎ Complete the following *tree diagram* probabilities involving the selection of toffees (T), minto (M) and jellies (J) from a bag of sweets containing 5 toffees, 3 mints and 2 jellies.

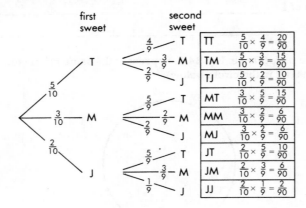

TT	$\frac{5}{10} \times \frac{4}{9} = \frac{20}{90}$
TM	$\frac{5}{10} \times \frac{3}{9} = \frac{15}{90}$
TJ	$\frac{5}{10} \times \frac{2}{9} = \frac{10}{90}$
MT	$\frac{3}{10} \times \frac{5}{9} = \frac{15}{90}$
MM	$\frac{3}{10} \times \frac{2}{9} = \frac{6}{90}$
MJ	$\frac{3}{10} \times \frac{2}{9} = \frac{6}{90}$
JT	$\frac{2}{10} \times \frac{5}{9} = \frac{10}{90}$
JM	$\frac{2}{10} \times \frac{3}{9} = \frac{6}{90}$
JJ	$\frac{2}{10} \times \frac{1}{9} = \frac{2}{90}$

✎ When all items have an equal chance of selection, we call this _____ sampling.

✎ When we choose a certain number of different types of persons to include in a sample, we call this _____ sampling.

✎ Sampling helps us to get a picture of the whole _____ from which the sample is taken.

✎ The standard deviation is a measure of _____, telling us how data varies around the average.

✎ Write down the *five steps* involved in finding the standard deviation.

a) _____

b) _____

c) _____

d) _____

e) _____

✎ A _____ is a sequence of operations that should be followed to reach a conclusion.

COURSEWORK

GETTING STARTED

All GCSE mathematics syllabuses include a coursework component, i.e. a component which seeks to measure your progress in 'using and applying mathematics' (AT 1). The way coursework fits into the whole programme of assessment will vary from exam board to exam board and from school to school. Yet there is a common underlying principle behind all coursework based activities, namely to help the student reach a better understanding of mathematics through investigation, problem solving and practical application.

Familiarity with the coursework activities expected of you will be of help towards the end of year 9 (as you begin to consider seriously your GCSE programme). Still more in years 10 and 11 as you embark on the activities themselves and have to present the outcome of your investigations in written form. The coursework may be assessed over the two years by many assignments or by one terminal exam.

You will find general aims in your GCSE mathematics syllabus which relate to coursework. These will include statements along the following lines. Coursework will help you as candidates to:

1   develop mathematical knowledge in a way which increases your interest and confidence;
2   write and talk about mathematics in a variety of ways;
3   apply mathematics to everyday situations and to start to understand the part that mathematics plays in the world in which you live;
4   see how a situation can be represented mathematically and then formulate the problem, selecting where necessary a mathematical method to solve it;
5   develop your mathematics by enquiry and experiment by means of practical and investigational work.

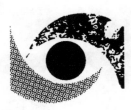

E S S E N T I A L   P R I N C I P L E S

Coursework should not be seen as an 'extra' activity which takes place *outside* the classroom. It should rather be understood that coursework seeks to encourage and reward good practice in mathematics, *wherever* it is performed. Good practical work and pieces of extended work or investigations will be recognised and assessed, and will now form part of the basis for the overall grade.

Coursework should encourage and support you in developing your knowledge and understanding of mathematics to the best of your ability. You will engage in a variety of 'experiences' of mathematics during your coursework programme. These should increase your *awareness* of how mathematics can be used to solve practical problems. It should also of course increase your *ability* to put these solutions into practice.

Coursework makes it possible for you to be examined on mathematical abilities which cannot easily or fairly be examined by *timed written papers*. The aim of coursework is 'to make what is important measurable, rather than to make what is measurable important'.

There will be *specific* tasks set and assessed as part of your coursework, and you should always be told if a particular piece of work is to be part of your coursework assessment or not. So *not all* the work you do during your mathematics course will be coursework; only those specific tasks given and *designated as such* will be called coursework. Although such coursework can be started in year 9 of school, it is usually in years 10 and 11 that coursework is counted towards the GCSE assessment.

Any part of your course (except written tests) can count towards your coursework assessment, and this can even include oral and aural work.

Your teachers are responsible for:

1   telling you which work is part of your coursework;
2   telling you what grades or level you have so far reached;
3   keeping a record of your work and the grades (marks).

The actual coursework done and assessed will vary from exam board to exam board, and from school to school. It will often vary from class to class, but *ALL* will be testing the same skills:

- reasoning, logic and proof;
- applications;
- communication.

The vast majority of tasks will be assessed on these three *skills*. They are the starting points to be used in deciding how the task is to be solved, and they determine what results you find.

These skills which are to be tested through coursework are listed below (not every task will require you to use every ability on this list).

REASONING, LOGIC AND PROOF

Ability to:

- understand what the given task or problem is about;
- find a suitable strategy to solve the problem or task;
- simplify a complicated situation by breaking it down into smaller tasks;
- choose the most appropriate equipment as necessary;
- find any patterns and to generalise;
- make and justify conclusions about the task or problem;
- think about how the task may be extended or varied.

APPLICATIONS

Ability to:

- sort out and organise any data from the situation;
- do the necessary calculations to a suitable degree of accuracy, making realistic

and sensible approximations;

- be clear in the way the work is set out (ability to be organised);
- use the appropriate mathematical language;
- prove the results obtained are accurate;
- estimate quantities and then to measure accurately with the equipment used.

COMMUNICATION

Ability to:

- present the whole work, problem, method of solution and conclusions in a clear and orderly way;
- talk about the work done and explain the results;
- discuss and to respond to 'mathematical' questions about the task or problem set.

In Chapter 3 we have already looked at the *levels of attainment* from 4 to 10 for AT 1 'Using and Applying Mathematics' (see Table 3.1).

<table>
<tr><td>

2 > TYPES OF COURSEWORK SKILLS

</td><td>

There are three main *types* of coursework that you could be given as assignments:

- investigational or problem solving;
- practical;
- extended pieces of work.

</td></tr>
</table>

There will inevitably be some overlap. For instance, there could well be an *investigation* that requires you to do some *practical* mathematics using appropriate equipment, and this could even be used as the basis of an *extended* piece of work. Nevertheless, it will help if we start by looking at these three types separately, bearing in mind that some overlap is likely to occur.

In each case you will be given the task, told the problem to solve or given the practical work to do. You may have some choice, especially on the extended piece of work, but almost *EVERY* task will be *given* to you.

1 Investigational or problem solving:

Here you are given a 'question' that needs to be solved by thinking through different strategies, often referred to as a puzzle.

2 Practical:

Here you are simply using equipment such as rulers, weighing scales or other mathematical equipment to measure or weigh things, etc.

3 Extended piece of work:

Here you are often given a fact then told to find out more about the situation. It is generally a long investigation.

Let us now look at each of these in more detail.

<table>
<tr><td>

3 > INVESTIGATIONS AND PROBLEM SOLVING

</td><td>

In both investigations and problem solving it is essential to be clear about what it is you have to do, so that you have in mind what the *complete* task is.

Your complete task is to:

1 read the problem;
2 do the problem;
3 write up the problem.

You may also have to *talk* about your solution once you've found it.

All these stages are important and of course are linked together since each of the later ones depends on the earlier ones. But

</td><td>

remember you may *solve* the problem in the best of ways, yet get few marks for it if you have not *written it up* properly.

Here we look more closely at these *three stages* and help you work through them with many sample tasks of the type you will meet during years 10 and 11 at school.

START BY READING

Read the question! I know that's obvious, but quite honestly the simplest mistakes are caused by candidates *not* reading the question properly. You need to understand

</td></tr>
</table>

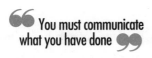
You must communicate what you have done

what the *problem* is about, and to know exactly what the problem is telling you and what it is really asking you. You need to read the *question* carefully so that you can sort out a route through the problem to come to a solution. You will need to organise and rewrite the facts (if any are given) into some simple, sensible order. Then think 'what is it I have to find?'.

■ **Task 1**

'Square' numbers are the average of the adjacent 'circle' numbers.

Task: What can you find out about the links between 'circle' numbers and the 'square' number for *all* such triangles?

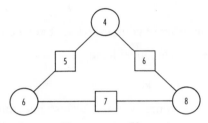

Fig. 15.1

To start:

1. **Read the question. Look at what's given and see what you know.**

a) Yes, each square holds the average of the two numbers either side of it.
b) 'Circle' numbers add up to give 4 + 6 + 8 = 18.
c) 'Square' numbers add up to give 5 + 7 + 6 = 18.
d) All 'circle' numbers are even, 'squares' are not.

These are the 'simple' things you can notice by 'looking' at the information.

2. **What is it you have to find?**

You are looking for links between 'square' numbers and 'circle' numbers. For example, we see that *both* 'circle' and 'square' numbers add up to the same. The most important thing is to 'investigate any links you see to find out if these are always true for such triangles, and to see what other possible links you can find'.

DOING THE PROBLEM

Now we've read the problem we need to sort it out and this will involve the following stages.

■ Looking for a *route* through our problem (or at least starting out on one).

■ Getting all the *information organised*.
■ Looking for *patterns and relationships*.
■ Finding an *end*.

Looking for a route

Now that you know what you are being asked, you have to sort out a route through your problem (there may well be more than one).

Here are a few questions that you could ask of your given task:

Question 1
'Am I looking for *one* answer only?'

Question 2
'Can I *simplify* the situation in any way?'

Question 3
'Can I *split the problem up* into a few separate parts?'

Question 4
'Can I *already see a pattern* or not?'

Question 5
'Do I need to find lots of *similar situations* to investigate?'

Then, depending on your answers to all these questions, you can start to organise your route through the problem.

If we were to answer these questions on Task 1, our *answers* would be:

Question 1
No, there are 'quite a few', so we know we are going to be involved in a number of different routes for different answers;

Question 2
'No' (This problem is as simple as it could be');

Question 3
'Yes', we could split it up into:

■ only even circle numbers (or squares)
■ only odd circle numbers (or squares);

(We've already seen that *adding* gives a nice link here, so what about subtracting, or multiplying, or even dividing? What about halves, even decimals!)

Question 4
'Yes' (I can see both type of numbers add up to the same);

Question 5
'Yes' (There are thousands you could try, but try to use reasonably small numbers, to keep it as simple as possible.)
Now we can work out a route to start us off.

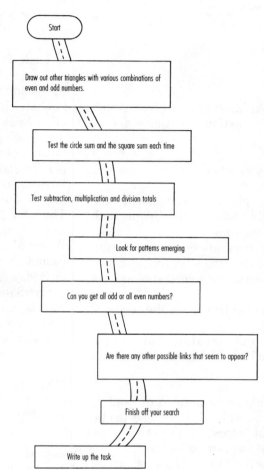

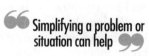
Simplifying a problem or situation can help

Fig. 15.2

Examiner's Note: How you start is important; you should try to start out on an organised route through your problem. Most of the questions raised should be asked 'in your head' and any constructive answers should be written down as *evidence* of your initial thoughts and the way you have gone about breaking the problem down. Starting with the *initial* answers to your questions will set you off on your route.

Let's look at what 'yes' could mean to your route from the previous questions.

Question 1
'Am I looking for one answer only?'
You may have a *yes* answer to this question for problems like the following:

■ **Task 2**
How many different combinations of

clothes can I wear if I choose from 4 different pairs of trousers, from 13 different shirts and from 7 different pairs of socks?

If, as here, you know that there is only *one* answer, your route will be entirely devoted to getting to that one answer. Therefore in this task we should avoid getting caught up in exploring interesting patterns that do *not* help us arrive at our single answer. (Keep that approach for another opportunity when you may need to extend a   problem of your own.)

However, if your answer here was 'no', as it would be to Task 1, then you *are* in a situation where you need to be exploring the various patterns that you can think of.

Question 2
Can I simplify the situation in any way?
Often if the problem is given in a 'real world' situation then the answer will be 'yes', as in the next task.

■ **Task 3**
A new town was being built with all the roads straight. The council, for safety reasons, needs to put an *extra large* lamp post at each crossroad. Find out the greatest number of extra large lamp posts needed by the council for the new town for the various number of roads that could be built.

This problem simplifies to one of drawing straight lines to cross each other rather than counting how many crossroads you have created.

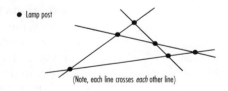
(Note, each line crosses *each* other line)

Fig. 15.3

Question 3
'Can I split the problem up into a few separate parts?'
Your task could give rise to a number of situations in which you would be advised to break it down into separate parts.

■ **Task 4**
Find a way of making a cone to a specified height and radius.

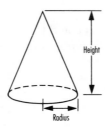

Fig. 15.4

The task looks short and simple, but will involve your sorting out quite a few problems.

1 How do you make a cone? (Answer, from a sector).
2 From the given dimensions of this sector what will be the height and radius of the cone?
3 From the previous question can you now 'turn the tables' so that you can predict what sector is needed for a given cone?
4 Prove it works by making the cone.

These are four separate but linked problems, each of which needs sorting out.

Question 4
'Can I already see a pattern or not?'
Well, here you will either see one (as in Task 1) or not. If 'yes', then you have your starting point and can explore that. If 'no', then you now need to look for a pattern to *check* whether or not one can be identified at this stage.

Question 5
'Do I need to find lots of similar situations to investigate
If 'yes', then you will need to think carefully about what similar situations you could investigate. Try to create some pattern or order in the situations you choose.

For example, in Task 2 you could investigate what happens with 1 shirt, 1 pair of trousers and 1 pair of socks, then 1 shirt, 1 pair of trousers and 2 pairs of socks up to 2 shirts, 3 pairs of trousers and 4 pairs of socks, and look for any *patterns* to help you *predict* the final answer you are seeking.

GETTING YOUR INFORMATION ORGANISED

Once you have set off on your route you will be finding data or information, usually as the result of experiment or from an organised trial of different situations.

The way you *record* your information is very important. It will gain or lose you marks, and good recording will help you to see patterns that arise from the situations.

Organise the information given
Look at the problem and see what links you can find.

■ Task 5
James, Philip, Jarrad, Ben, Michael, Alison and Suzy were the members of a Subbuteo league, and had to play each other twice only and not on the same date. Each game lasted for an hour and no one could play more than 2 games per day. James cannot play on Monday, Wednesday or Friday. Philip can only play on Tuesday, Wednesday and Thursday. Jarrad can play on Monday, Tuesday and Friday. Ben can play on Wednesday and Friday only. Michael cannot play on Wednesday, Thursday or Friday. Alison is free to play any day except Sunday. In fact none of them can play on Sunday, but they can all play on Saturday. Suzy cannot play on Tuesday or Thursday. Arrange a fixture list that will enable all the members of the league to play each other twice (not on the same day). Try to arrange it to last as few days as possible.

Solution
After reading through the question carefully, and maybe twice, you can produce a grid, as in Figure 15.5, to illustrate the information you have already been given.

	Mon	Tues	Wed	Thurs	Fri	Sat	Sun
James	✗	✓	✗	✓	✗	✓	✗
Philip	✗	✓	✓	✓	✗	✓	✗
Jarrad	✓	✓	✗	✗	✓	✓	✗
Ben	✗	✗	✓	✗	✓	✓	✗
Michael	✓	✓	✗	✗	✗	✓	✗
Alison	✓	✓	✓	✓	✓	✓	✗
Suzy	✓	✗	✓	✗	✓	✓	✗

Fig. 15.5

Then, from the information in Fig. 15.5, you can start to complete the problem.

■ Task 6
How many different routes are there from A to G, using the edges only? Each route must not use the same edge more than once.

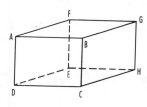

Fig. 15.6

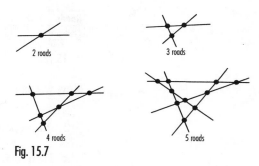

Fig. 15.7

Solution

It is not a good idea just to write down routes as you see them. Try to be organised; start with the routes using 1 edge only.

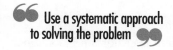
Use a systematic approach to solving the problem

- **1 edge** – You cannot do this route with only one edge – notice that AG is *not* an edge.
- **2 edges** – A → B → G and A → F → G are the only two routes to find. Put them in a list as
  ABG
  AFG
- **3 edges** – You cannot do this with three edges.
- **4 edges** – ABCHG
  ADCBG
  ADCHG
  ADEFG
  ADEHG
  AFEHG

Notice how you should be systematically looking from point A. Here it has been done alphabetically, AB …, then AD …, then AF …

Then we would look for the **5 edge** routes (but you wouldn't find any), then look for the **6 edge** routes, etc. So, to look for information efficiently you need to be organised in your search and your recording.

LOOKING FOR PATTERNS

Very often, the quicker you can find a pattern from your data, then the sooner you can stop experimenting and move on to the next stage of 'finding an end'.

Turn again to Task 3, the new town problem. Simplify the situation; record any findings, and then look for patterns.

Example
2 roads	need	1 lamp
3 roads	need	3 lamps
4 roads	need	6 lamps
5 roads	need	10 lamps

You need to be careful here that you try to draw each new road in such a way as to give the *most* crossroads needing *extra large* lamp posts.

Now look at Fig. 15.8 for any patterns.

Roads	2	3	4	5
Lamp posts	1	3	6	10

Fig. 15.8

If you look at the *differences* in the bottom table you will see that there *is* a pattern.

$$1 \xrightarrow{+2} 3 \xrightarrow{+3} 6 \xrightarrow{+4} 10 \xrightarrow{?} ?$$

Fig. 15.9

Hence the next number is $10 + 5 = 15$, so for 6 roads we will need 15 lamp posts.

You then need to see if you can find the link between the *number of roads* and the *number of lamp posts*, so that you could work out easily how many lamp posts you would need for, say, 150 roads. So, let's look at Fig 15.10 for our new extended table of results.

Roads	2	3	4	5	6	7	8	_ _ _ _ n
Lamp posts	1	3	6	10	15	21	28	?

Fig. 15.10

You are looking for the *relationship* that exists between roads and lamp posts.

1. Try simple *addition* or *subtraction* – nothing!
2. Try simple *multiplication* or *division* – nothing!
3. Look at the *factors* of each lamp post number, and you will find:

Roads	2	3	4	5	6	7	8
Lamp posts	1 (1 × 1)	3 (1 × 3)	6 (2 × 3)	10 (2 × 5)	15 (3 × 5)	21 (3 × 7)	28 (4 × 7)

Fig. 15.11

On first inspection you may see nothing, but then if you *double* the smallest number in each product you get:

Roads	2	3	4	5	6	7	8
2 × lamp posts	(1 × 2)	(2 × 3)	(3 × 4)	(4 × 5)	(5 × 6)	(6 × 7)	(7 × 8)

Fig. 15.12

Now we can see the pattern that gives

roads   n
2 × lamp posts $(n - 1) \times n$

> *Here is a* pattern *we have found*

■ Hence from n roads we get $\frac{1}{2} \times (n - 1) \times n$ lamp posts.

You can easily check this formula with any of the results we have already found, e.g. 7 roads = $\frac{1}{2} \times 6 \times 7 = 21$ lamp posts. Look for *patterns*, and then use these patterns either to find a relationship or to predict a certain result.

Have you now got an answer to your problem?

If not then you probably need to look at the problem in a *different way*. It can often happen that you seem to get nowhere, and when you *are* in this situation you need to look again and maybe turn the problem round.

■ Task 7

A mathematical milkman had to leave 18 pints of milk at a school each day. He always left the bottles in a 4 by 6 crate, as below:

Fig. 15.13

But *every* row and *every* column had in it an even number of bottles. How could he do this and can you find a number of different ways?

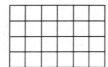

Fig. 15.14

Solution

The problem is best thought about by using counters or even pieces of paper to represent the bottles. Then by trial and error you can find one solution, then other solutions.
E.g.   There is an even number of bottles in each row and in each column of the crate shown here.

0	X	0	X	0	0
0	0	0	X	X	0
0	X	0	0	X	0
0	0	0	0	0	0

0 = milk bottle
X = space

Fig. 15.15

Yet, the problem is easier if it is looked at from the other end. That is, instead of the bottles, look for the *spaces* (there are only 6 of these).

Now, the problem is much easier – do one row at a time.
E.g. One of many solutions.

X	X				
X		X			
	X	X			

Fig. 15.16

So look out for the situations that can be looked at in quite a different way and so become much simpler.

FINDING AN END

You will get to a stage where you have got the answer to the task, or, if there are a number of possibilities, then you have arrived at a number of solutions.

If the problem was an open-ended investigation, like Task 1, then you must decide when enough is enough, i.e. when you have found *sufficient* relationships to end the task. Unfortunately there is no simple rule like 'three relationships will do' or 'four sides of paper is sufficient'. There will be times when one or two relationships will be sufficient; then other times when perhaps four or five can usefully be found.

Look through the 'model coursework solutions' later in the chapter. These will help to give you an idea as to how much material might be 'sufficient'. But remember – it will be the *quality* of your material and not the quantity that really matters.

Writing up

This is where you really do need to be very careful. You need to write up all the relevant things you did. You need three parts:

■ **Introduction** – state the problem and what it was that you planned to do.

■ **The route** – clearly show *all* the trials that you have done, with clear diagrams and tables illustrating the results. State the relationships found and their relevance. Do not just show results here – say what you *did* to find them.

■ **Conclusion** – You need here to say how you proved your results. Did you test out your findings? You need to give a clearly reasoned answer to the problem, or to summarise the relationships found.

> Important stages in writing-up your investigation

All the writing up must be of your *own* work. You may have been part of a group, but if you write up a result you must be able to understand where it came from and how it was found. This is important, for not only will you have to sign a declaration at the end of the course to say that it is your own work, but you may also be required to *talk* about your conclusions. This *oral work* can be part of the coursework and as such can be

included in your coursework assessment. Hence – read well → plan well → be thorough in your route → find conclusions then write it all up.

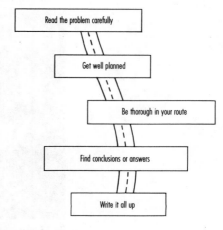

Fig. 15.17

It is usually very good technique to keep *rough notes* of your work at each stage – the reading, the planning, the patterns found and the conclusion, and *then* to write it all up neatly at the end.

If you have access to a word processor, then this can be very useful in recording and writing up your work. Remember to leave spaces for inserting your diagrams. Check with your teacher that you can use a word processor when writing up your material.

4 PRACTICAL WORK

Here you will generally be given either several small things to do, or one larger practical problem.

■ **Task 8**

From a piece of card, cut out a sector of radius 6 cm with an angle of 210°. Join your shape together so that it makes a cone with as large a radius as possible. Measure and state the length of the cone's height and diameter.

Solutions

You will be expected to use accurately (within 1 mm) a pair of compasses to draw a circle of radius 6 cm on your card. Then to draw in the angle of 210° to give a shape as shown here:

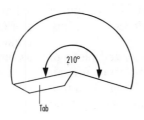

Fig. 15.18

Cut out the circle and the small sector from it. You could leave a tab on one end, as I have in the diagram, which will help you to glue the shape together, or to tape it.

If you try this for yourself you can check your accuracy by seeing if your cone has a diameter of 7 cm and a height of 4.9 cm.

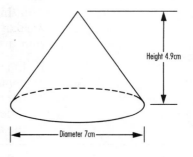

Fig. 15.19

In this situation there was only *one thing* to do, and you would be marked on:

1 how accurate you drew the first shape, and cut it out;
2 how neatly you put the shape together;
3 the accuracy of the final shape.

■ Task 9

Find six everyday containers, e.g., a cup, a beaker, or a milk bottle, and find out how many litres or millilitres each one holds.

Fig. 15.20

Solution

You have a choice of containers here, but a good variety of sizes is wanted, ranging perhaps from a small egg cup to a large bottle. Each measure should be to the nearest millilitre or centilitre, depending on what you find to measure them with. For small objects you could use a 5 ml spoon, but that is not as accurate as a measuring cylinder.

Use a measuring cylinder (if the work is done at school, this should be provided). Fill your container with water and pour it into the cylinder. For very small measures a good technique is to pour the same amount into the cylinder a few times (say 10) and then divide the total amount by how many times you have poured in a measure. If your answer comes to over 1000 millilitres, then give your answer in litres and millilitres. (For example, 1521 millilitres = 1 litre 521 ml).

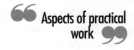

> *Aspects of practical work*

In this situation there are a number of ways of arriving at your final answer, and your marks will be awarded for:

1 the variety of different sized containers;
2 the method used to measure the different amounts;
3 the accuracy of your results.

■ Task 10

Find the weight of one piece of A4 paper.

Solution

It is anticipated that you do not have access to a very sensitive electronic digital weighing machine! Hence you need to choose a large quantity of A4 paper, preferably a ream, which would be a pack of 500 sheets. Weigh this as accurately as you can, and then divide the weight by 500, being careful with the units and the standard form notation on the calculator.

Again, you would be marked on:

1 your method of finding the weight of one piece of paper without measuring exactly one piece;
2 your accuracy (don't forget that different types of paper will weigh differing amounts).

Your answer

This can vary from task to task and from school to school. You could simply be asked the practical question *orally* (not written down), then have to perform the task while the assessor, who could be your teacher, watches you. While performing the task the assessor may ask you questions about *what* you are doing and *why.* Or the practical task could be given in *writing.* In this case, as with investigations, you may then have to write up your answers. Writing up can be done in a similar way to investigations. Start with an *introduction* to the problem; then explain *how* you worked out what you needed to do to solve the problem. Here be very precise as to why you chose that *particular piece of equipment* and how you used it. Then give the final answer(s) and comment suitably on your accuracy.

You will be assessed on:

1 how you use mathematical apparatus;
2 how well you choose appropriate apparatus;
3 how accurate you have been using this apparatus.

---

5 ▶ EXTENDED PIECES OF WORK

This will be a piece of work for which there is usually no one correct answer, but a *variety of different possibilities* depending on the situation

The treatment of an extended piece of work will be similar to that for an investigation or problem solving. Of course the activity of 'investigation' may be at the very heart of the extended piece of work. What is vital is that you select a piece of work that you can work on yourself and can make as long or as short, as complicated or as simple, as you wish. Of course, the more comprehensive the investigation is, the better the mark it can receive.

Researching

One example of an extended piece of work could be the following:

■ Task 11

Choose a busy roundabout or road junction near to you and find how much traffic uses this junction and what the likely effect of traffic lights could be (you decide on the timing of the lights).

Fig 15.21

Solution

Clearly you need a junction with a lot of traffic, and you need to find out:

1   how much traffic uses it from each direction;
2   the average waiting time to get into the main flow;
3   then try to simulate lights.

Quite a problem, but a real one as many town planners will tell you.

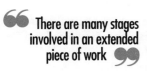
There are many stages involved in an extended piece of work

You need to select your junction. Make it one that you have easy access to, since you may be there quite often over a short space of time.

Then do a survey on *how much* traffic uses the junction from each direction. You can probably only sensibly count one road flow at a time.

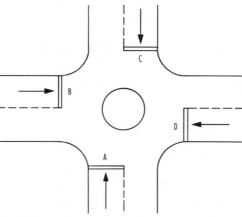

Fig. 15.22

So, as in the diagram, you need to count at A, B, C and D, on different days. To make

allowances for different days you would be advised to use a timetable similar to:

Monday	4.00 → 4.30	count at A
	4.30 → 5.00	count at B
Tuesday	4.00 → 4.30	count at C
	4.30 → 5.00	count at D
Wednes	4.00 → 4.30	count at B
	4.30 → 5.00	count at A
Thurs	4.00 → 4.30	count at D
	4.30 → 5.00	count at C

Fig. 15.23

This is already four hours of just counting, but do use a tally chart, i.e.

| Junction A | ⊞⊞ ⊞⊞ ⊞⊞ |
| Mon 4.00-4.30 | ⊞⊞ |

Fig. 15.24

Of course, you could get help in the survey. Friends, brothers or sisters will probably enjoy helping you (especially if you promised a Mars bar as a reward!)

Next, you need to calculate *how long* each car has to wait at a junction. Here you probably will need a friend to help you since you need a stopwatch to count the seconds that each car has to wait once it has got to the junction. Again, as before, you need to spread the count over a few days and do different junctions at different times.

Then you can work out on *average* how long each car waits, and you know how many cars use each junction.

Next, you *simulate* a set of traffic lights.

Let's suppose that we had the following figures from a survey.

Junction	Number of cars per minute	Number of seconds wait per car
A	15	5 sec
B	6	8 sec
C	11	4.3 sec
D	8	7.6 sec

Fig. 15.25

We can see that the flow from A and C is the largest, hence they should be given a longer time at green.

■   A starting point could be (for safety don't forget to allow for amber as well as green):
      AC green for 30 seconds
            amber for 5 seconds
      BD green for 15 seconds
            amber for 5 seconds   etc.
■   Consider the AC flow:

Use the largest traffic flow of 15 per minute, hence 8 every 30 seconds with no waiting.

After the next 25 seconds (5 + 15 + 5), 7 cars are waiting. It now becomes clear that we need to know how long it takes traffic to go through the lights when green to avoid a stoppage at a junction. So go to a junction where there *are* traffic lights to see how many cars usually go through at green and in what time.

Clearly this is becoming a large project – an *extended piece of work*, and a lot of time will be spent in research, looking at figures, simulating situations, trial and error for different times, until at last you reach a firm conclusion that:

either – lights would be a good idea and suggest the timing of them

or – lights would not help the flow at all.

Presentation

A lot of work will have gone into this project, so give it full value. Say what you have done, giving a good explanation of the nature of the problem and of the tasks you set yourself, and remember to give all your results. Show clearly the *use* you have made of the results and suggest any extra work you might now need to do.

■ Whatever you did in this project, put it down with clear explanations as to *why* you did it.

■ Then give your conclusions, with good clear reasons *why* you have come to the decision you have.

■ Present your work neatly and clearly. Again I will repeat that a word processor here could clearly be an advantage to you, but don't forget to insert your diagrams to help illustrate the points you are making.

Conclusion

In every type of coursework these three main principles will always apply.

■ Plan the work before you start.

■ Do the work thoroughly and thoughtfully, writing notes on what you have done.

■ Communicate all your work, in either oral or written form, depending on what you have been requested to do.

You can be given guidance by your teacher and help by parents or friends, but at the end of the day it is up to *you* to demonstrate what *you* can *do*.

<table>
<tr><td>**6** </td><td>**ORAL AND AURAL**</td></tr>
</table>

Part of your coursework assessment will be on how well you can speak mathematics, and on how well you can listen and think out mathematics. It is done in two quite different ways, *oral* and *aural*.

The differences between aural and oral always seem to confuse teachers, as well as students.

ORAL

An *oral* task might be you talking to someone about what you have done in a problem, or you giving a spoken answer to some questions.

For example, you could have been given the task we looked at earlier – 'how much does a piece of paper weigh?'

You might then be given the question 'explain why you did it that way'.

How you answer is of course important;

■ do you *know* why you did it that way?
■ can you *explain clearly* why you did it?

These are the main ideas that the assessor (who may well be your teacher) is looking for. In other words can you *communicate* your mathematical ideas verbally?

'Practice makes perfect' is an old saying, but one which contains a lot of truth. Do ask yourself (or perhaps each other) these types of question and get used to expressing yourself in response to such questions.

Try to *say* what you have done confidently. It may have been wrong, but the oral assessment is not about the right answer, it is about 'how well you can talk mathematics'.

Practise with your parents or friends. Get them to ask some of the following questions and then to comment on your answers. (Of course you could try some on them!)

66 The *oral* is about your ability to talk mathematics 99

■ **Situation 1**
1 What is a polygon?
2 What is the 'interior angle' and the 'exterior angle' of a polygon?
3 Describe a regular octagon.
4 Explain how you could find the size of the interior angle of a pentagon.

■ **Situation 2**
Write down any two odd numbers. Add them up and also find their difference.
1 What do you notice?
2 Do you think this will always happen?
3 How will you check out the last answer?
4 What do you think you will get with two even numbers?

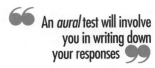
Practise talking about mathematical situations

■ **Situation 3**
Find the exact weight of one pint of milk, not including the bottle.
1 How did you do it?
2 Why did you do it like that?
3 Comment on your accuracy.
4 How could you have been more accurate?

Well, how did you, or your parents, get on? These are some of the types of questions you can expect from the 'oral' part of your assessment. Please, just try to *say* what you did, being as confident as you can. DON'T make up the explanation, because that is always noticed and will lose you marks.

After each piece of coursework has been done (or even during it), get someone to ask you some of the following questions. Practise *speaking* your answers to such questions.

1 What was the easiest part of the problem?
2 What was the hardest part of the problem?
3 How on earth did you start it?
4 What things did you assume?
5 What help did you need in solving the problem?
6 Can you explain exactly what it was that you had to find out?
7 What have you found out from this problem?
8 What possible extension of this problem could you suggest to try out?
9 What part of the task did you enjoy?
10 How did you record all the data found out?
11 How did you check your results?
12 What can you say about the accuracy of your figures?
13 Have you learnt anything special from this piece of work?

AURAL

An *aural* test will involve you in writing down your responses

An *aural* test is the name given to the situation where you listen to a question or a problem and *then write down* your response or answer.

I suppose these are what used to be called 'mental tests'. You could be given some reference sheets, such as timetables or charts, to use. The question will usually be the type that you could well be expected to do in your own head at the shops, on a journey or at work.

These aural tests will usually be assessed at your *particular level*, i.e. Basic, Intermediate or Higher. Try the following. Get someone to read the following aural tests to you and see how you get on. Each question should be read twice; then time should be allowed for you to *write down* your answer before giving you the next question. The answers are at the end of this chapter.

Basic tier aural test (for levels 4, 5, 6)

1 Mandy buys a magazine for 32p. How much change will she receive if she pays with two 20p coins?
2 What is the cost of six chairs at £21 each?
3 James buys a Michael Jackson tape at £7.75 and a Longman Revise Guide at £9.99. How much has he spent altogether?
4 Mary-Jo bought eight stickers for a total of 96p. How much did each cost?
5 Charles earns £5.50 an hour. How much would he earn in a day if he worked for eight hours?

6 It took me three minutes to drive two miles. If I do not alter my speed how long will it take me to drive a further eight miles?

7 How many minutes are there from ten past five until five to seven?

8 What is the area of a piece of carpet 3 metres by 5 metres?

9 The diameter of a cake is 9 inches. Approximately what is its circumference?

10 I have eaten $\frac{3}{4}$ of an 80 gram chocolate bar. What is the weight of the piece left?

Intermediate tier aural test (for levels 5, 6, 7, 8)

1 A car park has 15 rows of cars with 30 cars in each row. How many cars are there in the car park altogether?

2 My cat eats $\frac{3}{4}$ of a tin of cat food each day. How much does she eat in four days?

3 A road has marked out on it seven car-parking spaces, each 3 metres long, and a space at each end of $2\frac{1}{2}$ metres. How long is the road?

4 It takes Janet 20 minutes to walk to school. She walks back home at twice the speed. How long does it take her to walk home?

5 When hot, a metal bar will expand by 5%. What is the expansion of an 80 centimetre-long metal bar when hot?

6 The source of the Nile was discovered by Captain J. H. Speke in 1862. How long ago was that?

7 Write down an approximate answer to 789 divided by 42.

8 Valerie turned up for a date with Richard 12 minutes late. Richard had arrived three minutes early. How long did Richard have to wait for Valerie to turn up?

9 Victor bought a cassette player marked at £20 plus VAT at a rate of 15%. How much VAT did Victor pay?

10 The temperature at midnight was −6° C. At midday today the temperature was 7° C. By how much did the temperature rise between midnight and midday?

Higher level aural test (for levels 7, 8, 9, 10)

1 Archimedes discovered his theorem in the year 287 BC. How long ago was that?

2 What is the length of a side of a square of area 64 square centimetres?

3 Write down the next square number after 169.

4 Karen has to post 243 leaflets. They come in packs of 25. How many packs will Karen need?

5 John, who earns £810 a month, is given a 7% wage increase. What is John's increase in wages?

6 How many hours is 1000 minutes?

7 What is the approximate length of a diagonal of a square of side 8 centimetres.

8 Katie drove 150 miles in $2\frac{1}{2}$ hours. What speed was she doing?

9 Write down the next prime number after 37.

10 What is the cost of 21 booklets at 99p each?

Answers to basic level aural test

Check your answers

1	8p	1 mark	
2	£126	1 mark	
3	£17.74	1 mark	
4	12p	1 mark	
5	£44	1 mark	
6	12 minutes	1 mark	
7	105	1 mark	
8	15 square metres	2 marks	(lose one if the units are wrong)
9	27 or 28 inches	2 marks	(any other number between 27 and 29 give 1 mark)
10	20 grams	1 mark	

(Lose another mark if more than 3 units not given.)

Having marked yourself, then grade yourself below.

Level 6	11 or 12 marks
Level 5	8, 9 or 10 marks
Level 4	6 or 7 marks

Answers to intermediate level aural test

1	450	1 mark
2	3 tins	1 mark

3 26 metres   1 mark
4 10 metres   1 mark
5 4 cm   1 mark
6 131 years   1 mark   (add on a year, for each year after 1993)
7 20   2 marks   (18, 19 or 21 … give 1 mark)
8 15 minutes   1 mark
9 £3   1 mark
10 13 degrees   1 mark
(Add on 1 mark if no more than one unit not given.)

Having marked yourself, now grade yourself below.
Level 8   11 or 12 marks
Level 7   9 or 10 marks
Level 6   7 or 8 marks
Level 5   5 or 6 marks

Answers to higher level aural test

1 2280 years   1 mark   (add on a year for each year after 1993)
2 8 cm   1 mark
3 196   1 mark
4 10   1 mark
5 £56.70   1 mark
6 16 (and 40 minutes) or $16\frac{2}{3}$ 1 mark
7 11 cm   2 marks   (1 mark for answer between 11 and 11.5)
8 60 mph   1 mark
9 41   1 mark
10 £20.79   1 mark
    (Add on 1 mark if all the units are given.)

Having marked yourself, now grade yourself below.
Level 10   13 marks or over
Level 9   11 or 12 marks
Level 8   9 or 10 marks
Level 7   6, 7 or 8 marks

7 WHAT THE EXAMINER WANTS

You will usually present your coursework throughout the two-year course (or the one year of a one-year course) at times given to you by your teacher. Most pieces of coursework will only take you a few hours to complete. Of course some of the coursework is supposed to be 'extended work' and this will last considerably longer than two or three hours!

Do present your coursework on time. It will help if you keep to a schedule. You might set yourself *target* dates for doing the research, writing up some rough notes, writing a final version and so on. This will help you avoid having a lot of coursework to complete as the deadlines approach.

Your work should be presented as clearly as possible. As I have suggested before, a word processor could help your presentation, for your work does need to be as clear as you can make it. Use carefully-drawn, well-labelled diagrams wherever possible and try to explain what you *wanted* to do, what you *did* do and what you *found out*.

In most cases the first person to mark your coursework is your teacher, but it could also be looked at by an external examiner to see that all is well with the school's assessment.

Throughout your course, you will be presenting pieces of coursework that illustrate the different abilities being assessed. Any one task may contribute to one, some or all of these abilities (see below). For those parts that may have *no written evidence*, such as practical work, group work, discussion or oral work, a record will be kept by your teacher. But in most cases you will be presenting *written* evidence of what you have done so that your teacher can assess. it. Your teacher should be able to convey to you how well you did and what your strengths and weaknesses were even if they cannot give you the mark itself.

ABILITIES TO BE TESTED

The abilities being tested include the following:

Understanding the problem

1 How well have you shown your *understanding* of the problem? Have you understood it all; have you mis-understood it altogether, or have you only understood a part of the problem? The extent of your under-standing will be clear through your initial explanation of the problem in your introduction and in your final conclusions.

2 Did you manage to look at the initial problem and then to identify *exactly what it was* you needed to find out? Or did you just get on with it by trial and error? In other words, were you able to identify any mathematical principles that were relevant to the problem set?

3 Have you found the best *way* to tackle the problem, or, rather, a suitable way, for in many cases there is *no best* way? Have you gone a long way round the problem instead of finding a shorter route that was readily available? Sometimes you may have no choice of method, as only one will get you the answer, but usually there are a number of ways – some being better than others.

4 Have you been able to *break the task down* into smaller tasks or have you tried to solve it all at once? You should always be looking to see if you can simplify your problem by making it into a number of *smaller* problems.

5 Did you select *appropriate equipment* to solve your problem? For example, did you choose suitable weighing scales or units of measurement, or did you simply choose the pieces of equipment that were the easiest to find?

All these different aspects will indicate how well you were able to understand the given problem and what your response has been to that under-standing.

Using equipment

1 How *accurate* have you been in your use of the equipment? Remember that if you use equipment, then you will always be assessed on how accurate you have been with it. Of course this is linked to your using the most suitable equipment for the task in hand. This means that you must be aware of the inherent accuracy of various types of equipment. Take, for instance, the set of weighing scales illustrated below.

>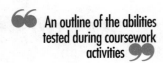
> An outline of the abilities tested during coursework activities

Fig. 15.25

Each small division represents 0.1 Kg which is 100 grams. Hence your only accurate reading from this scale is to the nearest 50 grams. So if you gave a weight as 3.534 Kg from these scales you are not being realistic and will lose marks. So use *appropriate measurements* from the *appropriate equipment*.

2 Have you been willing and able to use other suitable pieces of equipment where necessary? For example, did you test out a theory of cone sizes by *actually making* a cone from cardboard? Or did you use a computer to generate some data with *suitable software* that you either obtained or wrote yourself?

How you *decide* to use, and how you *actually* do use mathematical equipment and everyday equipment (scissors, string, etc.) is an important part of your coursework and will be assessed as such.

Working on the problem

1 Did you collect enough *information* for your enquiry? Were you able either to create your own data by suitable experiments or to find the data from reliable and suitable places?

2 How well did you then *'process'* this information? Were you able to use your collected data in a sensible and useful way?

3 Did you *carry out your calculations* sensibly? For instance, did you *round off* suitably, where necessary, to an appropriate degree of accuracy? In fact were you able to make sensible approximations beforehand so that you could tell if your results were *realistic* when you found them? This estimation could well be assessed orally, as it is not always easily written into your account. Did you also *check* your results and calculations?

4 How well did you *overcome difficulties*? Did you in fact state your difficulties and then explain how you got round them? You would not always have difficulties (I hope), but on many assignments they will be there (and will often be anticipated by your teacher).

How well you recognised them and sought to overcome them will be an important part of the assessment.

5 How *organised* have you been during the assignment? Have you clearly organised your *task* beforehand and gone through it in a logical way? Have you organised your *data* in such a way as to help you identify patterns or to pick out relationships? The more organised you were, the easier it should have been to complete the task and the more marks you are likely to earn.

6 Have you made efficient use of *mathematical language and shorthand* (symbols)? Or have you written everything out in longhand? Where it can be used, you should use the symbolism of mathematics (simple algebra for relationships, set notation, $+$, $-$, $\times$, $\div$, matrices, etc). This will all help to make the presentation less like an essay and more like a piece of mathematics coursework.

How you work out the problem is up to you, and you must therefore clearly state how you did it and why. Try not to leave out things that you did; even including those thoughts that did not seem to work will make a valuable contribution to your coursework.

Making conclusions

1 Could you *identify all the patterns* within the situation and how far could you *generalise* from the patterns identified? That is, could you write down some formula or relationship you have found out from the problem? For example, in the series of numbers:

2, 6, 10, 14, 18, 22 …

the pattern is 'going up in fours from the number 2' and the nth term can be expressed as $2 + 4 (n - 1)$. For instance the 5th term is $2 + 4 (5 - 1) = 18$. In fact, have you been able to generalise in mathematical language or did you have to use words?

2 How well could you make *logical deductions* from your sorted data? For example, you may have done some work on triangles, all with the same height and base length. Could you deduce that *all* the triangles with the same base and height have the same area?

3 When you state your conclusions, how have you *proved* them? Have you just stated what you noticed from your initial data, or have you then gone out to prove, or at least to check with other examples, that what you have found out is generally true?

4 How far have you been able to suggest any *possible extensions* to the task at hand? For instance if your work has all been on triangles, you could suggest what links this could have with quadrilaterals or parallelograms. You might be able to suggest further work which might be undertaken in this respect.

The whole object of problem solving is to come up with an answer of sorts. It is how you *arrive at* this answer, and how well you *set out your reasons* for your conclusions that will determine the final assessment of your coursework. It is *not* just a simple case of finding the answer. It is much more about your ability to reason out your conclusions mathematically and clearly.

All the exam boards will assess the coursework along similar lines. Here we look at a few actual coursework tasks and how they might be approached.

9 SAMPLE PIECES OF COURSEWORK

What might your coursework look like?

Let us look at a few tasks and see what the coursework could look like at the end.

TASK 1

A square grows in the following way

Start

Stage 1

Stage 2

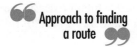 Fig. 15.26

1 Show how this growth continues.
2 What relationships can you find between the stage, the area and the perimeter of the shapes?

BEFORE STARTING

Consider the problem and read it through. We can see that a possible route through the problem is to:

1 draw the next few stages;
2 make out a table of stage, area, and perimeter (we could think about 'new areas of growth', i.e., the shaded squares, and about the total area of the shape.);

3 look for patterns within the table;
4 write up the solution, stating what was found out.

One solution to this is provided below, but try the problem yourself first. Only then see if what you have done is along the lines of my proposed solution.

Possible solution

The pattern of new growth can be seen to take the following form:

> **Identifying a pattern**

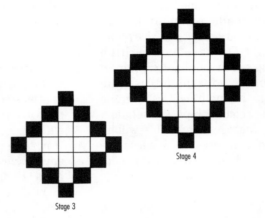

Fig. 15.27

Stage 3

Stage 4

A table of each stage with new growth area, total area and perimeter was constructed as shown:

Stage	New growth area	Perimeter	Total area
1	4	12	5
2	8	20	13
3	12	28	25
4	16	36	41

Fig. 15.28

1 Consider the relationship between 'stages' and 'new growth area'

Fig. 15.29

Stages	1	2	3	4
New growth	4	8	12	16

It looked to me as if each new growth had another four added on each time. This would then make stage 5 have 16 + 4 which is 20 new squares. I tested this out and as you see:

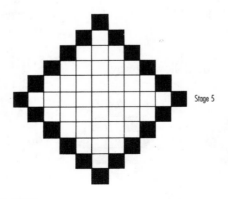

Stage 5

Fig. 15.30

stage 5 *does* have 20 new squares. Writing the table out as:

Stage	1	2	3	4	5
New growth	(1 × 4)	(2 × 4)	(3 × 4)	(4 × 4)	(5 × 4)

Fig. 15.31

led me to say that stage n would have $4 \times n$ new growth squares.
So the relationship between stages and new growth is:

- new growth = 4 times the stage number

or

- new growth stage n = 4n squares.

2 Consider the relationship between 'stages' and 'perimeter'

Stage	1	2	3	4
Perimeter	12	20	28	36

Fig. 15.32

It looks as if each stage has another 8 added on to the perimeter. This would suggest that stage 5 has a perimeter of 36 + 8 which is 44. Checking this in stage 5 (Fig. 15.32), I found it to be true.

Rewriting the table out as:

Stage	1	2	3	4	5
Perimeter	12 (8×1) + 4	20 (8×2) + 4	28 (8×3) + 4	36 (8×4) + 4	44 (8×5) + 4

Fig. 15.33

led me to say that stage n will have a perimeter of $(8 \times n) + 4$. So the relationship between stages and perimeter is:

- perimeter = eight times stage number, add on four

or

- perimeter of stage n = 8n +4.

3 Consider the relationship between 'stages' and total area

Stage	1	2	3	4
Total area	5	13	25	41

Fig. 15.34

Looking at the differences in the total area row;

Fig. 15.35

the next difference looks like being 16 + 4, which is 20. This gives the total area in stage 5 as 41 + 20, which is 61. By counting the squares in stage 5 (Fig. 15.30) this was found to be true.

Writing the table out as

Stage	1	2	3	4	5
Total area	5	13	25	41	61
I noticed	4 + 1	12 + 1	24 + 1	40 + 1	60 + 1
and then	(2×2) + 1	(2×6) + 1	(2×12) + 1	(2×20) + 1	(2×30) + 1

Fig. 15.36

I now tried to get the pattern of what multiplies to the 2

ie.   2   6   12   20   30

or 1×2 2×3 3×4 4×5 5×6

This is quite a nice pattern. Hence I can rewrite the earlier table as:

Stage	1	2	3	4	5
total area	5	13	25	41	61
	2 (1×2) + 1	2 (2×3) + 1	2 (3×4) + 1	2 (4×5) + 1	2 (5×6) + 1

Fig. 15.37

This led me to say that stage n would have a total area of

- $2 \times n \times (n + 1) + 1$ squares

or

- $2n(n + 1) + 1$ squares

So the relationship between stages and total area is:

- total area = 2 times stage times stage add one, then add another one.

This is written much better in algebra as:

- total area of stage n = $2n(n + 1) + 1$ squares.

Summary of conclusions

For any stage n:

- new growth area   = 4n squares

- perimeter   = 8n + 4

- total area   = $2n (n + 1) + 1$ squares

Hence taking as an example stage 10, this would have:

- new growth of 40 squares

- a perimeter of 84

- a total area of (20 ¥ 11) + 1 = 221 squares

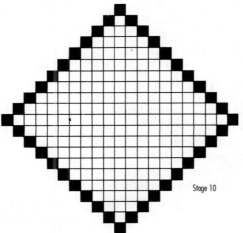

Stage 10

Fig. 15.38

The diagram is stage 10, and it does have these properties. This is evidence that the relationship is indeed correct.

The *level* or *tier* of your entry for mathematics GCSE will determine how much of that piece of coursework you would be expected to do. For example, only the *higher tier* students would be expected to find out the relationship between stage and total area! Only the *higher and the intermediate tier* students would be expected to find the algebraic relationship for the first two investigations.

Notice how I did not write an essay, but instead used tables of figures wherever possible. Also notice that as far as possible each suggested relationship was tested and the results shown.

TASK 2

Choose a book that does not have too many pictures in it, and estimate how many words it contains.

BEFORE STARTING

You need to choose a book that at least interests you. I chose *Hallowe'en Party* by Agatha Christie.
I then sorted out my route to an answer.

1   Estimate how many words to a line.
2   Estimate how many lines per page
3   Calculate final answer.

SOLUTION

My task was to find out how many words the book *Hallowe'en Party* by Agatha Christie had in it.

I could have counted them all, but decided that that would take too long and would be boring and a waste of my time.

So I decided to *estimate* the number of words in the following way:

1   estimate how many words per page;
2   multiply the number of pages by the estimated number of words per page to give the final answer.

Estimating how many words per page

- I chose a few pages at random and counted the number of words in a number of lines:
    page 67   114 words in 14 lines
    page 123   106 words in 12 lines
    page 179   121 words in 13 lines,
    giving a total sample of:
        341 words in 39 lines,

i.e. $\dfrac{341}{39}$ which is 8.74 words per line.

■ Now I had to estimate how many lines per page. Again I took a sample and found that:

page   27 had 37 lines
page   93 had 42 lines
page   141 had 37 lines
page   189 had 42 lines

giving an average of (37 + 42 + 37 + 42) ÷ 4 = 158 ÷ 4 = 39.5 lines per page.

Hence I can estimate that each page will have 8.74 × 39.5 words on it. This is 345.23 words.

■ The book consists of 192 pages, one of which is almost blank, giving a figure of 191 pages. So I estimate that each of the 191 pages has 345.23 words, giving a total of

191 × 345.23 = 65938.93.

This rounds off to 66000 words.

■ My conclusion then is that the Agatha Christie book *Halloween Party* was written using 66000 words.

There is no other way to check this other than to count them all, but it possibly could be made more accurate by taking a *larger sample* of lines and pages if this degree of accuracy were not thought appropriate.

This task could be given to any level of ability, and the grade you will receive for the work will depend on how you took your sample and on how well you have described it.

TASK 3

Using the 10 cm × 10 cm pieces of cm² paper as shown below, make at least four boxes with different volumes.

What will be the largest possible volume and what size will the box be?
Make this box with the greatest volume.

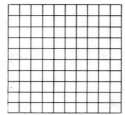

Fig. 15.39

BEFORE STARTING

We can see that to make boxes from these pieces of paper we need to cut out squares from the corners, then fold up and sellotape them together. I need to do this for different sized squares on the corner, then I need to see which has the biggest volume. After that I try to see if I can make the volume bigger.

SOLUTION

To make boxes from a 10 cm by 10 cm piece of paper, I need to cut out squares and tape them up. Below are the *nets* of the first four boxes that I made.

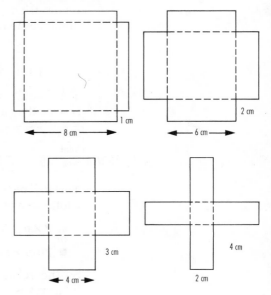

Fig. 15.40

The volumes are calculated by length × width × height. This gives the following results.

Side of square cut out (cm)	Volume of box (cm³)
1	8 × 8 × 1 = 64
2	6 × 6 × 2 = 72
3	4 × 4 × 3 = 48
4	2 × 2 × 4 = 16

Fig. 15.41

Clearly the largest volume here is 72 cm³, but I suspect that this is not the largest possible since I have so far only used whole numbers (integers) for the sizes of squares to cut out.

To help us find what the largest volume might be, I drew a graph of volume against length of square cut out.

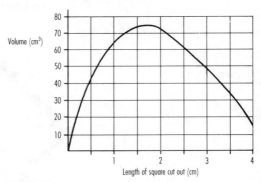

Fig. 15.42

This graph indicated that the volume gradually increased with larger squares cut out until just before 2 cm, when the volume then started to decrease.

From the graph I could see that this largest volume was going to be when the square cut out had length between 1 cm and 2 cm. I now calculated the volume from various squares being cut out from 1.1 cm to 1.9 cm with the rule:

volume = length × breadth × height
where x is the length cut out
volume = $(10 - 2x) \times (10 - 2x) \times x$
       = $x (10 - 2x)^2$

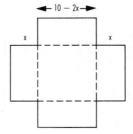

Fig. 15.43

My results were as follows:

Length of square (cm)	Volume (cm³)
1.1	66.924
1.2	69.312
1.3	71.188
1.4	72.576
1.5	73.5
1.6	73.984
1.7	74.052
1.8	73.728
1.9	

Fig. 15.44

I did not need to work out the volume with x = 1.9 since I can already see that the largest volume is between 1.6 and 1.8 cm. I then just tried squares of side 1.65 cm and 1.75 cm to be as close as I could.

Length of square (cm)	Volume (cm³)
1.65	74.0685
1.75	73.9375

Fig. 15.45

We now suspect that the largest volume lies between 1.6 and 1.7.

By now I could see that I was getting close. I wanted to be as close as possible, so I wrote the following computer program to calculate the volumes between 1.6 cm and 1.7 cm:

```
10 REM    VOLUME
20 FOR    X = 1.6 TO 1.7 STEP 0.01
30 LET    V = X*(10–(2*X) ↑ 2
40 PRINT  X, V
50 NEXT   X.
```

This gave me the following results

1.6	73.9840001
1.61	74.0091241
1.62	74.0301121
1.63	74.0469881
1.64	74.0597761
1.65	74.0685001
1.66	74.0731841
1.67	74.0738521
1.68	74.0705281
1.69	74.0632361
1.7	74.0520001

This showed the greatest volume was 74.0738521 cm³ when the square cut out is of side length 1.67 cm.

■ Conclusion

Greatest volume 74 cm³ with a box of dimensions 8.33 × 8.33 × 1.67. The net for this box is below (at a reduced scale).

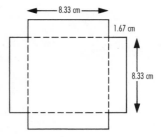

Fig. 15.46

This task could be given to any level of ability. It is the *extent* to which you have gone in trying to find the maximum volume and your ability in *explaining* what you have done that will determine your grade on this assessment. Also taken into account will be how well you constructed all the boxes, and how accurate you were, especially with the last one.

Of course, the use of a computer to do a lot of the calculations might be considered 'over the top', but if you *do* have the ability and the right equipment, then there is every reason to use it – as long as you have shown how and why and not just said 'the computer gave me this answer'.

These suggested 'model pieces of coursework' are, in each case, only one suggested way of arriving at your solution. It is quite acceptable to end up with similar results obtained by using different methods, so long as you are clear about what you did and have explained all you did.

SUMMARY

To sum up then, in your coursework you must always:

- read and think about the problem;
- plan a route through it;
- think about what equipment you might need for the problem;
- do the problem;
- check your results;
- generalise where possible to the best of your ability;
- write up exactly *what* you did, stating *why* you did what you did;
- read through the write-up to see if you have missed anything.

Try to avoid rushing the work. Give it the time to develop properly; otherwise you will be underselling yourself. Remember, the coursework marks are worth 20% of your total marks.

INDEX